CAMPAIGNS AN...

Date D

POWER, CONFLICT, AND DEMOCRACY SERIES

ROBERT Y. SHAPIRO, EDITOR

POWER, CONFLICT, AND DEMOCRACY:

AMERICAN POLITICS

INTO THE TWENTY-FIRST CENTURY

ROBERT Y. SHAPIRO, EDITOR

This series focuses on how the will of the people and the public interest are promoted, encouraged, or thwarted. It aims to question not only the direction American politics will take as it enters the twenty-first century but also the direction American politics has already taken.

The series addresses the role of interest groups and social and political movements; openness in American politics; important developments in institutions such as the executive, legislative, and judicial branches at all levels of government as well as the bureaucracies thus created; the changing behavior of politicians and political parties; the role of public opinion; and the functioning of mass media. Because problems drive politics, the series also examines important policy issues in both domestic and foreign affairs.

The series welcomes all theoretical perspectives, methodologies, and types of evidence that answer important questions about trends in American politics.

John G. Geer, *From Tea Leaves to Opinion Polls: A Theory of Democratic Leadership*

Kim Fridkin Kahn, *The Political Consequences of Being a Woman: How Stereotypes Influence the Conduct and Consequences of Political Campaigns*

Kelly D. Patterson, *Political Parties and the Maintenance of Liberal Democracy*

Dona Cooper Hamilton and Charles V. Hamilton, *The Dual Agenda: Race and Social Welfare Policies of Civil Rights Organizations*

Hanes Walton, Jr., *African-American Power and Politics: The Political Context Variable*

Amy Fried, *Muffled Echoes: Oliver North and the Politics of Public Opinion*

Russell D. Riley, *The Presidency and the Politics of Racial Inequality: Nation-Keeping from 1831 to 1965*

Robert W. Bailey, *Gay Politics, Urban Politics: Identity and Economics in the Urban Setting*

Ronald T. Libby, *ECO-WARS: Political Campaigns and Social Movements*

CAMPAIGNS AND THE COURT

The U.S. Supreme Court in Presidential Elections

Donald Grier Stephenson Jr.

COLUMBIA UNIVERSITY PRESS ◣◢ NEW YORK

Columbia University Press
Publishers Since 1893
New York Chichester, West Sussex
Copyright © 1999 Columbia University Press
All rights reserved
Library of Congress Cataloging-in-Publication Data
Stephenson, D. Grier.
Campaigns and the court: the U.S. Supreme Court in
presidential elections / Donald Grier Stephenson, Jr.
p. cm. — (Power, conflict, and democracy)
Includes bibliographical references and index.
ISBN 0–231–10034–5. — ISBN 0–231–10035–3 (pbk.)
1. United States. Supreme Court—History.
2. Electioneering—United States—History.
3. President—United States—Election—History.
I. Title. I. Series.
KF8742.S74 1999
347.73'2635—dc21 98–37351
CIP

For Claire and Jay in their new life together

CONTENTS

With a few minutes of reflection, anyone who can read would surely acknowledge that the United States Supreme Court is not only a legal body—an institution that says what the law is in the context of deciding cases—but a "political" body, too. That is, as it resolves conflicts between litigants who disagree over the correct meaning of a clause in the Constitution or a provision in an act of Congress, the Court affects the allocation of power and shapes public policy. In this sense, the Court has been political from practically the beginning. After all, the Court has consisted mainly of politicians who have been nominated and confirmed by politicians in order to perform what, at heart, are largely political tasks.

If the Court is necessarily "in" politics in this sense of the word, Americans use the word political to refer to something else as well: partisan politics—the continual struggle between those organized groups called political parties to control public offices, public resources, and the nation's destiny. In this more common use of the word, the federal courts, especially the Supreme Court, are ordinarily expected today to be "above politics," meaning that judges and justices are supposed to refrain from publicly taking sides in elections or otherwise jumping into the rough-and-tumble of partisan combat. (By contrast, in states with elected judiciaries, judges are frequently thrust into partisan combat by necessity.)

Yet, despite the belief that the Court should stand aloof from partisan struggles, most people would probably express little surprise were the United States Supreme Court to be an issue in the next presidential campaign. One candidate might fault the Court for evils supposedly either wrought or left uncorrected by one or more decisions, and might promise to "do something" about the Court if elected. The other candidate might come to the Court's defense. The future of the Court, the course of public policy, and even the meaning of the Constitution would accordingly all seem to depend on the outcome of the election.

For the Court to be in electoral contention in this way hardly seems novel, or so history suggests. After all, the Court figured prominently in the campaigns of 1968, 1980, and 1984, and was at least among the bones of contention in 1992. Put another way, an account of four of the last eight presidential contests would be strikingly incomplete without some discussion of the federal judiciary. And Court-driven election campaigns are hardly a recent phenomenon. The judiciary also found itself near or at the center of controversy as early as 1800 and again in 1832, 1860, 1896, 1912, 1924, and 1936.

These entanglements in presidential campaigns invite study for at least three reasons. First, partisan involvement has been intermittent, not constant. One should know, therefore, the institutional conditions and other circumstances and events that propel the Court into some national campaigns but not others. If the Court has been a major issue in at least ten elections since 1789, that is another way of saying that most election campaigns begin and end with little or no mention of the Supreme Court. Consequences are a second reason. That is, what are the effects of judicial campaign involvement on the Court itself, public policy, political parties, and constitutional government generally in the United States? This pair of reasons leads to a third: appraisal. Is electoral entanglement a necessary and beneficial feature of democratic politics, American-style? Should it be welcomed or feared? Surely any look at partisan involvement must consider its meaning for the democratic process and the continued vitality of the Court.

These matters are explored in the nine chapters that follow. As an introduction, the first chapter has three principal objectives. First, it outlines the Supreme Court's unique place in the constitutional system that only partly distances the bench from routine partisan conflict. The framers of 1787 went to considerable effort to enshrine an independent judiciary, but they also set in motion an arrangement of powers that both allows the Court, through its decisions, to intersect the political process and fosters opportunities for the Court's enemies to breach the wall of judicial independence. Second, the chapter offers an overview of the development of political parties in the United States. Parties are the engine that drives elections and facilitates the selection of members of the executive and legislative branches established by the Constitution, but they are an entirely extra-constitutional feature of the American political system. Nonetheless, like the Congress, the presidency, and the Court—all mandated by the Constitution—they have undergone change. Major and minor (or third) parties have disappeared and others have taken their place. Viewed historically, this evolution has defined six party "systems" or periods, with one system following another every generation or two.

The first chapter also lays out a series of five expectations or "propositions" about the Court's electoral entanglement to which the last chapter—the conclusion—returns. That last chapter assesses the five propositions against the record of presidential campaigns that unfolds in chapters 2 through 8. The concluding chapter also reflects on the significance of these events for the health of constitutional government in the United States. The intervening chapters, 2 through 8, generally share an organization. A sketch of the party system precedes a snapshot of the Supreme Court of the period. An analysis of the particular judicial decisions that sooner or later ensnared the Court in partisan warfare is followed by a narrative of the campaign. The chapter ends with an appraisal of what the Court's presence in the campaign meant for the Court, public policy, and the rest of the political system.

As such, the book is not a history of political parties or a survey of presidential elections. Nor is it a history of the Supreme Court or an overview of American constitutional law. Rather, the book selectively draws from all four—party evolution, presidential campaigns, and judicial and constitutional development—to tell the story of campaigns and the Court.

ACKNOWLEDGMENTS

N
o one completes even a modest undertaking like this one without the help of others, seen and unseen. The notes reflect my debt to prior scholarship and reveal the rich resources available to anyone exploring constitutional government in the United States. Students in my courses on American politics, constitutional law, and the Supreme Court at Franklin & Marshall College have made it possible for me to say, for nearly three decades, that I am indeed fortunate to be paid for doing what I enjoy. More directly, I owe much to John Michel of Columbia University Press. He first encouraged me to write this book and then provided the right combination of encouragment, prompting, and patience along the way. John also arranged for chapter-by-chapter reviews of the manuscript from Thomas J. Baldino of Wilkes University and Robert G. Seddig of Allegheny College. Their comments and suggestions proved valuable throughout, as did those from series editor Robert Shapiro of Columbia University. Sheldon Goldman of the University of Massachusetts at Amherst, Ellis Katz of Temple University, and John B. Taylor of Washington College were among those who, with Professors Baldino, Seddig, and Shapiro, reviewed the prospectus. Alexander Thorpe, Beth Wilson, and Susan Pensak have provided indispensable assistance through the production process. Nonetheless, any defects or errors or other sins of omission or commission that remain are my responsibility alone.

Finally, I am thankful for my family. My parents, Donald and Katherine Stephenson, along with everything else they have done for me, first interested me in politics and law. As a Georgia judge for a quarter-century who had to face the voters of Newton County every four years, my father gave me an early glimpse into the connection between campaigns and courts. My mother, a member of one of the first classes of women admitted to the University of Georgia, seems to have forgotten nothing from her survey course on the American political system. Next to them, my god-mother, Margaret Budd Stephenson, has been my biggest fan for the longest time. Always supportive, upon completion of my doctorate at Princeton in 1967 and just before I entered active service in the U.S. Army, she arranged my first lecture (to the Sergeant Newton chapter of the Daughters of the American Revolution) and even provided an honorarium of twenty-five dollars. After our thirty-one years of marriage, Ellen knows that no book writes itself and remains as long-suffering as ever. Todd and Claire—each now "away from home"—have been gracious when I have ended a telephone conversation all too often with the words "I've got to get back to work now."

Justice Louis Brandeis once said that one should make each task preparation for the next. Robert Louis Stevenson is supposed to have written that anyone can carry a burden, however heavy, until nightfall; that anyone can do a job, however hard, for one day; and that anyone can live lovingly until the sun goes down. I would add that doing the next task, carrying the next burden, and living lovingly on the second and successive days are made immeasurably easier by the strength one's family can provide.

CAMPAIGNS AND THE COURT

CHAPTER I

The Constitution, Politics, and the Supreme Court

The United States Constitution dictates, or at least allows, most of the recurring political phenomena in the nation. Through elections, voters choose their chief executive, senators, and representatives, plus a multitude of state and local officials. The Congress annually considers hundreds of pieces of legislation, rejects most of them, and forwards the rest to the president for his approval. Among other responsibilities, the president directs the foreign policy apparatus. With regularity, the Supreme Court hears and decides about 100 cases each term. And so on.

This book is about the intersection of two of these national political phenomena: Supreme Court decisions and presidential elections. As such, the book is not a history of political parties or a survey of presidential elections. Nor is it a history of the Supreme Court or an overview of American constitutional law. Rather, the book selectively draws from all four—party evolution, presidential campaigns, and judicial and constitutional development—to explore those instances when the Supreme Court and its decisions have been major issues in presidential elections.

One need only recall the presidential election of 1992. Campaigning for the White House, Governor Bill Clinton of Arkansas promised to apply a "litmus test" in selecting justices for the Supreme Court: only prospective nominees who supported a constitutional right to abortion would be considered.[1] In the same year, the platform adopted by the Republican National Convention promised efforts to secure ratification of a Human Life Amendment to the Constitution that would forbid all abortions.[2] The object of both Clinton's statement and the Republican platform was the United States Supreme Court and *Roe* v. *Wade*.[3] That landmark decision of 1973 first announced that the fundamental right to privacy protected by the Constitution encompasses abortion.[4] Clinton and many Democrats were alarmed by inroads the Court had begun to make on *Roe* in 1989.[5] For many

Republicans, the Court's newfound tolerance for significant restrictions on the abortion right did not go nearly far enough.

If Democrats and Republicans recognized the partisan significance of the Court's decisions on abortion, so did the justices. Barely weeks before the summer nominating conventions of the two major parties in 1992, the Supreme Court upheld most of a multifaceted regulatory scheme from Pennsylvania but left in place the "essential holding" of *Roe* that the Constitution provides at least some protection for women seeking abortions.[6] Nonetheless, there were only two justices (Harry Blackmun and John Stevens) willing to declare that abortion remained a "fundamental" right.[7] Moreover, four justices would have reversed *Roe* outright. Chief Justice William Rehnquist's opinion for himself and Justices Byron White, Antonin Scalia, and Clarence Thomas asserted that *Roe* was wrongly decided and that "States may regulate abortion procedures in ways rationally related to a legitimate state interest."[8]

In separate opinions, as well as for separate reasons, Justices Blackmun and Scalia acknowledged the connection between the Court's decisions on abortion and coming elections. According to Blackmun, who had written the majority opinion in *Roe*:

> While there is much to be praised about our democracy, our country since its founding has recognized that there are certain fundamental liberties that are not to be left to the whims of an election. A woman's right to a reproductive choice is one of those fundamental liberties. Accordingly, that liberty need not seek refuge at the ballot box.

> In one sense, the Court's approach [to the Pennsylvania statute] is worlds apart from that of The Chief Justice and Justice Scalia. And yet, in another sense, the distance between the two approaches is short—the distance is but a single vote.

> I am 83 years old. I cannot remain on this Court forever, and when I do step down, the confirmation process for my successor well may focus on the issue before us today. That, I regret, may be exactly where the choice between the two worlds will be made.[9]

The Court's political involvement was no surprise, retorted Scalia.

As long as this Court thought (and the people thought) that we Justices were doing essentially lawyers' work up here—reading text and discerning our society's traditional understanding of that text—the public pretty much left us alone. . . . But if in reality our process of constitutional adjudication consists primarily of making value judgments . . . then a free and intelligent people's attitude towards us can be expected to be (ought to be) quite different. . . . If, indeed, the "liberties" protected by the Constitution are, as the Court says, undefined and unbounded, then the people should demonstrate, to protest that we do not implement their values but ours. Not only that, but confirmation hearings for new Justices should deteriorate into question-and-answer sessions in which Senators go through a list of their constituents' most favored and most disfavored alleged constitutional rights, and seek the nominee's commitment to support or oppose them. Value judgments, after all, should be voted on, not dictated; and if our Constitution has somehow accidentally committed them to the Supreme Court, at least we can have a sort of plebiscite each time a new nominee to that body is put forward. Justice Blackmun not only regards this prospect with equanimity, he solicits it.[10]

Perhaps few thought it unusual that, because of issues such as abortion, the Supreme Court was a factor in the 1992 presidential campaign. After all, the Court figured prominently in the campaign of 1968 and only slightly less prominently in the campaigns of 1980 and 1984. Indeed, candidate Clinton's promise in 1992 to apply a litmus test must be considered in light of the commitment by Republican presidential nominee Ronald Reagan in 1980 and 1984 to build a Supreme Court majority hostile to *Roe*.[11] Seen another way, any account of at least three of the eight most recent presidential contests would be strikingly incomplete without some discussion of the Supreme Court.

The past two centuries of American presidential politics reveal that such references to the Court at election time are hardly novel. Judicial entanglement may have been the exception, nonengagement the rule, but examples of the Court's entanglement are almost as old as the Republic itself. Besides 1992, the federal judiciary has been a major focus in nearly one fifth of all other presidential elections: in 1800, 1832, 1860, 1896, 1912, 1924, 1936, 1968, 1980, and 1984.[12]

The phenomenon invites explanation. What are the circumstances that have pushed the Court into partisan political conflict? What have been the events, issues, forces, and personalities that have broken the norm of judicial absence from presidential campaigns? Understanding the intersection between the Supreme Court and presidential elections begins with a review of the development of political parties in the United States and of the political dimension of the federal judiciary.

CHANGING POLITICAL PARTIES

Possibly no feature or institution has reflected or shaped American politics as much as the political party. Defined as an organization that seeks to influence public policy by placing its members into positions of authority within the government, a party presents to the voters a slate of candidates who promise, if victorious, to translate proposed policies into governmental action. If parties function effectively, they serve popular government by enabling the electorate to make choices about the nation's future and by injecting responsibility into government. The notion of "the consent of the governed"—the core idea in the Declaration of Independence—presumes an opportunity for voters to hold their rulers accountable. By providing a simple label, parties make it easier for the electorate to control government by rewarding or punishing officials at the polls.

Parties are so ubiquitous on the electoral landscape that most Americans would have difficulty thinking or talking about politics and government for very long without mentioning or thinking about parties. This is so even though political parties receive not a single mention in the Constitution, a fact that makes the party system the most remarkable extraconstitutional feature of the political system. Moreover, the Constitution's official silence on the subject of parties was deliberate. Many of the founders, including James Madison and George Washington, actually feared political parties (or factions, as they were first called) because in a government in which ultimate political power lay in the hands of the people, a majority might run roughshod over the rights of a minority. Accordingly, one of the arguments advanced in support of the proposed Constitution was that the charter would minimize the influence of factions in the new government.[13]

In spite of this aversion to parties, political groupings emerged early in American national history and have persisted. Indeed, they were probably inevitable: if the right to rule rests on obtaining a majority of the votes, would-be rulers are bound to form organizations to marshal votes and win elections.[14] Moreover, some of the same devices built into the Constitution to thwart factions or parties, plus the practicalities of governing, encouraged their growth. The functional horizontal division of powers among the three branches and the vertical division of control between the central and state governments, combined with a large land area for which and over which public policy would have to be formulated and implemented, created hurdles for effective government right from the start. Parties soon formed to help overcome the fragmentation of authority caused by these divisions. Through parties, like-minded individuals could, by holding enough offices, move public policy in a common direction.

Like the nation itself, parties and voter preferences have changed over the decades to reveal as many as six major party systems, or periods "with characteristic patterns of voting behavior, of elite and institutional relationships, and of broad system-dominant decisions"[15] (see figure 1.1). Once parties were established, each party system has evolved from its predecessor following a few years of political turmoil, termed realignment. In a realigning (or "critical") election, voters perceive a distinct difference between political parties that gives them a "choice," and also shift in large numbers from the ranks of one party to another, thus handing control of most machinery of government—the presidency, Congress, and most state political systems—to the victorious party for a period of years spanning several presidential terms. According to one of the classic studies of party change, realignments

> arise from emergent tensions in society which, not adequately controlled by . . . politics as usual, escalate to a flash point; they are issue-oriented phenomena, centrally associated with these tensions and more or less leading to resolution adjustments; they result in significant transformations in the general shape of policy; and they have relatively profound aftereffects on the roles played by institutional elites. They are involved with redefinitions of the universe of voters, political parties, and the broad boundaries of the politically possible.[16]

In short, party realignment is revolution, American-style. Realignment may involve not only the major parties of the day but minor ones ("third parties") as well. Sometimes the latter have had a sizable influence on one or both major parties; once, a new or third party displaced a major one altogether. While there is not universal agreement on those elections that qualify as

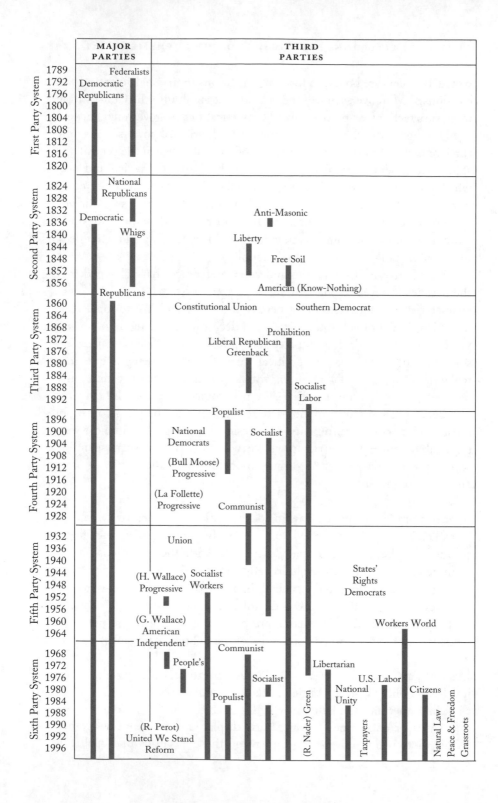

realigning events, many scholars include the elections of 1828, 1860, 1896, and 1932, and some count 1800 and 1968. The Supreme Court was a prominent issue in all of these campaigns or in campaigns adjacent to them.

An initial grouping of political forces took shape by the late 1790s. In the first party system, Federalists combated Antifederalists, later called Democratic Republicans or just Republicans. By the 1830s, some years after disappearance of the Federalists as an organized party, the second party system featured clashes between Democrats (formerly called Republicans) and Whigs. (The latter were the spiritual descendants of the Federalists; many Whigs had also comprised the short-lived National Republican party.) The second party system, and with it the Whig party, dissolved by 1860 over the issue of slavery. In its place was not only the new Republican party but, for most of the rest of the century, also an arrangement characterized by relatively close competition between Republicans and Democrats. Republican ascendancy, along with a significant alteration in the nature of the Democratic party, marked the fourth party system from 1896 until 1932. The calamity of the Great Depression brought on an era of Democratic rule in the fifth party system that persisted until 1968.

Republicans enjoyed unaccustomed success in winning presidential elections in 1968, 1972, 1980, 1984, and 1988, thus calling an end to the Democratic dominance that characterized the fifth system. Democrats, however, controlled Congress[17] and most of the state governments during

---

FIGURE 1.1 American Political Parties Since 1789

The life span for some political parties listed on the facing page can be only approximated because parties may exist at the state or local level before (or after) they run candidates in presidential elections. Most third-party candidates were on the ballots in only a few states. In 1992, for example, only four candidates were on the ballot in all fifty states: Bill Clinton (Democratic), George Bush (Republican), Ross Perot (Independent/United We Stand), and André Marrou (Libertarian). In 1996, and excepting only Ross Perot's Reform party vote, all third parties together received only 1.6 percent of the 96,277,634 votes cast for president.

Adapted from D. Grier Stephenson, Jr., et al., *American Government, Brief Edition* (New York: HarperCollins, 1994), p. 182. Sources: *Congressional Quarterly's Guide to the U.S. Elections*, 2d ed. (Washington, D.C.: Congressional Quarterly Press, 1985), p. 224; *Congressional Quarterly Weekly Report*, November 5, 1988, p. 3184; Federal Election Commission, "1992 Official Presidential General Election Results" and "1996 Official Presidential General Election Results."

this time, a pattern that suggested that no firm new party system, at least in the historical sense, had developed. Voters entrusted the executive branch mainly to one party and the legislative branch mainly to the other. This period of "dealignment" or divided government might be said to constitute a sixth party system in the sense that it stands in contrast to the pattern that prevailed in the fifth party system. Whether the Democrats' recovery of the White House in election of 1992 and retention of it in 1996 will result in a period of Democratic dominance, and hence the end of the sixth system, will not be known until after 2000 or 2004.

CONSTITUTIONAL PARAMETERS

Against a background of vacillating political fortunes and evolving party systems, at least two tensions in American government have allowed, perhaps even promoted, the intersection of presidential campaigns and the Supreme Court. One pits the principle of popular sovereignty against that of limited government; the other inheres in the idea of an independent judiciary.

Popular sovereignty, or government by the "consent of the governed," is institutionalized at all levels of the political system, from city councils to Congress. In his address at the Gettysburg battlefield in 1863, President Abraham Lincoln called this principle "government by the people."[18] Accordingly, voters possess the authority, facilitated by political parties, not only to choose those who will rule over them but also to remove those officials from office when they have betrayed a trust, when they have pursued unpopular policies, or when their policies have failed. After all, the right to vote—that is, the right of the many to confer the authority to govern on the few—would mean little if it did not also entail the right to withdraw that authority.

In contrast, the principle of limited government resides in the nature of a constitution itself. In John Adams's formulation on the eve of the American Revolution, the goal is a "government of laws and not of men."[19] A constitution, explained Justice William Paterson two decades later, "is the form of government delineated by the mighty hand of the people, in which certain first principles of fundamental laws are established."[20]

Ironically, the Constitution is at once both the consummation of popular sovereignty ("We the People . . . ," as the Preamble declares) and the embodiment of limits on what the people through their representatives may do. The Constitution of the United States therefore is much more than a structural blueprint of the national government that calls for institutions such as a bicameral legislature, a separately elected president, and a Supreme Court. The Constitution imposes limits on those who occupy the offices it creates. It simultaneously assigns primary responsibility for certain duties to particular branches, and forbids or sharply restricts certain policies altogether. Both structural limitations and prohibitions alike remain in place until formally changed by the Constitution's elaborate amendment procedure, the device whereby a later generation of "the people" may modify the "form of government" bequeathed by their forebears.

From the earliest years of the Republic, the Supreme Court has closely identified itself with the limits the Constitution imposes. Indeed, the Court matters as much as it does in American politics because it has seen itself as the unique custodian of constitutional limitations. At least since *Marbury* v. *Madison*[21] in 1803, when the Supreme Court for the first time invalidated an act of Congress as violative of the Constitution, the Court has insisted that, without the presence of the judiciary as an umpire of the political system, limited government would be more form than substance. Popular sovereignty left unchecked would, in Chief Justice John Marshall's words, "subvert the very foundations of all written constitutions" and "reduce to nothing, what we have deemed the greatest improvement on political institutions, a written constitution."[22]

Yet, the Court's guardianship of the Constitution—its contribution toward making limited government a reality—has revealed the tensions that inhere in the concept of an independent judiciary that the Constitution mandates. Applying the brakes to popular majorities increases the likelihood that the Court will be drawn nearer to the center of partisan combat.

When the Second Continental Congress, meeting in Philadelphia, approved the Declaration of Independence in 1776, one of the "Facts" the delegates "submitted to a candid world" through the literary handiwork of Thomas Jefferson was the predicament of the colonial judiciary: "He [the British monarch] has made Judges dependent on his Will alone, for the tenure of their offices, and the amount and payment of their salaries." Although the Articles of Confederation of 1777 (the new nation's first experiment with a national constitution) provided for no system of national courts, the Constitution of 1787 attempted by its design to correct the defects the Declaration had detailed. Not only would the Supreme Court and "inferior" courts that Congress might authorize constitute a branch separate from Congress and the executive, but justices and judges (who would be appointed by the president and confirmed by the Senate) would serve "during good Behavior" at a salary that could not be reduced during their time in office.

Accordingly, Alexander Hamilton argued in *Federalist* No. 78 (April 1788), during the struggle over ratification, that the "independence of the judges" was one more reason why citizens should favor the proposed Constitution. Judicial independence would be functional: it would be "an essential safeguard against the effects of occasional ill-humors in the society." The strong suggestion was that the Court would do more than engage in conflict resolution—essential in any political system. Its work, aided by the Constitution's arrangement of overlapping powers or checks and balances, would have a policy dimension. Of primary concern to Hamilton and others of similar mind were "infractions of the constitution" that the judiciary might remedy through the implied power of judicial review. (Hamilton was thus anticipating the same authority for the soon-to-be Supreme Court that Marshall would officially assert fifteen years later in *Marbury*.) In other words, the Court's structural independence was meritorious precisely because the Court would *not* remain independent of the political process. The insulation afforded by the Constitution would shield the Court from ordinary forms of retaliation (e.g., dismissal from office by the voters or the executive) and would help both to empower and to embolden the Court to oppose ill-chosen policies adopted by the people's government.

In deciding politically sensitive issues—questions that divide and perplex the nation—the Court cannot expect its independence to go unchallenged by those whom its decisions displease. The separated institutions mandated by the Constitution have therefore made judicial independence possible; its shared powers have allowed the federal judiciary to become a partner in governing the nation and have made occasional breaches of that independence possible. "Courts are the mere instruments of the law, and can will nothing,"[23] professed Chief Justice John Marshall in a self-effacing denial. But that claim stands alongside the candid acknowledgment that judges are not mere oracles and that courts affect the allocation of power: "We are under a Constitution, but the Constitution is what the judges say it is,"[24] asserted future Justice and Chief Justice Charles Evans Hughes while governor of New York.

There should be little wonder, then, that presidential campaigns and the Court sometimes intersect. Elections are the most visible recurring displays of popular sovereignty in the United States, and political parties exist to harness popular support for their candidates with an eye toward shaping public policy. The Constitution in turn places limits on what the people, through political parties and elected officials, may do. The Supreme Court's special link to those limitations makes the judiciary unavoidably political—not "political" in the sense of campaigning for votes on Election Day but political in the sense of affecting the allocation of power and the content of public policy. The Court's political dimension reveals itself either when the justices thwart the popular will or when they sustain that will against a challenge that the government has contravened or circumvented the law of the land. Thus, the judiciary may be sucked into partisan combat both in spite of and because of the "independence" the Constitution promises.

HISTORICAL PRECONDITIONS

Alongside the constitutional parameters of limited government, popular sovereignty, and an independent judiciary stand basic circumstances or preconditions without which the Court's electoral involvement might never have occurred. These are in addition to the events, forces, and personalities unique to different political eras that will be explored in later chapters.

One precondition embraces the judicial process: there must be an environment in which salient political issues are present in litigation and in which the Supreme Court is in a position to engage those issues. The other looks to the electoral process: presidential elections (1) that are organized by political parties and are characterized by appeals to the electorate for mass support and (2) that include a willingness by the parties and their candidates to use agreement or disagreement with the Court's decisions as a means of enhancing that support. These preconditions are independent of whether the Court actually desires or expects its rulings to become part of the partisan fray.

Salient political issues—that is, conspicuous concerns or subjects that a significant part of the public expects government to address—include both "position" and "valence" issues.[25] A position issue is one that permits at least two credible policy responses. For example, a person may favor or oppose spoken prayer in the classrooms of public schools. By contrast, a valence issue arises when people associate an official or a policy with a condition, symbol, or goal that almost everyone accepts or rejects. The economy and "safe streets" are valence issues. Nearly everyone favors prosperity and personal security. As a political objective or goal, there is, practically speaking, no "other side"—no organized constituency for muggings or economic misery. Still, if no sane individual campaigns for office by promising hard times or an escalating crime rate, few are surprised when one candidate tries to associate another candidate with precisely those conditions.

Similarly, judicial decisions may also be identified with both position and valence issues. The Supreme Court may allow or disallow official religious observances in public schools. A decision banning or severely restricting government regulation of monopolies may become associated with economic pain for some laborers, owners of small businesses, and even whole communities. Or a ruling curtailing interrogation of suspects by police may become a symbol of a criminal justice system that is "soft on crime."

Of the two preconditions, transfer of political disputes from the ballot box to the courtroom was the first to appear, and was well in place by the early nineteenth century. As Alexis de Tocqueville observed following his travels throughout the nation during the early 1830s, "Scarcely any question arises in the United States which does not become, sooner or later, a subject of judicial debate."[26] The predisposition in the United States to litigate policy disputes has continued nearly without interruption: conflicts that might bring a regiment of troops into the streets of some countries seem routinely to summon a battalion of lawyers into the courthouses of America.

Yet a cultural proclivity to convert disagreements over public policy into litigation does not guarantee action by the Supreme Court. This is because an effort by the Court to resolve a policy dispute is contingent on jurisdiction (the Court's authority under the law to decide a case) and volition (the Court's willingness to engage an issue). And as will be explained in the next chapter, the Court did not begin its existence in the familiar contemporary role of major participant in the policy-making process.

As an illustration of the impact of the presence or absence of jurisdiction, the now routine supervision by the Supreme Court of criminal justice in the states could not have developed had Congress not granted the Court authority to review certain decisions by a state's court of last resort and had the Fourteenth Amendment (or something like it) not become part of the Constitution. The latter extended federal protection against state infringement of indeterminate rights, and the former allowed review of state court decisions when a criminal defendant claimed a violation of one of those rights. Because the Fourteenth Amendment did not define the rights it protected, the task of giving meaning to the amendment largely fell to the Court. In lawyers' language, disputes over the fairness of criminal justice as administered by the states became "federal questions"—that is, matters that could be litigated in the Supreme Court.

Volition has plainly been essential during the twentieth century because—thanks to Congress—the cases the Supreme Court decides are today almost entirely limited to those it wants to decide. Moreover, when the Court has decided to decide a case, the justices have considerable latitude in how the case is resolved: one may win or lose a case in different ways. Such latitude in the resolution of cases was present even before discretionary review began to take shape near the end of the nineteenth century.[27] Disposing of a case did not necessarily entail authoritative rulings on all or even most of the issues present in the case. Perhaps the most notorious counterexample of a decision that communicated much more than was minimally necessary was *Scott* v. *Sandford*[28] in 1857, the central case considered in chapter 4. The majority could have disposed of the case with the same legal outcome by holding that Dred Scott, as a slave under the laws of Missouri, where the litigation originated, accordingly remained a slave. Such a ruling would hardly have pleased abolitionist groups, but it would have doubtless been far less inflammatory than the path the Court followed in Chief Justice Roger Taney's opinion: a denial of Congress's authority over slavery in the territories, coupled with an assertion of an intent by the framers of the Constitution to exclude all blacks, slave and free, from the blessings of national citizenship. In 1857, the Court may not have intended its decision to be a subject of debate prior to and during the campaign of 1860, but it had chosen to speak forthrightly on the most salient issue of the day.

The second precondition may at first glance seem to be a "given" in a democratic system with a separately elected chief executive and a high court that hands down politically charged decisions. Yet for the first years after government under the Constitution got under way in 1789, organized national political parties did not exist. In the beginning, to be sure, members of Congress and the state legislatures frequently held different opinions on matters that confronted them, but such groupings were initially little more than loose associations. Not until President Washington declined to seek a third term in 1796 did the United States have its first contested presidential election. Even after the first parties took shape, competition between them for the presidency was not regularized until the 1820s.

Furthermore, the size of the electorate was small relative to the whole population, and most of those with the right to vote did not actively take part in electing the president until well into the nineteenth century. The Philadelphia Convention rejected the most obvious means for election of the president: popular election (as provided for members of the House of Representatives), election by one or both houses of Congress (an element of the Virginia Plan laid before the Philadelphia Convention), or election by state legislatures (as in the case of members of the Senate). Instead, the framers placed election of the president in the hands of unique electors (comprising the electoral college) whom "[e]ach State shall appoint, in such Manner as the Legislature thereof may direct."[29] And for the early elections most state legislatures picked these presidential electors. Indeed, it was not until the election of 1824, when enough states had switched to the current practice of allowing the voters to elect the electors, that the custom developed of reporting the "popular vote" for president and vice president. In short, a system of presidential elections marked by party competition for votes coupled with a willingness of candidates to link judicial decisions with the campaign did not appear full-blown at the outset of the new nation. Like the Court itself, the electoral system took some time to develop.

PROPOSITIONS

The Supreme Court's occasional campaign presence suggests at least five propositions or expectations that this study seeks to examine.

- First, the Court is more likely to become ensnared in partisan combat when it has negated, rather than upheld, a policy choice made by a state government or another branch of the national government.
- Second, when the Court is on the "losing side" in an election in which it has been an issue, ensuing Court decisions in the short term will generate conflict between the Court and the new governing majority, resulting in presidential and/or congressional efforts to curb or otherwise to change the Court.
- Third, when the Court has been on the "losing side" in, or adjacent to, a realigning election, the Court will make significant policy changes within a decade that bring it into accord with the winning coalition.
- Fourth, the Court may facilitate the definition and clarification of candidates' and parties' positions on critical issues in a campaign.

- Fifth, instances when the Court becomes an issue in a presidential campaign tend to coincide with widespread debate over the legitimacy of judicial review and the Court's role in the political system.

Proposition 1: Negation and Validation

Reflection on the nature of the judicial process suggests the first proposition. Of course it is true that nearly any judicial decision will make some person or group unhappy. A case represents a dispute between parties. The Court's decision attempts to resolve the dispute, and resolution normally favors one party over another. In other words, there is a winner and there is a loser. The Supreme Court may rule, for example, that a policy adopted by Congress is entirely acceptable, acceptable only with certain modifications, or entirely unacceptable. Even in a collusive or "friendly" suit—litigation that the Court professes to disdain[30] but sometimes embraces nonetheless—where the parties do not have truly conflicting interests, a decision in reality leaves a policy in place or alters it.[31]

When the Court upholds a challenged policy, disappointed litigants remain free to work for legislative repeal or modification. They may be profoundly unhappy with the outcome of a case, but "blame" lies in the first instance with the legislators who adopted the policy. When a law is stricken as violative of the Constitution, however, the Court may not have ended debate about the policy, but it has effectively placed the policy out of reach, at least for the near future, by declaring certain objectives "off limits" or "out of bounds." Because negation of a statute will probably attract more public attention than its validation, the Court then becomes a lightning rod, attracting hostility and opposition. Greater awareness in turn means that, for any politician hoping to capitalize on popular disenchantment with the judiciary, the rudiments of an anti-Court campaign may already be at hand.

Proposition 2: Conflict and Reaction

The second proposition looks to consequences: the impact of electoral engagement on the Court, other political institutions, and public policy. Disputes over judicial decisions arise because the Supreme Court is an agency of *government* all the while it is an institution of the *law*. The Supreme Court is political, and in most respects unavoidably so.

Tension should of course be minimal if the Court is on the winning side. With no transfer in the control of government, little or no conflict between the Court and the other branches follows as a result of the election. The views that had prevailed on the bench before the election continue to be reflected in decisions after the election. The defeated party may persist in its criticism of the Court, but with little practical consequence for rulings in the immediate future.

Significant conflict, however, would seem probable, at least in the short run, when the opposition party is victorious, if the Court lags behind the changes that have overtaken the rest of the political system. Voters may turn one party out of power and hand control of Congress and the White House to another party, but, short of a wholesale turnover in personnel due to deaths and retirements, no such speedy displacement in the federal judiciary is assured. "The Court is almost never a really contemporary institution," cautioned Robert Jackson shortly before he became a justice. "The judiciary is . . . the check of a preceding genera-tion on the present one; . . . and nearly always the check of a rejected regime on the one in being."[32] Disharmony between the old and new regimes will not diminish until vacancies gradually allow one or more presidents to reshape the bench in their own image. Thus, this proposi-tion is akin to a body of opinion that assumes that the Court, as the embodiment of the old regime, stays its preelection course, a policy plac-ing it at odds with the new.[33] Accordingly, those now in power are no more satisfied with the Court after the election than they were before, and feel compelled to take steps to secure judicial decisions more consis-tent with their views.

Such steps may take a variety of forms. Even in the absence of official Court-curbing proposals, the Court may be used as a whipping boy or a scapegoat by members of Congress, as a repository of blame for various ills besetting the nation. Critics may direct a drumfire of criticism at the bench to convince the justices of the error of their ways. Pro-defendant decisions in criminal justice cases in the 1960s, for example, opened the Court to charges with far-reaching consequences that it was to blame for the rise in violent street crime. Judicial decisions may be politically significant as well when interest groups use them to galvanize members and potential mem-bers, or when interest groups attempt to influence public policy through litigation, as the abortion controversy demonstrates.[34] Amici curiae (friends of the court) briefs and law review articles routinely attempt to shape the course of legal doctrine.

In a potentially more serious scenario, Congress and/or the president may move against the Court officially in a variety of ways. While the Court enjoys considerable independence from outside control and has become a potent institution in American government, it by no means enjoys unlimited power. Several checks, external to the judicial process, exist that may limit what the Court does. For example, hostility in Congress to the Court's rulings has frequently led to calls for amending the Constitution to "correct" the Court. Although such efforts only rarely succeed, the justices have been expressly reversed by constitutional amendment on four occasions. The Eleventh Amendment, restricting federal court jurisdiction over the states, overturned *Chisholm v. Georgia*.[35] The Fourteenth Amendment, in part granting both national and state citizenship to "all persons" born in the United States, countered the Dred Scott decision. The Sixteenth Amendment, allowing for a national tax on incomes, reversed *Pollock v. Farmers' Loan and Trust Co.*,[36] and the Twenty-sixth Amendment, establishing a nationwide voting age of eighteen in state as well as national elections, set aside *Oregon v. Mitchell*.[37] The Court's flag-burning rulings in 1989 and 1990[38] were so unpopular that critics mounted an effort, thus far unsuccessful, to overturn them by constitutional amendment.[39]

Congress may also seek to accomplish through a statute what the Court has failed to do through constitutional interpretation. For instance, in 1978 the Court upheld the search, on the authority of a warrant, of newspaper offices for photographic evidence of crimes committed by others. In the Supreme Court's view, a newsroom enjoyed no greater constitutional protection than someone's home.[40] Within two years Congress passed the Privacy Protection Act, which barred unannounced searches of newsrooms by law enforcement personnel and that conditioned such searches on the issuance of a subpoena. Searches by warrants, deemed less friendly to press freedom, were to be allowed only in exceptional circumstances.

Such moves, however, can themselves be thwarted by the bench, as happened after Congress passed the Religious Freedom Restoration Act (RFRA) in 1993. RFRA reversed a 1990 decision by the Court that had made it easier for governments constitutionally to infringe on religious liberty in situations where laws of general application conflicted with the dictates of one's faith.[41] The statute restored a generous interpretation of free exercise of religion that the Court had first announced in 1963.[42] In *City of*

Boerne v. *Flores*,[43] however, the Court held that Congress's noble intentions exceeded its authority. The 1990 decision embodied the meaning of the free exercise clause, and according to it, no religiously based exception to an otherwise valid law was required. Because RFRA altered that meaning, the 1993 act was pronounced unconstitutional, at least as applied to state and local governments.

Less easily thwarted is new legislation that Congress enacts to correct the Court's interpretation of an existing statute. (Statutory interpretation accounts for a large part of the Court's work today. At least half the cases the justices receive from the lower federal courts turn not on the meaning of the Constitution but on the meaning of a federal statute or regulation.) However, because some groups almost certainly have been favored by the Court's reading of Congress's meaning, vigorous lobbying usually develops to derail attempts to override the Court legislatively. One study that looked at over 200 constructions by the Court of antitrust and labor statutes found a congressional attempt to override in only 12 percent of the cases and a successful override in only 4 percent.[44] During recent decades, however, congressional override has been more common, with 121 such "reversals" taking place between 1967 and 1990.[45] By contrast, between 1945 and 1957, only 21 reversals occurred.[46]

For example, the Civil Rights Act of 1991 overturned no fewer than twelve of the Supreme Court's statutory constructions, including the controversial ruling in *Wards Cove Packing Co.* v. *Atonio*,[47] on the meaning of Title VII of the Civil Rights Act of 1964. In 1971, the Court had read Title VII to proscribe "not only overt discrimination but also practices that are fair in form, but discriminatory in operation. . . . Good intent or absence of discriminatory intent does not redeem employment procedures or testing mechanisms that operate as 'built-in headwinds' for minority groups and are unrelated to measuring job capability."[48] Under this rule, employers had the burden of showing that a questionable device was "a reasonable measure of job performance." *Wards Cove*, however, made it more difficult for an employee to prove a violation of Title VII. Statistical disparities remained important, but the plaintiff bore the burden of establishing that the employer had no "legitimate business justification" for the device, thus making it easier for the employer to win a discrimination suit. The 1991 action by Congress shifted the burden of proof back to the employer by stipulating that the employer had to show that the device was "job-related for the position in question and consistent with business necessity."

The ordinary process of filling vacancies is another way—perhaps the most effective way—in which a president and the Senate may influence judicial decisions. From Washington's day to the present, presidents have been acutely aware of the importance of appointments to the High Court and have made some appointments precisely as a response to certain decisions, in an effort either to maintain or to reverse them.[49] Even the prospect of a judicial vacancy can become part of an election campaign as candidates promise to select the "right" persons for the bench.

Other Court-curbing measures are ordinarily far less successful. On grounds of misconduct, Congress has removed seven judges of lower federal courts through impeachment, including District Judges Walter Nixon of Mississippi and Alcee Hastings of Florida in 1989, but never a Supreme Court justice. (Five other federal judges either have been acquitted by the Senate or have had charges against them dismissed before a Senate trial began.) In fact, only once has the Senate held an impeachment trial for a justice. That occurred in 1805, when the Jefferson administration attempted to have arch Federalist Justice Samuel Chase removed.[50] The House of Representatives might have begun impeachment proceedings against Justice Abe Fortas after certain improprieties came to light in 1969, but Fortas resigned.[51] This record would not have surprised Thomas Jefferson. "Having found from experience that impeachment is an impracticable thing, a mere scarecrow, they [the judiciary] consider themselves secure for life."[52]

Congress may also attack the Court by withdrawing jurisdiction to hear certain types of cases. Article III grants appellate jurisdiction to the Supreme Court but "with such exceptions, and under such regulations as the Congress shall make." Thus, opponents of the Court's position on particular issues can try to prevent cases raising those issues from reaching the Court. This is an extreme measure, frequently threatened but only very rarely carried out.[53] Moreover, the Court long ago intimated that it would not abide by repeals of its jurisdiction where those repeals were designed to determine the outcomes of cases.[54] Such intimations, however, have not deterred representatives and senators from trying. In 1957, Senator William Jenner campaigned to withdraw the Court's jurisdiction in five categories of cases, all involving loyalty–security matters.[55] In 1979, Senator Jesse Helms pushed a measure through the Senate that would have withdrawn High Court jurisdiction in school prayer cases, but the House tabled the bill and it died.[56]

Finally, even judicial organization has political implications. Of all the federal courts, the Constitution requires only the Supreme Court. Article III left the creation of other ("inferior") courts to the discretion of Congress. Ever since, political factors, not mere housekeeping consider-ations, have infused debates over the number and types of courts and the kinds of cases they would be authorized to decide.[57] Moreover, the num-ber of justices allotted for the Supreme Court has been driven by more than the practical needs of a growing country. Between 1789 and 1869, Congress changed the number of justices from six to five, five to six, six to seven, seven to nine, nine to ten, ten to seven, and seven to nine—each time at least partly with an eye to influencing the Court's constitutional jurisprudence.

Proposition 3: Policy Change

Like the previous proposition, the third looks to the effects of electoral entanglement on the Court, other political institutions, and public policy. In contrast to the second proposition, however, this proposition focuses on relations between the judiciary and the rest of the political system in the longer run, anticipating that the Court will soon be responsive to changing political winds. "[T]h' supreme coort follows th' iliction returns," observed Finley Peter Dunne's newspaper column character Mr. Dooley near the turn of the twentieth century.[58] The proposition assumes that time is on the side of the party that has come to power, either precipitating a change of mind by the "old Court" or allowing the appointment of justices who reflect the views of the new ruling coalition. The proposition thus is akin to a body of opinion that depicts the Court as ordinarily aligned with, not against, the prevailing political forces of the day. "The political views on the Court," Robert Dahl concluded in the 1950s, "are never for long out of line with the views dominant among the lawmaking majorities of the United States."[59] Instead of playing a countermajoritarian role, at odds with the popular mood, the Court soon reverts to a legitimizing role in which the justices place the stamp of approval on policies once deemed constitution-ally unacceptable.

Nonetheless, in reflecting on this and the previous proposition, several cautions seem in order. To say that the Court is an issue in a campaign does not necessarily mean that the Court is in reality identified entirely with one party or another. The Court may not have supported all aspects of a party's or an administration's policies before the election. There also may be con-siderable agreement between the two major parties on a variety of policy matters. Rather, to say that the Court is engaged in a campaign typically means that one or more of its decisions have affected a prominent concern: that is, that the decision directly touches a subject over which the parties divide and about which the electorate holds, or comes to hold, strong opinions.

Second, what the Court does between elections in which it is embroiled may be just as important as what it does immediately before and after those elections.[60] As will be seen, between the elections of 1896 and 1936, for example, the Court was neither static nor monolithic. Some decisions appeared surprisingly progressive or pro-regulatory, and when the conservative or antiregulatory view prevailed, there were often powerful dissents. Moreover, one study has found that nearly half of the instances when the Court invalidated state and national legislation between 1837 and 1964 involved issues *not* salient to the elections that demarcate the eras of American political party development.[61]

Third, even when the Court undergoes noticeable change, as happened after 1936, the causes may be many. After all, the "Roosevelt Court," as it came to be known in the early 1940s, was not characterized merely by its consistency, in contrast to its predecessor, in upholding social welfare and economic measures. Although the Court's propensity to invalidate such programs had drawn the judiciary into the partisan fray in 1936, the "new Court" encountered an increasing number of cases involving nonproprietarian aspects of civil liberties and civil rights—issues barely visible on the Court's docket before 1937. Furthermore, the Roosevelt Court was more disposed than previous courts to rule in favor of such rights. So, while one might safely conclude that the Court's "defeat" in the election of 1936 *allowed* or even encouraged these sweeping changes to go forward, one must be wary in attributing *all* of the change to the election alone. As chapter 6 will show, there were other factors at work as well.

Proposition 4: Campaign Impact

Whereas the second and third propositions examine the postelection consequences of the judiciary's electoral involvement, the fourth probes the effects of the Court on the campaign itself. The bench ordinarily becomes ensnared in an election only because of particular decisions that it has made or seems about to make. Candidates galvanize voters by taking the bench to task, first by focusing attention on the justices as the culpable persons and then, by linking the outcome of the election to the direction of future decisions and policies, and promising corrective measures. Moreover, because the legal process seems almost invariably to characterize even the most complex problems as if they consisted only of two sides—one for, the other against—what the Court says and does may in turn make it easier for parties and candidates to sharpen and clarify opposing positions. Policy-making by litigation seems ready-made for a two-party system where the "outs" seek to seize power by attacking the "ins." Furthermore, as will be developed in more detail with respect to the fifth proposition, certain peculiarities of the Court itself make it an inviting target for a politician in search of votes.

In one scenario, the Court becomes a factor in a campaign because it has generated an issue. That is, a decision proclaims policy on which parties and their candidates feel compelled to take opposite positions. The issue probably will not literally be new, in the sense that a division now exists among people on a subject where none existed before, but it will be new to congressional and presidential politics. For example, almost everyone knows that abortion was a contentious moral and political issue in the United States long before 1973, but as chapter 8 explains, it was the Supreme Court's decision in *Roe* v. *Wade* in that year that transformed the abortion debate and, with it, the political system as well. The Court not only *nationalized* what had heretofore been a matter for each state to resolve for itself but, by taking the position that it did, *constitutionalized* abortion policy. Opponents and supporters of the rule announced in *Roe* thus had little choice but to attack and defend the bench.

A second scenario follows a somewhat different path. An issue may be "national" in the sense that it has already engaged the attention of Congress and/or the presidency. The issue is thus salient in the absence of any intervention by the Supreme Court. For instance, as chapter 4 shows, the extent of national authority over slavery in the territories and what the policy on that subject should be were at or near the top of the congressional agenda for a dozen years after 1848. But judicial entanglement in presidential electoral politics began only after the Court took sides in the Dred Scott case, bestowing constitutional legitimacy on one side of the debate and constitutional illegitimacy on the other side, and foreclosing all options but one for Congress in attempting to cope with the most divisive political issue of the century. Thereafter, no political leader could address slavery without also addressing the Supreme Court.

Proposition 5: Court, Nation, and Judicial Review

The fifth proposition focuses on judicial review and constitutional inter-pretation: the authority the Court possesses to say what the Constitution means and to invalidate statutes that, in the justices' view, contravene the nation's fundamental law. This is the judicial function that most sets Amer-ican courts apart from the courts of many other lands and that, along with interpretation of statutes, assures a policy-making role for American courts. The proposition assumes that criticism of the Court will not always be directed solely to specific decisions but may also include debate, at a more fundamental level, over the Court's authority to make such decisions in the first instance and its place in the political system. While the debate may sometimes be confined to the scholarly community, it may extend more broadly to encompass political and opinion leaders and the general public as well. When the latter occurs, the probability increases that the debate will affect the Court and public policy. The point is *not* that entan-glement in a presidential campaign itself causes the debate. Rather, the point is that criticism of the bench that is sufficiently widespread to become part of a presidential campaign may arise from, and even con-tribute to, doubts about the propriety or legitimacy of the Court's role.

The possibility that the fifth proposition anticipates stems from what might be called the Supreme Court's "triple debility." The first is its ambivalent authority: the constitutional underpinnings of the Court's role as chief interpreter of the nation's fundamental law are equivocal at best and suspect at worst. The second is its antidemocratic function: judicial review assumes the authority of this unelected branch to invalidate deci-sions made by the elected branches. The third is its operational and struc-tural aloofness. Not only do the justices do much of their work away from the public eye and shun the sort of publicity that most politicians crave, but a decision of the Court on constitutional grounds cannot be altered through the devices one ordinarily employs to change public policy. That can be done only by the Court itself or by the extraordinary resort to amendment of the Constitution. That the Court has long appeared delib-erately to be different in its behavioral and political isolation from the rest of the national government may make the Court an inviting target for someone eager to convince voters that the justices have thwarted the will of the people.

Fundamentally, the Court is susceptible to a kind of challenge to its work that Congress does not share. While citizens may complain about the wisdom of policies Congress adopts or oppose the manner in which a committee conducts hearings, there is surely little doubt that one of Congress's chief functions is to legislate: that is, to consider and then to adopt or reject various policies. The very first sentence of Article I in the Constitution declares, "All legislative Powers herein granted shall be vested in a Congress." Section 8 of Article I contains a catalog of subjects to which the legislative power extends, a list vastly expanded by the "elastic" or necessary and proper clause that concludes the section.

The Constitution's text offers less expressivity to the Court. While Article III vests the "judicial Power of the United States" in "one Supreme Court," the words do not specifically authorize judicial review. Besides the absence of express authorization, judicial review seems "undemocratic" because it allows unelected judges to block actions of the people's elected representatives. (This charge should not be levied, however, against those *state* judiciaries that are elected or that are subject to periodic "retention" ballots.) Did the framers at the Philadelphia Convention of 1787 intend for the U.S. Supreme Court to have such power? The question cannot be answered with certainty.

While it was not until 1803 and the case of *Marbury* v. *Madison* that the Supreme Court first invalidated an act of Congress, some delegates at the Philadelphia Convention assumed that the Court could, and would, set aside laws that ran counter to the Constitution. As noted, in *Federalist* No. 78, Alexander Hamilton made an argument in support of judicial review that Chief Justice John Marshall followed closely in his *Marbury* opinion fifteen years later. Moreover, references to judicial review abound in the records of the state ratifying conventions, and some state courts made use of the power before Marshall did. Several U.S. Supreme Court decisions in the 1790s assumed judicial review but did not explain, justify, or apply it.[62] Nonetheless, if the Court was to possess the potentially important power of ascertaining constitutional limitations, it is strange that the Constitution would be largely silent. It is even stranger that the Constitution would be silent had the Court been expected to be the major policy player that it is today.

Within the language of the document, one can at most infer judicial review. The judicial power conferred on the Court by Article III extends to "all Cases . . . *arising under this Constitution.*"[63] Moreover, Article VI designates the Constitution, federal statutes pursuant to the Constitution, and treaties made under the authority of the United States as "the supreme Law of the Land," adding that "the judges in every State shall be bound thereby, any Thing in the Constitution or Laws of any State to the Contrary notwithstanding." Inserted to assure the supremacy of federal over state law (otherwise the union would have promptly disintegrated into chaos), the words appear to assume that state judges would be expected to invalidate state laws that conflicted with national law. Since Congress defined the Supreme Court's appellate jurisdiction in 1789 to include review of some state court decisions where the outcome turned on the meaning of the Constitution, Congress surely presumed some form of oversight of state policy by the U.S. Supreme Court. Nonetheless, as the next chapter will show, Marshall's justification of judicial review in *Marbury* rests less on what the Constitution says and more on the idea of a written Constitution: its expedience and the theory of limited government.

Aside from lingering doubts about the legitimacy of judicial review, other questions arise. There is, for example, the matter of the finality of constitutional interpretation. If the Supreme Court's decisions bind lower courts, are those decisions about the meaning of the Constitution also binding on other branches of government? This was one part of the controversy, discussed above, over Congress's authority to grant a greater degree of religious liberty through passage of the Religious Freedom Restoration Act than the Court had granted through construction of the free exercise clause. Is the Supreme Court merely *an* authority or is it *the* authority on the meaning of the Constitution? Should a decision by the Supreme Court be regarded as having ended debate over the proper construction of a provision in the Constitution?

Yet a third controversy arises over method: *how* are judges supposed to interpret the Constitution? The Constitution does not say. The problem arises from two characteristics of the Constitution. First, the document enumerates both the powers it grants and the limitations it imposes, but it defines neither. Thus, it may be clear from Section 8 of Article I that Congress possesses the authority to regulate "commerce" among the states, but it is by no means clear what this "commerce" encompasses and does not encompass. Second, the Constitution contains open-ended phrases such as "due process of law" and "equal protection" that not only convey little in the way of specific meaning but also invite interpretation to be supplied. If judges are to furnish a meaning in the context of deciding cases, where do they look for that meaning? Should a judge be confined to the "intent of the framers" of the Constitution in assigning meaning to a passage in the document or to the actual words of the document? May either of those be augmented by custom and usage, the Constitution's overall design, general principles derived from the American national experience, and the political and social needs of the current day? If so, does the Constitution then become little more than a repository for a judge's own values? Does interpretation convert constitutional supremacy into judicial supremacy? These questions are consequential: different answers and methods may well result in divergent conclusions about the powers of government and the liberties of individuals.

It is within the history of elections and the evolution of American political parties that the following chapters will place constitutional interpretation and the Supreme Court. The elections of 1800, 1832, 1860, 1936, and 1968 are examined individually in separate chapters. The remaining Court-centered elections—1896, 1912, 1924, 1980, and 1984—are together the subjects of a pair of chapters. The story demonstrates that the Court intersects with politics not merely because of the impact of its decisions on public policy but also because of its occasional place in the partisan life of the nation.

CHAPTER 2

Partisan Beginnings

A lthough it had been in existence for barely a decade, the federal judiciary first entangled itself in partisan conflict through events culminating in the presidential election of 1800. Opponents pointed to judicial inattention to limits on national power and to a collaboration with Congress and the presidency to repress the political opposition. The episode nudged the Court after the election into a posture of independence, stimulated articulation of an institutional role, and established the Supreme Court as a politically significant branch of government. The setting for these events was the maturing of the first party system in which the judiciary both influenced and was influenced by the partisan life of the nation.

THE FIRST PARTY SYSTEM

Characterized by contests between Federalists and Republicans (initially called Antifederalists), the first party system took shape at the national level soon after government under the Constitution got under way in 1789.[1] Party development proceeded from the top down rather than moving upward from the grass roots. In supporting or opposing policy proposals in Congress, members found themselves increasingly voting with the same group of colleagues on one side of an issue or the other.[2] In turn, members sought reelection by defending their positions on legislation and so carried to the electorate the disputes that had divided Congress. Partisanship thus filtered down to the voters, leading them to associate one kind of policies with one group and different policies with another. The result was that congressional factions acquired local followings that duplicated congressional divisions.[3] The same divisions were apparent in the 1796 contest between Federalist John Adams and Republican Thomas Jefferson—the third presidential election but the first in which the identity of the person to be chosen was not a foregone conclusion. Nonetheless, these original parties were not the mass-based organizations designed to mobilize the electorate, that would develop in the 1820s and 1830s. The earliest parties existed more as parties in the government than as parties in the electorate.[4]

Until the early 1800s, the main issues of the first party system focused on political and economic structure. Federalists typically favored more centralization, and therefore a larger role for the national government. Republicans wanted state governments to remain the dominant power in the political system, as they had been under the Articles of Confederation. Federalists were comfortable with a relatively closed (or "elite") political system, while Republicans preferred a more open system with a broader franchise. Unlike the Republicans, Federalists wanted the national government to pursue an active economic policy. Moreover, after the fall of the monarchy in France, Federalists were pro-British in foreign policy; Republicans were pro-French.

The Republicans (also known as Democratic-Republicans) replaced the Federalists as the ruling party after 1800, when Thomas Jefferson became president. The Federalists gradually faded away as a credible political force and by 1820 there was no candidate for the presidency running as a Federalist. Federalists were still elected to the House and Senate, but only in very small numbers. (Of course, the people who had been Federalists did not vanish but gradually became a faction within the Republican party.)

After Jefferson, Republicans nominally continued to govern as a party under Presidents James Madison and James Monroe (see appendix 1). Yet, while various political divisions continued to exist at the state level and while there were shifting coalitions among Republicans at the national level, the years 1816–1824 lacked major national issues of the intensity that had earlier sparked partisan combat. The period thus came to be called the "Era of Good Feeling," although, as will be seen in the next chapter, the "good feeling" did not fully embrace the Supreme Court. Rivalry among Republican leaders for the presidency and the reemergence of major national policy issues marked the end of the first party system in the mid-1820s.

THE SUPREME COURT BEFORE JOHN MARSHALL

The Supreme Court's first decade was characterized by obscurity, weakness, and uncertainty. To a degree, each was both a cause and an effect of a high turnover in membership and an absence of effective leadership. Moreover, the Court had relatively little of significance to do. Three years passed before it decided its first case, and during the entire decade the number of decisions totaled only about sixty.

After President Washington initially filled the six positions Congress had authorized for the Supreme Court, he and President John Adams encountered eight vacancies between 1790 and 1800 (see appendix 2). Moreover, the Court had three chief justices during the same period.[5] By contrast, of the twelve chief justices between Marshall's appointment in 1801 and Warren Burger's retirement in 1986, only two (Harlan Fiske Stone and Fred M. Vinson) served for fewer than nine years. For some early jurists, other positions were clearly more appealing. Washington's first choice for one of the initial appointments in 1789 was Robert Harrison. Five days after his confirmation by the Senate, he was selected chancellor of Maryland, a position he deemed preferable to a seat on the Supreme Court. John Jay, the first chief justice, did not attend a session of the Court after 1793, accepted a diplomatic mission to England in 1794 that led to an accord that bears his name, and resigned in 1795 to become governor of New York. John Rutledge resigned as associate justice in 1791 to become chief justice of the South Carolina Court of Common Pleas.

Detracting from the attractiveness of the high bench was the circuit-riding that Congress imposed on the justices, a duty not finally eliminated until 1891. In addition to sitting collectively as the Supreme Court, justices sat as judges of the circuit courts, one of two "inferior" federal courts established by the Judiciary Act of 1789. Though the act provided for three types of courts (district courts, circuit courts, and the Supreme Court), it authorized the appointment of judges only for the district courts and the Supreme Court. Except for a brief period in 1801–1802, no separate circuit judgeships existed until 1869. Each circuit court was at first staffed by two justices (a number soon reduced to one) and one district judge. Consequently, the early justices spent more time holding circuit court than they did sitting on the Supreme Court. Moreover, circuit-riding was onerous and sometimes dangerous, given the long distances to be traveled and the primitive transportation of the day.

Despite a handful of noteworthy decisions during the period,[6] by the close of the eighteenth century the Court only barely resembled the political force it would later become. If the Congress and the presidency had already begun to assume a modern shape, the Court had not. So in 1800, when John Adams asked John Jay to return to his old job as chief justice,

Jay turned the president down. The Court, Jay explained, "would not obtain the energy, weight and dignity which are essential to its affording due support to the National Government."[7]

THE ELECTION OF 1800

Both the victorious challengers (the Republicans) and the vanquished incumbents (the Federalists) labeled the election of 1800 a "revolution,"[8] and indeed the event was highly significant on at least four counts. First, the nation experienced its first realigning election. Not only did Republicans displace Federalists and maintain control of the government for years afterward, but the Federalists would never recover as a organized political force. (Ordinarily, a realigning election would mark the beginning of a new party system. In this instance, however, most scholars include the decade prior to the election of 1800 as part of the same party system because political parties had only begun to develop.)

Second, in none of the preceding elections had presidential electors displayed such party cohesion. In 1796, Federalists and Republicans had cast votes for Adams and Jefferson, respectively, for president but divided their second vote among eleven party figures for vice president. By contrast, in 1800, with one exception, all electors voted either for the Republican ticket of Jefferson and Burr or for the Federalist ticket of Adams and Pinckney.

Third, the election brought about the nation's first experience with "divided government" whereby each party controlled at least one of the three branches. Although the Republicans had won the presidency and now had a majority in both houses of Congress for the first time, the Supreme Court and the rest of the federal judiciary remained staffed by the Federalists whom Washington and Adams had appointed. This state of affairs did not go unnoticed by the new president and Congress.

Fourth, the election occasioned the world's first peaceful transfer of political power from one party to another.[9] This was a greater achievement than is sometimes acknowledged. True, the Federalists conveyed control of both houses of Congress and the presidency to the Republicans, but they did so only reluctantly. Federalists staged a frantic last-minute effort to keep Jefferson out of the White House by creating a constitutional impasse.

The impasse was a consequence of the effect of the development of political parties on the procedure for selecting a president that the Philadelphia

Convention of 1787 had devised. Until modified by the Twelfth Amendment in 1804, the Constitution required presidential electors to vote for two persons for president: the individual with a majority of votes became president, and the runner-up became vice president. Electors cast their ballots for president on December 3, 1800, but it was not until near the end of the month, when news trickled in from the closely contested states, that the Federalists knew with certainty of their defeat. However, while a Federalist defeat meant a Republican triumph, it did not necessarily mean a Jeffersonian triumph. Of the Federalist electors, all sixty-five had cast a vote for John Adams, sixty-four also voted for Charles Cotesworth Pinckney, and the remaining vote went to John Jay. Republicans should have followed a similar pattern but did not. Instead, the seventy-three Republican electors each voted for Jefferson and Aaron Burr. Republicans thus had a majority of the electoral votes and a tie vote for president.

As president of the Senate, Vice President Jefferson presided over the joint session of Congress on February 11, 1801, when the certificates of the electors from the sixteen states were tabulated, making official the count that had been known for six weeks. Because Jefferson and Burr were tied, selection of the president devolved upon the House of Representatives, where voting would be by state. However, this was the Federalist-dominated House chosen in 1798,[10] not the newly elected House the Republicans would control, and Federalist members had decided as early as mid-January that they would vote for Burr in an attempt to deny Jefferson the presidency. Through thirty-five ballots on five days, the result was the same: eight states for Jefferson and six for Burr, with two states not voting because their delegations were equally divided. (The fact that Burr did not remove himself from consideration, thus beating the Federalists at their own game, doubtless did little to endear him to Jefferson.) Finally, on February 17, during the thirty-sixth ballot, Federalists in the divided, and hitherto nonvoting, delegations of Vermont and Maryland abstained, thus handing control of those delegations to the Republicans. Breaking the deadlock averted the distinct possibility of anarchy and meant that the inauguration, then only two weeks away, could proceed on schedule.[11]

The Alien and Sedition Acts

Issues that dominated campaign debate in 1800 sprang from policies pursued by the Adams administration. Following implementation of the Jay

Treaty between the United States and Great Britain, French privateers seized American ships, and the French government refused to receive Washington's envoy, C. C. Pinckney, as minister to France. This rebuff led Adams in 1797, the first year of his presidency, to name three commissioners (Pinckney, John Marshall, and Elbridge Gerry) to attempt negotiations with France. The result was the "XYZ affair," which provoked a wave of anti-French feeling in the United States once Congress authorized publication of the commissioners' dispatches in April 1798.[12]

As the pro-British party, the Federalists stood to gain from this widespread resentment against France. Not only did they enlarge their majority in the House in the elections of 1798,[13] but they succeeded in enacting four statutes in June and July that were ostensibly designed to cope with foreign menaces. Bipartisan support existed for only one: the Alien Enemies Act, which would operate only in wartime against subjects of the hostile country who were present in the United States. Republicans objected to the other three because the laws might well include the political opposition within their reach.

The first of the controversial pieces of legislation, the Naturalization Act, nearly tripled the residency period required for state and national citizenship. The measure thus deprived Republicans in the short run of an increasingly important source of political strength, particularly among Irish immigrants. The Alien Act followed seven days later. Unlike the Alien Enemies law, it gave the chief executive extraordinary, if temporary, peacetime control over aliens: the president could order the deportation of any alien deemed "dangerous to the peace and safety of the United States" or involved "in any treasonable or secret machinations against the government thereof."[14] "Aliens" of course applied to all who were not citizens, including some Republican sympathizers.

Less than three weeks later, the Sedition Act became law on July 14. Cleverly crafted to expire on March 3, 1801, it "cut perilously near the root of freedom of speech and of the press," Woodrow Wilson commented a century later.[15] Section 2 was particularly worrisome to Republicans. Carrying maximum penalties of a two thousand dollar fine and a two-year imprisonment, it forbade "any person," among other things, to

> write, print, utter or publish . . . any false, scandalous and malicious writing or writings against the government of the United States, or either house of Congress of the United States, or the President of the United States, with intent to defame the said government, or either

house of the said Congress, or the said President, or to bring them, or either of them, into contempt or disrepute; or to excite against them, or either or any of them, the hatred of the good people of the United States.

More than the other two statutes, it would soon demonstrate how the judiciary could become a weapon in partisan warfare.

Federalists insisted upon passage of a sedition law not merely because they regarded their Republican opponents as "heralds of calumny and apostles of insurrection,"[16] but also because of uncertainty whether the prosecutorial authority of the United States subsumed a criminal law jurisdiction at common law.[17] Punishment of libels against the government may have been controversial, but it was hardly novel. The law of seditious libel was well established in eighteenth-century England, and it had been selectively employed in colonial America.[18] Some of the states of the Union utilized it even after the turn of the nineteenth century.[19]

In spite of the First Amendment's command that "Congress shall make no law . . . abridging the freedom . . . of the press," Federalists argued that no government should be without authority to protect itself from unwarranted verbal abuse. Their view was that the First Amendment forbade only prior restraints—that is, censorship of material before publication—which had been common in England before the eighteenth century. Because the Sedition Act imposed no restraints in advance, the law was not inconsistent with freedom of the press. Moreover, in mitigation of the rigor of the English law of seditious libel, the 1798 statute allowed truth as a defense, thus forcing the law's opponents to defend the right to make false accusations.[20] Among prominent Federalists only John Marshall opposed the measures, but his objections were based on expediency, not constitutionality.[21] Nonetheless, partisanship was so acute that such dissent caused Federalists in New England to brand him a "half Federalist."[22] Later Marshall publicly defended the constitutionality of the laws, maintaining that the national government possessed the power to protect "the nation from the intrigues and conspiracies of dangerous aliens; [and] . . . to secure the union from their wicked machinations."[23]

From its introduction in Congress, Republicans opposed the Sedition Act on two separate constitutional grounds, one jurisdictional and the other substantive. First, since the national government was a government of delegated powers and since the Constitution had conferred no authority over political expression to Congress—indeed, the First Amendment had expressly withheld that power—Congress lacked jurisdiction to punish libels against itself, the president, or the government generally. Rather, under the Tenth Amendment, authority to punish seditious libel remained with the states. The second argument, inconsistent with the first, involved free speech. Since popular government rested on the consent of the governed, expression of public opinion was essential. Punishing criticism of the government or those in authority was therefore at odds with republican principles, a point that presumably applied with equal vigor to state, as well as national, prosecutions. At heart, expediency drove both arguments: as the opposition, Republicans would be the targets of any concerted effort by the national government to squelch dissent.

Directed principally by Secretary of State Timothy Pickering, enforcement of the Sedition Act commenced soon after passage; the first trials followed in the fall of 1798.[24] "The Alien and Sedition Laws are working hard,"[25] Jefferson wrote to George Mason in August.[26] Eventually, the government obtained indictments of fourteen individuals and convictions of ten. Numerous others were arrested or threatened with prosecution. The "chief enforcement effort was tied directly to the presidential campaign of 1800."[27] Pickering's strategy included legal action against the five leading Republican newspapers in the nation. They circulated widely, and many smaller newspapers routinely reprinted material from them. Thus, "a blow at any of the 'big five' Republican presses would be a severe setback to the Democratic–Republican party in 1800,"[28] or so Federalists and Republicans alike assumed.

The Judicial Response

Republican fears were particularly exacerbated by the partisan conduct of the judiciary that confirmed suspicions Jefferson had expressed as early as 1795: that judges had become an arm of the presidency. The executive "has been able to draw into this vortex the Judicare branch of the Government, and by their expectancy of sharing the other offices in the Executive gift to make them auxiliary to the Executive in all its views, instead of forming a balance between that and the Legislature, as it was originally intended."[29] That assessment was hardly less credible in 1800.[30] A union of the executive and the judiciary appeared aimed at maintaining Federalists in power.

Judicial partisanship manifested itself in three ways in enforcement of the Sedition Act, even though the Supreme Court never ruled on the constitutionality of the legislation.[31] Recall that trials of serious federal criminal matters, including offenses under the Sedition Act, occurred in the circuit courts. Each circuit court was staffed by a district judge and a Supreme Court justice.

First, the justices let their interest in enforcement of the Sedition Act be plainly known, routinely charging federal grand juries to be alert for "all offenses" against the statute.[32] Perhaps no jurist was more ardent at this task than Justice Samuel Chase, whose enthusiasm would later almost cost him his seat on the Supreme Court. At the trial in 1800 of James T. Callender, a vituperative pamphleteer and writer for the Richmond *Examiner*, Chase not only urged the grand jury to bring an indictment but supplied the grand jurors with a copy of the writing at issue.[33] Republicans could fairly believe that the federal judiciary acted as prosecutor as well as judge.

Second, the general demeanor of the judges in the conduct of trials and other court business communicated outright hostility to Republicans. Surviving trial records are replete with intemperate remarks to defense counsel and witnesses. According to one account of a grand jury charge delivered by Justice William Paterson:

> The *Law* was laid down in a masterly manner: *Politics* were set in their true light by holding up the Jacobins [Republicans] as the disorganizers of our happy country, and the only instruments of introducing discontent and dissatisfaction among the well meaning part of the community. *Religion & Morality* were pleasingly inculcated and enforced as being necessary to good government, good order, and good laws; for "when the righteous [Federalists] are in authority, the people rejoice."[34]

Judges also tolerated partisan behavior by U.S. marshals. Rather than selecting grand jurors and petit jurors according to the laws of the states where the circuit court met, as they were supposed to do, marshals typically packed the panels with Federalists, including local politicians.[35]

Third, the Federalist judiciary refused seriously to entertain motions by counsel for the defense that the Sedition Act was unconstitutional. The record of the trial of Matthew Lyon that Justice Paterson conducted in Vermont, for example, includes the following entry: "The [jury] box having been filled, and the jury sworn, the defendant interposed an additional plea, to the effect that the sedition law was unconstitutional, which plea was stricken off by the court."[36] Paterson's refusal stemmed not from a perceived absence of authority to act but from a disinclination to do so in this instance. While the Supreme Court had yet to declare a statute unconstitutional, the justices (Paterson included) had implicitly accepted their power to do so in 1796 when the Court upheld the validity of a congressionally imposed tax on carriages.[37]

In Callender's case, tried before Justice Chase in Virginia, defense counsel, in an apparently desperate move, attempted to inform the jury that jurors could consider the constitutionality of the Sedition Act in passing on Callender's guilt. "Take your seat, sir, if you please," Chase instructed. "Now I will tell you that this is irregular and inadmissible; it is not competent to the jury to decide on this point." Rather, "I draw this conclusion, that the judicial power of the United States is the only proper and competent authority to decide whether any statute made by Congress (or any of the state legislatures) is contrary to, or in violation of, the Federal Constitution."[38] While Chase did not explain in this case why the Sedition Act conformed with the Constitution, the implication of his elaborate defense of judicial review was that the statute's constitutionality was hardly open to question. Indeed, Chase had declared that to be true two months earlier, at Thomas Cooper's trial in Philadelphia:

> All governments which I have ever read or heard of punish libels against themselves. . . . A republican government can only be destroyed in two ways; the introduction of luxury, or the licentiousness of the press. This latter is the more slow, but most sure and certain, means of bringing about the destruction of the government. The legislature of this country, knowing this maxim, has thought proper to pass a law to check this licentiousness of the press.[39]

Consequently, it was difficult for Republicans to resist the conclusion that the judiciary was conducting its own campaign to keep the Federalists in power. Statements by federal judges both in and out of court sounded more like campaign oratory than legal commentary. Chief Justice Oliver Ellsworth was sarcastically critical of John Marshall's opposition to the Sedition Act.[40] Chase, and perhaps other justices,[41] electioneered for Adams at political gatherings in Maryland during August 1800, and as a result the Supreme Court had to adjourn for several days for want of a quorum.[42] Justice Bushrod Washington actively campaigned in support of Federalist candidate C. C. Pinckney.[43]

Through the sedition trials particularly, justices of the Supreme Court had jumped into a political cauldron. Moreover, other "delicate questions" that so sharply divided the two parties had come before the justices sitting on the circuit benches in 1798–1800, and "on each of these questions the decisions had been invariably adverse to the view held" by the Jeffersonians.[44]

The Republican Counterattack

The judiciary's refusal seriously to entertain constitutional objections to the Sedition Act provoked countermeasures by Republicans. These steps both framed a key issue for the campaign of 1800 and set in motion the first debate since 1788 over judicial review and constitutional limitations. Experience had taught Republicans that Congress could not be trusted to be the arbiter of limits on itself and that the courts would not intervene to block palpable transgressions of the Constitution. The Republican conclusion was that the states must act, as Kentucky and Virginia did in passing two sets of resolves in the fall and early winter of 1798. The resolves were the opening shots in the conflict that would culminate in Jefferson's electoral victory.

Secretly drafted by Jefferson and James Madison,[45] respectively, the Kentucky and Virginia Resolves (or "Resolutions," as they have also been called) represented attempts to create a forum for debate that would focus attention on abuses of power and lead to a repeal of the detested alien and sedition statutes. Besides asserting that the Sedition Act was a violation of the Constitution, the resolves tendered an answer to a question the Constitution left in doubt. If the Constitution was the supreme law of the land, as by Article VI it declared itself to be, who or what would determine the Constitution's meaning? Phrased differently, who or what would settle constitutional disputes?

By 1798 some thought that those responsibilities would lie with the judiciary. Even Jefferson, whom historians have not regarded as a friend of judicial authority, thought as much, at least in connection with the protection of individual rights. In March 1789, he had urged James Madison to support Bill of Rights amendments to the Constitution because of an argument "which has great weight with me, the legal check which it puts into the hands of the judiciary. This is a body, which if rendered independent, and kept strictly to their own department merits great confidence for their learning and integrity."[46] In 1798, he still advised that "the laws of the land, administered by upright judges, would protect you from an exercise of power unauthorized by the Constitution of the United States."[47] Yet, events had now revealed the judiciary's inadequacies. Champions of state power "began to appreciate for the first time the added sanction given to national authority by judicial decision."[48]

The answer the Kentucky and Virginia Resolves proffered was that the states through their legislatures would be the arbiters of the Constitution's meaning. Accordingly, the legislatures of the two states proclaimed that "in case of a deliberate, palpable, and dangerous exercise of other powers not granted by the said compact [the Constitution], the states, who are parties thereto, have the right and are in duty bound to interpose for arresting the progress of the evil, and for maintaining within their respective limits the authorities, rights, and liberties appertaining to them."[49] Because the Alien and Sedition Acts had exceeded Congress's powers, they were "not law" and therefore were "altogether void and of no force."

Both sets of resolves called on the legislatures of the other states to act similarly. Left unclear was a method by which such legislative declarations of unconstitutionality were to be operationalized. The Kentucky Resolves, for example, had omitted one means Jefferson's draft had included: "co-States . . . will concur in declaring these acts void and of no force, and will each take measures of its own for providing that neither of these acts . . . shall be exercised within their respective territories."[50] At the very least, the assumption must have been that, faced with a phalanx of adverse official opinion from state legislatures, Congress would be moved to repeal the laws.[51]

Judged solely by their call for action by the states, the Kentucky and Virginia Resolves failed. The legislatures of only seven states—all Northern and mainly Federalist—responded, each rejecting the view that state legislatures were the proper forum for resolving constitutional disputes. In the remaining states, opinion was so divided over the remedy Kentucky and Virginia had advanced that no resolutions were adopted to counter the Federalist response.[52]

Ironically, one outcome of the debate sparked by the Kentucky and Virginia Resolves was wholly unintended by the sponsors: a vindication of judicial prerogative, state and federal. Whatever defects lay in the Alien and Sedition Acts, the cure advanced by the resolves must have seemed too extreme to too many: state legislative oversight and review of congressional acts implied legislative supremacy within the states as well. As the House and Senate in Massachusetts declared, "the decision of all cases . . . arising under the Constitution of the United States, and the construction of all laws made in pursuance thereof, are exclusively vested by the people in the judicial courts of the United States." Were the states to assume the role claimed by Kentucky and Virginia, the Constitution

> would be reduced to a mere cipher . . . ; every act of the federal government which thwarted the views or checked the ambitious projects of a particular state, or of its leading and influential members, would be the object of opposition and of remonstrance; while the people, convulsed and confused by the conflict between two hostile jurisdictions, enjoying the protection of neither, would be wearied into a submission to some bold leader, who would establish himself on the ruins of both.[53]

The Campaign

Although the resolves were a constitutional failure, they were a political success. Denunciation of the Alien and Sedition Acts comprised a key part of the policy alternatives Republicans offered voters in 1800. Those laws were not the only issue of the campaign, to be sure (other major grievances included Adams's expansion of the military and the increased taxation to pay for it), but without them it is far from certain that Republicans would have won.[54] The election, after all, was close. No other issue cast the Republicans as victims of political persecution; no other issue drew a clearer distinction between the parties; no other issue was better designed to energize opposition against the Federalists. Alone, the Sedition Act "furnished a ready text which the Democratic-Republicans used to incite the American people to legal 'insurgency' at the polls."[55] The "mass of the people, especially in the Miiddle [sic] and Southern States, regarded the sedition trials as something more than a mere tussle between the administration and a horde of foreign libellers."[56] Moreover, the judiciary's behavior in those trials made the Sedition Act appear all the more menacing.

There was no party "platform" in the modern sense, but Jefferson wrote letters, circulated political pamphlets, urged friends to write essays for newspapers, and generally encouraged his supporters to emphasize, among other things, opposition to the Alien and Sedition Acts. "I am for . . . freedom of the press, and against all violations of the constitution to silence by force and not by reason the complaints or criticisms, just or unjust, of our citizens against the conduct of their agents,"[57] he explained early in the campaign.

Numerous campaign documents in the Middle Atlantic and Southern states repeated the theme. "What do the republican interest want by so zealously attempting a change of men?" queried Charles Pinckney (a cousin of Federalist C. C. Pinckney) in a pamphlet distributed in South Carolina: "Never to have such acts as the alien and sedition laws."[58] The Philadelphia *Aurora* on October 14, 1800, paired a list of eleven "Things As They Have Been" under the Federalists with an equal number of "Things As They Will Be" under the Republicans. In place of "Judges incorporated with the Government for political purposes, and . . . polluting the . . . seats of Justice" would be " Justice administered without political intolerance." In place of "A Sedition Law to protect corrupt magistrates and public default-ers" would be "The Liberty of the Press, and free enquiry into public char-acter, and our constitutional charter."[59] A declaration approved by a con-vention in New Jersey in September 1800 reminded voters "We have had an Alien and still have a Sedition law; by which many citizens have been deprived of their rights, and native Americans consigned to loathsome prisons for exercising the constitutional right of public enquiry."[60]

In reply Federalists avoided mention of the Alien and Sedition Acts but sought to identify the policies of the Adams administration with Wash-ington's and with the "present prosperous situation." Republican com-plaints were wide of the mark. The "fleet, the army, the taxes, *all the little evils* which were necessary to the attainment of these great and invaluable objects, make a strong impression, and are attributed as crimes to the gov-ernment,"[61] declared an appeal in Virginia. Signing himself "A Christian Federalist," a publicist in Delaware inquired,

> When they talk of a violation of the constitution, is there a many among you who can say he *ever saw it or felt it*; will you believe such things before you *see* or *feel them*? Will you be governed by your *own eyes and feelings*, or *those of other people*? . . . This is the 12th year of our government, and it has been in the same hands, and is it not as free and republican as it was the first year? If the *Jeffersonites* wish more republicanism, what must it result in? Not in the freedom of equal laws, which is true republicanism; but in the licentiousness of anar-chy, which in fact is the worst of tyranny. Let me press this question upon you, are not the offices of the government open to all, and do not the laws rest equally on the shoulders of all?[62]

The Federalist *Connecticut Courant* admonished its readers not to stoop "to learn the principles of liberty of the slave-holders of Virginia."[63] A pamphlet distributed in Rhode Island repeated that theme, reminded voters that they "enjoy a greater portion of civil and political happiness, than was ever enjoyed by any nation of which we have any account," and played upon their fears of domination by the most populous states.

> The great and powerful State of Virginia seems to take the lead in the present opposition to the measures of administration. The plausible and specious cry that the liberties of the people are in danger . . . originates in and emanates from that State. But will New-England-men . . . ever confess that they are in danger of slavery? Will such men . . . take lessons . . . from the State . . . where slavery constitutes a part of the policy of the government! . . . [W]hen she appears as the advocate of liberty and equality, and the enemy of aristocracy, we may be excused if we doubt her sincerity, and suspect that some other object, more agreeable to her prejudices and ambition, lies under the covering of the veil.[64]

The campaign of 1800, to be sure, was more than a campaign of rhetoric. Party committees and other types of organizations, especially for the Republicans, played a crucial role for the first time. Yet the rhetoric about the Sedition Act, sedition trials, and a general threat to liberty seemed important in helping to define what the parties declared to be at stake in the contest.

EFFECTS

The federal judiciary's entanglement in partisan conflict during 1798–1800, followed by the Republican electoral victory in 1800, allowed for several scenarios. Federalists might attempt to entrench themselves further into the judiciary as a fortress from which they might defend against Republicans. Perceiving the importance of the judiciary as an instrument of power, the newly empowered Republicans might try to remold the federal courts in their own image. Regarding the years 1798–1800 as a time of profound constitutional uncertainty, Supreme Court justices might aspire to shed the judiciary's partisan reputation, reassess its role, and assert independence from the other branches of government. To some degree, the decade after the "revolution of 1800" witnessed movement toward all three objectives, with lasting consequences for the political system.

The Federalist Initiative

After Adams's electoral defeat became fact, but before Jefferson's term began, Federalist actions again made the judiciary an object of Republican displeasure. Upon receiving word in early December of Oliver Ellsworth's resignation as chief justice, Adams made sure that he, not Jefferson, would name Ellsworth's successor. Ellsworth had written to Adams from France on October 16, 1800, citing declining health as his reason for leaving the Court.[65] His decision to resign, therefore, seems to have been independent of the political events of the fall. Given the slow pace of transatlantic mail in those days, the most recent news Ellsworth could have possessed of events in the United States would have been of very late summer. Jefferson apparently believed as much, supposing that Ellsworth resigned when he did only because he expected an Adams victory. Had Ellsworth anticipated a different outcome, Jefferson thought that decency would have dictated inaction so that the new president could fill the vacancy.[66]

Adams, however, persevered to make sure that the Supreme Court remained Federalist. On December 18, the president picked former Chief Justice John Jay for the post, and the Federalist-controlled Senate confirmed the appointment on December 19. Jay, however, declined to accept, citing deficiencies in the judicial system that, ironically, Congress was about to address. Party leaders then urged that the nod go to a staunch Federalist such as William Paterson, who was the most senior associate justice on the Supreme Court, or to C. C. Pinckney.[67] Instead, on January 20, with minimal consultation, Adams turned to his forty-five-year-old secretary of state, John Marshall[68] of Virginia, one of Jefferson's distant cousins, whom the president-to-be sometimes referred as "that gloomy malignity."[69]

The second move belonged to Congress, with enactment of a major reorganization of the federal judiciary three weeks after Marshall's appointment. The Judiciary Act of 1801 (1) relieved justices of the Supreme Court of their circuit-riding duties; (2) created sixteen circuit judgeships (Republicans would call those named to these seats "midnight judges" because of the timing of the appointments in the last hours of the Adams administration); (3) enlarged the jurisdiction of the circuit courts, at the expense of state courts, to include, among other things, adjudication of "federal questions"; and (4) stipulated a reduction in the number of justices, at the next vacancy, from six to five.

On February 27, Congress passed a far more minor bill, but one that would soon figure prominently. "An Act Concerning the District of Columbia" authorized an unlimited number of justices of the peace for the nation's capital. Adams appointed forty-two (including William Marbury) on March 2, and the Senate confirmed them on March 3, only a day before Jefferson took office. Under the two acts combined, Adams made ninety-three judicial and legal appointments in the closing days of his term.[70]

The provisions in the Judiciary Act had been discussed in Congress for several years, and most could be justified as examples of reasonable reform. For example, the circuit judgeships not only freed the justices from a physically taxing burden but also eliminated the untowardness of a justice's sitting in an appellate capacity to review his handiwork in a trial capacity. The planned reduction in the number of justices might be defended as a step to avoid tie votes or as recognition that the new circuit courts would reduce demands on the justices. Yet its obvious immediate effect was to postpone by one death or one retirement the third president's first opportunity to put a Republican jurist on the Supreme Court. Coming, as the statute did, only a few weeks before the end of Adams's term, it and the District of Columbia Act reeked of partisanship. (As events unfolded, had the Court's size remained at five, Jefferson would not have been able to make an appointment to the Supreme Court until well into his second term.)

Republican Countermoves

The federal courts were becoming "a hospital of decayed politicians," exclaimed John Randolph.[71] Jefferson was worried, too, but his concern went beyond Randolph's. Republicans had generally opposed an enlargement of federal judicial power, precisely the objective of the act of 1801. Worse, the new judges with the expanded authority would doubtless come from the other party. "They have retired into the judiciary as a stronghold . . . and from that battery all the works of republicanism are to be beaten down and erased. By a fraudulent use of the Constitution, which has made judges irremovable, they have multiplied useless judges merely to strengthen their phalanx."[72] William Giles of Virginia called for "the absolute repeal of the whole judiciary system" and advised Jefferson that "the revolution is incomplete so long as that strong fortress is in possession of the enemy."[73]

It came as no surprise that the new administration acted at once to reduce Federalist influence in the judiciary. Among the president's first directives was the removal of U.S. attorneys and marshals who had displayed "high federalism," so as to protect "Republican citizens" against "the federalism of the courts."[74] But as for Federalists on the Supreme Court and lower federal courts, including the new circuit courts, he proceeded cautiously, commenting ten days after his inauguration that "the tenure of [the judiciary] makes it difficult to dislodge them."[75] However, by April he had decided to move the repeal of the act of 1801.[76] "The judiciary system of the United States, and especially that portion of it recently erected, will of course present itself to the contemplation of Congress,"[77] he advised legislators when they next convened in December. Indeed, some of the gleeful preelection judicial partisanship remained: two new circuit judges in the District of Columbia had directed a prosecutor to initiate a criminal libel action against the editor of the *National Intelligencer*, the administration newspaper,[78] for publishing a letter from "A friend to impartial justice" that attacked the judiciary.

Then on December 21 the Supreme Court issued an order to Secretary of State Madison to "show cause" why a writ of mandamus should not issue, directing him to deliver commissions of office to William Marbury and three other would-be justices of the peace who had not received their commissions from the acting secretary of state (John Marshall) following their appointments in the waning moments of the Adams administration.[79] The order may have given Jefferson one more reason "that the growing pretensions of the Judiciary must be curbed."[80] "What think you of the rule entered upon the Federal Court last week against the Secretary of State to show cause?" wondered Kentucky's Senator John Breckinridge. "I think it is the most daring attack which the annals of Federalism have yet exhibited. I wish the subject of the Courts to be brought forward in the Senate next week."[81]

The result was the Repeal Act. Introduced in the Senate on January 6 and signed into law on March 31, it abrogated the act of 1801, effective July 1. Aside from the merits and demerits of returning to the status quo ante, the bill posed at least one serious constitutional question: Could Congress abolish a tier of courts and the judicial offices that went with them? Not surprisingly, Federalists answered that question in the negative, as Republicans did in the affirmative. Because the former also predicted that the

Supreme Court would invalidate the Repeal Act, Republican representatives and senators from four states pressed a further argument: that the Court lacked the authority to invalidate an act of Congress and that Congress was sole the judge of the constitutionality of its own acts. "The Legislature have the exclusive right to interpret the Constitution in which regards the law-making power," asserted Senator Breckinridge, "and the Judges are bound to execute the laws they make."[82]

However, this theory failed to command the support of a congressional majority. Indeed, to forestall the opportunity of the Supreme Court to invalidate the act before it went into effect, Congress passed the Judiciary Act of 1802, a legislative shot across the judicial bow that postponed the justices' next term until February 1803. Nonetheless, the articulation of congressional supremacy in constitutional interpretation meant that within a span of three years, serious people had tendered three answers to the question of who or what was to settle disputes under the Constitution: state legislatures, the judiciary, and Congress.[83]

The widespread Republican perception of the judiciary as a partisan institution was also reflected in Jefferson's behavior when he had his first opportunity to make an appointment to the Supreme Court. The occasion was the resignation of Justice Alfred Moore in early 1804 because of ill health. Since Moore sat in the Sixth Circuit, Jefferson looked for a successor from Georgia or South Carolina who possessed not only integrity and legal acumen but also party loyalty. As Albert Gallatin, Jefferson's treasury secretary, advised the president, "The importance of filling this vacancy with a Republican and a man of sufficient talents to be useful, is obvious."[84] Gallatin's message was clear: any Republican whom Jefferson named would join a bench of five Federalists; to be "useful," the nominee would have to be talented. Within two days after receiving Gallatin's advice, Jefferson asked two members of Congress from South Carolina to assess possible candidates.[85] Of the several persons they reviewed, their obvious preference, and Jefferson's as well, was William Johnson: "a state judge, an excellent lawyer, prompt eloquent, of irreproachable character, Republican connections, and of good nerves in his political principles about 35 years old. was [sic] speaker some years."[86]

Jefferson's selection of Johnson helped to establish a pattern in Supreme Court appointments that has persisted. It is true that Washington and Adams had consciously picked justices supportive of their view of the Constitution, but Jefferson was the first president to use a Supreme Court appointment for the purpose of reorienting the bench. Jefferson was also among the first to experience an obvious judicial disappointment. While Johnson effectively articulated some Republican values during his tenure on the Court,[87] he was no automated mouthpiece for the administration. In an important mandamus case in circuit court testing the Embargo Act in 1808, Johnson not only ruled against the administration but gave the president a chiding. "The offices of our government, from the highest to the lowest, are equally subjected to legal restraint," he declared.[88]

As satisfying as filling the Supreme Court vacancy and passing the Repeal Act must have been to Republicans, most of the federal judiciary remained as the new administration had found it on March 4, 1801. To reach the Federalist judges whom they regarded as the most offensive, Republicans wielded the congressional power of impeachment.

Accordingly, in February 1803, the House initiated impeachment proceedings against U.S. District Judge John Pickering of New Hampshire, who had become mentally incapacitated and an alcoholic. While he was doubtless unfit to serve, his incapacity highlighted one of the Constitution's deficiencies: removal by impeachment and conviction extended only to "treason, bribery, or other high crimes and misdemeanors,"[89] not old age, infirmity, or incompetence. Some Republicans, however, considered impeachment as a general device to rid the judiciary of undesirables, including judges who had voted to invalidate an act of Congress or who held politically unacceptable views. As Virginia's Senator William Giles bluntly explained, "[A] removal by impeachment [is] nothing more than a declaration by Congress to this effect: you hold dangerous opinions, and if you are suffered to carry them into effect, you will work the destruction of the Union. We want your offices for the purpose of giving them to men who will fill them better."[90]

As soon as the Senate convicted and thereby removed Pickering from the bench in March 1804, the House directed its scrutiny to Justice Samuel Chase. While the public record of the charges against Chase alleged departures from the law in some of the sedition trials he had conducted, and not ideological differences,[91] the justice would probably have escaped an impeachment trial had he not been so blatantly partisan in the campaign of 1800. Worse, Jefferson's victory had not quieted him. In May 1803, he used the occasion of a charge to a grand jury in Baltimore to attack Republicans for passing the Repeal Act of 1802[92] and, according to one newspaper, to denounce "the present Administration" as "weak, relaxed and not adequate to a discharge of their functions, and that their acts flowed, not from a wish for the happiness of the people but for a continuance in unfairly acquired power."[93]

With Aaron Burr (still under indictment for murder in New Jersey, for having killed Alexander Hamilton in a duel in July) presiding, Chase's trial before the Senate began on February 4, 1805, and concluded on March 1. Despite the justice's questionable behavior on and off the bench both before and after the election of 1800, Republicans, who held twenty-five of the Senate's thirty-four seats, could not obtain more than nineteen votes on any single count of the indictment. That was a majority, but not the two-thirds majority the Constitution demanded.

Acquittal of Chase was constitutionally significant when considered alongside the alternative. If any member of the Supreme Court was vulnerable to impeachment proceedings in 1804, Chase was surely the one. If he could not be removed, neither could the others. Had the Senate convicted Chase, ardent anti-Court Republicans probably would have urged impeachment of another, although there is no way to know whether the effort would have succeeded. Nonetheless, it is noteworthy that Marshall, who had no hand in the sedition trials, was worried about the impact a Chase conviction might have on the Court. Marshall's concern was so great that he shared in a letter to a colleague his willingness to allow Congress the authority to overturn Supreme Court decisions of which it disapproved in exchange for abandoning impeachment as a method of disciplining jurists who made unpopular rulings.[94] Whatever else might be said, acquittal of Chase dampened the Republican drive to use impeachment as a tool to reshape the federal judiciary. Even had a Senate conviction not resulted in impeachment of any of Chase's colleagues, Chase's conviction might have become a precedent for ideologically driven removals from the bench in later administrations. This development would have seriously dampened the judiciary's independence and would have marked a movement toward a different model: a judiciary subservient to Congress.

Even before Pickering had been removed, Jefferson considered impeachment inefficient. In its place he preferred an amendment to the Constitution "so that the President should be authorized to remove a Judge from office, on the address of the two Houses."[95] Chase's acquittal made him certain of that, and he would later speak of the impeachment power as "not even a scarecrow."[96]

Chase's acquittal, Congress's failure to pursue an easier way of removing judges, and its refusal to declare itself the final arbiter of the meaning of the Constitution are indicative of the respect the more moderate Republicans had for the concept of an independent judiciary—that is, a judiciary that not only was set apart institutionally from the elective branches of government but also was not itself to be a partisan agent. This was so despite the fact that by 1801 the concept was far more an ideal than a reality. The failure of these congressional moves against the judiciary may also have been encouraged by the Supreme Court itself.

Court Actions

The judiciary's partisan entanglement during and preceding the election of 1800, combined with the minority position it occupied in the national government after 1801, may have provided plenty of incentive for the justices to rethink their place in the political system. The election of 1800, after all, produced for the first time partisan distinctions among the branches of government. Not coincidentally, perhaps, it is in the Marshall years that a lasting and distinctly "American judicial tradition" took shape. The tradition gives the Supreme Court a peculiar relation to politics: conscious aloofness from direct participation in politics alongside an "active and weighty" political presence. As such, the tradition involves a tension between "independence and accountability" and "a trade-off between acknowledged powers and freedoms in the individual judge, and acknowledged constraints on the institution of the judiciary."[97] Examples of the beginnings of this tradition appear in two early decisions by the Marshall Court.

The first was the resolution of the suit filed by William Marbury and three others to become justices of the peace for the District of Columbia. In December 1801 the Supreme Court issued an order to Secretary of State Madison to show cause why he should not deliver their commissions of office. (Chief Justice Marshall was of course embarrassingly involved in the origins of this case, since it was he who had not delivered the commissions prior to Jefferson's swearing-in.) At the outset, Marbury's suit appeared mainly partisan—an attempt to ruffle the new administration. However, by the time the litigation concluded fourteen months later, the case had accomplished something more.

On the premise that the minor judgeship was his, Marbury requested a writ of mandamus from the Supreme Court to the secretary of state. But the premise of the writ was that the executive branch was answerable to the judicial process in the course of exercising presidential powers such as appointments. In this instance that meant a Republican executive official answering to a Federalist bench. By early 1803, when the case was argued, the atmosphere was such that Marshall and his colleagues must have concluded that Madison, with the president's blessing, would almost certainly ignore a writ. The administration, after all, had boycotted the hearing, with counsel only for Marbury and the other petitioners attending. The justices' recourse was a decision that avoided a confrontation with the executive, addressed the Court's role, and handed Marbury nothing more than a moral victory.

The Court achieved the third objective by excoriating the Jefferson administration for not giving the commissions to the would-be magistrates. It achieved the first objective by concluding, however, that it was powerless to order delivery of the commissions because Section 13 of the Judiciary Act of 1789, which authorized the Court to issue writs of mandamus as part of its original jurisdiction, violated Article III of the Constitution. (The reasoning was that since Article III spelled out the Court's original jurisdiction and made no mention of mandamus as part of it, Congress could no more add to that jurisdiction than take it away.) If there was no order for Madison to disregard, there could be no confrontation.

Marshall's opinion addressed the second objective in two ways: first, in support of the position that the statute conflicted with the Constitution, the Court for the first time articulated a defense of the doctrine of judicial review. That is, the Court explained why the judiciary could not apply a statute passed by Congress that, in the justices' view, conflicted with the Constitution. In so doing, Marshall implicitly countered the competing theories that state legislatures or Congress was the appropriate forum to judge the constitutionality of national policy. Second, Marshall's opinion explained why the executive must be answerable to the Court, although in doing so, Marshall was careful to distinguish between discretionary (that is, "political") actions that were not judicially cognizable and nondiscretionary actions that were. "By the constitution of the United States," he conceded, "the President is invested with certain important political powers, in the exercise of which he is to use his own discretion, and *is account-able only to his country in his political character and to his own conscience.*"[98] But delivery of commissions fell into the other category. "The question whether a right has vested or not, is, in its nature, judicial, and must be tried by the judicial authority."[99]

The essence of Marshall's opinion was that the Court was an independent entity of government. Rather than sit as the agent of one political force against another, the Court was the agent of the Constitution. An independent judiciary, moreover, was not the same as an administration-friendly or a party-friendly judiciary. Individuals claiming violations of rights might pursue judicial remedies. Judicial review was expedient: "the substitute offered by political wisdom for the destructive right of revolution."[100] For years Jefferson resented Marshall's opinion in *Marbury*, although not because of the chief justice's defense of judicial review.[101] More objectionable to him was that Marshall had gone out of his way to speak to the merits of Marbury's suit and to assert the judiciary's power to interfere with executive functions.[102]

The second of the pair of significant decisions by the early Marshall Court came down within days of *Marbury*. *Stuart* v. *Laird*[103] rejected a challenge to the constitutionality of the Repeal Act of 1802. Significantly, the Court was able to avoid the troubling constitutional question of whether the statute deprived judges of tenure "during good behavior" as granted by the Constitution. Instead, the case was framed in terms of Congress's power to organize the judiciary, including the assignment of Supreme Court justices to the circuit courts. This was so because Stuart was not a judge who claimed deprivation of a right. Rather, he was a litigant whose case had been transferred when the court where it had been filed had been abolished. Even though Marshall personally believed the 1802 act to be unconstitutional, he and his colleagues chose the safer path.[104] He was fully aware of the political dimension any challenge to the Repeal Act would contain. "This is a subject not to be lightly resolved on. The consequences of refusing to carry the law into effect may be very serious."[105] One can only speculate on the long-term institutional consequences had the Court chosen to articulate its defense of judicial review in *Stuart* rather than in *Marbury*.

Under Marshall's leadership, the Court's nurture of judicial power and the appearance of independence lapsed at least once, however, during the decade following the election of 1800—in the litigation surrounding the Burr conspiracy.[106] Jefferson believed that his first-term vice president had conducted an expedition in the Southwest in order to precipitate a war with Spain and/or to set up a new government independent of the United States. Over the dissents of Johnson and, ironically, of Chase, however, the Supreme Court in February 1807 granted a writ of habeas corpus to two of Burr's associates, Erich Bollman and Samuel Swartwout, that severely tightened the definition of the crime of treason. As a result, the government was left with insufficient evidence that either had levied war against the United States.[107]

Burr himself went on trial in Richmond in August 1807, with Marshall presiding as circuit judge. The narrow construction of the crime of treason that Marshall included in his charge to the jury led to the former vice president's acquittal, much to Jefferson's displeasure. The disdain that Jefferson and Marshall held for each other may have encouraged the chief justice to be especially scrupulous in protecting the defendant's rights, and the president to interpret Marshall's conduct of the trial as a partisan affront to the administration. As Jefferson had said in April, "The fact is that the Federalists make Burr's cause their own, and exert their whole influence to shield him from punishment. . . . It is unfortunate that Federalism is still predominant in our judiciary department, which is consequently in opposition to the legislative and executive branches and is able to baffle their measures often."[108] Jefferson would not be the last president to complain that the courts were "inclined to construe the law too favorably for the accused and too rigidly against the Government."[109]

After Burr's acquittal in September, Jefferson made his feelings known to Congress. In his annual December message, the president laid before the body the evidence against Burr, asked the members to judge "whether the defect was in the testimony, in the law, or in the administration of the law," and urged them to consider a remedy.[110] Anti-Court Republicans in Congress then introduced a constitutional amendment in March 1808 providing for a fixed term for federal judges and for their removal by the president on a two-thirds vote of each house. The measure resurfaced in Congress in 1811, 1812, and 1816, but miscarried each time.

Neither Jefferson nor his immediate successors succeeded in remolding the Supreme Court into a distinctly Republican image. Indeed, efforts they made to alter the Court's jurisprudence by way of new faces on the bench were marginal at best. Jefferson was able to make two additional appointments to the High Court—Henry B. Livingston in 1806 and Thomas Todd in 1807, the latter's seat being made possible when Congress enlarged the Court from six to seven. Only Johnson, however, proved to be an effective countervoice to Marshall. James Madison, who followed Jefferson in the White House, selected as a justice Joseph Story, who, over the span of a career that extended to 1845, outdid Marshall in articulating principles distasteful to true Republicans. The Republican effort to shape the Court was so unproductive that in 1820 Jefferson would refer to the Court (on which all three of his appointees still sat) as a "subtle corps of sappers and miners" that consisted of "a crafty chief judge" and "lazy or timid associates."[111]

Nonetheless, for a time Republicans might have measured success less in terms of what they were able to do to the Court and more in terms of what the Court itself did not do. The federal judiciary's success in establishing a considerable degree of institutional independence may be due in part to the fact that, with only a handful of exceptions, the Supreme Court under Marshall did not fully reengage Republican principles until long after Jefferson had returned to his beloved Monticello.

CHAPTER 3

The Election of 1832: Partisanship Revived

As the previous chapter explained, the federal judiciary's first major partisan entanglement coincided with events surrounding the election of 1800 and the beginning of John Marshall's tenure as chief justice. Its second major partisan entanglement culminated in the election of 1832, near the end of Marshall's long Supreme Court tenure. In place of Thomas Jefferson as Marshall's chief antagonist stood Andrew Jackson. At stake was no less than the definition of American constitutional government. If the federal judiciary made political difficulties for itself in 1798–1800 by being perceived as insufficiently attuned to individual liberty and to judicial independence, it was now perceived as being insufficiently attuned to the prerogatives of state governments and excessively independent of changing political winds.

The setting for this turmoil was the metamorphosis of the first party system into the second. The result was a reopening of the question of the Court's place in the political system and a modification in constitutional interpretation.

ORIGINS OF THE SECOND PARTY SYSTEM

Some of the first evidence of the decline of party distinctions surfaced in Congress after the War of 1812 demonstrated a need for energetic national policies.[1] In 1816 Congress responded to President James Madison's recommendations and chartered the second Bank of the United States, passed a major tariff act, and decreed that revenues derived from the bank be spent on the construction of new roads and canals. All three measures flew in the face of Jeffersonian orthodoxy,[2] but only the third failed to become law:

Madison changed his mind and vetoed the road and canal bill on the last day of his second term.

What the legislative package of 1816 suggested was made plain by the virtually uncontested reelection of President James Monroe in 1820. Not only did a serious challenge fail to arise from within his own Democratic-Republican party but the Federalists had so dwindled in numbers and influence as a national party that they offered no opponent. The first party system faded from sight.[3] As the old Virginian John Randolph explained the outcome, Monroe's second term came about from "the unanimity of indifference, and not of approbation."[4]

Monroe's reelection and the absence of partisanship, however, were not signs that the United States was relatively free of problems of national scope. From 1818 into 1819, the country sank into an economic depression. Foreclosures mounted, and dozens of state-chartered banks, in the South and West especially, went out of business. Antibanking sentiment took hold in many locales among farmers and other working people, and would remain a force until at least the 1840s. Sectional animosities against financial interests in the East intensified in the more recently settled regions of the South and West. These economic dislocations profoundly affected state and local races but, amazingly, had little immediate impact on congressional actions or on presidential politics.

Instead, the "Missouri question" preoccupied Congress. Opposed by Southern interests, Northern senators and representatives wanted the admission of Missouri into the union conditioned on an antislavery provision in its constitution.[5] A compromise, credited largely to Henry Clay, became law on March 2, 1820. It called for Missouri to be admitted as a slave state but for the rest of the land acquired in the Louisiana Purchase north of Missouri's southern boundary to be nonslave. To offset Missouri's entrance in 1821, Congress admitted Maine in 1820, thus assuring the maintenance of an even division between slave and free states in the Senate.

What the election of 1820 lacked in terms of candidates, the presidential election of 1824 provided in abundance. But the election was fought without party distinctions and labels, the last such event in American national politics. Five prominent figures, each with substantial sectional backing, initially vied for the highest office. William Crawford of Georgia, secretary of the treasury in the Monroe administration, was a favorite of Old (states' rights) Republicans in New York and Virginia. Henry Clay of Kentucky, a member of the House of Representatives, was well known as an advocate of internal improvements and central banking. John Quincy

Adams, son of the second president, served as secretary of state under Monroe and was especially popular in New England. Andrew Jackson, since 1823 a senator from Tennessee, enjoyed the status of a military hero from the War of 1812 and war with the Seminoles, and had been the first governor of the Florida territory. His strongest support lay in the Southwest and South. While his views on some issues were not widely known, Jackson was able to attract the disaffected and the dissatisfied in all regions, who tended to look on him as one of their own.[6] John C. Calhoun, who had not yet become the Southern sectionalist, was Monroe's secretary of war, shared many of Clay's nationalistic ideas, and was the clear favorite in his home state of South Carolina and, for a time, in Pennsylvania. Calhoun withdrew from the presidential race in March 1824, however, when his Pennsylvania backers deserted him in favor of Jackson, thus leaving four contenders in the race and Calhoun the leading candidate for vice president.

With Crawford as the nominee of the congressional caucus, state conventions and legislatures—increasingly influential in presidential nominations—put forward the candidacies of the others. (National party conventions as presidential nominating devices would not make their appearance for another eight years.) The 1824 electoral results reflected the absence of the cohesion that two-party competition would have provided: no candidate received a majority of electoral (or popular) votes, although Jackson garnered a plurality of both. That meant that, for a second time in a quarter-century, the House would elect the president under the Constitution's stipulation that the delegation from each state cast a single vote. Even though Jackson claimed all or a majority of the electoral votes in eleven of the twenty-four states, Clay, who had finished a distant third in both popular and electoral votes, threw his support to Adams. With Clay as House speaker presiding over the polling of the state delegations, the House named runner-up Adams as president on February 9, 1825: thirteen state delegations voted for Adams, seven for Jackson, and four for Crawford.

When Adams soon picked Clay as secretary of state in the new administration, Jackson's followers accused the former speaker of having made a "corrupt bargain." The post was not merely the most prestigious one in the cabinet but also an obvious boost to Clay's chances someday to claim the presidency as his own.[7] The charge was one that Clay was never able convincingly to refute and immediately became a rallying cry for the Jackson camp. The 1828 election furnished Jackson's ranks an opportunity to gain what they believed should have been theirs in 1824.

A new party system—the second—began to take shape, although it did not emerge suddenly throughout the country and would not be fully developed until 1840.[8] Although Adams's support for internal improvements, sound banking, and a national university distressed Old Republicans in the North and many in the South as well, the second party system was probably brought on less by doctrinal conflicts than by candidate-centered contests for the presidency.[9] Accordingly, when Jackson challenged Adams in the election of 1828, personalities, not issues, dominated the campaign. Jackson's champions recounted the "corrupt bargain" of 1825 and painted Adams as an aristocrat who was out of touch with ordinary people. Adams's publicists depicted Jackson as "impetuous and uncontrollable,"[10] and labeled his mother a "common prostitute." Others verbally abused his wife, Rachel.[11]

Parties in the second system emerged as organizations to mobilize mass support for presidential favorites. And in 1828 getting out the vote was the key to victory to an unprecedented extent. In only two of the twenty-four states did legislatures still elect presidential electors.[12] Moreover, the franchise included virtually all adult white males; only in Virginia and Rhode Island had property qualifications survived.[13] Jackson and his supporters, who called themselves Democrats, excelled at voter mobilization and were the clear beneficiaries of the enlarged electorate: Jackson's 56 percent of the popular vote in 1828 exceeded that of any other presidential candidate in the nineteenth century. "Friends of Adams" (and Clay), who became known as National Republicans,[14] may have outdone the Democrats in the battle of insults, but they had no candidate to rival Jackson in popularity and no party organization to match his in getting out the vote.

Jackson's political foes were unsuccessful again in 1832 when the president sought reelection. Their defeat brought about the demise of the National Republican party and the appearance of the Whig party as the second party system came into place. Whigs consisted of opponents of Jackson's economic policies, particularly those distressed by his war on the Bank of the United States. This dispute, combined with an attack on the Supreme Court, helped the two parties to define themselves. Also into Whig ranks moved Democrats who could not abide New York Democratic leader, and now vice president, Martin Van Buren. Further, Whigs would shortly claim members of the Anti-Masonic party once it faded away.[15] The first example of a third-party movement in American politics, the Anti-Masonic party was strongest in New York and Pennsylvania. Its 1832 presidential candidate, William Wirt, collected nearly 8 percent of the popular vote.

By the mid-1830s, the Democrats had declared themselves to be the intellectual descendants of the Jeffersonian Republicans. They professed to share the latter's vision of an agrarian democracy and a working or artisan class that needed protection from the financial establishment. They added to that vision the need for a strong president as a national party leader. Democrats became known as the party of patronage and "machine" government. In contrast, Whigs campaigned on a vision of a nation modernized by government-encouraged commerce and became the party of the upwardly mobile, the successful farmer and businessperson, and the reform-minded. Its ranks included Senators Henry Clay and Daniel Webster and a young lawyer from Illinois named Abraham Lincoln. Democrats and Whigs were "two new parties, not two old parties in new dress."[16]

If Jefferson's party began to lose its identity after his presidency, the same did not happen to the Democrats when Jackson left the White House in 1837. Because of a system of national conventions and patronage, partisanship in national elections had become routine.[17] The party system that began to take shape in 1828 and 1832 persisted for over two decades until it was undone by slavery (see appendix 1).

THE MARSHALL AND EARLY TANEY COURTS

Whereas the Supreme Court had three chief justices in its first decade, the combined service of the next two chief justices—John Marshall and Roger Brooke Taney—spanned sixty-three years. As an institution of American government, the Supreme Court owes much to John Marshall, sometimes called "the Great Chief Justice," as if no other occupant of that office could ever be his equal. Of the sixty-three years, Marshall served thirty-four, longer than any other chief justice to date. He led the Court like no chief justice before or since. Partly this was the result of his personality and political acumen. Partly it was the result of Marshall's determination to use the Supreme Court to reinforce constitutional principles he thought vital to the advancement of the nation. And partly it was the result of the justices' living conditions in Washington. During most of Marshall's tenure, they resided and took their meals at the same boardinghouse, and traveled together across town to the courtroom in the Capitol, making it easier for a strong-willed individual like Marshall to influence most of his colleagues.

By the 1820s, Marshall and Bushrod Washington were the surviving Federalist appointees (see appendix 2). Marshall had acquired a strong ally in Joseph Story, named to the bench in 1811 by James Madison. Only William Johnson, Jefferson's first pick for the high court, had maintained independence and was in a position to challenge Marshall intellectually. The other Jefferson, Madison, and Monroe appointees reflected the decline of partisanship that characterized the election of 1820 and seemed content to follow Marshall's leadership much of the time, at least until the late 1820s.[18] It is hardly surprising, then, that Marshall's name became practically synonymous with that of the Court, even if no monolithic bench under his domination ever existed.[19] Of the 1,090 cases the Supreme Court disposed of through an opinion of the court during the Marshall years (1801–1835), Marshall spoke for the Court in 530, or 49 percent.[20]

Three themes characterized the Court's constitutional decisions during Marshall's tenure: judicial review, national supremacy and power, and private rights. As noted in the previous chapter, *Marbury* v. *Madison*[21] marked the Court's first invalidation of an act of Congress. While this decision alone hardly assured the Court's lasting influence, Marshall's vision of its place in the constitutional order persisted. In other cases the Marshall Court defended national prerogatives against inroads by the states and rendered such an expansive reading of Congress's powers under the Constitution that a century would go by before Congress took full advantage of them. The United States sometimes seemed more promise than fact, and Marshall's jurisprudence was a counterforce to ever-present forces of disunion. This was still an era when state legislatures overshadowed Congress as the policy-making bodies of the nation. Perhaps for this reason the justices were also concerned about intrusions by the states on private rights, and used the contract clause[22] of the Constitution to limit interference with certain vested rights of property, especially as lodged in corporate charters. Such decisions fueled controversy about the Court and seemed to place it at odds with some of the most powerful political forces of the day.

Roger Brooke Taney, Marshall's successor, was chief justice from 1836 until 1864, and was the first chief justice appointed for the express purpose of undoing some of the handiwork of his predecessor. The constitutional docket during his tenure was dominated by three issues: economic expansion, federalism, and slavery. With the first, the Taney Court strove to achieve a balance between vested financial interests and the needs of a growing population and new forms of wealth. Sometimes the difference between the Marshall and Taney courts on this subject is described in terms of protection of, versus hostility to, property. More accurately, the Court in Taney's time reassessed its understanding of property, choosing to view it as dynamic and entrepreneurial, not static and inhospitable to risk takers.

The Taney Court was also solicitous of state prerogatives. In place of Marshall's emphasis on national supremacy, the Court preferred dual federalism, a legal conception of the union that juxtaposed the central and state governments as equals, with the Court standing between as constitutional referee. An enlarged understanding of state powers not only allowed states to cope with problems of economic growth but also permitted the Court to protect the institution of slavery. Indeed, pro-slavery decisions, to be explored in the next chapter, helped to ensnare the Court in partisan combat as the second party system dissolved into the third.

JUDICIAL ACTIONS

As much as John Marshall's name is associated with American constitutional law, the number of landmark—that is, truly significant and groundbreaking—constitutional decisions of his Court amounted to no more than a dozen. Several of these were clustered in the years 1819–1824, and sparked controversies that simmered locally and in Congress before becoming part of presidential politics surrounding the election of 1832. One leading case challenged the scope of Congress's power to legislate, another tested the appellate authority of the Supreme Court, and a third probed the limits on the power of the states to manage their internal affairs.

The Bank

McCulloch v. *Maryland*[23] highlighted Maryland's war on the second Bank of the United States. The origins of the litigation lay in one of the first disputes over the meaning of the Constitution to arise in President Washington's first term. In 1791, Alexander Hamilton supported both the desirability and the constitutionality of a central bank[24] as vigorously as James Madison and Thomas Jefferson objected to both.[25] Congress accepted Hamilton's recommendation and chartered the first Bank of the United States for a period of twenty years. By 1811 Jeffersonian principles and a call for an easier monetary policy by farmers and entrepreneurs led the Madison administration to allow the first bank's charter to expire. As noted, Madison approved the rechartering of the bank by Congress in 1816, once the need for a central financial institution issuing a national currency had been demonstrated by its absence.[26]

The bank's rebirth in 1816, however, hardly meant that its opponents had vanished. Opposition to the bank had three bases: philosophical, commercial, and constitutional. Hatred of all banks, especially big ones, was a tenet of Jeffersonian Republicanism and was a view Andrew Jackson held even before coming to the presidency.[27] This hatred was so widespread and deeply felt that as late as 1852, there would be no incorporated banks in seven of the nation's thirty-one states.[28]

Even among those who approved of banking in principle, a central bank with branches in many cities across the land was objectionable because distant financiers in effect set local banking policy. Moreover, a central bank and its branches dwarfed the much smaller state-chartered banks. A central bank could cripple a state bank by refusing to accept its notes on the grounds that the former thought the latter unsound.

For a third group, the national government lacked authority even to create a bank. If the government of the United States possessed only those powers conferred by the Constitution, the chartering of a national bank was illegal because Congress's powers did not include the creation of a corporation. Even the "necessary and proper" clause[29] in the Constitution was insufficient since the creation of a financial institution was not "necessary" (that is, *essential*) to carrying out the duties that the Constitution expressly allotted to Congress.

With such a reservoir of negative opinion toward the bank even in the best of times, it was not surprising that the onset of an economic downturn in 1818, ironically made more severe by the bank's tightening of credit, was reason enough for a few states to attempt to drive the bank out of business or, at the least, out of their midst. Those who disliked all banks and those who disliked only the bank were willing to cooperate temporarily because, once they had achieved victory, each faction was convinced that it could prevail over the other.[30] One of the states where antibank sentiment was strongest was Maryland.[31]

Under the guise of a revenue measure, a Maryland statute of February 11, 1818, stipulated that the bank must buy special stamped paper from the state on which to print its notes or pay a fee of $15,000 per year.[32] Alternatively, the bank could close its branch in Maryland. Stamps would range from $.10 on a $5 note to $20 on a $1,000 note.[33] If the bank refused to pay the annual fee and to use the stamped paper, state officials would assess a penalty of $100 for every note that the bank issued on unstamped paper.

The objective was clear. Maryland wanted to make the bank's cost of doing business in the state prohibitive.[34]

When James McCulloch, the cashier of the bank's branch in Baltimore, refused to comply with the law, the state brought suit to compel obedience. Following defeats in two Maryland courts, the bank appealed to the United States Supreme Court. The questions the case presented were simply stated but profound in their implications: Did Congress possess the authority to charter the bank? If so, could Maryland tax the bank?

Treasury Secretary Crawford convinced the Monroe administration to support the bank in its litigation, and Attorney General William Wirt assisted the bank's counsel, Daniel Webster, in preparing for argument set to begin on February 22, 1819—barely more than a year after Maryland had passed the law. Decision by the Supreme Court followed on March 6. The pace was remarkable by both nineteenth- and twentieth-century standards of practice: attempted enforcement of the measure, rulings by two state courts, plus docketing, argument, and decision in the Supreme Court all took place in the span of fifty-seven weeks.

The bank won and Maryland lost on both questions. But the significance of the decision went well beyond an affirmation of congressional authority to create a bank and a denial of Maryland's authority to tax it. Marshall rested Congress's authority on an exceedingly expansive reading of national powers echoing, but not acknowledging, Hamilton's own argument to Washington in support of a bank twenty-eight years before. The necessary and proper clause not only gave Congress a choice of means in carrying out the powers that the Constitution expressly granted, but by "necessary" Marshall reasoned that the powers need be merely convenient and appropriate, not "essential."[35] Thus, Congress possessed not only those powers *granted* by the Constitution but also an indefinite number of others as well, unless *prohibited* by the Constitution. Moreover, the breadth that the Constitution allowed in a choice of means was largely a matter for Congress, not the judiciary, to decide.

As for Maryland's tax on the bank, Marshall's reply practically assumed that the state had taxed a department of the national government, not merely a corporation chartered by Congress in which the national government held a minority interest. A part of the union could not be allowed to cripple the whole.

For defenders of state prerogatives, Marshall's opinion was a double dose of bad news. First, the ordinary remedy for unacceptable *national* legislation lay not with the Court but with Congress; second, the judiciary would be attentive to alleged victims of *state* policies. *McCulloch* therefore stood for the proposition that the Supreme Court was to be less a forum to judge the limits of national power than a forum to protect national interests from local interests. Once Congress acted, the bank (and, inferentially, any other national instrumentality) enjoyed constitutional immunity from hostile state actions. "[A] state of things has now grown up in some of the states," Justice Johnson would write in another case, "which renders all the protection necessary, that the general government can give to this bank."[36]

The Lottery

Decided two years after the Maryland bank case, *Cohens v. Virginia*[37] presented a substantive issue that was frankly trivial alongside the constitutional legitimacy of the bank. Yet on the important jurisdictional issue in *Cohens* turned the future of the American constitutional system. The case precipitated one of the last major debates on the nature of the Constitution by the generation that wrote and ratified the document.

Cohens would not have developed as it did without the intersection of several forces. First among these was the growth of the lottery as a major device for the generation of capital. The Jacob I. Cohen Jr. and Brother Lottery Office, a Maryland firm, was one of the largest lottery concerns in the United States at that time: the company published *Cohen's Gazette and Lottery Register*, engaged in an extensive mail-order business, and offered a wide range of financial services.[38] Philip and Mendez Cohen managed the firm's branch office in Norfolk, Virginia. The case arose when the Cohens were fined $100 for selling lottery tickets in violation of a Virginia statute that banned the sale of all tickets for lotteries not approved by the state assembly. The tickets in question were chances in the congressionally authorized Grand National Lottery for the District of Columbia.

A second force was the depression or "panic," the hardships of which largely accounted for passage in 1819 of Virginia's antilottery law. Legislators saw the ban as a means of halting the export of capital to finance improvements out of state at a time of financial exigencies at home.[39]

A third force was the usual suspect: the Bank of the United States. The Old Republican faction in Virginia, inspired by Jefferson and led by Judge Spencer Roane and political theorist John Taylor, capitalized on this opportunity to increase its political influence by uniting those distrustful of the bank with those suspicious of national power. Because *McCulloch* coincided with the panic, the Supreme Court became a convenient tool as tim-ing and context invested *Cohens* with considerable importance.[40]

Litigation proceeded quickly—so quickly that it had all the signs of an arranged case.[41] If Virginia Republicans stood to gain politically, win or lose, the lottery firm was anxious to establish its right to continue to do business. Moreover, Marshall and other members of the Court may have viewed the case as an opportunity to respond to the antiunion sentiments that resurfaced in debates over the Missouri Compromise. "The attack upon the judiciary is in fact an attack upon the union,"[42] the chief justice confided to Story four months after *Cohens* came down. Indeed, the Court seems to have agreed in early August 1820 to hear the case before the Cohens even came to trial in Norfolk at the end of that month. The Court's request for a record in the case in time for its forthcoming session in Feb-ruary 1821 indicates that, as far as the justices were concerned, the Cohens had already been convicted and their appeals in state court rejected.[43]

The case generated an intensity and quantity of constitutional discourse in pamphlets and newspapers in Virginia not seen since the days of the Alien and Sedition Acts, and its ferocity may have ultimately shaped Mar-shall's opinion in the case. The Cohens argued that congressional autho-rization of the District lottery overrode any conflicting state statute. But defenders of the Virginia law offered the fundamental objection that the Supreme Court lacked jurisdiction to hear the case because the Court's appellate jurisdiction could constitutionally extend only to the lower fed-eral courts, and because the Eleventh Amendment barred litigation brought against a state without its consent by a citizen of another state.

The first objection meant that Section 25 of the Judiciary Act of 1789, which authorized Supreme Court review of state court decisions when a claim under federal law had been rejected, was unconstitutional.[44] A hold-ing for the state would effectively make state courts the final authority on the meaning of the United States Constitution in that state, a position that the Supreme Court had rejected five years earlier.[45] It is indicative of the strong antinationalist climate prevailing in some quarters that counsel for Virginia[46] nonetheless treated the validity of Section 25 as an open question and that Marshall took the argument seriously.[47] A victory on the second objection would have severely constricted federal jurisdiction generally.

Marshall's opinion deftly held for Virginia on the merits of the case; that is, Virginia could validly apply the antilottery law to the Cohens. While Congress might have superseded state law in this instance (a conclusion the opinion suggested but formally left open), Congress had indicated no intention to do so. As in *Marbury* v. *Madison*, there was thus no decision that could be officially resisted or defied. On the jurisdictional issues, however, the decision was a thorough victory for national authority and the Supreme Court—"one of the strongest and most enduring strands of that mighty cable woven by [Marshall] to hold the American people together as a united and imperishable nation."[48] State court judgments on matters of federal law were not immune to review by the Supreme Court, and an appeal by a defendant against a state judgment was not a suit against a state as contemplated by the Eleventh Amendment. *Cohens* was thus consistent with *McCulloch*: the Supreme Court possessed the authority to sit in judgment on actions by state legislatures and courts on matters that affected the nation.[49]

The Compact

The United States of the early nineteenth century was still a nation where the economic base was mainly agricultural and wealth was defined largely in terms of land. Because westward movement meant settlement on "new" land and because settlement often preceded established authority, confusion over land titles generated large amounts of litigation.

One such dispute grew out of the agreement between Virginia and Kentucky when the latter was separated from its parent in 1789. According to the compact between the two states, "all private rights and interests of lands" in the new state "derived from the laws of Virginia, shall remain valid . . . and shall be determined by the laws now existing" in the parent state.[50] Later, the Kentucky legislature passed two statutes, one in 1797 and the other in 1812, that attempted "to inject order into a chaos"[51] of conflicting land titles by softening the consequences that enforcement of the 1789 agreement had wrought. The first measure protected occupants, upon eviction by claimants holding a superior title, from being held liable for rents and profits during their occupancy. The second law strengthened the first by requiring reimbursement for improvements should title to the land in dispute be found to be vested in others.

Richard Biddle was one whose legal occupancy of a piece of land was in question, and his rights under the Kentucky statutes were challenged in federal court by the heirs of John Green, whose estate claimed ownership under the compact of 1789. After ruling against the validity of the Kentucky laws in March 1821, the Supreme Court agreed to reargument of the case in

1822 and affirmed its original holding a year later, on February 23, 1823.[52] The Kentucky statutes violated the Constitution's ban on state laws impairing the obligation of contracts, announced Justice Washington for himself and two colleagues.[53]

By construing the contract clause for the first time to encompass agreements between states, the Court negated policy Kentucky thought desirable. The case involved neither a contest between national and state governments, as in the bank cases, nor a dispute over the relationship between the state and federal courts, as in the lottery case. Rather, it was a holding by the Supreme Court that the language of the Constitution alone forbade a state from enacting its relief legislation.[54]

POLITICAL REACTION

Decisions by the Supreme Court in the bank, lottery, and compact cases were vexatious. Reaction in Congress against the Court alternately simmered and boiled during the 1820s. Given the heat of the debate, it is surprising both that Congress passed no legislation restricting the Court and that the Court was not a principal issue in the presidential elections of 1824 and 1828. Why the expected did not come to pass may be just as intriguing as understanding what did occur.

Sources of opposition to the Court in the 1820s were varied. Some Republicans, mainly in the South, feared the implications of the justices' generous interpretation of congressional powers in *McCulloch*. Their concern arose not because of the assertion of judicial authority but because of its absence. Alongside those who disliked the decision because of its results—Marshall's opinion revealed not a whisker of doubt about the constitutionality of the bank or about the unconstitutionality of the state tax on it—were those who worried more about the reach of Marshall's reasoning. Few informed observers really thought that a bench so Federalist in its outlook would reject an institution inspired by Federalist ideas and reestablished by a Republican administration.[55] News of the bank's survival in Court was probably anticipated,[56] but accounts of the justification of the bank's existence were plainly distressing. Marshall's opinion removed any constitutional doubt about congressionally sponsored internal improvements and held out prospects for far-reaching congressional authority over tariffs as well as the status of slavery in the territories and new states.[57]

Focus on the reasoning and not the result would seem to account for the brutal verbal lashing the decision received, particularly in Virginia.[58] Marshall announced his decision in *McCulloch* on March 6. Before the end of the month, the *Richmond Enquirer* published two essays attacking the chief justice's opinion over the pseudonym "Amphictyon" (probably Judge William Brockenbrough). Marshall then published a response over the signature "A Friend to the Union" in the Philadelphia *Union* in April. There soon appeared in the *Enquirer* four essays, more threatening than the first pair. Signed "Hampden," they were written by Marshall's nemesis, Spencer Roane[59] of the Virginia Court of Appeals, whom Marshall once called the "champion of dismemberment."[60] Marshall thus felt compelled to reply again. Beginning in June, a nine-part response to "Hampden" appeared in the *Gazette* of Alexandria, Virginia, over the pen name "A Friend of the Constitution."[61] Proprieties may have driven Marshall to defend his opinion anonymously, but concern for the future of the nation overrode any scruples he may have had about resorting to the newspapers as an extra-judicial forum.

The Marshall Court was as troubling to defenders of state prerogatives as to those who were concerned about its generous construction of congressional authority. *McCulloch*, after all, negated a state tax at the same time it upheld the bank, and *Cohens* reaffirmed the Supreme Court's duty to make sure that state policies conformed to federal constitutional standards. Those cases symbolized the federal judiciary's threat to state interests. By 1820, the Supreme Court had already invalidated laws in seven states, and by 1825 the number of directly affected states would grow to ten.[62]

"That [bank] charter . . . has been justified by the Supreme Court, on principles so bold and alarming, that no man who loves the Constitution can fold his arms in apathy . . . principles calculated . . . to change the whole face of our Government, and to generate a thousand measures which the framers of the Constitution never anticipated,"[63] thundered John Taylor in 1820. "[W]hen [the Constitution] operates upon collision between political departments," he argued in 1822, "it is not to be construed by the Court."[64] "[T]he law of Congress declaring that the supreme court shall have appellate jurisdiction from the courts of the several states" was, Taylor asserted the following year, "precisely as unconstitutional, as state laws for bestowing an appellate jurisdiction from the decisions of the federal courts, upon the supreme courts of the states."[65] This backlash meant that by 1823 there were already substantial arguments widely in print against both Marshall's broad construction of national power and his position that state courts were subordinate to the Supreme Court on interpretation of federal law. The outcome of this clash would determine the meaning of union for the American states.

The verbal furor about the Court had risen to a level sufficient to lead Congress to consider seriously various devices to rein in the justices.[66] Proposals generally took three forms: jurisdictional, institutional, and procedural.[67] The first consisted of outright repeal of Section 25. The second included configuration of the Senate as an appellate body to the Supreme Court when a state was party to a case. Others advocated elimination of the justices' tenure "during good behavior" and substitution of fixed terms of six years coupled with the possibility of reappointment by the president on the approval of both houses of Congress. An instance of the third was a stipulation that the Court could invalidate a statute only by unanimous vote or by vote of two-thirds of the full bench (that is, with the concurrence of a minimum of five). Of the group, elimination of Section 25 proved to be the most durable of the Court-curbing measures, and therefore the one most feared by supporters of Marshall's doctrines. The Court's surest defense proved to be its critics' inability to agree on a single remedy: many in Congress seemed as dissatisfied with any particular limitation as they were with the Court.[68]

At the heart of the debate was frustration over the evolution of the Supreme Court as arbiter of the meaning of the Constitution during a period when "popular sovereignty" was taking on a new meaning in American life. This was the era of the arrival of the "common man." Some states underwent significant constitutional changes that broadened the franchise to include almost all adult white males and altered apportionment to represent the more newly settled western or "upcountry" regions more equally.[69] Judicial review as fashioned by Marshall thus seemed to be on a collision course with popular majorities and local autonomy: Congress could pass almost any law unless the Constitution prohibited it, yet the Court would be far less tolerant of laws enacted by popularly chosen legislatures in the states. The combination of the two allowed the Court to superimpose a national perspective over dominant interests in the states.

"It is not my desire to excite prejudice against the Supreme Court," Senator Robert Hayne of South Carolina would confess a few years later. "I object only to the assumption of *political power* by the Supreme Court, a power which belongs not to them and which they cannot safely exercise."[70] What Hayne had stumbled onto was the fact that while constitutional cases might appear to be like ordinary legal disputes in that they pitted party A against party B, they possessed unique political (that is, policy and power) dimensions as well. The Court had amply demonstrated that it could render decisions affecting a large part of the public. For those unhappy with the outcomes and the supporting rationales, it was also apparent that the justices were not accountable to "the people" through the usual electoral channels. "There are two parties in the United States, most decidedly opposed to each other," one commentator from the period observed, "as to the rights, powers, and province of the Judiciary." One "almost claims infallibility for the Judges, and would hedge them round about in such a manner that they cannot be reached by popular opinion at all"; the other "would subject them to the vacillations of popular prejudice" and would "require . . . them to . . . interpret the Constitution according to the real or apparent expediency of things."[71] For one side the Court was expounder of the law and defender of the Republic; for the other it was elitist and threatening.

Despite the uproar, the Court was not a notable issue in the presidential elections of 1824 and 1828.[72] To be sure, the Court was occasionally a scapegoat in congressional races,[73] and candidates and their followers could sometimes be identified by their stands on constitutional issues. For example, the Old Republicans in Virginia were among the strongest backers of Crawford in the 1824 race, and many critics of Marshall Court doctrines joined the Jackson ranks in 1828. Similarly, those who looked to the courts to control the excesses of popular rule sensed a threat from the rise of Jacksonian democracy. Moreover, various events in Jackson's life suggested a lack of respect for the rule of law.[74] A National Republican campaign statement published in Virginia in January 1828, for instance, acknowledged a willingness to preserve "the Constitution . . . from the too liberal interpretation of Mr. Adams" but advised that the party "would yet more zealously defend [it] against the destroying hand of his rival. . . . [W]e ask whether you will [lay] all your conquests, and all your former possessions—the Constitution itself, and the freedom it was intended to protect—at the feet of a despot?"[75]

Fully conscious of their critics in Congress and elsewhere, in 1828 justices of the Supreme Court succumbed to a level of partisanship not seen since 1800. Chief Justice Marshall told friends that he would vote for the first time in twenty-four years, and there was little mystery how he would cast his vote.[76] For the chief justice, Jackson "typified the recrudescence of that unbridled democratic spirit which he so increasingly feared and distrusted."[77] Justice Story vigorously supported Adams, used the excuse of a book review to write a powerful pro-Adams polemic,[78] regretted not being able to do more, and described the upcoming election as "momentous, both in principles and consequences."[79] Justice Smith Thompson remained on the Court while he ran for governor of New York, hoping that his popularity would allow Adams to carry the state.[80] Justice Bushrod Washington took part in an Adams convention in Virginia. Justice Johnson, Marshall's senior associate, backed Jackson. Only Justice Gabriel Duval remained outwardly uncommitted.[81] While their posturing probably swayed few voters, their overt preference for Adams's reelection hardly endeared the bench to the victor.[82]

Nonetheless, several factors kept the Supreme Court away from the center of the campaign. Recall that partisanship—defined as competition *between* organized parties—was absent from the presidential races of 1820 and 1824. Also recall that Monroe ran unopposed for a second term in 1820 while Congress was preoccupied with the Missouri question. In 1824, the personal followings of the four candidates were not party organizations. While antibank sentiment could have translated into anti-Court proposals in the race, the economic distress of 1819 and 1820 had moderated, and so the bank appeared less of a threat. Even in 1828, the clearly partisan race between Adams and Jackson quickly focused on personalities, making the campaign the "most venomous in American history."[83] These distractions overshadowed the Court while Jackson avoided clear-cut stances on constitutional and other specific policy matters, lest he alienate potential supporters.[84]

Furthermore, the states' rights issues at the heart of cases like *Cohens* and *Green* were not the stuff from which popular campaigns were easily forged. In 1800 Democratic-Republicans could point to the judiciary's eager application of the Sedition Act as an example of a threat to personal liberty, but in the 1820s the link was tenuous. Any threat posed by the federal judiciary to one's personal liberty was indirect and remote at most. Converting the Court into a whipping boy for the campaign would have been difficult in any event, because only a handful of newspapers during the decade paid any attention even to the most significant of the Court's decisions.[85] Even among those periodicals that followed the Court, commentary moderated between 1825 and 1830 so that, according to one study, the Court appeared less as a partisan instrument and more as an "impartial, incorruptible buffer against cultural disintegration."[86]

Besides, inconsistency and self-interest undercut the Court's critics. For example, as much as the Old Republicans in Virginia might complain about *McCulloch* and *Cohens, Green* v. *Biddle* drew no such condemnation. Because Virginia landowners and their heirs would be the probable beneficiaries, many in Virginia applauded the decision.[87] Not until later, when the institution of slavery would seem to be threatened by national power, would a cooperative spirit of states' rights develop among a large number of states at the same time. In the 1820s, opposition to judicial decisions still depended less on political theory and more on the immediate interest that a decision might advance or hinder.[88] While a decision might generate loud protests within a state, there were also those whom the outcome benefited. Furthermore, although a state might lose in one case, there was still much to be said for retaining a federal forum for defense of the state's interests in later litigation. *Green*, after all, was vindication of Virginia's interests over Kentucky's.

Finally, longevity of the justices kept to a minimum the occasions to debate the composition of the bench that a wholesale and rapid turnover in personnel might well have provoked.[89] In what stands as a record in the stability in the membership of the Supreme Court, only two seats changed hands in the years between 1812 and 1829: Smith Thompson and Robert Trimble replaced Henry Brockholst Livingston and Thomas Todd in 1823 and 1826, respectively. That neither appointment was free of concern about the role of the Court suggests that additional vacancies might have more sharply focused senators on the constitutional values of those selected for the bench.[90]

THE CAMPAIGN OF 1832

As much as the election of 1828 had been characterized by personal attacks, the election of 1832 was defined by war over the Bank of the United States.[91] The drive "to rescue the American people from the federal bank overshadowed all other issues."[92] The Marshall Court, placed on the defensive again by a series of developments, could not escape this conflict.

Revival of partisanship in 1828 had imbued Democratic leaders with the idea that the Court was a repository of obnoxious views.[93] Attacks on the Court materialized in Congress in January 1830, in what became known as the Hayne-Webster debate. As the Senate considered a resolution on public lands, Senator Robert Y. Hayne of South Carolina asserted the authority of a state to declare unconstitutional a law that the Supreme Court had held constitutional. To Daniel Webster's reply that the Court was properly the arbiter of the meaning of the Constitution, Senator Thomas Benton of Missouri decried the results to which that theory led, "a despotic power over the States" and "a judicial tyranny and oppression."[94]

In the middle of the five months during which the Senate from time to time debated the role of the Court, the justices announced the outcome of *Craig* v. *Missouri*,[95] a case Senator Benton had argued in early March on behalf of his state. He had maintained that a Missouri statute authorizing loan certificates was not a violation of the Constitution's ban on state bills of credit.[96] More fundamentally, he asserted a point that he and others had recently made in the Senate debates: the unconstitutionality of Section 25, by which the case had reached the High Court.

Craig did nothing to reassure the Court's critics. Not only did Marshall's opinion reaffirm the constitutionality of Section 25 but the Court invalidated the Missouri law, four votes to three. The ruling so energized opponents of Section 25 that Marshall was dismayed: "It requires no prophet," he confessed to Justice Story, "to predict that the 25th Section is to be repealed or to use a more fashionable phrase, to be nullified by the Supreme Court of the United States."[97]

Hayne and Benton were emboldened in their attacks on national authority in part because of the doctrine of nullification, which lay at the core of the "South Carolina Exposition." Secretly drafted by ex-nationalist John C. Calhoun—vice president in the Adams administration as well as in Jackson's first term—and issued by the legislature of South Carolina in response to the tariff of 1828,[98] the document built on the ideas of the Kentucky and Virginia Resolutions to claim the authority of a state to "nullify" unconstitutional acts of Congress. "The majority in Congress, with the Executive and the judiciary, will habitually be true to the majority of the States, and where they prove otherwise, we need no other remedy but the ballot box," Calhoun explained to Postmaster General John McLean. "But where the disease is in the community itself, such as is the case, . . . the great minor interest can have no security, in any tribunal constituted by the majority of the States. . . . [T]he remedy is in the States themselves, each judging for itself."[99] Accordingly, Section 25 was unconstitutional: "Such a construction of the powers of the Federal Court, which would raise one of the departments of the General Government, above the sovereign parties, who created the Constitution, would enable it in practice to alter at pleasure the relative powers of the States and General Government."[100]

The "Exposition" no doubt emboldened officials in Georgia in their expulsion of the Cherokee Indians from the state, an objective made more urgent by discovery of gold on Cherokee lands in northern Georgia in 1828. Legally the struggle was between extension of state law into tribal lands and state recognition of tribal integrity under a treaty the national government had made with the Cherokees in 1791.

In a series of cases, Georgia officials defied the Supreme Court. One involved a Cherokee named Corn Tassel who was convicted of murder under state law and sentenced to death. When the Court granted a writ of error in 1830 to consider the state court's jurisdiction to conduct the trial, the governor ignored the order and, in a kind of applied nullification, Corn Tassel was promptly executed.[101]

Another incident involved white Christian missionaries Samuel Worcester and Elizur Butler. A Georgia statute of 1831 required all white persons living in the disputed areas to obtain a license from the state in order to remain on Cherokee lands. When Worcester and Butler failed to comply, they were arrested, tried, and sentenced to four years in prison. When the U.S. Supreme Court issued a writ of error to review the case, the governor replied that any compliance would "be usurpation of a power never granted by the States." Moreover, the legislature directed the governor to disregard any order from the High Court and required him "with all the power and means placed at his command, . . . to resist and repel any and every invasion from whatever direction it may come, upon the administration of the criminal laws of this State."[102] Following argument at which no counsel appeared for Georgia, the Court held the state licensing statute unconstitutional on March 3, 1832, and reversed Worcester and Butler's convictions.[103]

When Georgia officials refused to comply,[104] President Jackson declined to enforce the ruling, noting that he would thereby exceed his own authority and compound the erroneous decision the Supreme Court had made.[105] "John Marshall has made his decision:—*now let him enforce it!*" the president is supposed to have said.[106] It may well be that Jackson thought he lacked authority to act on the Court's behalf, but that conclusion was made all the easier to reach for several reasons. First, he was hardly a supporter of the rights of Indians, east of the Mississippi at least. Second, he may well have concluded that enforcement was beyond his reach without unacceptable violence and loss of life.[107] Third, it was an election year. Among his supporters there was little to be gained by coercing Georgia into compliance and perhaps much to be gained by watching the Supreme Court endure its comeuppance. Finally, Jackson was fully aware of the nullification spirit that was ascendant in South Carolina. He would have endangered his own authority had he given Georgians common cause with their neighbors east of the Savannah River.

The context for reopening the bank question was, therefore, suspicion of national authority in general and of federal judicial authority in particular. The bank had played little role in the campaign of 1828, and Jackson entered office publicly "uncommitted" on the future of that institution.[108] However, in his first annual message to Congress in 1829, he suggested a reevaluation of the bank, and in 1830 called for creation of a new bank in place of the old that would have fewer resources and powers. Although the bank's charter was good until 1836, its president, Nicholas Biddle, was understandably alarmed. In 1831, with cooperation from some members of the cabinet, he asked for early renewal of the charter. If Congress moved quickly, Biddle calculated, Jackson would acquiesce in the renewal to avoid alienating potential supporters in an election year.

Meanwhile, the National Republicans had nominated Henry Clay for president and John Sergeant for vice president.[109] Like their party, both were committed to a continuation of the bank and claimed that reelection of Jackson would mean its destruction. After Democrats had given their nod to Jackson for a second term, the Senate passed Biddle's charter renewal on June 11 and the House acted favorably on July 3. The bill then went to the president for his signature. Relying heavily on a memorandum written by Attorney General Roger Brooke Taney,[110] Jackson vetoed the charter renewal on both constitutional and policy grounds.[111] "It is maintained by the advocates of the bank," Jackson maintained, "that its constitutionality in all its features ought to be considered as settled by precedent and by the decision of the Supreme Court. To this conclusion I cannot assent." *McCulloch* v. *Maryland* was not dispositive.

If the opinion of the Supreme Court covered the whole ground of this act, it ought not to control the coordinate authorities of this government. The Congress, the executive, and the court must each for itself be guided by its own opinion of the Constitution. . . . It is as much the duty of the House of Representatives, of the Senate, and of the President to decide upon the constitutionality of any bill or resolution which may be presented to them for passage or approval as it is of the supreme judges when it may be brought before them for judicial decision. The opinion of the judges has no more authority over Congress than the opinion of Congress has over the judges, and on that point the President is independent of both. The authority of the Supreme Court must not, therefore, be permitted to control the Congress or the executive when acting in their legislative capacities, but to have only such influence as the force of their reasoning may deserve.[112]

Jackson's veto message made the bank *the* issue for the election[113] and placed the constitutional role of the Supreme Court in doubt. The choice for the electorate was clear: it would be Jackson or the bank. Jackson thus became the first American president to bypass Congress through a direct appeal to the electorate. He envisioned the presidency as the repository of the wisdom and virtue of the people, and the people should never be excluded from the councils of government. As Jackson had written in March, if anything "can paralyze the course of the executive, it will be done . . . and Clay, Calhoun, and Webster have [never?] ceased to endeavour to put me down and the supreme court in a late decision declaring the Cherokees an independent nation, have united, to embarrass me. *It all will not do.* I have always relied on the good intelligence and virtue of the people. They will decide."[114] Even the Court was to heed the message of the ballot box. As the *Globe*, a mouthpiece for the administration, editorialized within days of the veto, surely no one believed that "four men who form a majority of the Supreme Court" should have "dominion over the rights of the states and the rights of the majority of the people of the United States."[115]

The National Republican reply to Jackson's veto opened with a counterattack by Webster on the Senate floor in a message that was partly written by Justice Story himself.[116] The bank reprinted 30,000 copies of Webster's message for distribution around the country, and donated nearly $100,000 to Clay's campaign.

The bank helped the Democrats to sharpen their appeal. The bank was not merely bad in itself but was a symbol of the aristocracy that the people and Jackson had to master. "The veto works well," Jackson said, for "instead of crushing me as was expected and intended, it will crush the Bank." As the *Globe* proclaimed, "From time immemorial to the present date, the great mass of mankind have been struggling to preserve their conventional rights against the usurpations of a *few*. . . . This governing party has been denominated the Aristocracy. . . . The new-fangled name 'National Republican,' is a *ruse de guerre*."[117]

The Clay campaign in turn used the veto as a symbol of the threat Jackson posed to the Constitution and the Republic: "THE KING UPON THE THRONE: *The people in the Dust*!!!" proclaimed one newspaper headline.[118] Even before Jackson's rejection of the bank bill, National Republicans emphasized the danger the Democrats posed for the Court.

> The judiciary department . . . seems . . . to be seriously threatened by the perverse policy of the present administration. . . . When a proposition to repeal . . . the section of the judiciary act which authorizes the appeal from the state to the federal courts, and forms the foundation of the jurisprudence of the union in this respect, was made in congress, it was favored by the immediate friends of the president, and by the journals under his control. . . . These proceedings seem to indicate a settled intention in the administration to shake the independence and destroy the efficiency of this most important branch of the government.'[119]

Anti-Masonic groups joined the anti-Jackson chorus, depicting the president as one who possessed "monstrous pretensions," and attacked the "supremacy of the law."[120]

Such views must surely have aligned the Court more closely with the bank in the popular mind once the campaign was fully under way in late summer and fall of 1832. In the end, Biddle's renewal strategy backfired. While Jackson's share of the popular vote declined slightly, he still received an impressive 54.5 percent; of the 286 electoral votes cast, he collected 219. He could fairly claim to have a mandate to dismantle the bank.

EFFECTS

Jackson's victory meant changes for the Supreme Court and public policy. Most immediately, however, the political atmosphere that assured a Democratic triumph in 1832 helped to precipitate a constitutional crisis for Jackson and the country. Ironically, its resolution witnessed the president embracing Marshallian nationalism.

On November 24, before the electoral votes were cast and Jackson was officially reelected, the South Carolina legislature passed the Ordinance of Nullification to block enforcement of the Tariff of 1832. This measure attempted to mollify Southern states by reducing some of the rates in the "Tariff of Abomination" enacted in 1828, but many Southerners deemed the new tariff unacceptable as well. The ordinance declared that tariff acts of 1828 and 1832 were "null and void," denied the authority of the Supreme

Court to review any state court decision on the constitutionality of the ordinance, and threatened armed resistance should the national government attempt to collect the new tariffs. Jackson must have realized that South Carolina's defiance was partly of his own making: leaders of the nullification movement had witnessed his passivity after the Cherokee decisions and had read his statements about the Court in the bank veto message. If Jackson had not actively lobbied for repeal of Section 25, neither had he discouraged the drive or spoken in defense of the Court. "[By making [the Court] a topic of party and electioneering discussion, and representing it to the people . . . as a despotic department of the Government," Missouri Senator David Barton had warned, "it loses its great utility in quieting instead of inflaming the public mind."[121]

Nonetheless, it was one thing for the president to trump the Supreme Court and another for a state to trump the executive by resisting collection of revenue. On December 10 Jackson issued a proclamation that denounced the ordinance and called on Congress to enact legislation to meet any acts of defiance. At least one paragraph could have been written by Marshall himself:

> The Constitution declares that the judicial powers of the United States extend to cases arising under the laws of the United States and that such laws, the Constitution, and treaties shall be paramount to the State constitutions and laws. The judiciary act prescribes the mode by which the case may be brought before a court of the United States by appeal when a State tribunal shall decide against this provision.[122]

"Who would have dreamed of such an occurrence?" Justice Story wrote to his wife after dinner at the White House in January. "[S]ince the . . . proclamation and message, the Chief justice and myself have become his warmest supporters."[123]

Jackson's stand squelched the nullification crisis as he distanced himself from states' rights extremists in his own party. That, however, did not mean a wholesale turnabout on other questions. With the bank, Jackson steadfastly pursued its end, instructing Roger Taney in the fall of 1833 (Taney was then holding a recess appointment as secretary of the treasury) to withdraw all federal deposits and transfer them to state banks. If the bank was going to survive until its charter ran out in 1836, Jackson wanted to make sure that it did so in a weakened state.[124] Yet Taney's obedience soon cost him his job; a majority of the Senate, still irate over Jackson's antibank policies, rejected the nomination.

Indeed, the bank controversy probably crystallized Jackson's thinking about the judiciary and the Constitution in a way that had a significant effect on the Supreme Court. Because of the election of 1832, Jackson was able to affect its composition, and hence some of its decisions, for more than a generation. During his two terms, Jackson placed six justices on the bench,[125] more than any of his predecessors except Washington and more than any of his successors except Franklin Roosevelt.[126] Two of these nominations occurred in Jackson's first term, the remaining four near the end of his second. With all six, party and political fealty was of importance to the president, but with the four appointments that followed the bank episode, Jackson appears to have taken greater care to assure that their fealty was genuine.[127]

The first nomination was possible because of the vacancy Jackson inherited from the Adams administration, and his choice was Adams's postmaster general, John McLean. Not only did McLean turn out to be unpredictable in his judicial leanings,[128] but he failed to keep his promise to Jackson to eschew presidential ambitions. Henry Baldwin joined the Court in 1830 to replace Bushrod Washington, but while the new justice had been a stalwart Jacksonian in Pennsylvania in the campaign of 1828, on the bench he was less faithful to the president's views. Perhaps most distressing to Jackson, Baldwin was an outspoken critic of the president's war on the bank in 1832. Nonetheless, his judicial views followed a middle course between the extremes of states' rights in his own party and Marshall's nationalism in the opposition.[129]

It was perhaps good fortune for the Court that the next vacancy did not open during the first volleys of the bank war. Jefferson's first appointee, Justice William Johnson, died in August 1834. As a South Carolinian, Johnson had had the nullification crisis on his doorstep[130] even as the president doubtless had the episode still on his mind. Jackson believed that his party had to avoid the extremes symbolized by the National Republicans and the advocates of nullification.[131] He therefore felt compelled to pick a Southerner with unionist sympathies, but the risk was that such a person would be too enamored of central authority. His choice of James Moore Wayne of Georgia sent the right message to the nullificationists, but the risk proved real. Especially in cases after 1840, Wayne frequently rejected the states' rights position.[132]

With the three other vacancies, however, Jackson was more successful in strengthening the states' rights perspective on the bench. When Gabriel Duval retired in 1835, the president sought revenge on the Senate by selecting Roger Taney. The Senate, however, had its revenge on Jackson both by "postponing" action on Taney on the last day of its session and by voting to abolish Duval's old seat, a move the House rejected. Then in July 1835, fate created a second seat to fill when Chief Justice Marshall died. Waiting until December, Jackson responded by nominating Philip Barbour, a judge and loyal party man from Virginia, to take Duval's place and Taney to fill Marshall's. This time the Senate acted favorably on Taney, voting 29 to 15 on March 15, 1836.[133] Approval of Barbour followed in May. Jackson selected his last appointee for the Court on his last day in office in March 1837, one of the two new seats added to the bench. Not confirmed until after Martin Van Buren, Jackson's vice president, had become president, John Catron would, along with Taney and Barbour, generally take positions of which Jackson approved.[134]

"Judge Story . . . thinks the Supreme Court is *gone* and I think so too,"[135] wrote Daniel Webster while the Senate had Taney's name under consideration. Events proved both Story and Webster wrong. Yet the Jackson justices altered the course of the nation's constitutional jurisprudence. Ironically, they reinforced a trend that had begun under Marshall during the J. Q. Adams administration. "The trend of Marshall's decisions after 1826 was unmistakably in the direction of state power, as it was with the entire Court."[136] In *Providence Bank* v. *Billings*,[137] for example, the Court retreated from the rigorous construction of the contract clause seen in cases such as *Green* v. *Biddle* of 1823.[138]

Now with Taney as chief justice, the trend became even more indisputable, particularly in three of the new Court's initial decisions. Each loosened the constitutional reins by acknowledging greater regulatory power in the states and seemed to go against precedents set by the Marshall Court. With Justices Story, McLean, and Thompson in dissent, *Charles River Bridge Co.* v. *Warren Bridge Co.* refused to use the contract clause to recognize implied rights in a charter granted by a state to one company that was later crippled by a charter granted to a second company.[139] With only Story dissenting, *New York* v. *Miln* upheld a regulation on passengers on incoming ships in face of a challenge that it was a regulation of commerce, and hence an impermissible interference with a power of Congress. Instead, Justice Barbour's opinion placed the ordinance within the "police power" that the states possessed. Similarly, *Briscoe* v.

Bank of Kentucky involved a challenge under the bills-of-credit clause to notes issued by a state-chartered, state-owned, and state-directed bank.[140] *Craig* v. *Missouri* weighed heavily against the practice, but, with Story again as the sole dissenter, the Court so "distinguished" the present case from *Craig* as to make Marshall's handiwork virtually impotent. The decision was significant in light of Jackson's war on the bank, because it signaled broad judicial tolerance of state regulation of banking practices.

However, the Taney Court's hostility to Marshall's doctrine of national supremacy did not mean a shrunken role for the Supreme Court. By acknowledging a greater role for the states, the Court multiplied the occasions when the justices would have to decide whether state laws had gone too far in treading upon national prerogatives.[141] Nor did rulings by the Taney Court preclude an expansion of judicial power, one of the banes of the uprising in the 1820s that helped to make possible Jackson's election. For example, *Swift* v. *Tyson*[142] broadened the discretion of federal judges in diversity cases by allowing them to look to general principles of commercial law rather than to the law of the state in which they were sitting, as seemed to be dictated by Section 34 of the Judiciary Act of 1789. The effect was to make the law of business transactions more uniform among the states, at least in those cases decided in federal court. Three years later, the justices significantly expanded the jurisdiction of the federal courts. A decision by the Marshall Court in 1825 had followed English law and limited federal admiralty jurisdiction to tidal waters.[143] In order to promote trade on inland waters, however, Congress in 1845 extended federal admiralty jurisdiction to the Great Lakes and connecting navigable bodies. In *Genesee Chief* v. *Fitzhugh*[144] the Taney Court overturned the Marshall era ruling, upheld the statute, and declared that admiralty jurisdiction was not limited to tidal regions. The English rule adopted by Marshall was deemed unworkable in a land with many navigable inland waterways. Federal court jurisdiction thus became a function of navigability and not the ebb and flow of the tide, and effected an enlarged national intrusion into what had been matters of state law.

The anti-Court agitation that climaxed in the election of 1832 worked changes on public policy and the judiciary, but the changes were at the margin. In terms of its place in the political system, the Supreme Court that Jackson helped to shape not only maintained its influence but also enlarged it. The bank vanished as a national institution, but Section 25 remained the law of the land. Jackson discovered firsthand what Tocqueville reported: that the Supreme Court, with the jurisdiction to decide its jurisdiction, was an essential link in the American union.[145] Jackson's bank veto message, however, remained a precept for successors equally disinclined to cede constitutional finality to the Supreme Court.

If the Taney Court was more favorably disposed than the Marshall Court toward state legislation, that disposition must be considered in light of Congress's general unwillingness to use the powers the Marshall Court had declared it possessed. If legislation was needed, it would be, more often than not, state legislation that was passed. Moreover, with increased judicial influence came prestige. That prestige, however, would not protect the Court in later entanglements with politically sensitive issues. Indeed, a heightened sense of institutional self-importance would make such involvement less resistible.

CHAPTER 4

The Election of 1860: Limits of Partisanship

A pair of cases decided after the election of 1856 thrust the Supreme Court into the campaign of 1860. Both cases involved slavery, which by the late 1850s threatened to dismember the union. The justices not only took sides on this explosive question but did so in a way that invalidated the organizing principle of the new Republican party. These developments occurred as the second party system disintegrated and the third party system emerged.

ORIGINS OF THE THIRD PARTY SYSTEM

The second party system lasted for about a quarter-century, with Democrats prevailing in national elections most of the time. Only in 1840 and 1848 did Whigs win the White House, and they controlled Congress only occasionally: both houses in the 27th Congress, the Senate in the 28th, and the House in the 30th. (See appendix 1.) Yet in terms of the development of American parties, the years were noteworthy in at least two respects. First, in contrast to the sectional orientation that would later characterize both Democrats and Republicans, Democrats and Whigs in the second party system drew from both North and South. Second, the period was a vigorous political garden, rich with the flowering of third parties. Indeed, the Democratic–Whig competition ended with the ascendancy of one of them (the Republicans), the only instance in American history when a third party supplanted a major party. The underpinnings of the major parties' national base encouraged these competitors.

As early as 1820, when Congress considered the Missouri question (discussed in the previous chapter), Thomas Jefferson regarded the controversy over slavery in territories and new states as a "fire bell in the night" and "the knell of the union."[1] National parties would be a way of keeping slavery off the national agenda, as Martin Van Buren of New York, Andrew Jackson's successor as president, counseled Virginians in 1827 when he helped mold Jackson's followers, North and South, into a party.[2] The reverse would be true as well. With slavery on the agenda, two parties would be hard pressed to maintain a national base of support were they to advocate different positions. And at least through the 1830s, dominant sentiment in the North supported Southern insistence that the subject remain officially muted, even in face of growing abolitionist opposition to slavery. Indeed, from 1836 until 1844, the House of Representatives enforced a "gag rule" that automatically tabled every antislavery petition, and the Senate took similar steps to avoid consideration of abolitionist proposals.[3]

While vocal opposition to American slavery predated even the Constitution,[4] abolitionism as a movement began in 1833 with creation of the American Anti-Slavery Society. Its aims were radical: not only did it advocate eradication of slavery throughout the United States, but its charter called for freed slaves to "share an equality with the whites, of civil and religious privileges."[5] The political wing of the society later organized the Liberty party, which put forward James G. Birney for president of the United States in both 1840 and 1844. The party's chief strength was that it "provided a way of not voting for the parties which sinfully governed."[6] The party's chief weakness was its single-issue obsession. While it appealed to ardent abolitionists, it was not attractive to antislavery Northerners who had other political concerns. Birney's total vote in the 1840 and 1844 contests, therefore, was only a minor fraction of the number of adult males in the Anti-Slavery Society. His vote in New York State in 1844, however, which came mainly from antislavery Whigs, was large enough to hand that state's electoral vote, and with it the election, to Democratic nominee James Polk rather than to Whig nominee Henry Clay.

Democrats had denounced all efforts to interfere with slavery, and the Whig platform of 1844 referred not once to the issue. As the dominant party during the second party system, Democrats knew that patronage and other rewards of power depended on victory. And victory depended on a united party, which in turn required the cooperation of the Southern wing. Northern Whigs, who may well have been more disposed than Northern Democrats, by class and religion, to oppose slavery,[7] must have thought similarly. A contrary view risked the loss of the Whig base in the South.[8] Nonetheless, while third-party movements drew from both Democratic and Whig ranks, the Whigs proved less monolithic. Countering flirtations with a third party were long-standing agreements within each party on economic and other issues that temporarily, like glue, held the large parties together.

That slavery eventually occupied the congressional and national agendas was as much a by-product of other events as it was the result of the spread of antislavery sentiment. One could not debate the annexation of Texas in the early 1840s, for example, without talking about slavery. It was not merely that Texas, which had become independent of Mexico in 1836, would join the Union as a slave state; its land was so vast that many expected a division of Texas into as many as four states. That would strengthen the slavery interests at the national level. The controversy, therefore, stemmed only partly from moral objections to slavery or its extension; at heart it was a question of power, both between regions and within the Democratic party.[9]

Annexation of Texas provoked war with Mexico in the spring of 1846 when the Polk administration supported Texas's claim of a southern border along the Rio Grande River. In August, David Wilmot, a Democratic representative from Pennsylvania, introduced an amendment to an appropriation bill—quickly dubbed the Wilmot Proviso—that would prohibit the introduction of slavery into any territory purchased or won from Mexico. Passed by the House several times, Wilmot's measure never succeeded in the Senate. Outside the South it had wide appeal, since more voters opposed the extension of slavery than favored its abolition in those states where it already existed. Moreover, it was responsible for initiating what would be a fourteen-year debate on congressional authority over slavery in the territories. Those who favored slavery's extension and those who opposed it were agreed on one thing: as a social and economic institution, slavery would be extended or it would gradually die.

Nonetheless, the proviso divided both Democrats and Whigs, generally but not entirely along regional lines. Among the former, pro-administration and pro-Southern "Hunkers" opposed the "Barnburners," who were willing to cooperate with the foes of slavery.[10] Among the latter, "Conscience Whigs" could claim the moral high ground over "Cotton Whigs."

When Democrats nominated Lewis Cass of Michigan for the presidency in 1848, Barnburners bolted because the party had turned its back on Martin Van Buren, whom they favored. Moreover, Cass, who had been one of the few Northern senators to vote against Wilmot's proviso, eagerly joined Southern members of the party in backing "popular sovereignty," by which settlers of new areas would choose whether their land would be slave or free. Renegade Democrats could not look to the Whigs, however, since they offered no platform in 1848, only Zachary Taylor as a presidential candidate. Taylor was popular in the South as a slave owner and hailed nationally as a hero ("Old Rough and Ready") who had defeated General Santa Anna in the war with Mexico.

Disgruntled Whigs and Democrats then combined with remnants of the Liberty party and founded the Free Soil party in August 1848 at Buffalo, with Van Buren as their presidential candidate. While proposing "no interference by Congress with slavery within the limits of any state,"[11] the new party demanded "no more Slave States, no more Slave Territory."[12] Accordingly,

> the federal government [should] relieve itself from all responsibility for the existence or continuance of slavery wherever that government possesses constitutional authority to legislate on that subject, and is thus responsible for its existence. . . . [T]he only safe means of preventing the extension of slavery into territory now free, is to prohibit its existence in all such territory by an act of Congress.[13]

The Free Soil ticket, headed by Van Buren and Charles Francis Adams (a Conscience Whig and son of another former president), got no electoral votes but garnered 10 percent of the popular vote, and ran second to Taylor in New York, Massachusetts, and Vermont. Since only thirty-six electoral votes separated the victorious Taylor from Cass (the number of electoral votes cast by New York), and since the Free Soil vote in New York came mainly from the Barnburners,[14] entry of the Free Soilers into the campaign of 1848 may fairly be said to have determined the outcome.

Soon after the new Congress convened in December 1849, Whigs and Democrats led by Senators Henry Clay of Kentucky and Stephen Douglas of Illinois worked for legislation that would defuse the controversy. Their package of bills, called the "Compromise of 1850," became law in September and provided for admission of California into the union as a free state (as stipulated in that state's constitution), organization of the Utah and New Mexico territories without restriction on slavery, abolition of the slave trade (but not slavery itself) in the District of Columbia, and a more stringent fugitive slave law. Like any compromise, the legislation avoided the extremes: extension of slavery was possible, not guaranteed.

The legislation at first seemed to lay the matter to rest. In the presidential race of 1852, both the Democratic and the Whig platforms backed the compromise, although the latter's support was decidedly lukewarm. Indeed, at the Whig convention in Baltimore, two weeks after Democrats had nominated darkhorse Franklin Pierce of New Hampshire in the same city, all the votes against endorsement of the compromise came from Northern supporters of the party's nominee, General Winfield Scott ("Old Fuss and Feathers"), another hero of the Mexican War. Among Democrats, the prospects of power triumphed over the pursuit of principle when most Barnburners returned to the Democratic fold. Pierce won handily, and the Free Soil ticket (now labeled the Free Democratic party) mustered only about half of what it had achieved in 1848.

The compromise might have extended the life of the second party system for another generation had further westward settlement not intervened. By 1854 organization of territorial governments for Kansas (the land west of Missouri) and Nebraska (the land west of Iowa) seemed essential. Under the Missouri Compromise of 1820, however, that region was free soil. As chairman of the Senate's committee on territories, Stephen Douglas proposed to organize the new territories under the principle of popular sovereignty. This would carve out an implicit exception to the Missouri Compromise, but Southerners successfully insisted on an outright repeal of the 1820 ban. Popular sovereignty (that is, congressional nonintervention) thus became the rule for all territories.

Even before passage of the Kansas–Nebraska Act on May 30, a fusion movement had begun to take shape that included the likes of Liberty and Free Soil Senator Salmon Chase (who had Democratic leanings on the tariff question), New Hampshire Democrat John P. Hale, Free Soil Democrat Charles Sumner of Massachusetts, and Ohio Whig Benjamin F. Wade. Realignment in Congress was simultaneous with local meetings to form a new party. By the summer of 1854, the Republican party was born. In a convention "under the oaks" in Jackson, Michigan, on July 6, the first Republican platform absolved its supporters "from all 'compromises,' except those expressed in the Constitution, for the protection of slavery and slave-owners"; derided the Fugitive Slave Act of 1850 as "odious"; demanded its repeal as well as the repeal of the Kansas–Nebraska Act, and called for a federal law banning slavery in the territories and in the District of Columbia.[15]

Disintegration of the Whig party, North and South, soon followed. Whigs were not even able to put forth a separate candidate for president in 1856. As a Republican journalist wrote of the Whigs, "These gentlemen are evidently incapable of the idea that the process now going on in the politics of the United States is a *Revolution*."[16] The Whigs' demise was speeded by the growing popularity between 1849 and 1856 of yet another third party, the "Know-Nothings."[17] At first a secret movement that stressed nativism and drew heavily from the ranks of Whigs, Know-Nothings had come into the open as the American party and run former president Millard Fillmore as a candidate in 1856. And it was in Fillmore's candidacy that the Whigs acquiesced. With a Whig platform that was silent on the slavery issue and asserted only that Fillmore could save the nation, and with an American convention that was unable to unite its membership on slavery, the Whig–American ticket carried only Maryland.

The real contest centered on Democrats and Republicans, and for the first time two major parties took diametrically opposite positions on slavery. The Republican platform of 1856 stated its case succinctly: "We deny the authority of Congress, of a Territorial Legislature, or any individual, or association of individuals, to give legal existence to Slavery in any Territory of the United States, while the present Constitution shall be maintained." Accordingly, "it is both the right and the imperative duty of Congress to prohibit in the Territories those twin relics of barbarism—Polygamy, and Slavery."[18] In contrast, Democrats promised "to abide by and adhere to a faithful execution of the acts known as the compromise measures, settled by the Congress of 1850," to "resist all attempts at renewing . . . the agitation of the slavery question," and to accept "the principles contained in the organic laws establishing the Territories of Kansas and Nebraska as embodying the only sound and safe solution of the 'slavery question' upon which the great national idea of the people of this whole country can repose in its determined conservatism of the Union—*Non-Interference by Congress with Slavery in State and Territory, or in the District of Columbia*."[19] With the Whigs gone as an effective party, a new party system materialized, even as the nation poised on the brink of dissolution.

THE TANEY COURT

Roger Brooke Taney, named chief justice in 1836 by Andrew Jackson, during the early years of the second party system, presided over the Supreme Court for twenty-eight years. That was long enough to witness the emergence of the third party system, the disintegration of the union, and the catastrophic effects of the clash between abolitionism and sectionalism: civil war. The Court was bound up with the first of these developments and accelerated the other two.

There had been twenty-four states when John Marshall died in 1835, and the territory of the United States did not extend west of the Louisiana Purchase of 1803. On the eve of war in 1860, the nation counted thirty-three states, an increase of more than a third, and acquisitions of territory from Mexico and Great Britain had given the United States the continental boundaries it retains today. Justices of the Taney Court were the first routinely to travel by rail to conduct some of their circuit court duties.[20] After 1844, as telegraph lines spanned the country, news of political events could travel in seconds—not days or weeks. Improvements in printing technology and increased literacy resulted in inexpensive and mass-circulation newspapers. News could be disseminated more widely and more rapidly than ever before.

Partisan controversy swirled around Taney's last years, as it had Marshall's. But unlike the onset of John Marshall's tenure, which found a beleaguered bench in the thick of a clash between Federalists and Jeffersonians, the Court in Taney's first years was spared much of the venom that had been aimed at its predecessor. Indeed, for almost two decades, amid various national political storms, the judicial waters remained relatively calm. Compared with what had been and to what was to come, it was an "era of good feeling" for the Supreme Court. By one estimate, the Court's prestige had never been higher as the 1850s began.[21] Bitterness over Taney's role in the bank episode in 1832 (see the previous chapter) had dissipated, as had congressional efforts to restrict the High Court's appellate jurisdiction.

That prestige rested on the Marshall legacy that had carved out a place for the Court in the political system, on the dynamics of the second party system, and on the Taney Court's ability to shape constitutional doctrine to meet the needs of an expanding, and changing, nation. Without this prestige the Court after 1860 might not have survived as an independent branch of government. This does not mean that the Taney Court was constitutionally and politically unimportant for much of its life or that its decisions escaped criticism. Still, for several reasons the Court usually managed to steer clear of electoral campaigns.

First, the Taney Court was staffed mainly by Democrats during an era when Democrats were the dominant party. In 1836, five of the Court's seven members—Taney included—were Jackson appointees. From then until the mid-1850s there would be only eight new faces on the bench, and two of those were occasioned by enlargement of the Court from seven to nine justices in 1837. Moreover, only two of the eight appointments (Samuel Nelson in 1845 and Benjamin Curtis in 1851) were made by Whig presidents

(Tyler and Fillmore). And Nelson's occurred soon after Tyler, now out of favor with the Whigs, had unsuccessfully sought nomination on the Democratic ticket.

This Democratic complexion was important when one remembers that Democrats, and before them the Jeffersonians, had been the antijudiciary party in national politics. The Whigs, in contrast, were the intellectual heirs of the National Republicans and the Federalists, who had been strong supporters of the federal judiciary. Unless the Court displayed no breaks with the Marshall era, Democrats presumably would be disinclined to attack a member of the family, so to speak, just as Whigs would refrain from fundamental attacks on the Court, short of a series of sharp departures in constitutional law.[22]

Second, for two decades the Taney Court managed to accommodate both camps. The Court was generally acceptable to Democrats because it was mainly majoritarian in outlook as it examined the constitutionality of state laws.[23] And it was the states that remained the principal sources of new policies in the United States; Congress was little disposed to make use of the generous constitutional authority that Marshall had tendered. While the Court under Taney hardly abandoned judicial review of state laws, proportionally it resorted to the judicial veto far less often than it had under Marshall. While the Taney Court invalidated twenty-one state laws during its twenty-eight years, in contrast to nineteen such invalidations in the thirty-four years of the Marshall Court, the volume of cases in the later period was substantially greater. The 1,712 cases decided by the Taney Court represented a 57 percent increase over the 1,090 cases decided while Marshall presided.[24] So, if the Taney justices appeared more tolerant than their predecessors of state laws that impinged on contracts,[25] the Court made it clear that the Constitution nonetheless imposed real limits.[26] If the Taney justices on balance rejected the theory that regulation of commerce was a power residing exclusively with Congress, there were still policies affecting commerce that the states could not pursue.[27] State governments did not necessarily prevail in arguable conflicts with national prerogatives,[28] and in *Ableman* v. *Booth*[29]—its sharpest clash with claims of states' rights—the Taney Court proved to be no more of a friend than Jackson had been to the doctrine of nullification. Statistically, the Taney Court was just as tolerant of congressional power as the Marshall brethren; its first (and only) invalidation of an act of Congress did not occur until 1857, in the Dred Scott case.[30] (Both *Booth* and *Scott* are examined in the next section.) Furthermore, Chief Justice Taney was the first to define a "political question doctrine" that excused the Court from decisions in inappropriate cases, particularly those that might sweep the Court into uncharted political waters.[31]

The Taney Court, however well deserved its reputation for restraint, nonetheless pushed the federal judicial power—and hence the role of the Supreme Court—beyond the boundaries in place at the time of Marshall's death. The Court's Democratic complexion helped to legitimize this expansion in the eyes of the old anti-Court party all the while it pleased most Whigs. One ruling, for example, increased the probability that suits involving corporations would come within the diversity jurisdiction of the federal courts.[32] This was a significant step because of *Swift* v. *Tyson*,[33] decided in 1842, that freed federal courts from state-court interpretations in commercial law matters and allowed the former to develop a nationwide body of law that was far more convenient for business.[34] A third decision recognized the impact of steam on water transportation when it repudiated a decision of the Marshall Court and expanded the scope of federal admiralty jurisdiction to include all navigable freshwater rivers and lakes, not merely tidal areas.[35] Except for a single dissent in one, the votes in all three cases were unanimous, cutting across party, region, and generation.[36]

JUDICIAL ACTIONS

The Court had avoided electoral entanglement for a fourth reason as well. Until 1857 it treated the slavery issue with "meticulous circumspection."[37] This accomplishment was noteworthy when one remembers that the issue appeared on the national political agenda soon after Taney became chief justice. Circumspection, however, was overtaken by events that moved the Court into the partisan arena. Four cases illustrate how its decisions were eventually perceived generally as favoring one side over the other.

Prigg v. *Pennsylvania*[38] posed a problem slaveholders frequently encountered: some persons "held to Service or Labour,"[39] as the Constitution delicately described slaves, understandably tried to escape; when they succeeded, their owners understandably wanted them returned. The problem was compounded by personal liberty laws in free states that made recaption more difficult, often by requiring a trial or other hearing on the question of title before the owner or the owner's agent could remove the captured slave from the state of refuge. Such laws existed alongside the federal fugitive slave law enacted in 1793. Under this statute, the owner or designee could apply to either a federal or a state judge for a certificate that would authorize removal, a procedure that was considerably less protracted than under the personal liberty laws.

A challenge to both the federal and the state laws developed when Edward Prigg, a professional slave catcher, located Margaret Morgan, a runaway slave, in Pennsylvania. A state judge refused to issue the required certificate under the 1793 act, and Prigg forcibly carried Morgan into Maryland. Pennsylvania then charged Prigg with kidnapping under its personal liberty law of 1826.

When Prigg's appeal reached the Supreme Court, Justice Story's opinion for the majority upheld the constitutionality of the federal act and struck down Pennsylvania's law (and, by inference, similar laws in other states). Not only had Pennsylvania burdened recovery of slaves, but Story suggested that recaption was exclusively within the domain of the national government. Thus, while states might cooperate in the enforcement of the 1793 act, as its terms expressly allowed, they were not compelled to do so.

Prigg was fully satisfactory to neither side, but it offered something to both. Slave states were pleased because free states could no longer deploy legal processes to interfere with the recovery of slaves. Indeed, Story had said that the 1793 law even gave the owner a right, independent of the certificate, to remove the slave if that could be done without a breach of the peace. On the other hand, if federal power was exclusive, then the validity of state laws assisting recaption was also in doubt.[40] *Prigg* offered something to free states even as it invalidated their personal liberty laws. Not only were states not legally obligated to assist in the enforcement of the 1793 act, but some states forbade their officers to enforce the federal law or barred slave rendition proceedings from state facilities.[41] The absence of state cooperation would be particularly noticeable because there were so few federal judges in each state. Not surprisingly, enforcement of the 1793 act declined, a consequence that led to Southern insistence on a revised fugitive slave procedure as part of the Compromise of 1850.[42] *Prigg* also had the probably unintended effect of making abundantly clear, in a way that no judicial decision had done, the national government's role in the preservation of slavery.

Abolitionist Salmon Chase (a future chief justice) soon led another unsuccessful assault on the 1793 law after a conductor of the Underground Railroad was penalized for violating it.[43] The existence of slavery in the United States, declared Justice Woodbury for a unanimous bench, was "a political question, settled by each State for itself." Federal power over slavery was therefore "limited and regulated by the people of the States in the

Constitution itself, as one of its sacred compromises, and which we possess no authority as a judicial body to modify or overrule." Woodbury then revealed the discomfort that antislavery jurists such as himself felt over charges by abolitionists that the Court was in collusion with slavery interests.

> Whatever may be the theoretical opinions of any as to the expediency of some of those compromises [in the Constitution], or of the right of property in persons which they recognize, this court has no alternative, while they exist, but to stand by the Constitution and laws with fidelity to their duties and their oaths.[44]

In 1851 *Strader* v. *Graham*[45] asked whether slaves became free when they entered free states or territories. Lurking within the case was the perilous issue Congress was then confronting: its power over slavery in the territories. The owner of a band of slave musicians had brought a suit for damages against several men who were accused of helping the slaves flee from Kentucky to Canada. The defendants' defense was that the musicians were not slaves at the time of their flight because an earlier musical tour into Ohio had made them free. The Kentucky courts had ruled in favor of the slave owner, reasoning that whatever the musicians' status in Ohio, they were slaves under Kentucky law once they returned home. The U.S. Supreme Court dismissed the appeal: the Northwest Ordinance of 1787, under which the Ohio territory had been declared free soil and upon which the accused abettors built their argument, had no force in Ohio after statehood. (The holding won the Court no friends among antislavery groups because it meant that Ohio could now introduce slavery within its borders if it wished, however improbable that might be.) Without a federal question, the High Court therefore lacked jurisdiction. Chief Justice Taney's opinion for the unanimous bench, however, said more—much more—than was necessary, considering that he declared that his Court had no authority to decide the case. Agreeing with the Kentucky courts, he placed the Supreme Court's imprimatur on the doctrine of reversion: upon return to the home state, the slave reverted to its authority. The status of a slave back in bondage depended on the law of that state. *Strader* thus preached judicial restraint. Federal courts would not interfere with state court rulings on this subject, even when the former had jurisdiction.

Although *Strader* theoretically allowed a slave state to declare a recaptured slave to be free, it and the other rulings furnished evidence to critics who argued that, at heart, the Court was pro-slavery. Even the structure of the federal judicial system tilted the Court to the pro-slavery side. After 1837, there were nine circuits, and by custom presidents appointed justices from the states within a circuit. There were five circuits with slave states and four circuits with free states (no circuit combined both). Ordinarily, then, one would expect a majority of the Court to come from slave states.[46] In the year *Dred Scott* was decided, that was precisely the Court's composition: Taney was from Maryland (4th circuit), Wayne from Georgia (6th circuit), Catron from Tennessee (8th circuit), Campbell from Alabama (9th circuit), and Daniel from Virginia (5th circuit). Seats from free circuits were held by Grier from Pennsylvania (3d circuit), Nelson from New York (2d circuit), Curtis from Massachusetts (1st circuit), and McLean from Ohio (7th circuit).

Yet the Court had carefully refrained from foreclosing options for the nation on the subject of slavery. Nothing the Court had done (1) disallowed the free soil principle, that is, Congress's power to forbid slavery in the territories; (2) addressed territorial or popular sovereignty over the status of slavery in newly organized regions; (3) addressed Congress's authority or obligation to allow slavery in the territories; or (4) cast any doubt on the authority of any state to determine the status of slavery within its own borders.

In the year following *Strader* the Missouri Supreme Court concluded the first half of the litigation known as the Dred Scott case. His case was actually two cases, one pursued in the state courts of Missouri and the other in the federal courts. Combined, the cases commenced in 1846 and ended in 1857. At one level, the litigation involved efforts by a black man to obtain his and his family's freedom as well as back pay for services rendered. At another level, the litigation became a vehicle for resolution of an issue that divided the land. At both levels, the litigation failed. "[T]he questions involved . . . ," Georgia Whig (and future Confederacy vice president) Alexander H. Stephens presciently advised, "will have a greater political effect and bearing than any others of the day."[47]

Scott was born into slavery, probably in Virginia around 1800.[48] He later became the property of Dr. John Emerson, an army surgeon. In 1834 Emerson took Scott from Missouri to Illinois, where, under both the Northwest Ordinance and state law, slavery was forbidden. In 1836 Emerson and Scott traveled to Fort Snelling in what is now the state of Minnesota. Lying well above 36°30' north latitude, the territory was in that part of the Louisiana Purchase where, under the Missouri Compromise of 1820, slavery was forbidden. In 1838 Emerson returned to Missouri with Scott, who had now acquired a family. After Dr. Emerson died, Scott brought suit against Mrs. Emerson in state court, maintaining that his residence in free territory had made him a free man. The trial court held for Scott, but the state supreme court reversed in 1852.[49] Whatever Scott's legal status outside Missouri, he remained a slave under that state's law.

It is not clear why litigation proceeded as it did at this point. Ordinarily, the losing party in a case like Scott's would file a writ of error in the United States Supreme Court under Section 25 of the Judiciary Act. Counsel, however, did not. Perhaps *Strader* seemed to be an insurmountable barrier, even though, strictly speaking, the holding in that case was inapplicable to Scott's. Recall that the Supreme Court denied jurisdiction in *Strader* because statehood had supplanted the Northwest Ordinance, the federal link that would qualify the case for the High Court. But in Scott's case, the Missouri Compromise applied. Perhaps it was Taney's digression into the controlling force of Kentucky law that discouraged an appeal. Why litigation was then begun anew in federal court remains perplexing. Funds expended to gain Scott's freedom through the courts might have been employed to purchase it outright.

If a suit was to begin in federal court, a requisite for jurisdiction was diversity of citizenship. By this time, Mrs. Emerson had married Dr. C. C. Chaffee, a Massachusetts abolitionist who would shortly be elected to the U.S. House of Representatives. Accordingly, to reopen the case and to shield Chaffee's reputation, ownership of Scott passed to Mrs. Chaffee's brother, John Sanford,[50] of New York. In 1853, Roswell Field, an abolitionist attorney in St. Louis, filed suit on Scott's behalf against Sanford in the U.S. Circuit Court in Missouri. This court ruled against Scott, deeming dispositive both *Strader* and the state supreme court's holding in Scott's first case.

In the U.S. Supreme Court, *Scott v. Sandford* was argued twice: in February and December of 1856. Setting the case for reargument thus guaranteed that a ruling could not come down until after the presidential election. In fact, the Court announced its decision against Scott on March 6, 1857, two days after James Buchanan's inauguration as the fifteenth president. The case involved three questions that might be, but did not necessarily all have to be, addressed. First, was Scott's status settled by Missouri law, under which he had already been declared to be a slave? Second, was Scott a citizen of the United States, for the purpose of maintaining a suit in federal court against a citizen of another state? Third, what was the effect of his sojourn in territory declared free by the Missouri Compromise on his status as a slave? If the Court decided one or the other, or both, of the first two questions against Scott, there would be no need to answer the third.

After reargument, the Court seemed to have agreed to focus on the first question alone, with Justice Nelson assigned the task of writing the opinion. As first cast, then, *Dred Scott* would have avoided the most sensitive issues and would perhaps have been no more controversial than *Strader*. Several justices, however, wanted the decision to do more, "to quiet all agitation on the question of slavery in the Territories," Justice Curtis explained later.[51] Boldness displaced caution as necessity dictated a wider swathe.

Nine justices filed nine opinions, seven holding for Sanford and two (McLean and Curtis) for Scott. Traditionally viewed as the majority opinion,[52] Chief Justice Taney's addressed all three questions. First, while a state might grant state citizenship to blacks, they were not "citizens" of the United States within the meaning of the Constitution, and so could not press a suit in federal court. The circuit court therefore had no jurisdiction in Scott's suit. Second, Scott was a slave because he had never been free. The provision of the Missouri Compromise of 1820 banning slavery in certain areas was unconstitutional because of the absence of language in the Constitution granting Congress authority to prohibit slavery in the territories, and because the law interfered with rights of property the Constitution protected through the Fifth Amendment.[53] Furthermore, Taney reasoned, "if Congress itself cannot do this—if it is beyond the powers conferred on the Federal Government—. . . it could not authorize a Territorial Government to exercise them. It could confer no power on any local Government, established by its authority, to violate the provisions of the Constitution." Last, and almost as an afterthought, whatever the status of slaves in a free state or territory, once they returned to a slave state, their status depended on the law of that state. And Missouri had decided that Scott was a slave.

It would be difficult to exaggerate the significance of the second part of Taney's opinion. True, his position was hardly novel; questions about Congress's authority to ban slavery in the territories had been raised for decades. Moreover, the direct short-term effect of the pronouncement on *national* law was minuscule. Congress had expressly repealed the free soil provision of the Missouri Compromise three years earlier. Yet just because the Congress of 1854 had substituted a policy of popular sovereignty for a policy of free soil did not mean that a future Congress might not choose to do otherwise. *Scott* v. *Sandford*, however, declared that congressionally mandated free soil was constitutionally unacceptable, and it did so within months of a presidential campaign during which a major political party had made free soil in the territories its overriding objective. As construed by the Court, the Constitution now placed that objective out of the Republicans' reach.

In declaring the statutory law of the land to be the constitutional law of the land, however, the Court did more than pull the legal props from under the Republican party. Taney's opinion took sides on a matter that had divided Democrats[54] and thus had been deliberately left in doubt by the Kansas–Nebraska Act. Thanks to the Court, Democrats would soon be divided once more.

A clause in the 1854 act declared that the "true intent and meaning" of the statute was "not to legislate slavery into any Territory or State, nor to exclude it therefrom, but to leave the people thereof perfectly free to form and regulate their domestic institutions in their own way, *subject only to the Constitution of the United States.*"[55] The words prior to the emphasized phrase are unclear. They grew out of an understanding among Democrats in Congress at the time to agree to disagree: Could a *territorial* legislature constitutionally prohibit slavery, or was a prohibition of slavery allowable only at or after the time that *statehood* was achieved? A free state was more likely to result from the first interpretation than from the second. By addressing the authority of a territorial legislature in his opinion, Taney was not only stating his views on a question that had absolutely nothing to do with Dred Scott's case (it was Congress, after all, that had enacted the Missouri Compromise), but he was doing so in a way that made the Court—that "citadel of slavery," Senator John Hale had called it[56]—appear more pro-slavery than even a majority of the 1854 Congress itself.[57] Of the three positions one might take on the subject—congressionally mandated free soil in all territories, slave or free soil at the option of a territorial legislature, and a choice between slave or free soil only at or after statehood—the Court held that only the third was constitutionally acceptable.[58] Taney's position was only one step shy of the most extreme Southern position on slavery in the late 1850s: namely, that Congress not only was powerless to prohibit slavery in the territories but also was under an affirmative constitutional obligation to protect it.[59]

What did the emphasized portion of the clause from 1854 mean? Since the Constitution would apply to any act of Congress, the phrase technically was superfluous. Was it a congressional invitation to the federal judiciary to resolve the ambiguity of the previous clause? Perhaps a divided Congress passed a hot potato to the justices. In 1848 Senator John Clayton of Delaware had introduced a bill that would have allowed an appeal to the Supreme Court from territorial courts, without regard to the monetary value at stake, in all cases involving title of slaves and personal freedom. What seemed dubious[60] to most in Congress in 1848, however, was incorporated into both the Compromise of 1850 and the Kansas–Nebraska Act. Since by 1854 Congress had lifted its own restrictions on slavery in the territories, these two pieces of legislation communicated congressional willingness for a judicial decision on the authority of territorial legislatures.

That inducement, coupled with the Court's inflated assessment of its capacity to resolve the controversy, led the justices to try.[61] Coming as it did at the start of a new administration, they could have hoped that the decision might shelve these contentious matters for a while, since by being made a matter of constitutional law, they were placed beyond the reach of political majorities. Even Abraham Lincoln had professed toleration for a judicial resolution.

> Do you say that such restriction of slavery [in the territories] would be unconstitutional and that some of the States would not submit to its enforcement? I grant you that an unconstitutional act is not a law; but I do not ask, and will not take your construction of the Constitution. The Supreme Court of the United States is the tribunal to decide such questions, and we will submit to its decisions; and if you do also, there will be an end of the matter.[62]

In fact, the institutional stature that drove the Court to conclude that it could succeed where others had not, made *Dred Scott* matter. The case would not have been such a catalyst had the Court itself not mattered politically.

Meanwhile, a second case was under way that had an even greater immediate legal impact. On March 6, 1857, the same day that Taney announced the result in *Dred Scott*, Attorney General Caleb Cushing filed papers to obtain the High Court's review of actions by the Wisconsin Supreme Court in *Ableman* v. *Booth*.[63] Taney's Court had entered water over its head in the first case by constricting congressional power; it was about to step into equally deep water by asserting the supremacy of federal over state law.

Following passage of the Fugitive Slave Act of 1850, Wisconsin and six other Northern states enacted new personal liberty laws that, among other things, provided counsel for supposed fugitives, and guaranteed them access to state habeas corpus proceedings and trial by jury. Benjamin Garland, a slaveowner from Missouri, went to Wisconsin and located Joshua Glover, a runaway slave, in Racine. At Garland's request, the United States commissioner in Milwaukee issued a warrant for Glover's arrest. After a deputy marshal had incarcerated Glover in a local jail, Sherman Booth, an abolitionist newspaper editor, procured a writ of habeas corpus on Glover's behalf from a state judge. Believing that a state writ could not discharge someone from federal custody, the sheriff refused to release Glover. A crowd then broke into the jail and did what the sheriff would not. For having aided and abetted Glover's rescue in violation of the Fugitive Slave Act (Glover was never recaptured), the U.S. district court fined Booth $1,000. The Wisconsin Supreme Court issued a writ of habeas corpus, freed Booth, and declared the 1850 act unconstitutional. U.S. Marshal Ableman then sought review in the U.S. Supreme Court of the Wisconsin court's actions. Not only did the state supreme court refuse even to acknowledge the U.S. Supreme Court's order that it would review the case, but the state ignored review of its decision altogether. No one appeared for Wisconsin at the oral argument in January 1859.

Taney must have felt that his public career had come full circle. A part of the Jackson administration during the South Carolina nullification crisis twenty-seven years earlier, as chief justice he now faced similar defiance from a Northern state. In the several months before and after the decision in March 1859, bills were introduced in Congress to repeal Section 25 of the Judiciary Act that gave the Court jurisdiction over decisions by state courts. Not since 1831 had that threat been raised.[64]

In a unanimous ruling, the Supreme Court upheld Booth's conviction, denied Wisconsin's authority to interpose itself against implementation of federal law, and reasserted its authority over state courts. Unless the national government was supreme in its own sphere, it would be "inadequate to the main objects for which the Government was established," wrote Taney.

[L]ocal interests, local passions or prejudices, incited and fostered by individuals for sinister purposes, would lead to acts of aggression and injustice by one State upon the rights of another, which would ultimately terminate in violence and force, unless there was a common arbiter between them. . . . So long, therefore, as this Constitution shall endure, this tribunal must exist with it, deciding in the peaceful forms of judicial proceedings the angry and irritating controversies

between sovereignties, which in other countries have been determined by the arbitrament of force.[65]

While it may be that the opinion was one that "Marshall himself never
excelled in loftiness of tone,"[66] its champions and detractors at the time
surely read Taney's words in the context of *Dred Scott*. Not only did the
Court sustain the validity of the Fugitive Slave Act of 1850 but it effectively
pulled the teeth from personal liberty laws everywhere. The Court and the
enforcement machinery of the national government once more proved to
be agents of the slave states. Furthermore, because the decision was as
much (or more) a declaration of federal judicial authority as a defense of
congressional authority, Taney sent a clear message that valid state interests
would be just as protected from national interference as the nation's would
be guarded from state intrusion.[67] Finally, Taney's words about the authority of Supreme Court pronouncements were a plain, if unintended, assertion of the binding force of *Dred Scott* throughout the political system.

THE CAMPAIGN OF 1860

In one important respect, the presidential campaign of 1860 failed. Large
numbers of people in a single geographical region of the country refused to
accept the outcome of the election, and secession and war followed. The
results of that war mooted the issue that drove candidates and rent the
nation. Had reaction to the election been less extreme, it remains only a
matter of speculation how, or even whether, Americans might have been
spared the ensuing catastrophe. None of the four men running for president that year seemed to have perceived how deep the abyss was and how
close the union had moved to its edge. In 1860 the electoral process
encountered the single most important issue to face the country in its brief
history. Slavery captured the public agenda and divided the people in a way
unprecedented in American history. The situation called into question a
fundamental question of democracy: the capacity of competing political
parties to manage and to diffuse an issue of great magnitude.

The first round in the campaign had begun in 1858. "The prairies are on
fire,"[68] commented a New York newspaper in describing a heated race in
Illinois for the United States Senate. Republicans in the state wanted
Abraham Lincoln to replace two-term Democrat Stephen Douglas. This
being long before the Seventeenth Amendment brought direct election of

United States senators, the Illinois legislature would make that choice. Accordingly, if voters elected more Democratic delegates to the state house in 1858, Douglas would "defeat" Lincoln; if Republicans obtained a majority, Lincoln would "win," even though neither man's name was on any formal ballot that any voter would cast.

Although the legislature returned Douglas to the Senate for another term, the campaign proved to be more important for a series of seven debates that occurred at Lincoln's invitation across the state in the summer and fall of 1858.[69] It is the only time in American history that two persons have sought the same Senate seat and then run against each other for the presidency two years later. *Dred Scott* and slavery consumed so much of the candidates' attention that one wonders what the two men would have discussed without them. The debates in turn helped build a national reputation for Lincoln; without the visibility (in the South as well as in the North) that they provided, it seems improbable that he would have become the Republican party's second candidate for president.

Dred Scott was both opportunity and challenge for Lincoln. As a target on which to focus the public's attention, the ruling allowed Lincoln, who opposed *Dred Scott,* to distinguish himself from Douglas, who supported it. Douglas started from the premise that local control over slavery was essential if the union was to last. "I care more for the great principle of self-government . . . ," Douglas asserted, "than I do for all the niggers in Christendom."[70] In contrast, Lincoln began from the premise that slavery was "a moral and political wrong,"[71] and predicted that slavery and freedom could not coexist. "[T]his government cannot endure, permanently half *slave* and half *free.* . . . It will become *all* one thing, or *all* the other."[72]

"We believe, as much as Judge Douglas, (perhaps more) in obedience to, and respect for the judicial department . . . ," Lincoln declared in early summer 1857.

> We think its decision on Constitutional questions, when fully settled, should control, not only the particular cases decided, but the general policy of the country. . . . More than this would be revolution. But we think the Dred Scott decision is erroneous. We know the court that made it, has often over-ruled its own decisions, and we shall do what we can to have it to over-rule this.

Implicit in his words was the need for a Court that would see the matter differently. "[W]hen . . . we find it wanting in all these claims to the public confidence, it is not resistance, it is not factious, it is not even disre-spectful, to treat it as not having yet quite established a settled doctrine for the country."[73]

Moreover, Douglas appeared to contradict himself. How could he both call for acceptance of *Dred Scott* and believe in full local sovereignty? Taney had denied the latter at least until statehood. Pressed by Lincoln, Douglas countered with the "Freeport doctrine," a position based on practical, not constitutional, grounds.[74]

> Whatever the Supreme Court may hereafter decide as to the abstract question of whether slavery may go in under the Constitution or not, the people of a Territory have the lawful means to admit it or exclude it as they please, for the reason that slavery cannot exist a day or an hour anywhere unless supported by local police regulations, furnish-ing remedies and means of enforcing the right to hold slaves. Those . . . regulations can only be furnished by the local legislature. If the people of the Territory are opposed to slavery they will elect members of the legislature who will adopt unfriendly legislation to it. . . . Hence, no matter what may be the decision of the Supreme Court on that abstract question, still the right of the people to make it a slave Territory or a free Territory is perfect and complete under the Nebraska bill.[75]

That "amounts to nothing more nor less," Lincoln retorted later, "than the naked absurdity, that you may lawfully drive out that which has a lawful right to remain."[76] Under *Dred Scott*, " 'squatter sovereignty' squatted out of existence."[77]

The Freeport doctrine, however, also demonstrated why *Dred Scott* presented a challenge to Lincoln. In this struggle for public favor, Lin-coln needed to identify Douglas firmly with the pro-slavery camp. That was difficult not only because of Douglas's known position on local sov-ereignty but also because of his Lecompton connection. The senator was widely credited—and soundly castigated by the Buchanan administra-tion and its supporters in Congress—with preventing congressional acceptance in early 1858 of the pro-slavery Lecompton constitution[78]— and hence statehood—for Kansas. Although the Democrats controlled both houses of the 35th Congress and President Buchanan favored admission of Kansas with the Lecompton constitution, the House nar-rowly failed to concur with the Senate's approval. For Southern Democrats in particular, Douglas's Lecompton stance amounted to a betrayal. It may have cost the South two additional pro-slavery votes in the Senate. Douglas and the Lecompton constitution became symbols of the growing rift between Northern and Southern Democrats. Indeed, some prominent Republicans in the Northeast were so delighted with what Douglas had done on Kansas that the New York *Tribune*'s Horace Greeley even suggested to party members in Illinois that Douglas be returned to the Senate unopposed.[79] Lincoln's task in the Illinois senatorial race and the presidential campaign that followed was thus the classic one of defining his opponent, but the image that he fashioned came from *Dred Scott*, not Lecompton.

Accordingly, Lincoln argued that the Kansas–Nebraska Act, as well as the timing and substance of *Dred Scott*, pointed to a conspiracy among "Stephen [Douglas], Franklin [Pierce], Roger [Taney] and James [Buchanan]." They "all understood one another from the beginning, and all worked upon a common *plan* or *draft* drawn up before the first lick was struck." Their objective was to nationalize slavery. Not only had Taney said that territorial governments were powerless to prohibit slavery, his opinion failed "to declare whether or not the same Constitution permits a *state*, or the people of a State, to exclude it. *Possibly*, this as a mere omission; but who can be *quite* sure."[80] The specter was "the next Dred Scott decision . . . that no state under the constitution can exclude slavery."[81]

> We shall *lie down* pleasantly dreaming that the people of *Missouri* are on the verge of making their State *free*; and we shall *awake* to the *reality*, instead, that the *Supreme* Court has made *Illinois* a *slave* State.

> To meet and overthrow the power of that dynasty, is the work now before all those who would prevent that consummation.[82]

"Douglasism," Lincoln explained the following year, "is all which now stands in the way of an early and complete success of Republicanism." It would prove to be the "way that leads straight to final surrender."[83]

The Lincoln-Douglas skirmish continued until November 1860. The Democrats were the first to hold their convention in the spring of that year, but the meeting in Charleston, South Carolina, broke up over *Dred Scott*. A majority report from the resolutions committee (where each state had one vote) stood by the 1857 decision and called on Congress to act to protect slavery in the territories.[84] A minority report backed local sovereignty but promised acceptance of any future Supreme Court decisions on the subject. The convention adopted the latter, upon which most of the delegates from eight Southern states withdrew. With no candidate able to win a majority of the remaining delegates, the convention adjourned and reassembled in Baltimore on June 18. Those delegates who had withdrawn set a convention date for June 11 in Richmond. The Baltimore group nominated Stephen Douglas, and the Richmond faction picked John Breckinridge, Buchanan's vice president, as their nominees for president. The largest political party in the United States (the Republican ticket, though victorious in the 1860 election, received only a minority of the popular vote) thus split over slavery in the territories.[85] Paradoxically, Southerners were only months away from the ultimate rejection of national authority because of the Charleston convention's rejection of their demands for enhanced national authority. Charles Warren may have been right when he surmised that Taney elected Lincoln to the presidency.[86] If so, it was surely due more to the havoc the decision wrought in Democratic ranks than to voters lost to the Republican side.

In the meanwhile, the Republicans and a new party convened. On May 9, former members of the old Whig party from twenty-one Northern and Southern states met in Baltimore as the Constitutional Union party. With Tennessee's John Bell as presidential nominee, their platform recognized "no political principle other than the Constitution of the country, the union of the States and the enforcement of the laws."[87] It had little else to say. Its main objective was to hold out continuation of the union as the common ground.

Republicans opened their convention in Chicago on May 15 and nominated Lincoln on the third ballot. His party's platform condemned the Buchanan administration for its defense of "an unqualified property in persons" through enforcement of the Fugitive Slave Act in the federal courts—"the extreme pretensions of a purely local interest." While the document mentioned neither Taney nor *Dred Scott* by name, Republican campaign literature surely did.[88] Besides, the platform was clear on the issue that had consumed public debate:

> That the normal condition of all the territory of the United States is that of freedom: That, as our Republican fathers ... ordained that "no persons should be deprived of life, liberty or property without due process of law," it becomes our duty, by legislation, whenever such legislation is necessary, to maintain this provision of the Constitution

against all attempts to violate it; and we deny the authority of Congress, of a territorial legislature, of any individuals, to give legal existence to slavery in any territory of the United States.[89]

This plank that proclaimed freedom as the constitutional norm looked to the same words in the Constitution on which Taney had relied to invalidate the free soil principle.

For three years *Dred Scott* had been a boon for Lincoln as he riddled it while speaking throughout the North. The decision also set Stephen Douglas's agenda and colored the candidacies of John Breckinridge and John Bell. In 1858 and 1859—Lincoln made few formal addresses in the campaign year of 1860—the decision and the prospects of a "second case"[90] were devices to engender loathing not only for Southern slaveholding but perhaps for the slaveholding South, too. That perception in turn made all the more urgent the Southern demands at Charleston for affirmative congressional protection of slavery. As depicted by Lincoln, the threat posed by the South was both moral and political. "Holding as they do, that Slavery is morally right, and socially elevating, they cannot cease to demand a full national recognition of it, as a legal right, and a social blessing."[91] Expansion of slavery, whether in the territories or in free states, would have altered the political balance of power against national values of freedom to which, in Lincoln's eyes, the North had fallen heir.

EFFECTS

The resort to arms that followed the election of 1860 temporarily displaced politics as usual. The North's victory in the conflict compelled a resolution of issues that otherwise might have absorbed the partisan and legal systems for years. The 1860s therefore had unprecedented consequences for the Court, public policy, and the Constitution itself.

From the Republicans' perspective, the Supreme Court's reputation had been badly tarnished. *Dred Scott* placed the Court on the losing side in the election, and during the war years lent the institution a somewhat pro-Southern hue. Indeed, the 1860s are widely viewed as the nadir of Supreme Court influence.[92] "Very different . . . that court will now be from the court as I have heretofore known it," lamented Taney, who lacked "hope that it will ever again be restored to the authority and rank which the Constitution intended to confer upon it."[93] But how much damage had really been done to the Court's place in the political system? Assessments range from substantial to superficial.[94]

One would expect the Court's wartime role to have been minimal—even today the justices rarely intrude into defense policies during hostilities—and it was.[95] The Court's few rulings on war policy during the fighting gave the administration the answers it wanted.[96] Nonetheless, in the immediate postwar Reconstruction years the Court, on balance, practiced discreet restraint. To be sure, judicial review was very much alive. From 1861 until 1870, the Court invalidated twenty-four state statutes or local ordinances, a rate substantially above that of previous decades. Moreover, from Taney's death in 1864 until 1870, the Court set aside no fewer than seven acts of Congress, compared with only one each in the Marshall and Taney courts.[97] Without doubt, *Dred Scott* ranks first among the Court's "self-inflicted wounds,"[98] but the victim plainly remained ambulatory.

Still, none of the postwar rulings struck at a major piece of the Republican party's Reconstruction program, arguably the major legislative undertaking of the decade. Even the invalidation in 1870 of legal tender legislation dating from the Lincoln administration was reversed by the Court itself the following year.[99] For the most part, then, the Court was inclined to impede neither the president nor the Congress.[100] When the justices declared in Ex parte *Milligan*[101] that civilians could not be tried by military courts in wartime if the civil courts were functioning, they did so after the war was over. When congressional leaders feared that the Court might use *Milligan* to invalidate rule by military commissions in the South, Congress repealed the Court's jurisdiction at the moment the justices had the case under advisement. The Court then unanimously ruled that it had no authority to decide the case.[102] Thus, if the Court was not banished and disowned by the rest of the political family, it does seem, like an errant child, to have been sent from the table or, perhaps more accurately, to have excused itself.

At the very least, the Court that had been predominantly Democratic in its membership and perceptibly pro-Southern in slavery cases became mainly a Republican, or Lincoln, Court. Inheriting an unfilled vacancy from the last months of the Buchanan administration and with four additional vacancies on his watch, Lincoln was able to appoint five justices by 1864, four Republicans and one Democrat.[103] All five easily met Lincoln's main criterion: each was a firm Union man. Even the Court's size was in flux, as Congress raised the number of justices to ten in 1863, only to cut the allotment to seven in 1866 (the reduction would take place through retirements) and then in 1869 to fix the number at nine, where it has remained ever since. While several reasons account for these adjustments (including an understanding that the justices' salaries would go up if there were fewer of them to pay),[104] the effect was to deny the Union Democrat from Tennessee, Vice President Andrew Johnson, any appointments to the Supreme Court once he succeeded Lincoln in the White House.[105]

Congress undertook reorganization of the circuits in 1862 and 1866, to incorporate westward expansion and especially to reduce the Southern states' dominance in the circuits. By 1866, only one circuit was composed exclusively of states that had seceded; only two of the nine circuits comprised only states that had allowed slavery in 1860. So far as future Supreme Court appointments might be "by circuit," the new arrangement would drastically cut the number of Southern justices. And as this tradition declined, the Supreme Court became off-limits to Southerners. After the death of Jackson appointee Wayne of Georgia in 1867, twenty-one years passed before another Southerner graced the high bench. Congress wanted to make sure that the judiciary remained "safe for the North—and Republicans."[106]

Indeed, the changes that fortuity allowed in the Court's membership— particularly with Taney's death—as well as those that willfulness averted, combined with the overall discretion that the justices displayed in their rulings to obviate the need for more drastic action by Congress against the Court.[107] If one places serious Court-related legislative proposals in the 1860s alongside those in the 1820s, for example, the contrast is sharp. While some potentially threatening Court-curbing proposals surfaced in 1867 and 1868, they were not as numerous as in the earlier period. Except for the withdrawal of appellate jurisdiction to derail an anticipated hostile decision, Republicans were no more successful at agreeing on appropriate measures than Democrats had been when the latter took aim at the Marshall Court. Moreover, with few exceptions, Republicans had no quarrel with judicial power in principle; as the intellectual heirs of the Whigs, many appreciated the need for a strong federal judiciary. It was Taney, his colleagues, and some of their handiwork that they detested. Institutionally the Court was safe from fundamental harm so long as the justices steered shy of foolhardiness by refraining from blocking something central to the Reconstruction agenda. Thus, although the Lincoln justices did not comprise a majority of the bench until 1865, the surviving holdovers from 1860 did not combine to restrain Republican policies. The Court may not always follow "th' illiction returns,"[108] but on this occasion it did.

One should hardly be surprised, therefore, that the constitutional and policy changes most associated with the 1860s were legislatively, not judicially, inspired and driven. Four such changes stand out in particular. Overall, Northern victory accomplished what John Marshall's jurisprudence had not: by defeating secession it established unequivocally the constitutional supremacy of the national government over the states without obliterating state power. "The Constitution, in all its provisions," Chief Justice Chase anticipated in 1869, "looks to an indestructible Union, composed of indestructible States."[109]

More specifically, it was a foregone conclusion that Republicans surely, somehow, would undo *Dred Scott* and all that it stood for. The initial step came with a statute of 1862 that countermanded the Compromise of 1850, the Kansas–Nebraska Act, and *Dred Scott* by outlawing slavery in the territories.[110] Ratified in late 1865, the Thirteenth Amendment then expanded and provided a constitutional foundation for Lincoln's Emancipation Proclamation[111] of 1863 by banishing slavery throughout the United States. Finally, the status of former slaves was addressed by the Fourteenth Amendment of 1868. Its very first sentence interred a particularly odious part of *Dred Scott* and provided constitutional underpinning for the Civil Rights Act of 1866 that had declared the former slaves to be citizens: "All persons born or naturalized in the United States . . . are citizens of the United States and of the state wherein they reside." The rest of Section 1 for the first time extended federal protection to certain undefined individual rights against infringement by the states.[112] As the Fourteenth Amendment nationalized civil rights, it held out the potential of a vastly increased role for the Supreme Court.

Ironically, the Republican party, founded on a single issue, succeeded so thoroughly so soon in achieving—indeed, surpassing—its free soil objective of 1860 that other concerns would soon dominate the national political agenda of the third party system. When it evolved into the fourth in the 1890s, the Court would again be a factor as a jurisprudential legacy of *Dred Scott* reappeared.

CHAPTER 5

The Elections of 1896, 1912, and 1924: Partisanship Redirected

A trio of cases decided in 1895 exemplified a quickening of judicial activism and symbolically cast the Supreme Court with the victorious Republican party in the election of 1896. Seemingly arrayed against Populists and then a refashioned Democratic party, the Court became identified institutionally as an agent of the forces of law and order, respectability, and economic wealth. These decisions, combined with later ones, placed court-curbing on the agenda of the reform movement called Progressivism in the elections of 1912 and 1924. It would be the first serious campaign against judicial review itself—as opposed to efforts to reverse particular decisions—in nearly a century. Progressivism fostered a climate of skepticism about the legitimacy of the judiciary's role in democratic government that would have far-reaching effects. Together, 1896, 1912, and 1924 marked a watershed in campaign response to the Supreme Court. The context for this turmoil was the fourth party system, in which Republicans consolidated the gains which they had achieved in the third and secured an ascendancy in national politics that lasted, barely interrupted, until 1932.

ORIGINS OF THE FOURTH PARTY SYSTEM

As the previous chapter showed, the Republican party emerged from the Civil War with a firm grip on the White House and Congress. Not until 1874 did Democrats recapture control of the House of Representatives for a term, and not until the election of 1878 did they dominate both houses of Congress. The executive branch remained out of their hands entirely, except for Grover Cleveland's bifurcated administration following the elections of 1884 and 1892.

Republican dominance in national politics, however, did not assure

Republican hegemony. Democrats were almost always serious contenders, frequently within reach of victory. In fourteen postwar congressional elections between 1868[1] and 1894, inclusive, Democrats controlled both the House and the Senate as a result of two (1878 and 1892) and held a majority in the House as a result of six (1874, 1876, 1882, 1884, 1886, and 1890), for a combined House/Senate success rate of 35.7 percent. In the seven presidential contests from 1868 to 1892, inclusive, Democrats garnered a majority of the popular vote in three (1876, 1884, and 1892).[2] Moreover, the average percentage difference in the popular vote received by Republican and Democrat candidates in those seven elections was but 3.5. On only one occasion was the difference greater than 5.4 percent: when Ulysses Grant outpolled Horace Greeley by 11.7 percent in 1872. On three occasions—two of them Republican victories (1880 and 1888)—the percentage difference in popular vote between the parties was less than 1.0.

Razor-thin margins symbolized the similarity of Democrats and Republicans on substantive issues during most of the third party system. The end of the Civil War had suddenly made obsolete the issues of the 1850s and early 1860s. Instead of forward-looking platforms that might address new concerns, the two parties appealed more often than not to emotion, personality, and the past. The Republican platform of 1876, for example, charged the Democratic party "with being the same in character and spirit as when it sympathized with treason." In 1884 Protestant clergy in New York City declared their support for Republican nominee James G. Blaine rather than, in the words of Presbyterian pastor Samuel D. Burchard, "identify ourselves with the party whose antecedents have been Rum, Romanism and Rebellion."[3] For their side, Democrats opposed sectional hatred and accused Republicans of fostering "secret sectarianism" in the states. Their platform of 1880 protested the "great fraud" of 1876 that had cost them the White House, and in 1884 labeled the opposition an "organization for enriching those who control its machinery." Both parties promised honest and competent government, and called for curbs on Chinese immigration and, later, for civil service reform. Only on the protective tariff was there a substantive difference: Democrats favored a tariff for revenue purposes only; Republicans looked to the tariff to protect American industry and jobs. Both parties seemed less concerned with principle and more concerned with patronage. Democrats by the 1880s appeared less Jeffersonian and more Hamiltonian (and therefore Republican), increasingly identifying with "wealth, industry and commerce, nationalism, more vigorous defense, and honest money."[4]

It was largely around money—specifically, more plentiful, and therefore cheaper, dollars—that protest movements formed in the 1870s. Inspired by the success of the Grangers in some Midwestern states in securing railroad and grain elevator rate regulation, the National Independent (or Greenback) party toiled for currency reform.[5] When the Greenback party faded after 1880, groups such as the Union Labor and Antimonopoly parties picked up the torch of reform and added new ideas to the agenda for change that ranged from a graduated income tax to government ownership of railroads. But currency remained the focus point. Tight money policies brought on by restrictions on the supply of greenbacks as legal tender, and on the purchase and coinage of silver, caused a price deflation by the late 1880s that was as ruinous to farmers as it was often beneficial to their creditors. Even though both the Democratic and the Republican parties had a "silver wing" (candidates and office holders in the West and South were more likely than those in the Northeast to share soft money and antimonopoly views), neither major party seemed especially receptive to the farmers' plight. So third-party activity flourished,[6] just as had occurred when the Whigs and Democrats tried to sidestep slavery before 1850.

Eventually Democrats and Republicans responded positively at the national level to the discontent. The Democratic platform of 1892 advocated bimetallism and a law banning child labor in factories. Republican congressional leadership had lately been chiefly responsible for legislation that partly addressed some grievances: the Interstate Commerce Act of 1888 provided for a degree of federal regulation of interstate rail transportation, and the nation's first antitrust measure, bearing the name of Senator John Sherman of Ohio, became law in 1890. The same senator achieved passage of a compromise bill more than doubling the government's purchases of silver. Such measures, however, struck the new reformers as going not nearly far enough.

By 1890, a new movement called the Farmers' Alliance and later the People's party, or the Populists, took shape in parts of the Midwest and the South; its ranks were swelled by defecting Democrats and Republicans, and in some urban centers by the Knights of Labor (the leading labor movement of the day that would be wholly supplanted by the American Federation of Labor by 1900). Almost from the beginning, People's party activists divided over a strategic question: Would they remain a distinct party of their own (as preferred by many Midwesterners and Westerners) that might displace the Democrats, or would they fuse with the Democrats (as preferred by many Southerners)?[7] Grover Cleveland of New York helped to provide an answer.

It seemed almost certain that the Democrats would nominate the former president at their 1892 national convention, but Cleveland—branded "a true and consistent friend of the money power"[8]—had no appeal whatsoever to Alliance activists. For the time being, antifusion advocates largely prevailed. To oppose Cleveland and the Republican incumbent, Benjamin Harrison, the first national convention of the People's party nominated General James B. Weaver of Iowa for president. Its platform promised currency expansion through "free" coinage of silver; a graduated income tax; government ownership of railroad, telephone, and telegraph companies; direct election of U.S. senators; and a few pro-labor measures such as restriction of "undesirable immigration." The tariff debate between Democrats and Republicans was called a "sham battle" and was otherwise ignored.

The new party polled more than 1 million (about 8.5 percent) of the votes cast. More significantly, by winning a plurality in five states, the Populists won 22 (of 444) electoral votes, the first time since 1860 that electoral votes had been divided among more than two parties.

The administration's response to the acute depression (or "panic") of 1893 that ensued soon after Cleveland reentered the White House drew a sharp contrast between the Populists and the Cleveland (or "gold") wing of the Democratic party, and between the latter and its "silver" wing. Moving against his own party's 1892 platform, Cleveland prevailed upon Congress to repeal the Silver Purchase Act of 1890 as a means of restoring prosperity. When hard times persisted well into 1894, midterm elections diminished a nearly two-thirds Democratic majority in the House of Representatives to a one-third minority. The party appeared to be on the verge of being pulled apart, as the Whigs had been nearly four decades earlier: there seemed little practical difference on the currency issue between the Cleveland wing and most Republicans, just as there seemed little practical difference between the party's silver wing and the Populists. As Nebraska's William Jennings Bryan—nominally a Democrat, but a Populist at heart—declared on the floor of the House:

> the Democratic party stands between two great forces, each inviting its support. On one side stand the corporate interests of the nation. . . . They demand that the Democratic party become their agent to execute their merciless decrees. On the other side stands that unnum-

bered throng . . . . Work-worn and dust-begrimed, they make their sad appeal.[9]

By 1896 one force had proved clearly to be stronger: silver Democrats captured the party. Delegates to the national convention soundly defeated a motion commending the Cleveland administration, and nominated Bryan for the presidency and Sumner Sewall of Maine for the vice presidency on a platform with a strong Populist orientation. Populists also picked Bryan, with Thomas Watson of Georgia for vice president. The timing seemed ideal: silver Democrats, Populists, and silver Republicans could unite to defeat the Republican ticket of William McKinley and Garret Hobart.

With polarized parties, the election gave voters a clear choice on economic policy. "The economic rationale for the party system that had been displaced in midcentury by the issues of slavery, war, and reconstruction had reemerged at last."[10] Yet the significance of the election went well beyond the choice it presented or even the fact that the Republicans regained the White House and retained both houses of Congress.

First, the Populist party allowed itself to be absorbed by the Democrats, with the result that the Democrats redefined themselves as the economically radical of the two major parties. Second, the election witnessed a fundamental shift of voters in the Northeast and Midwest into the Republican ranks that persisted for more than three decades. Especially in urban areas, Northern Democrats appeared to have a much easier time becoming Republicans than silver Republicans in the Midwest had becoming Democrats. Populists who had once been Republicans were disinclined to wear the Democratic cloak. States that had been battlegrounds between the parties—Connecticut, New York, New Jersey, Indiana, California, Pennsylvania, Illinois, Wisconsin, Michigan, and Iowa—became predominantly and predictably Republican. Thus, the fourth party system came about because the Republicans consolidated, enlarged, and hence strengthened the dominance that they had achieved in the third party system. This phenomenon is called a converting election: a significant shift of voters strengthens, not displaces, a declining major party.

The fourth party system, however, did not end significant third-party agitation. The new party system would not have persisted, as it did, until 1932 had the Progressive[11] movement of the early twentieth century prompted a realignment in the two elections—1912 and 1924—when it fielded its own presidential candidates. This movement included three kinds of reformers: agrarian, political, and social. First were Bryan's followers and their converts from 1896, who pursued an antimonopoly and debtor-relief agenda designed mainly to help farmers. Some Progressives in urban centers were typically "honest government" (independent) Republicans, who fought urban political machines thought to be corrupt and in unholy alliance with local monopolies such as transit companies and utilities. They were joined by a variety of social reformers, who wanted government to ameliorate the living and working conditions of the poor who had crowded into cities as a result of the nation's expanding industrial base.

A realignment was averted partly because Progressives reflected such diversity.[12] No single central organization ever succeeded in combining the many elements into a new national party behind a single electoral strategy. Moreover, there were Progressive-minded people in both major parties who were responsive at different times to Progressive concerns.

Reformer and Spanish-American War hero Theodore Roosevelt, for example, was the Republican vice presidential candidate in 1900 when President McKinley sought a second term against a repeat challenge by Bryan. McKinley's assassination in September 1901 thrust Roosevelt into the presidency, which he retained in 1904 by robustly defeating Democratic nominee and fellow New Yorker Alton B. Parker. Roosevelt was so popular by 1908 that he practically dictated the nomination of his successor, William Howard Taft, who ran successfully against three-time Democratic nominee Bryan. However, Democrats gained control of the House of Representatives in the midterm election of 1910, and it seemed clear that Taft would be unelectable in 1912. When "Old Guard" Republicans renominated him anyway, more liberal Republicans bolted, formed the Progressive (or Bull Moose) party, and nominated Roosevelt. This division opened the door to victory for Democratic nominee Woodrow Wilson, who, as governor of New Jersey, had both professed and practiced Progressivism.[13] Bull Moose Progressives returned to the Republican fold in 1916 after Republicans nominated Justice Charles Evans Hughes, who, as New York governor, had impressed reformers, and after Roosevelt withdrew as the Progressive party nominee in favor of Hughes.

Thus, not only were Progressives unable to emerge as a strong "second party," displacing one of the other two, but neither of the two major parties became home to all Progressives. Moreover, while both Democrats and Republicans retained a reform-minded wing, Progressives could not count on controlling either. Accordingly, neither major party nominated a Progressive in 1920 or 1924. In the latter year, Democrats picked corporate lawyer John W. Davis and Republicans were content with Calvin Coolidge, who had become president upon Harding's death in 1923. Progressives then combined with farmer-labor groups in the Northwestern states as a third party behind Robert La Follette, Republican senator from Wisconsin, who polled a smaller fraction (but a larger number) of votes than Roosevelt had gleaned in 1912.

THE WAITE, FULLER, AND WHITE COURTS

In the forty-seven years from 1874 until 1921 that encompassed most of the third and fourth party systems, Morrison R. Waite, Melville W. Fuller, and Edward D. White served as chief justice of the United States. Composition of the Supreme Court reflected Republican dominance of the executive and legislative branches. After Lincoln, presidents filled seventeen vacancies on the High Court during the third party system, and twelve vacancies from the beginning of McKinley's administration in 1897 to the start of the Harding administration in 1921.[14] With four exceptions—and these were due to special circumstances in each—presidents picked from the ranks of their party, resulting in twenty Republican and nine Democratic justices.

In at least one respect the Court of the late nineteenth century was much like its predecessors under Marshall, Taney, and Chase: as important as they were, typically only a small share of cases each term raised constitutional questions. The proportion, only 6 percent in 1875, would rise to about a fifth in 1921. The Court of the late nineteenth century was still largely a tribunal for the final settlement of common law and similar disputes between individual parties. In terms of the volume of cases, its role as policy maker was decidedly secondary. Not until well after 1925 would the Court emerge in its modern role as mainly a public law institution where, through constitutional and statutory interpretation, it makes public policy for uniform application across the nation.

In two respects, however, the Court of a century ago was a harbinger of the Court in the contemporary era. First, the federal judiciary underwent important structural changes. By 1880 the Supreme Court confronted a case backlog of several years.[15] A cartoon of the day depicted the justices wading about their courtroom in a sea of briefs and other documents, pleading for relief. A docket in arrears was not simply the product of an expanding population. Congress had gradually enlarged the jurisdiction of the federal courts, meaning that a greater variety of questions had access to a federal forum. Potentially this development meant that the Court could hardly escape embroiling itself in virtually every political movement of the day. Swollen dockets finally moved Congress to act. In 1891 Congress authorized intermediate appellate courts called the courts of appeals. For the first time the federal judiciary had permanent appellate tribunals below the Supreme Court.[16] Moreover, the 1891 statute introduced some certiorari, or discretionary, jurisdiction for the Supreme Court,[17] meaning that there were fewer categories of cases that the justices were legally obliged to hear, that the new courts of appeals gradually became the courts of last resort for many cases, and that the percentage of constitutional decisions the Court rendered each term began to rise.

Second, particularly after 1890 a major part of the Supreme Court's constitutional business involved the commerce clause and the Fourteenth Amendment, under which various congressional and state enactments, respectively, were challenged. As noted in the preceding chapter, this amendment of 1868 not only conferred both state and national citizenship on the newly freed slaves but also provided federal protection of civil rights against violation by state governments. Indeed, the long second sentence of Section 1 is addressed specifically to the states: "No state shall make or enforce any law which shall abridge the privileges or immunities of citizens of the United States; nor shall any State deprive any person of life, liberty, or property, without due process of law; nor deny to any person within its jurisdiction the equal protection of the laws." These words invited interpretation through litigation.

Although worries over abuses committed by the many against the few through legislation had partly animated the drive for the Philadelphia Convention of 1787, the Constitution contained only a trio of general limitations on the powers of state legislatures that might apply to regulations of property: the clauses banning "any ... ex post facto Law, or Law impairing the Obligation of Contracts,"[18] and the implied limitations on state laws that were found unduly to interfere with interstate commerce, authority over which was among the enumerated powers of Congress. In 1798, the Supreme Court construed the first limitation to include retrospective criminal laws only.[19] While later deciding that corporate charters were among those contracts the obligations of which states could not impair,[20] the Court made it clear by 1837 that the rights protected by a contract against state impairment included only those that the contract expressly granted, not those that might be implied.[21] In 1852, the Court allowed states a considerable degree of commercial authority, provided the regulation was not one that needed to be national in scope or one that conflicted with an existing act of Congress.[22] Thus, before the Civil War, states had ample leeway under the federal Constitution to enact laws on various subjects under their reserved "police powers."

The question prompted by the Fourteenth Amendment was what new restrictions, if any, beyond those protecting the newly freed slaves might be encrypted within the second sentence of Section 1. The question had particular relevance after the Civil War as lawmakers in many states responded with an unprecedented volume of legislation to cope with social ills and other grievances occasioned by population growth, a national economy, and the industrial age.

The Court's first answers were hardly encouraging to opponents of such regulation. When butchers from New Orleans challenged a state law limiting the slaughtering of animals in the affected area to a single facility, a majority of five held that the right allegedly violated—the right to engage in a lawful business—was not a right encompassed within the amendment.[23] Four years later, *Munn* v. *Illinois*[24] tested the constitutionality of Granger-inspired legislation that imposed various regulations and fixed maximum rates to be charged by grain elevator companies in Chicago and by railroads doing business in the state. Yet the significance of the ruling went well beyond counsel's failure to convince the majority of seven that the regulations and rates were unreasonable, and hence a violation of the "due process of law" that the Fourteenth Amendment guaranteed. According to Chief Justice Waite's opinion for the majority, the state's police power extended to private property "in which the public has an interest."[25] Asking whether the facts of the situation justified the legislature's action in this case, Waite deferred: "For our purposes we must assume that if a state of facts could exist that would justify such legislation, it actually did exist."[26] Moreover, the degree of regulation was a matter for the legislature to determine. "For protection against abuses by legislatures, the people must resort to the polls, not to the courts."[27] The conspicuous reality was that there was now a growing sphere of public policy against which no national constitutional limitations existed.

Railroads, other businesses, and much of the newly formed American Bar Association then began a campaign, lasting thirteen years, to undo *Munn*. Victory came in the Minnesota Rate Case,[28] which challenged a regulatory structure that conferred rate-making authority on a commission and expressly denied judicial review of its decisions. For the majority of six, Justice Samuel Blatchford turned *Munn* on its head.

The question of the reasonableness of a rate of charge for transportation by a railroad company, involving as it does the element of reasonableness both as regards the company and as regards the public, is eminently a question for judicial investigation, requiring due process of law for its determination.[29]

This step was made easier—perhaps possible—by the arrival of new justices in the years after 1877. Of the nine justices who voted in *Munn*, only Stephen Field, Samuel Miller, and Joseph Bradley survived in 1890. New faces included Blatchford, Fuller, David J. Brewer, John Marshall Harlan, Horace Gray, and L. Q. C. Lamar. Of the holdovers, Field and Bradley took positions in 1890 consistent with their opposing stances in 1877; concurring with Blatchford, Miller did not. Thus, of the six who arrived after *Munn*, only two (Gray and Lamar) joined Bradley's dissent.[30]

An analogous development revealed that the Supreme Court was similarly unwilling to allow Congress complete discretion in exercising its considerable powers over the economy under the commerce clause. In 1824 Chief Justice Marshall reasoned that only political checks limited Congress in its exercise of powers under the commerce clause.[31] To these, later justices added the judicial check. Because challenges to Congress under the commerce clause often raised issues of federalism, the terminology was different from that employed in cases under the Fourteenth Amendment, where the focus was liberty. But the effect could be the same. Accordingly, the Court occasionally invalidated or otherwise restricted national legislation because the thing regulated either was not commerce or was not sufficiently related to commerce. As such, the regulation intruded into a domain reserved to the states. For the Court of this period, the distinction between national and state power was fundamental. Unlike state governments, the national government possessed no undefined power to advance the public good. Except as limited by the Constitution, that remained with the states.

These developments had effects beyond the results reached in individual cases. If the Fourteenth Amendment and the commerce clause enshrined their own limitations against which all manner of national, state, and local regulations could be measured, judges would henceforth be the ultimate arbiters of whether those boundaries had been crossed. If opponents of reform laws lost battles in the legislative halls, they could now turn to the courts. The Supreme Court had thus acquired an unprecedented role in shaping public policy.

JUDICIAL ACTIONS

Courtroom Encounters of 1895

Beginning on January 21, 1895, the Supreme Court rendered three decisions within the space for four months that propelled the bench into the presidential election of 1896. In re *Debs*[32] and *Pollock* v. *Farmers' Loan & Trust Co.*,[33] the second and third in the sequence, figured prominently in campaign rhetoric. The first, *United States* v. *E. C. Knight Co.*,[34] reinforced the view that the Court had taken sides in the clash between contending economic forces. All three enhanced judicial power and, when viewed in light of decisions on the Fourteenth Amendment, suggested that the Court had become the national censor of undesirable legislation.

In the context of the growth of large industrial, rail, and financial corporations, the Sherman Antitrust Act of 1890 authorized the U.S. attorney general to proceed against any "combination in the form of trusts or otherwise, or conspiracy, in restraint of trade." Its purpose was not to promote economic efficiency but to protect the market from itself by curbing business practices that limited competition and led to monopolies. The statute recognized the tendency in free-market economies for successful enterprises to acquire an ever greater share of a market by eliminating competitors.

The E. C. Knight case, popularly known as the Sugar Trust Case, began in 1892 after the American Sugar Company, which commanded about 65 percent of the market for refined sugar in the United States, attempted to acquire five additional refineries (four in Pennsylvania, including the E. C. Knight Company, and one in Massachusetts), a step that would give it 98 percent of the market. When President Harrison's attorney general, William Miller, moved to block the acquisition, however, the trial court dismissed the suit. In the Supreme Court, defense of the government's action fell to Cleveland's attorney general, Richard Olney, who, having opposed the law and worked for its repeal,[35] may not have given the case "a very thorough or a very vigorous prosecution."[36]

If that was so, Olney was not disappointed when the decision came down. For a majority that included everyone but Justice Harlan, Chief Justice Fuller explained that the Sherman Act could not constitutionally be applied in this instance. Since the law derived its authority from Congress's power to regulate commerce "among the states," the law could properly be applied only to activities that constituted that commerce. "[T]hat which does not belong to commerce is within the jurisdiction of the police power of the state."[37] Refining of sugar, however, was manufacturing, and manufacturing was distinct from commerce, the former affecting the latter "only incidentally and indirectly. Commerce succeeds to manufacture, and is not a part of it." To hold otherwise threatened the nature of the union. "Slight reflection will show that if the national power extends to all contracts and combinations in manufacture, agriculture, mining, and other productive industries, whose ultimate results may affect external commerce, comparatively little of business operations and affairs would be left for state control."[38] State governments were thus constitutionally empowered to act where the national government could not. Reality, however, meant that most states were reluctant to move against a combination in their jurisdiction, given the possible loss of jobs and revenues were enterprises to shift from one locale to another.

Aside from Fuller's introduction of the "direct-indirect" distinction into the jurisprudence of the commerce clause, a dichotomy that would persist for forty-two years, the ruling had symbolic importance. In the context of the political struggles already under way, it cast the justices as defenders of the most powerful economic forces in the nation.[39] As one legal journal of the day noted, "The decision is the most deplorable one which has been rendered in favor of incorporated power and greed and against popular right since the Dartmouth College Case [of 1819]."[40] While the Supreme Court was willing in later decisions to allow application of the law to other forms of "restraints in trade,"[41] *E. C. Knight* for many years dampened attempts "to invoke the statute in relation to commercial business."[42] As late as 1914, former President Taft noted its effects "upon the popular mind, and indeed upon Congress as well, . . . to discourage hope that the statute could be used to accomplish its manifest purpose and curb the great industrial trusts."[43]

In contrast to the declaration in *E. C. Knight* that the federal government was constitutionally powerless to bar combinations in manufacturing, a decision on May 27, 1895, found ample federal authority to inhibit certain combinations in labor. The ruling grew out of one of the most significant events in American labor history, the Pullman strike of 1894.

By the 1880s American industry was no stranger to strife, even armed confrontations between employers and employees. In 1886 workers in Chicago struck over demands for an eight-hour day. Protests turned into a riot in Haymarket Square that caused the deaths of several strikers and policemen, and led to death sentences for seven rioters. In 1892, strikers at Carnegie Steel's plant in Homestead, Pennsylvania, engaged in a pitched battle with several hundred Pinkerton detectives hired by the company.

State troops were summoned to restore order, and the strike was broken. Amid the Panic of 1893, unemployment averaged 30 percent overall and as high as 50 percent in construction and some manufacturing sectors.[44] James Coxey of Ohio formed an "army" of some 500 of the unemployed; they descended upon Washington in 1894 to demand relief from Congress.

In this climate of hard times and unrest, workers in May 1894 struck the Pullman Palace Car Company in Illinois after this maker and operator of railroad sleeping cars cut wages as much as 40 percent without also reducing stock dividends, executive salaries, or rents in company-owned housing. To bolster the strikers' insistence on arbitration, the American Railway Union, headed by Eugene V. Debs, called a "sympathetic strike" (or secondary boycott), directing its 150,000 members to refrain from handling any train in the United States with Pullman equipment in its consist. The effects were widespread, crippling rail transportation and the postal system in many parts of the country. On July 2, Attorney General Olney obtained an injunction from a federal court, predicated on the Sherman Antitrust Act, ordering union members to cease their interference with the rail system and specifically barring Debs from issuing further directives to continue the interference. The response to the injunction, however, was more resistance. As Debs's counsel Clarence Darrow said, it was about as effective as "read[ing] a writ of injunction to Lee's army."[45] Even with hundreds of deputized assistants on hand, the U.S. marshal telegraphed Washington for troops. Debs's rhetoric added to the tension.

> The first shot fired by the regular soldiers at the mobs here will be the signal for a civil war. . . . Bloodshed will follow, and 90 per cent. of the people . . . will be arrayed against the other 10 per cent. And I would not care to be arrayed against the laboring people in the contest, or find myself out of the ranks of labor when the struggle ended.[46]

When troops arrived to protect the rail yards in Chicago, a riot ensued. Twenty people were killed, trains were derailed, and some 2,000 rail cars were destroyed.[47] To restore order, President Cleveland, over the objection of Illinois reformer and pro-labor Governor John Peter Altgeld, dispatched some 2,000 troops from New York, Kansas, Nebraska, and Michigan, and deputized an additional 5,000 marshals.

In December, Debs was tried and convicted in federal court for violating the injunction, the first successful criminal prosecution under the Sherman Act.[48] On May 27, 1895, the Supreme Court unanimously affirmed, although not on statutory but on constitutional or even supraconstitutional grounds. The justices may have been sensitive to the fact that they had only recently turned back the government's statutory efforts in the Sugar Trust Case, leaving attacks on combinations in manufacturing in the hands of state authorities. Now they were called upon to uphold a federal court's injunction against "forcible obstructions"; that was another way of talking about maintaining order, quintessentially a function of state and local governments. It may also have been that the broader grounds seemed wise because, in the words of Justice Brewer's opinion for the Court, the government found itself in "the throes of rebellion and revolution."[49] Thus, the attorney general could properly ask for the injunction not simply because the American Railway Union was interfering with interstate commerce and movement of the mails. If what had happened in Chicago did not threaten the political union of the United States, it had surely endangered the economic union.

Brewer's opinion carried a heavy burden. Unlike the statute on which the government had relied in the Sugar Trust case, which seemed to fit the facts but which the Court found wanting when applied to manufacturing, there was no obvious federal constitutional or statutory basis for holding Debs accountable for his actions. The Court thus had to go to considerable lengths to legitimize federal authority in the Debs case, ironically just as the Court had denied it in *E. C. Knight*.

The events of 1894 proved Brewer nearly prescient. A year before the Pullman strike, but with the excesses of the Homestead strike fresh in the memories of his listeners, he had addressed the New York State Bar Association on the "coercion" inherent in the "effort of the many" to "compel the one to do their bidding." "[T]he black flag of anarchism, flaunting the destruction of property," and the "red flag of socialism, inviting a redistribution of property," threatened the social order.

> Who does not perceive that the mere fact of numbers is beginning to assert itself? Who does not hear the old demagogic cry, "*Vox populi vox Dei*," constantly invoked to justify disregard of those guaranties which have hitherto been deemed sufficient to give protection to private property?

The answer was to "strengthen the judiciary" and to realize that impending changes "must be guided in justice to safety and peace or they will culminate in revolution."[50]

For nearly thirty years the injunction in the Pullman strike was the model for others, the first effective example of what soon came to be called "government by injunction." Previously considered chiefly a device to protect the private rights of individuals, the injuction quickly became a tool to cope with social and economic problems. It became a symbol of "the propertied classes' fear of social revolution."[51]

The government's victory in *Debs* stood in contrast to its defeat precisely a week earlier in the rehearing that the Court had mandated in the income tax case, *Pollock* v. *Farmers' Loan & Trust Company*. As part of the Wilson-Gorman Tariff Act of 1894, Congress imposed a tax of 2 percent on income, derived from a variety of sources, above $4,000. This was not the nation's first experiment with such a tax. Congress had imposed an income tax during the Civil War (but failed to renew it in 1872), and the Supreme Court had upheld this type of taxation in 1881 as applied to a lawyer's professional earnings.[52] Nor was the tax levied in 1894 a burdensome one. Whereas the tax in 1865 incorporated both progressivity and a rate as high as 10 percent, was paid by 1.3 percent of the population, and constituted 19 percent of federal revenues, the tax of 1894 was flat, was paid by barely 0.1 percent of the population (almost all of whom lived in the Northeast), and contributed less than 4 percent of revenues.[53] The law was thus neither redistributory nor lucrative but largely symbolic. It essentially preserved the status quo against attacks from those on the economic and political right and left. The great bulk of federal expenditures continued to be paid from revenues generated by tariffs. Nonetheless, advocates of redistribution and greatly enlarged federal appropriations could look at the 1894 law as a "foot in the door," and those who, like attorney Joseph H. Choate, saw the tax as a harbinger of "socialism" and "communism"[54]—"class legislation" and an "assault on capital," Justice Field called it[55]—would oppose the tax for precisely the same reason.

In April 1895, with Justice Howell Jackson absent because of terminal illness, the Court invalidated parts of the new tax law. As applied to income from bonds issued by states and municipalities, all eight justices declared the tax to be unconstitutional since it amounted to a tax on state and local governments themselves, and hence violated the principle of state sovereignty. As applied to income from real property, six justices (White and Harlan dissenting) thought that the tax was no different from a tax on land itself. As such, it was a "direct tax" that according to Article I, Section 9, of the Constitution, had to be apportioned among the states on the basis of population. (Apportionment would of course inject irrationality into the scheme, making it bizarre and therefore unpassable. The federal tax one paid would vary not only with the rents received but also with the population of the state in which the rental property was located.[56]) As for the validity of the tax on other income, such as wages and income derived from corporate bonds and stocks (the latter being that part of national income most affected by the tax), the Court was evenly divided. The most probable alignment placed Fuller, Brewer, Field, and Gray against the tax, and White, Harlan, Shiras, and Brown for the tax.

With Jackson making a special trip to Washington from his sickbed for a hearing on this issue on May 6–8, the justices announced a 5 to 4 vote against the validity of the rest of the tax statute on May 20. When Jackson, the supposed tiebreaker, joined only White, Harlan, and Brown, it became immediately apparent that one justice who previously had voted to uphold this part of the law had changed his mind. Court lore assigns that distinction to Justice Shiras.[57]

A tax on personal property was a direct tax, reasoned Chief Justice Fuller for the majority, and so must be subjected to the rule of apportionment, thereby making the tax unworkable.[58] As for wages in various occupations, most justices agreed that Congress could tax them as an excise, although the Court avoided saying that a tax on earned income was either direct or indirect. However, since all other provisions of the tax law had been found constitutionally deficient, this part fell, too, because Congress probably would not "pass the residue independently." If the tax on earned income was left standing, Fuller argued, "what was intended as a tax on capital would remain in substance a tax on occupations and labor."[59] Thus the Court put the proceeds of invested wealth beyond the reach of Congress.

Progressive Setbacks in the Court

As the next section will show, the timing of *Pollock* and *Debs* in particular meant that the campaign of 1896 could not overlook the Court. No similar combination immediately preceded the campaigns of 1912 and 1924. However, a pair of decisions—one in 1905 and the other in 1918—demonstrated that the enhanced role assumed by the Supreme Court in the 1890s persisted. The Court appeared intent on remaining an active policy maker for the nation, but not always in ways acceptable to political majorities.

Among the key components of the Progressive agenda—whether pursued within one of the major parties or in a third party—were limits on hours of work and the elimination of child labor. Both were advanced on grounds of health, safety, and quality of life. For organized labor such legislation would protect jobs as well. In the Court's eyes, both were suspect.

An attack on maximum hours legislation under the federal Constitution became possible after the Supreme Court declared in an insurance case in 1897 that a "liberty of contract" was implicit in the "liberty" that the Fourteenth Amendment shielded from state interference.[60] Thus, in a step that has had profound meaning for public policy ever since, the amendment was construed not only to impose a standard of reasonableness on rates set by the states for private businesses, as the Court had declared in 1890, but to contain substantive rights as well. An hours statute interfered with liberty of contract because it dictated that employees and employers might not agree to certain terms of labor—for instance, twelve hours of work per day.[61] Nonetheless, the justices seemed prepared to uphold hours laws where sufficient justification existed, as happened when seven justices upheld a Utah law that specified an eight-hour day for miners and workers in smelters.[62]

If hours legislation could be justified at all, one would suppose it would be justified in mines and smelters. Could hours laws be applied to other workplaces as well? In one politically important case the Court's answer was no. Five justices declared faulty, on Fourteenth Amendment grounds, a New York law that limited employment in bakeries and confectionery establishments to ten hours per day and sixty hours per week.[63] While the Constitution allowed states to impose reasonable restrictions on liberty of contract, it remained the judiciary's task to decide finally whether such legislation was appropriate. "The law must be upheld, if at all," wrote Justice Rufus Peckham, "as a law pertaining to the health of the individual engaged in the occupation of a baker. Clean and wholesome bread does not depend upon whether the baker works but ten hours per day or only sixty hours a week."[64] But "the trade of a baker" was not so unhealthful as to "authorize the legislature to interfere with the right to labor, and with the right of free contract on the part of the individual, either as employer or employee." To uphold the statute would be to say that the legislature could control the hours of labor in any occupation that was not "absolutely and perfectly healthy." Since "almost all occupations more or less affect the health . . . are we all, on that account, at the mercy of legislative majorities?"[65]

The judicial task had become essentially legislative: independently to evaluate the need for the regulation, presumably the same task in which the legislature had engaged. But in court the burden of proof lay with the state. Liberty of contract was the rule; restraint, the exception.

A year before *Lochner* was decided, reformers organized the National Child Labor Committee to mobilize public opinion against employment of children in factories and mines. By 1907 two-thirds of the states had either enacted their first laws on the subject or had strengthened existing protections.[66] In the same year Senator Albert Beveridge of Indiana was among the first seriously to propose federal legislation under the commerce power that would abolish "child slavery."[67]

A federal statute seemed desirable because state laws varied widely in both content and enforcement.[68] Ample evidence existed of children still at work in Pennsylvania coal breakers, Ohio glass plants, New Jersey sweatshops, and North Carolina textile mills.[69] Businesses in states with tough laws complained that competitors in states with lax regulations placed them at an economic disadvantage. Moreover, an act of Congress on the subject seemed constitutional because of a 1903 Supreme Court decision upholding, 5 to 4, a law of 1895 that banned the interstate shipment of lottery tickets.[70] Within a decade the Court had also upheld the Pure Food and Drug Act of 1906 (designed to stamp out interstate shipments of misbranded or adulterated foods, among other things)[71] and the Mann Act of 1911 (aimed at prostitution by criminalizing the interstate transportation of a woman for immoral purposes).[72] Such decisions suggested judicial approval of a de facto "federal police power"—national regulation by way of the commerce clause of matters traditionally within the purview of the states.

In 1916 Congress passed the Keating-Owen Act, banning the interstate shipment of goods manufactured with child labor within thirty days of their production. Twenty-one months later, in *Hammer* v. *Dagenhart*,[73] the Supreme Court struck down the statute. For the majority of five, Justice Day distinguished this regulation from valid ones by noting that the latter restricted products harmful in themselves, an element not found in goods made by children.[74] The Keating-Owen law also was defective because it "exert[ed] a power as to a purely local matter to which the federal authority does not extend." Were the statute to be upheld, "the power of the states over local matters may be eliminated, and thus our system of government be practically destroyed."[75] Thus a key element of the Progressive platform of 1912 and the Democratic and Republican platforms of 1916 had been declared constitutionally illegitimate.

Furthermore, the Court announced in 1922 that what Congress could not do under its commerce power, it could not do under its taxing power.

After Congress tried to combat child labor again in 1919 by imposing a tax on goods made with child labor (thus greatly diminishing the financial incentive to employ children), eight justices viewed the measure as constitutionally indistinguishable from the 1916 law. The tax was invalid both as an intrusion on state domain and as a penalty in disguise.[76]

CAMPAIGNS

While the money question was the dominant issue of the presidential election of 1896, the Supreme Court nonetheless mattered in that campaign in at least three ways. First, the decisions of 1895, *Pollock* and *Debs* in particular, were rallying points for Populists and anti-Cleveland Democrats, fresh reminders of the need for political action. Second, attacks on the judiciary allowed Republicans and other anti-Bryanites to depict Democrats as extremists intent not merely on passing new laws but also on undermining constitutional government. Third, the resulting polarization of the campaign and the successful Republican exploitation of it made Bryan appear entirely too risky—an enemy of law and order—frightening away votes he might otherwise have received, and thus helping to elect McKinley.

Beginning in the summer of 1895, Populists and some Democrats unleashed their displeasure with the Supreme Court. "Our government has been supplanted by a judicial oligarchy," asserted former governor of Oregon Sylvester Pennoyer, as he called for Congress "to impeach the nullifying judges." The result would be humbling: "the Supreme Court of the United States would never hereafter presume to trench upon the exclusive power of Congress."[77] Governor Altgeld of Illinois declared that the Court "has come to the rescue of the Standard Oil kings, the Wall Street people, as well as the rich mugwumps."[78] The justices would be well advised, he added, to wear two black gowns, so that the people would not so easily see through them. At a Populist rally, Lyman Trumbull, who had been one of Debs's attorneys in the Supreme Court, rendered the justices as "sappers and miners" (as Thomas Jefferson had once done) who "will soon undermine the very pillars of the constitution and bury the liberties of the people beneath their ruin."[79]

In July 1896 the Democratic national convention opened with an address by Virginia Senator John Daniel criticizing the income tax decision, a theme that Bryan then reinforced. The tax "was not unconstitutional when it was passed. . . . It did not become unconstitutional until one judge changed his mind, and we cannot be expected to know when a judge will change his mind."[80] Texas Governor J. S. Hogg branded the Court an instrument of Republican corporate power. "This protected class of Republicans proposes now to destroy labor organizations . . . proposes through Federal courts, in the exercise of their unconstitutional powers by issuance of extraordinary, unconventional writs, to strike down, to suppress, and to overawe those organizations."[81] The Democratic platform proclaimed not only that *Pollock* was in error but also that it departed from previous rulings issued "by the ablest judges who have ever sat on that bench." Furthermore,

> We declare that it is the duty of Congress to use all the constitutional power which remains after that decision, or which may come from its reversal by the Court as it may hereafter be constituted, so that the burdens of taxation may be equally and impartially laid, to the end that wealth may bear its due proportion of the expense of the government.[82]

As for *Debs*, the platform "especially" objected "to government by injunction as a new and highly dangerous form of oppression by which Federal judges, in contempt of the laws of the states and rights of citizens, become at once legislators, judges and executioners."[83] Concern over judicial excesses spread into the silver question, too. In a parallel to anxieties in 1860 over a "second Dred Scott decision," some now claimed that the Court might well declare unconstitutional a silver law expanding the currency.[84] It may have been for this reason that the money plank in the platform recalled the reference to silver coin in the Constitution and the minting of silver dollars under the first coinage law passed by Congress.[85]

For Republicans like McKinley's manager, Mark Hanna, the Democratic platform and campaign rhetoric were a "covert threat to pack the Supreme Court of the United States."[86] Hanna's accusation echoed Democratic Senator David Hill's objection to the income tax plank at his party's convention: "That provision if it means anything, means that it is the duty of Congress to reconstruct the Supreme Court of the country. It means . . . the adding of additional members to the Court, or the turning out of office and reconstructing the whole court."[87] With the abrupt turn to the left, Hill and like-minded cohorts remained "Democrats still—very still."[88] Gold Democrats (the "Gold Bugs") all but verified Hanna's observation when, having bolted the party, they nominated Illinois Senator John M.

Palmer and wrote a platform reaffirming the Court's independence and authority. "We condemn all efforts to degrade that tribunal," it declared, "or impair the confidence and respect which it has deservedly held."[89]

After Bryan formally accepted the nomination in New York City on August 12, former President Harrison addressed Republicans in Carnegie Hall on the danger that Democrats posed.

> In my opinion there is no issue presented by the Chicago convention more important or vital than the question they have raised of prostituting the power and duty of the national courts and national Executive. Tariff and coinage will be of little moment if our constitutional government is overthrown. . . . I cannot exaggerate the gravity and the importance and the danger of this assault upon our constitutional form of government; [upon] the high-minded, independent judiciary that will hold to the line on questions between wealth and labor, between the rich and poor.[90]

Harper's Weekly on September 12 published a cartoon on its cover entitled "A Forecast of the Consequence of a Popocratic Victory to the Supreme Court of the United States." Complete with Benjamin Tillman holding his pitchfork was a bench filled with personalities such as Altgeld and General Coxey and adorned with a large "50 cent Bunco Dollar." In October, Chauncey Depew made the same Court-money connection in a Chicago address.

> There are two places in this country where all men are absolutely equal: One is the ballot-box and the other is the Supreme Court. Bryan proposes to abolish the Supreme Court and make it the creature of the party caucus whenever a new Congress comes in, because it decided the income tax to be unconstitutional.[91]

It mattered little that most such assertions were distortions. Because Bryan and other Democrats coupled their denial of extreme positions with their right to criticize the Court, they furnished substance to the accusations. Criticizing the bench presumably meant doing something about it, as Altgeld implied in a Cooper Union speech in New York on October 17: "The Supreme Court cannot by mere decision upon a constitutional question rob the people of the powers of self-government."[92]

The Republicans beat Bryan and reclaimed the White House in 1896 because the Democrats failed to attract sufficient numbers of urban voters, especially laborers.[93] Even Bryan's famous "Cross of Gold" speech that electrified the Chicago convention spoke of "our farms" and "your cities." The Democratic campaign was consumed too much with the money supply and too little with the job supply, leaving the party divided. But the Democrats also failed because Republican scare tactics worked. Republicans came across as the party of moral respectability (sound money and support for the Court) and prosperity. It was not merely that the demise of the tariff promised by Democrats would cost factory jobs; for urban dwellers generally, Democrats symbolized too much risk. An outsider seeking to become the insider at the White House, the Republican party behaved more like the incumbent, while the incumbent party in the executive branch, having so transformed itself since 1892, ran like the challenger. "To the image of the Democrats as the party of rum, Romanism, rebellion, and economic recession was added another R—radicalism."[94]

With few exceptions, attacks on the Court in 1896 and immediately afterward focused on specific decisions.[95] In contrast, Progressives later became alarmed over judicial power itself, as well as the ends that it served. Judicial review was questionable and even unsound, not only when it sometimes reached the "wrong" result but even when it reached the "right" result. It was at odds with what Theodore Roosevelt labeled "[T]he first essential in the Progressive programme": "the right of the people to rule."[96] Moreover, some scholars had concluded that judicial review was a perversion of the Constitution—something that was not supposed to be part of the American constitutional system.[97]

At the very least the Supreme Court cloaked the reform agenda in constitutional doubt. Understandably, party platforms in 1912 reflected the debate over the judiciary. Winning the presidency with almost 42 percent of the popular vote, Democrats "regret[ted] that the Sherman anti-trust law [had] received a judicial construction depriving it of much of its efficiency."[98] Placing third with 23 percent (the only instance in American history when a continuing major party polled fewer votes than a third party), Republicans affirmed the importance of "an untrammelled and independent judiciary" and stated their "intention to uphold at all times the authority and integrity of the Courts, both State and Federal."[99] In fact, the nomination of Taft in place of Roosevelt at the Republican convention occurred in part because of the belief, widespread among centrist Republicans, that Roosevelt's views on the courts were too radical.[100] Roosevelt had written to *Lochner* dissenter Justice William Day, "If the spirit which lies behind [the decision] obtained in all the actions of the Federal and State Courts, we should not only have a revolution, but it would be absolutely necessary to have a revolution, because the condition of the worker would become intolerable."[101]

Polling almost 1 million votes, Socialists, with Eugene Debs as their candidate, called for the elimination of all federal courts below the Supreme Court, as well as the "abolition of the power usurped by the Supreme Court of the United States to pass upon the constitutionality of the legislation enacted by Congress." National statutes would "be repealed only by act of Congress or by a referendum vote of the whole people."[102]

Receiving over 27 percent of the vote (the highest third-party percentage recorded thus far in the twentieth century), the Progressive party "demand[ed] such restriction on the power of the courts as shall leave to the people the ultimate authority to determine fundamental questions of social welfare and public policy." Two provisions then took aim squarely at the judiciary: one called for a referendum whenever a state court invalidated legislation under the state constitution; the other demanded review by the U.S. Supreme Court whenever a state court declared a state law invalid as a violation of the national Constitution.[103] Both provisions reflected a new reality. The heightened scrutiny that the Supreme Court applied to social legislation had been contagious. State courts presented an even greater barrier to reform.[104] Indeed, Congress in 1914 enacted the substance of the second provision into law by allowing High Court review of state court judgments that *upheld* the federal constitutional claim.[105] It was the first enlargement of the Supreme Court's appellate jurisdiction with respect to state courts since 1789.

The first provision, however, represented a sharper break with tradition and a compromise among Progressives as well. Roosevelt was on record as favoring the recall of judicial decisions—that is, their negation by popular vote—("subject only to action by the Supreme Court of the United States"[106]) as well as the recall of judges—their removal from office prior to the expiration of their term.

> [E]ither the recall will have to be adopted or else it will have to be made much easier than it is now to get rid, not merely of a bad judge, but of a judge who, however virtuous, has grown so out of touch with social needs and facts that he is unfit longer to render good service on the bench.[107]

The intent of both recall devices was to force on state judges a majoritarian interpretation of the federal Constitution. However, recall of decisions arguably ran against the supremacy clause of Article VI, which bound state judges to the national Constitution, "any Thing in the Constitution or Laws of any State to the Contrary notwithstanding." Thus the platform prudently limited recall to state judicial decisions resting on the authority of the *state* constitution alone.

Following Woodrow Wilson's two terms and Republican Warren Harding's truncated one, significant third-party politics, sparked by Progressives, reemerged in 1924.[108] With Senator La Follette as their candidate, farmer and labor groups plus a variety of other reformers fused into a separate, reborn Progressive party. By this time concern over the judiciary had become even more acute. Not only had the Supreme Court twice barred the door against any congressional regulation of child labor, but it had overturned on due process grounds an act of 1918 that mandated a minimum wage for women working in the District of Columbia.[109] For the most constitutionally contentious parts of the Progressive agenda the clear import was (1) that no minimum wage statute nor any general hours legislation applying to all workers could survive an attack under the federal Constitution and (2) that hours statutes were sustainable only when narrowly tailored to the health or welfare of particular categories of laborers.[110] Both generalizations would remain true until 1937.

"I may not know much law," remarked Theodore Roosevelt on one occasion, with more hope than assurance, "but I do know that one can put the fear of God in judges."[111] Now La Follette was intent on creating his own godly fear. The Progressive party platform went well beyond the planks of 1912. Besides calling for the popular election of the federal judiciary, the platform adopted the Socialist position of 1912 that judicial review itself was illegitimate.

> The federal courts are given no authority under the Constitution to veto acts of Congress. Since the federal courts have assumed to exercise such veto power, it is essential that the Constitution shall give the Congress the right to override such judicial veto, otherwise the Court will make itself master over the other coordinate branches of the government. The people themselves must approve or disapprove the present exercise of legislative power by the federal courts.[112]

Thus the politics of the amendment process would determine whether the American people accepted the Court's supervisory role over policy. If they did not, the Supreme Court would be transformed into a cousin of the British House of Lords: the justices might delay but they could not block.

Democrats acknowledged that judges could sometimes make mistakes, as did their presidential nominee, John W. Davis, in criticizing excessive use of injunctions in labor disputes.[113] With Calvin Coolidge as their nominee, Republicans advocated an amendment to authorize Congress to regulate child labor. But only the Progressives pointed to the judiciary as part of the problem. Indeed, a major address by La Follette in New York City on September 18 devoted more to the judiciary than to any other subject. The campaign "witnesses a conflict between two principles of government as old as human history," he declared. On the one hand was the principle embodied in the Declaration of Independence that "the people are sovereign." On the other was the protection of "privileged interests above the political and economic rights of the people." The Supreme Court represented the latter, as he proceeded to show through a recitation of "the cases wherein during the last few years the Court by usurping legislative power has nullified the acts of Congress." The laws were struck down not because they violated the Constitution but because they

> enunciated a rule contrary to the economic or political beliefs of a majority of the men who happen to make up the Supreme Court.... Always these decisions of the Court are on the side of the wealthy and powerful and against the poor and weak, whom it is the policy of the law-making branch of the Government to assist by enlightened and humanitarian legislation.[114]

Statistically, the statement was an exaggeration,[115] but politics (then and now) is as much symbol as fact. La Follette had made his point: the Supreme Court showed few signs of relinquishing its role as a key determinant of social policy.

Republicans seemed in difficulty at the outset of the race because of the lingering effects of an economic downturn in 1922 and because of revelations about Teapot Dome that were coming to light. Democrats, however, soon found some of their own implicated in the scandal, and Harding's death saved Republicans "from the follies of a careless President." Moreover, Democrats divided their party and weakened their public position by a convention that was both confused and seemingly interminable. Not only did the band play "Marching Through Georgia" as accompaniment to a demonstration by the Peach State's delegation, but it took an exhausting 103 ballots before delegates settled on John Davis. Besides, Coolidge proved to be a far more popular figure than many had anticipated. He so overwhelmed Davis at the polls that "the Democratic Party appear[ed] to be on the way out."[116]

Handicapped by a shortage of funds, difficulty in getting on the ballot, and weak or nonexistent organizations in some states, the Progressive party carried only La Follette's home state of Wisconsin, but ran well in most states west of the Mississippi. By one estimate his vote count fell "far short of the total strength of the country's progressive forces."[117] But for the death of La Follette in 1925, the party conceivably could have built on its 1924 revival.

EFFECTS

The election of 1896, reinforced by the election of 1924, ensured a significant period of Republican domination in American history. Every presidential election but two in the fourth party system—from 1896 through 1928—generated a Republican president, usually by a substantial margin. The difference in the votes received by the Democratic and Republican nominees ordinarily surpassed the difference noted in the third party system. If one omits the three-way races of 1912 and 1924 (one of which produced a Republican defeat and the other a Republican victory), the average spread in the remaining seven contests was 12.1 percent. In Congress, Republican domination was the rule as well. In the eighteen congressional elections from 1896 until 1930, inclusive, Democrats won control of both houses in only three, and in the House alone but twice.

Not surprisingly, Republicans shaped the Supreme Court. Of the twenty justices who went on the Court during the fourth party system, only Wilson's three were not Republican choices. Of the sixteen appointed between 1896 and 1924 (the period examined in this chapter), five were serving as late as 1937—the start of President Franklin Roosevelt's second term—well after the fourth party system had dissolved. Of the sixteen, ordinarily no more than three were disposed to accept the more controversial reform measures that were challenged in the Court (although there were occasional surprises, such as Chief Justice Taft's dissent in the minimum wage case of 1923). One of the three was Theodore Roosevelt's first appointee, Oliver Wendell Holmes, Jr., who, while hardly a Progressive himself,[118] articulated a philosophy of judicial restraint in cases like *Lochner* and *Dagenhart*.

Woodrow Wilson's election led to the selection in 1916 of two reform-minded jurists: Louis D. Brandeis and John H. Clarke. (Wilson's first appointee, James McReynolds, served the longest of the three, outlasting Brandeis by two years and Clarke by nineteen years, on the bench. He was ordinarily a dependable vote against the constitutionality of social legislation.) Brandeis in particular, who had worked hard in 1912 to achieve Senator Robert La Follette's nomination in place of Roosevelt on the Progressive ticket, was among the most famous reformers in the nation. Indeed, until the Senate fight over the nomination of Robert Bork to the Supreme Court in 1987, Brandeis held the dubious distinction of being the subject of the century's most rancorous Supreme Court confirmation battle. While antisemitism was a factor, conservatives, former president Taft included, opposed Brandeis chiefly because of his ideas and his zeal: a "business-baiter, stirrer up of strife, litigious lover of hate and unrest, destroyer of confidence, killer of values, commercial coyote, [and] spoiler of pay envelopes,"[119] said one critic.

Overall, most justices who arrived on the bench after 1896 accepted the enlarged role that the Court had begun to craft for itself in the late nineteenth century. The justices ushered in a jurisprudential era of what might be termed "constitutional reasonableness," by which they had the last say on the acceptability of all manner of social and economic legislation. If this was a new role for the Court, much of the legislation that drove the litigation was also new, in degree and often in kind.

Having lost at the polls or in the legislative chambers, litigants typically framed their objections under one or more constitutional rubrics: due process of law, commerce, taxation, reserved powers, and so on. Although draped in the same constitutional garb, judicial decisions and the ratiocinations in the opinions became increasingly viewed at the time as turning primarily on the justices' views of the appropriateness, desirability, or need for the regulatory policy under attack.[120]

Invigorated judicial review after 1890 had several important jurisprudential and institutional consequences. First, doubts over the legitimacy of judicial review that permeated Progressive thinking did not lead to the demise of judicial power. Populists, Progressives, and labor leaders might all be critics of federal judicial power, but the would-be reformers were unable to concert their efforts to yield effective remedies.[121] Second, the political tumult nonetheless generated a debate over the purposes of judicial review in a democracy that has continued almost unabated.[122] Ironically, as the next chapter will demonstrate, Progressives lost the battle but won the war. Judicial review survived, but on many fronts the judiciary ceased to be a barrier to the people's will. At least regarding the implementation of social values dearest to their hearts, the judiciary's sharpest critics would prevail outright within a generation, without a constitutional amendment.

The Court of the fourth party system was also a factor in the emergence of sociological jurisprudence that emphasized the consequences of judicial decisions. Challenging legal formalism (sometimes called the "declaratory" theory or, disparagingly, "mechanical jurisprudence")—the dominant school of the day that depicted law as rules objectively discovered and applied by courts—was a view of law as norms shaped by social forces. Legal rules were therefore expedient, not timeless. Judges were to be aware that in interpreting the law, their decisions shaped social policy. Accordingly, judges were to take social conditions into account when declaring what the law was.[123]

Fourth, near the end of the fourth party system, scholars called legal realists concentrated on judicial causation, maintaining that constitutional or statutory interpretation was mainly a cover to mask the judges' own predilections and the exercise of raw power. Accordingly, the declaratory theory by which judges "discovered" the law was little more than myth. For the realist, law and the legal process were politics by other means.[124] The cumulative impacts of all three perspectives have been far-reaching, profoundly affecting the thinking about the Court, constitutional interpretation, and the judicial process.

While the factors and forces that guide judicial decisions remain the subject of debate, the Court's expanded place in the political system during the fourth party system is a fact. This phenomenon is significant for at least five reasons.

First, while the Court upheld the large majority of statutes it confronted, in absolute terms the number of statutes struck down was unprecedented.[125] In the years 1898–1902, for example, sixty-nine cases tested the limits of the state police power under the Fourteenth Amendment, and the Court found a constitutional violation in fourteen. During 1903–1906, of ninety-six such statutes reviewed, the constitutional challenge was successful in thirty-three.[126] The data suggest not only that the volume of regulatory measures enacted in the states was on the rise[127] but also that more were being challenged in court. Second, uncertainty therefore surrounded the constitutionality of any single enactment, particularly a novel one, until the Court had spoken finally.

Third, the Court made clear it that it was a partner in governing the nation. No party bent on reform could truly have its way until it had the Court on its side. This new reality became plain once the fifth party system replaced the fourth, as the nation struggled with the calamity of the Great Depression.

Fourth, power did not engender humility. That the Court weathered this swell of protest from Populists, Progressives, and labor leaders without having to inter a single one of its most troublesome decisions may have encouraged an aura of institutional invincibility. The judiciary, it appeared, could effectively stem the tide against the excesses of majoritarianism as "the only breakwater against the haste and passions of the people—against the tumultuous ocean of democracy."[128]

Finally, this air may have contributed to the even more severe political turbulence that the justices were to encounter in the 1930s, as the next chapter will show. The Court charted a new constitutional course as a consequence and was able to maintain an activist posture partly because of, not just in spite of, the decisional legacy of the preceding half-century.

CHAPTER 6

The Election of 1936: A Constitutional Divide

I n the midst of the Great Depression, a dozen decisions by the Supreme Court invalidated all or parts of eleven statutes enacted by a Democratic Congress to promote economic recovery. For the first time since the Jacksonian era, the Court squarely opposed the defining policies of the administration in power. For the first time since 1860, the Court found itself on the losing side in a presidential election. In this situation, would the Court be the restraining hand of the old regime, or would it quickly align itself with the new? The consequences were unprecedented: (1) the boldest attempt by a president to alter constitutional law by a direct assault on the Supreme Court; (2) the most abrupt fundamental change in constitutional interpretation; and (3) the first steps toward a new role for the Supreme Court in the American political system. The context for this jurisprudential imbroglio was the sudden collapse of the fourth party system and the rapid emergence of the fifth. Roosevelt was not only the third Democrat to move into the White House since James Buchanan departed in 1861; his electoral triumphs inaugurated an era of Democratic dominance in national affairs that persisted, with few lapses, until 1969.

ONSET OF THE FIFTH PARTY SYSTEM

"Onset" aptly describes the arrival of the fifth party system.[1] Except perhaps for the Democratic collapse wrought by Lincoln's election in 1860 and then the Civil War, never has one party's domination been so rapidly eclipsed as when Democrats displaced Republicans in the 1930s. The fourth party system had unfolded in the 1890s because voters rejected a Democratic party that had been partly remade by the Populists. The fifth party system arose abruptly because voters embraced a Democratic party that circumstances and leaders had transformed yet again.

Without the economic dislocations that engulfed the nation following the stock market crash in October 1929, it is impossible to know how much longer the fourth party system might have lasted. There was little in the presidential election of 1928 that pointed to impending realignment. The appeal of Republican nominee Herbert Hoover was his identification with prosperity, for which Republicans gladly accepted responsibility. Americans were "in sight of the day when poverty will be banished from this nation," Hoover announced in his acceptance speech, if only his party could be "given a chance to go forward with the policies of the last eight years."[2]

Democrats remained a party safely in the collective hands of plantocrats in the South and Irish Catholics in urban areas of the North, a pairing unlikely to induce a presidential victory. The nomination of Governor Alfred E. Smith of New York, the nation's first Irish Catholic slum-bred presidential candidate and a "wet" as well, demonstrated the Democrats' dilemma. While Smith polled 6.6 million more votes than John W. Davis had in 1924, Republican nominee Herbert Hoover in 1928 topped President Calvin Coolidge's draw in 1924 by 5.7 million votes. However, Smith's total amounted to only 41 percent of the popular vote, and the Democrats lost six Southern or border states that they had carried in 1924. Encouraging signs were few. Democrats managed to win Massachusetts and Rhode Island, Smith drew well in many cities outside the South, but his 41 percent was still the fourth weakest showing nationally of any Democrat in the first quarter of the twentieth century.

Economic conditions that assured a Republican victory in 1928 had vastly changed by 1932, with Depression hardships reaching their peak in midyear. Republicans would now pay a high price for the nation's afflictions. Thanks to Democratic gains and the post-election departure of a few Republican members, the midterm elections of 1930 had already handed Democrats narrow control of the House of Representatives, and had left them one vote shy of formal control of the Senate.

Still, it was hardly clear from the presidential campaign itself that a Democratic sweep would mark a sharp break with the policies of the past and would effect a realignment. The party seemed an unlikely vehicle to carry out the full potential of its 1932 platform promise of "a drastic change in economic governmental policies."[3] The Republican party's "weaker twin ... differs from the G.O.P.," *The Nation* had opined, "only in that its desire to become the party of privilege has never been satisfied."[4]

During Hoover's term, Democrats tended to be to the left of Republicans mainly on the question of relief: whether the national government itself, as well as state and local governments, should directly come to the aid of citizens or whether it should do so indirectly by encouraging voluntary activities and, as a last resort, engaging in economic "pump-priming." "Economic depression cannot be cured by legislative action or executive pronouncement," Hoover had explained to Congress in December 1930. "Economic wounds must be healed by the action of the cells of the economic body—the producers and consumers themselves,"[5] a view echoed by the Republican platform in 1932: "The people themselves, by their own courage, their own patient and resolute effort in the readjustment of their own affairs, can and will work out the cure."[6] This position had long been an article of faith among most leaders of both parties. After all, "panics," or depressions, had always righted themselves, usually sooner than later.

Although known as a progressive, Democratic nominee Franklin Roosevelt was no crusader. "He is no tribune of the people," wrote Walter Lippmann, the most influential publicist of the day. "He is no enemy of entrenched privilege. He is a pleasant man who, without any important qualifications for the office, would very much like to be President."[7] As late as 1931 Roosevelt, like Hoover, subscribed to the belief that relief should remain a private and local matter, and he criticized Hoover's proposal for increased public works spending as risking dangerous deficits and abandoning of laissez-faire in favor of "a wholly new economic theory that high wages and high pressure selling could guarantee prosperity at all times regardless of supply and demand."[8] Both FDR and the Democratic platform called for a "federal budget annually balanced."[9] Moreover, the Democratic campaign was longer on promise than on detail. FDR's speeches "so often veered either right or left and contained so many generalities that to contemporaries it would have been hard to have predicted from them what the New Deal might be."[10]

With unemployment at about 24 percent and with about one fourth of the farmers having lost their holdings, a Roosevelt victory in November was hardly a surprise, even though Republicans had entered the campaign year with a 2–1 lead in voter registration.[11] More surprising was the scope of the Democratic victory. Roosevelt and running mate John Nance Garner of Texas collected more than 57 percent of the popular vote and 88 percent of the electoral vote.[12] Incumbents Hoover and Vice President Charles Curtis carried only six states, and of these only Pennsylvania and Delaware lay outside New England. In Congress, the Democrats acquired

193- and 25-seat majorities in the House and Senate, respectively. The New Deal era was about to begin.[13]

Historians typically divide the New Deal into two stages. The first, during 1933 and 1934, was concerned more with relief and recovery and less with reform. For example, the National Industrial Recovery Act (NIRA) authorized the executive branch to establish "codes of fair competition" for businesses engaged in interstate commerce. The Agricultural Adjustment Act (AAA) imposed production controls, and hence supported prices, through marketing agreements and processing taxes. Other legislation took the country off the gold standard, shored up the banking system, funded public works, and regulated the securities industry.

With these in place by the midterm elections of 1934, the New Deal seemed so widely accepted that the campaign centered not nearly so much on what had been done as on what remained to be done. The division in the country was "not between the New Deal and the Old, but between the New Deal and one newer still."[14] The results at the ballot box were unprecedented: Democrats had a majority of 216 in the House and 44 in the Senate.

In his message to Congress in January 1935, FDR claimed "a clear mandate from the people, that Americans must forswear that conception of the acquisition of wealth which, through excessive profits, creates undue private power over private affairs and . . . public affairs as well."[15] Thus, the second stage of the New Deal developed policies that created permanent systems of income support, expanded government regulation, and strengthened both government and organized labor as countervailing centers of power to business. The National Labor Relations (Wagner) Act guaranteed collective bargaining in most large industries and established an agency to enforce the rights bestowed on organized labor. The Social Security Act instituted a system of income maintenance for the disabled, the unemployed, and the elderly. Other enactments included the first nationally sponsored public housing and the Fair Labor Standards Act with provisions for minimum wages and maximum hours.[16] A revolution (American-style)[17] was under way both because of what government was doing and because it was the federal government doing it. Would voters return FDR for a second term?[18]

Republican campaign rhetoric in 1936 portrayed Roosevelt and the Democratic Congress as dangerous radicals who had forsaken constitutional government. Former President Hoover was more strident than even Republican nominee Governor Alfred Landon of Kansas. The New Deal wore the "color of despotism . . . the color of Fascism . . . the color of Socialism"; was "dipped from the caldrons of European Fascism or Socialism"; drew on "the philosophy of collectivism and . . . greed for power"; and embodied "a revolutionary design to replace the American system with despotism" and "the poisoning of Americanism."[19] Materials distributed by the Republican National Committee made references to Soviet Premier Joseph Stalin and American Communist party leader Earl Browder in an attempt to "equate social security with European totalitarian ideas."[20]

Democrats were at least an equal match in the war of words. "We have begun and shall continue the successful drive to rid our land of kidnappers and bandits," the 1936 platform declared. "We shall continue to use the powers of government to end the activities of the malefactors of great wealth who defraud and exploit the people."[21] The pairing of "kidnappers and bandits" with "malefactors of great wealth" was surely not unintentional. President Roosevelt repeated the theme in his acceptance speech at the national convention in Philadelphia:

> These economic royalists complain that we seek to overthrow the institutions of America. What they really complain of is that we seek to take away their power. Our allegiance to American institutions requires the overthrow of this kind of power.[22]

At Madison Square Garden on October 31, the same thought drove FDR's final address of the campaign. In an "almost vengeful" tone,[23] he asserted that the forces of

> organized money . . . are unanimous in their hatred for me—and I welcome their hatred. I should like to have it said of my first Administration that in it the forces of selfishness and of lust for power met their match. I should like to have it said of my second Administration that in it these forces met their master.[24]

At the polls, the politics of fright succumbed to the politics of class.[25] Electoral numbers could hardly have produced a more resounding ratification of FDR's first term. Roosevelt's 60.8 percent of the popular vote exceeded any share in the history of American presidential politics. He carried every state but Maine and Vermont, and his 523 electoral votes surpassed the share of any candidate since the advent of the party system in the late eighteenth century. In the House of Representatives, Democrats added twenty-one seats to an already swollen majority; in the Senate the gains were even more impressive with sixteen new seats. In Congress, Republicans were an endangered species. They had been reduced to so small a number that their survival as a national party was in doubt. Prominent Republicans talked of changing the party's name, as a way of forging a coalition with conservative Democrats.[26]

Beyond electoral victory was evidence of a new Democratic party that would outlive FDR by two decades. "Issue-oriented, working-class-based, even more urban-centered than before, activist, liberal, and wholly devoted to Rooseveltian leadership," it bore little resemblance to the Democratic party of 1924 or even 1928.[27] Its ethnic diversity was broader as well, including a higher percentage of Jews, Italians, blacks, and those of various eastern European origins. The greatest transformation in American politics since 1860 was a fact. Roosevelt accomplished in 1936 what Bryan could not in 1896.

THE TAFT AND HUGHES COURTS

The Supreme Court that Roosevelt found upon taking office on March 4, 1933, had been shaped by five presidents. Named in 1910 by William Howard Taft, who himself served as chief justice from 1921 until 1930, Willis Van Devanter was the most senior. Two justices—James McReynolds and Louis Brandeis—had gone on the Court in Woodrow Wilson's first term. George Sutherland and Pierce Butler were legacies of Warren Harding's abbreviated presidency, and Harlan Stone was Calvin Coolidge's sole appointee to the High Court. Charles Evans Hughes (who succeeded Taft as chief), Owen Roberts, and Benjamin Cardozo (a Democrat) were Hoover's choices.

Statistically, Roosevelt could expect to shape the Court's composition to some degree in a first (or complete single) term, as had each of his predecessors since James Monroe.[28] Between 1869—when Congress set the bench size at nine—and 1933, fourteen presidents had filled thirty-seven Supreme Court vacancies.[29] On average, therefore, a vacancy occurred once every 1.7 years (about twenty months). At this rate, FDR would name at least two, and perhaps three, justices during his first term. But this was not to be.

Had the new president been prescient, the prospect of this privation would have been disturbing for two reasons. First, FDR was not merely a

new president: he was a new president who proposed strikingly novel policies. Second, there was no assurance that the Supreme Court of 1933 was
prepared to accommodate his initiatives. True, six of the nine justices had
been appointed within the past decade, but their sponsors were Republican
presidents. Roosevelt had recognized as much in the campaign of 1932
when, on the eve of the election, he reminded his audience that "[a]fter
March 4, 1929, the Republican party was in complete control of all
branches of the government, executive, Senate and House, and, I may add
for good measure, in order to make it complete, the Supreme Court as
well."[30] That Republicans expected the Court to remain independent of
the presidency were the Democrats to prevail at the polls was reflected in
President Hoover's reply three days later:

> He implies that it is the function of the party in power to control the
> Supreme Court. . . . Does it disclose the Democratic candidate's con-
> ceptions of the function of the Supreme Court? Does he expect the
> Supreme Court to be subservient to him and his party? Does that
> statement express his intention, by his appointments or otherwise, to
> attempt to reduce that tribunal to an instrument of party policy and
> political action?[31]

The bench did not appear altogether hospitable to reform. Three
jurists—Brandeis, Stone, and Cardozo—either approved of the need for
reform or saw few constitutional reasons why the popular call for new policies could not be heeded. Four—Van Devanter, McReynolds, Sutherland,
and Butler—were the judicial embodiment of the fourth party system and
were constitutionally hostile to such measures. It remained to be seen how
Roberts and the new chief justice would respond.

The tentative alignment of the Court across the jurisprudential spec-
trum was noteworthy, since constitutional doctrine in 1933 was mixed in its
reaction to social and economic reform. As the previous chapter explained,
certain decisions had recognized ample regulatory authority in Congress
and the states. Other reform measures had hit a constitutional brick wall.
Campaigns to enact wage and hours legislation and congressional bans on
child labor, for example, had been around for decades, but of these, only
hours legislation had sometimes succeeded in winning Supreme Court
favor. What would be the High Court's reaction to measures more novel
still? In 1933, a fog of doubt thus enshrouded the courtroom fate of state
and national legislation predicated on the need to combat the depression.[32]

The trend was ominous. "If the system of judicial law that is being written in defiance of state legislation and of congressional legislation is continued," Senator Clarence Dill had warned, "there is no human power in America that can keep the Supreme Court from becoming a political issue, nation-wide, in the not far-distant future."[33]

JUDICIAL ACTIONS

Despite Republican charges that Roosevelt had taken "the first steps" in 1933 and 1934 to "emasculate" the Constitution,[34] it was not until early 1935 that the Court passed upon the first New Deal statutes. In the meantime, the president's supporters could take heart in the fact that the Court had upheld some state programs aimed at coping with economic distress.

In March 1934, for example, five justices[35] upheld New York's Milk Control Law, which prohibited the sale of milk below a specified minimum price. The statute's purpose was to inflate the retail price of milk as a way of aiding the state's dairy farmers. Justice Roberts declared for the majority that a state "may regulate a business in any of its aspects, including the prices to be charged for the products or commodities it sells," adding that a state "is free to adopt whatever economic policy may reasonably be deemed to promote public welfare. . . . With the wisdom of the policy adopted, with the adequacy or practicability of the law enacted to forward it, the courts are both incompetent and unauthorized to deal."[36] The message of Roberts's words seemed clear enough: states had ample discretion under the Constitution in regulating their economies.

Three months later, the same five justices found even greater pliancy in the Constitution when they sustained Minnesota's Mortgage Moratorium Law that rescued beleaguered debtors by extending a mortgage's redemption period. Yet the contract clause of the Constitution seemed to prohibit precisely what Minnesota had done: "No State shall . . . pass any . . . Law impairing the Obligation of Contracts."[37] In the most significant interpretation of those words in almost a century,[38] Chief Justice Hughes held that the prohibition was not intended to deny states the authority to safeguard the vital interests of the community. He recognized a "growing appreciation . . . of the necessity of finding ground between individual rights and public welfare." The sanctity of an agreement between private parties would have to make way for "reasonable means to safeguard the economic structure upon which the good of all depends."[39]

Those favoring interventionist policies could hardly have asked for more unqualified judicial endorsement. "As it stands," observed the *New Republic* after the milk case, "the decision has created the . . . impression that the Supreme Court sees no unconstitutionality in the Roosevelt program."[40] Yet any elation should surely have been tempered in at least three respects. First, the vehemence of the dissents may have exaggerated the extent of economic regulation that a majority was prepared to accept. Second, both the milk and the mortgage decisions made clear that there were four firm votes (Van Devanter, McReynolds, Sutherland, and Butler) against ameliorative legislation. Third, the Court had approved *state*, not national, legislation. The distinction was important because of the different nature of state and national legislative powers in federal constitutional law. Under the doctrine of reserved powers, states legislate at will *unless prohibited* by the U.S. Constitution. In contrast, under the doctrine of enumerated powers, Congress legislates *only* on the basis of *express* or *implied* grants of power to it by the Constitution.

Yet even when the Court spoke contrarily on the first congressional New Deal enactment it encountered, the constitutional defect seemed reparable. Coming three days after FDR's forward-looking message to Congress in January 1935, *Panama City Refining Co.* v. *Ryan*[41] invalidated the "hot oil" provisions of the National Industrial Recovery Act, a minor part of the centerpiece of the first phase of the New Deal, which proscribed the interstate shipment of petroleum in excess of specified amounts. For eight justices, Chief Justice Hughes pointed to a standardless, and hence unconstitutional, delegation of rulemaking power from Congress to the president. However, Hughes said nothing about the main objection that the oil companies put forward: that production of oil was "local" in character and therefore not part of the commerce among the states that the Constitution empowered Congress to regulate.

Not quite six weeks later, a trio of decisions in what are commonly called the Gold Clause Cases suggested more fundamental judicial objections to the New Deal. As part of a sweeping monetary reform in 1933, Congress imposed controls on ownership of, and trade in, gold; abrogated the clauses in all public and private contracts, including currency of $20 and higher (gold certificates) and the U.S. government's own obligations, requiring payment in gold; and authorized a presidential devaluation of the dollar to 60 cents of its former value, relative to gold. Among other things, the intent was to boost foreign trade, to raise commodity prices at home, and to permit debts to be paid with cheaper money.

The same five justices who had upheld the milk and mortgage statutes strained to find sufficient constitutional authority to regulate the currency and to abrogate the gold clauses in private contracts, but refused to condone the government's alteration of its own obligations. The government was enriching itself at the expense of its creditors. That was a breach of a moral duty, said Hughes, but the plaintiffs were not entitled to recover because Congress was not obliged to furnish judicial relief to the government's creditors. The outcome was too much for the minority. The "Constitution as many of us have known it, the Instrument that has meant so much to us, has gone," declared McReynolds in a passionate oral dissent. This is "Nero in his worst form. . . . Horrible dishonesty! . . . Shame and humiliation are upon us now."[42]

The administration deemed the legislation so crucial that, anticipating defeat at the Court, Roosevelt had drafted a speech for broadcast explaining why he would disregard the decision. "[T]he Nation will never know," he wrote to Joseph P. Kennedy, "what a great treat it missed in not hearing the marvelous radio address the 'Pres' had prepared for delivery to the Nation Monday night if the cases had gone the other way."[43]

The gold litigation proved to be a pyrrhic victory for Roosevelt. Since the five justices in the majority "were forced by circumstances and expediency into a clearly reluctant backing of the New Deal in the gold cases," the *New Republic* predicted, "the natural tendency of at least one or two of them will be to react in the other direction at the earliest opportunity."[44] That opportunity materialized on May 6 when Roberts joined the four dissenters from the milk and mortgage cases to strike down the Railroad Retirement Act of 1934,[45] which mandated pensions for the employees of the nation's railroads. Even Hughes, Brandeis, Stone, and Cardozo agreed with the majority that Congress had acted arbitrarily in that part of the law that extended pensions to persons no longer employed by the companies. While the administration's defeat worked an immediate hardship only on railway employees, the logic of Roberts's opinion cast doubt on the fate of the Social Security bill, then pending in Congress.

Three weeks later, a unanimous bench dealt the administration another setback in *Schechter Poultry Corp.* v. *United States*[46] which invalidated the rest of the National Industrial Recovery Act that remained intact after the "hot oil" decision in January. The "codes of fair competition" authorized by the act derived, as in the earlier case, from an unconstitutional delegation of power to the president, said Hughes. It was "delegation run riot," Cardozo admonished in a concurring opinion. More significantly, the codes, which the Schechter brothers had violated by selling an "unfit chicken" in Brooklyn, were unconstitutional as well because they regulated local activities absent a direct effect on interstate commerce. To "find directness here is to find it almost everywhere," Cardozo added.[47]

The so-called Sick Chicken Case was a major defeat for the administration not solely because of the embarrassment of having a cornerstone of national policy undone.[48] Indeed, by 1935 even some of the president's advisers had second thoughts about the law's wisdom and effectiveness. With the death of NIRA, they could embrace even more warmly the regulatory and empowerment policies of the New Deal's second phase, then just beginning.[49] However, the truly disturbing aspect of *Schechter* was the Court's pronouncement on Congress's commerce power. "If this decision stands and is not met in some way," mused Attorney General Homer S. Cummings, "it is going to be impossible for the Government to devise any system which will effectively deal with the disorganized industries of the country, or root out, by any affirmative action, manifest evils, sweatshop conditions, child labor, or any other unsocial or anti-social aspects of the economic system."[50]

Professor Felix Frankfurter counseled FDR to welcome the prospect of additional defeats.

> Decisions in other cases may accumulate popular grievances against the Court .... That is why I think it so fortunate that the Administration has pending before Congress measures like the Social Security bill, the Holding Company bill, the Wagner bill, the Guffey bill. ... Put *them* up to the Supreme Court. Let the Court strike down any or all of them next winter or spring.... *Then* propose a Constitutional amendment giving the national Government adequate power to cope with national economic and industrial problems. That will give you an overwhelming issue of a positive character arising at the psychological time for the '36 campaign, instead of [the] mere negative issue of being "agin" the Court which, rising now, may not be able to sustain its freshness and dramatic appeal until election time.[51]

Frankfurter portended the Court's response more accurately than he did the president's, but neither man had long to wait before the next judicial salvo. The 1935–1936 term was the Court's first in the "magnificent" surroundings of its new building,[52] but the spacious quarters proved no more receptive than the old to FDR's agenda.

On January 6, 1936, six justices invalidated the Agricultural Adjustment Act of 1933.[53] In contrast to NIRA, the administration was privately, as well as publicly, committed to the act for the twin reasons that the AAA was both popular with farmers and their suppliers[54] and effective, having already "brought about a considerable transfer of income from the non-agricultural sector into farming."[55] In short, the act was FDR's lever to revive the nation's farms.[56] The immediate impact of its undoing was clear: some $2 billion in benefit checks to farmers would not be mailed.

Incorporating notions of parity prices and production controls that had been discussed for at least a decade, the statute nonetheless ventured down "a new and untrod path for American agriculture and for the American government"[57] in terms of the extent of governmental intervention it contemplated. To raise the market price of corn, cotton, wheat, tobacco, and rice, farmers entered into voluntary agreements with the Agricultural Adjustment Administration to reduce cultivated acreage, in return for which they received payment from the government. These payments were financed by a tax levied on the first domestic processing of the commodity. Litigation challenging the constitutionality of the scheme arose when the receivers of the Hoosac Mills Corporation refused to pay the processing tax on cotton.

Justice Roberts's majority opinion explained that the processing tax could be upheld only as an exercise of Congress's power to "lay and collect Taxes, . . . , to . . . provide for the . . . general welfare of the United States."[58] Was the power to tax and spend for the general welfare a substantive, independent power, as Alexander Hamilton had maintained at the founding, or was it merely a means to implement Congress's enumerated powers, as James Madison had contended? The Court had never answered this question. While Roberts embraced the Hamiltonian view, he proceeded in effect to apply the narrow Madisonian theory. Congress, Roberts agreed, might appropriate money for an objective designated as the general welfare, but it could attach no terms or conditions to the use of funds unless such terms or conditions were themselves authorized by another specific power. And curtailing agricultural production lay outside the province of national authority. The scheme thus invaded the reserved domain of the states.

A decision in the next month that upheld the Tennessee Valley Authority[59] did little to soften the judicial blow delivered on March 18: the destruction of the Bituminous Coal Conservation (or Guffey Coal) Act of 1935, which attempted to ameliorate distressed conditions in the bituminous coal industry through a combination of price-fixing and labor regulations. Coal mining was plagued by overproduction and ruinous competition that resulted in appallingly low wages, strikes, and violence. The statute was flawed constitutionally, Justice Sutherland explained in *Carter v. Carter Coal Co.*, because mining was not interstate commerce and had only indirect effects on that commerce.[60] Both the decision and its reasoning were reminiscent of the Sugar Trust Case, forty-one years before, which rested on a distinction between manufacturing and the "commerce" that Congress was empowered to regulate.[61] Congress's motives might be laudable, but the law amounted to a seductive subversion of states' rights.

> Every journey to a forbidden end begins with the first step; and the danger of such a step by the government in the direction of taking over the powers of the states is that the end of the journey may find the states so despoiled of their powers, or—what may amount to the same thing—so relieved of the responsibilities which possession of the powers necessarily enjoins, as to reduce them to little more than geographical subdivisions of the national domain.[62]

Because the coal case, like the chicken case, turned on an assessment of national power in relation to state power, the Court's defenders could say that the majority was not opposed to regulation; it was merely protecting the federal system. Congress had moved outside the perimeter of its own powers and intruded into those of the states. The obvious message was that the evils to be corrected lay within the latter's authority.

On June 1, however, the Court placed its defenders in an awkward position by invalidating a state minimum wage law for women in *Morehead v. New York ex rel Tipaldo*.[63] Roberts's opinion in the 1934 New York milk case had signaled that the Court was prepared to accept legislation that removed effects of unequal bargaining power. Now, Roberts joined the four dissenters from the milk case who reasserted the authority of the *Adkins*[64] decision of 1923, which had struck down a minimum wage law for women and minors in the District of Columbia. It made no difference, apparently, that New York had sought to meet Justice Sutherland's main objection in *Adkins*, that the law "exacts from the employer an arbitrary payment for a purpose and upon a basis having no causal connection with his business."[65] Instead, Justice Butler insisted for the majority that *Adkins* was meant to apply to all minimum wage laws,[66] suggesting either that New York had illegitimate goals or that it had chosen inappropriate means to attain them, or both.

And if a state was powerless to pass minimum wage laws, then under the coal and chicken decisions, Congress was as well. Little wonder Justice Stone, who dissented in both the coal and minimum wage rulings, was despondent. "We finished the term of Court yesterday," he wrote to his sister on June 2,

> in many ways one of the most disastrous in its history. . . . Our latest exploit was a holding by a divided vote that there was no power in a state to regulate minimum wages for women. Since the Court last week said that this could not be done by the national government, as the matter was local, and now it is said that it cannot be done by local governments even though it is local, we seem to have tied Uncle Sam up in a hard knot.[67]

THE CAMPAIGN OF 1936

Uncertainty over the constitutionality of the New Deal legislation "will increase the importance of the Supreme Court in the Presidential campaign next year," predicted one commentator in the summer of 1935. "In fact, there are many who think the Supreme Court, in a sense, will dominate the Presidential election of 1936."[68] Measured solely by the volume of comments emanating from the White House during 1936, however, the Court seemed at most a passive participant in the election. But that would be about as accurate as characterizing the night of April 14–15, 1912, by saying that the crew was relieved when the starboard side of the S.S. *Titanic* only brushed the iceberg but perplexed when the ship sank a few hours later. In fact, the Court framed the principal question that the election would answer: the constitutionality (and hence the future) of the New Deal.

The Supreme Court largely remained a shadow in the race between Roosevelt and Landon because FDR, for the most part, maintained a deliberate public silence on his judicial nemesis. In the eighteen months prior to the election there were but two occasions when Roosevelt uttered criticism of the Court for popular consumption. The first[69] of these occurred during a rambling press conference on May 31, 1935, when the president asserted that *Schechter*'s implications for the commerce power

> are much more important than almost certainly any decision of my lifetime or yours, more important than any decision probably since the Dred Scott case. . . . We have been relegated to the horse-and-buggy definition of interstate commerce. Now, as to the way out—I suppose you will want to know something about what I am going to do. I am going to tell you very, very little on that.[70]

Public presidential silence on the Court persisted for a full year, until June 1, 1936.[71] Within hours of *Tipaldo*, Roosevelt declared that the Court had created a "No-man's land where no government can function."[72] When then asked what he would do to "meet the situation," the president only smiled and said that he had nothing further to say.[73] The *Tipaldo* sortie marked the end of public criticism by FDR, or his cabinet, until after the election. Even publication of Agriculture Secretary Henry Wallace's systemic critique of the Court was delayed.[74] Considering how badly the Court had mauled his legislative agenda, the president seemed remarkably restrained. In the short run at least, FDR was deft in denying Republicans exactly what they needed. (There was no such restraint in Congress, however. By one count, there were more Court-curbing bills introduced in 1935–1937 than in any other three-year period, or thirty-five-year period, for that matter, in American history.)[75]

The Republican campaign to recapture the White House in 1936 had two thrusts. The first accused FDR of spending the nation into bankruptcy without having restored prosperity and full employment. The second faulted FDR and the Congress for undermining constitutional government by concentrating power in Washington, and took aim at the president for aspiring to be a dictator. As columnist Arthur Krock described their argument:

> The Republicans say officially that the President is an impulsive, uninformed opportunist, lacking policy or stability, wasteful, reckless, unreliable in act and contract. . . . Mr. Roosevelt seeks to supervene the constitutional processes of government, dominate Congress and the Supreme Court by illegal means and regiment the country to his shifting and current ideas—a perilous egomaniac.[76]

A presidential assault on the Court during the campaign would have been a blessing to Republicans in at least two respects. First, courtroom defeats had hardly dampened FDR's enthusiasm for social reform. Within a few weeks of *Schechter*, for example, the Senate passed both the Social Security and the Wagner labor bills. (And to make matters gloomier for conservatives, the president on the same day endorsed "the very sound public policy of encouraging a wider distribution of wealth"[77] by sending to Capitol Hill an income tax bill embodying graduated rates that some Republicans denounced as confiscatory.) The president was becoming more daring, not less, in the face of judicial opposition. Second, Court-curbing proposals from the White House would surely have fueled the dictator charge. To express disagreement with judicial decisions was one thing; to tamper with the Constitution's system of checks and balances was another. Yet as long as Governor Landon was unsuccessful in smoking out any plans the president might have for the Supreme Court, Republicans could push their second theme only by conjecturing what Roosevelt's real intents might be.

Accordingly, the Republican platform of 1936, while calling for state-sponsored social welfare legislation and modest federal relief efforts, bewailed the administration's record. "The integrity and authority of the Supreme Court have been flouted. . . . The New Deal Administration constantly seeks to usurp the rights reserved to the States and to the people. . . . It has insisted on the passage of laws contrary to the Constitution." The party therefore pledged

> [t]o maintain the American system of Constitutional and local self government, and to resist all attempts to impair the authority of the Supreme Court of the United States, the final protector of the rights of our citizens against the arbitrary encroachments of the legislative and executive branches of government. There can be no individual liberty without an independent judiciary.[78]

Landon reemphasized the theme before a crowd of 20,000 at Madison Square Garden in New York City shortly before the election.

> He has publicly belittled the Supreme Court of the United States. . . . [I]f changes in our civilization make amendment to the Constitution desirable it should be amended. . . . And what are the intentions of the President with respect to the Constitution? Does he believe

changes are required? If so, will an amendment be submitted to the people or will he attempt to get around the Constitution by tampering with the Supreme Court? The answer is: No one can be sure.[79]

Landon's reference to constitutional amendment was an acknowledgment that the Court had not been an entirely reliable ally during the campaign year. *Tipaldo* had come down practically on the eve of the Republican National Convention in June, and had undercut the campaign's twin reliance on Court and Constitution. "Where are the rights of the States," queried columnist Dorothy Thompson, "in whose name the Supreme Court has reversed other legislation?"[80]

Republicans did not want to appear opposed to all reform, only to reform imposed from the top down. Yet here was judicial invalidation of a state law, and it left the party's platform in an awkward position. Two pages after the pledge of fealty to the Court was a promise to

[s]upport the adoption of *state* laws and interstate compacts to abolish sweatshops and child labor, and to protect women and children with respect to maximum hours, minimum wages and working conditions. We believe that this can be done within the Constitution as it now stands.[81]

Republicans thus found themselves in an uncomfortable position: they, too, were now at least implicitly critical of the Court. Moreover, *Tipaldo* forced them into an echo of Roosevelt orthodoxy.

"Our Constitution is so simple and practical," FDR had explained in his first inaugural address, "that it is possible always to meet extraordinary needs by changes in emphasis and arrangement without loss of essential form."[82] Even after his policies foundered on the rock of unconstitutionality, he did not waver. The problem was outmoded interpretation, not an outmoded Constitution. So while Republicans were gathered in convention, accusing the president of acting unconstitutionally, Roosevelt upstaged the opposition. The Constitution "is intended to meet and to fit the amazing physical, economic and social requirements that confront us in this modern generation," he retorted. Reform and the Constitution were entirely compatible, he argued, equating "the enjoyment by all men and women of their constitutional guaranties of life, liberty and the pursuit of happiness" [*sic*] with federal control over "[p]rices, wages, hours of labor, fair competition, conditions of employment, social security."[83]

The Democrats in 1936 claimed to make war on privilege, not the Constitution. Yet the administration's string of courtroom routs could not be ignored altogether. Accordingly, just as he uttered no overt criticism of the Court from June 1 until the election, Roosevelt worked hard to weaken a plank in the platform promising a constitutional amendment. "If these [economic and social] problems cannot be effectively solved by legislation within the Constitution," read the final version,

> we shall seek such *clarifying amendment* as will assure to the legislatures of the several States and to the Congress of the United States, each within its proper jurisdiction, the power to enact those laws which the State and Federal legislatures, within their respective spheres, shall find necessary, in order adequately to regulate commerce, protect public health and safety, and safeguard economic security. *Thus we propose to maintain the letter and spirit of the Constitution.*[84]

So qualified, the language was intended to reassure all but the most ardent defenders of states' rights. Democrats promised at most to "clarify" the Constitution, not to tamper with it. The intent was to avoid a pro-Constitution backlash. "The proposer of an amendment would be heralded as a monster," Senator Elbert Thomas had predicted in January. "The gentlest proponent imaginable would be greeted by three-fourths of the headlines of the Nation's papers as 'Wants to Smash the Constitution.'"[85]

Given the dimensions of Roosevelt's victory, the Republican scare stratagem failed as greatly as that of 1896 had succeeded. At most, Republicans kept alive a question that Democrats did not answer: How would the president cope with the recalcitrant Court? The new year provided no immediate answer. "During the past year there has been a growing belief that there is little fault to be found with the Constitution . . . as it stands today," declared FDR in his annual message to Congress. "The vital need is not an alteration of our fundamental law, but an increasingly enlightened view with reference to it."[86] His audience may have wondered how that "enlightenment" would be effected.

EFFECTS

The realignment confirmed by the election of 1936 ushered in an era of Democratic hegemony that persisted for three decades. Of the nine presidential elections between 1932 and 1964, inclusive, Republicans won but two, and then only because Democrats had no match for war hero Dwight Eisenhower. Of the seven Democratic victories, the average margin of difference in popular votes over the Republicans was 12.3 percent. Only one—John Kennedy's 0.1 percent in 1960—was whisker thin. Of the remaining six, the closest was Truman's 4.4 percent edge over Governor Thomas Dewey in 1948, a race in which Governor Strom Thurmond of South Carolina and former Vice President Henry Wallace both cut into the New Deal coalition Truman had inherited by running, respectively, as third-party Dixiecrat and Progressive candidates. Democrat occupancy of the White House was mirrored in the party's domination of Congress. Of the eighteen Congresses between 1933 and 1969, inclusive, Republicans controlled only two: 1947–1949 and 1953–1955. Democrats thus became the default party: voters ordinarily entrusted them with the nation's destiny, choosing the Republicans only when the former could be shown to have led the country down the wrong road.

More immediately, the presidential campaign between Roosevelt and Landon had profound consequences for the Supreme Court and constitutional interpretation. Although they appeared on no ballot, the justices plainly lost the election. The election, commented one newspaper, yielded "a roar in which cheers for the Supreme Court were drowned out."[87] Voters overwhelmingly validated what the Supreme Court had invalidated. The result was the most abrupt, the most sweeping, and the most far-reaching constitutional upheaval in American history, off the battlefield.

The Court-Packing Plan

Roosevelt had four options. Least attractive was to stay the course. "Father time, with his scythe, is one your side. Anno Domini is your invincible ally,"[88] Senator Henry Ashurst counseled FDR in 1936. But the previous four years had yielded not a single vacancy. While it seemed improbable that another four years would be equally unrelenting, FDR feared that the most conservative justices would hang on until death.[89] Neither was FDR willing to count on an election-induced conversion by one or more justices. Reliance on either the Grim Reaper or a change of mind carried high risks: if he was wrong, more of his legislative agenda would perish in the meantime.

Two additional options entailed substantive or procedural amendments to the Constitution.[90] The former would empower Congress to regulate aspects of the national economy, such as labor relations or agricultural production, that the Court had placed off limits. While appealing because it would presumably be efficacious, an empowering amendment was far easier to imagine in principle than to reduce to writing. What, exactly, would it say? If it was insufficiently inclusive, it would fall short of meeting the nation's needs and might not receive support from necessary constituencies. If it was too inclusive, or "a meaningless jumble of weasel words,"[91] opponents could attack the amendment as a grant of nearly unlimited power to Congress. Besides, any amendment would be subject to interpretation by the Supreme Court.

Procedurally, an amendment could eliminate or restrict judicial review itself.[92] Harold Ickes described one proposal discussed at a cabinet meeting that would confer

> explicit power on the Supreme Court to declare acts of Congress unconstitutional. . . . If the Supreme Court should declare an act of Congress to be unconstitutional, then—a congressional election having intervened—if Congress should repass the law so declared to be unconstitutional, the taint of unconstitutionality would be removed and the law would be a valid one. By this method there would be in effect a referendum to the country. . . . At the intervening congressional election the question of the constitutionality . . . would undoubtedly be an issue.[93]

Such modification of judicial power by amendment, however, had less than certain prospects for success. Fundamentally it would shift the American political system closer to the British model of legislative supremacy. Constitutionally, the Court would have no more power than the House of Lords. That liberals might be unhappy with *this* Court did not mean that they were unhappy with the concept of constitutional limitations on *all* manifestations of majority rule. Moreover, any proposed change in the Constitution—procedural or substantive—had to be ratified. Even if Roosevelt assumed that he could count on two-thirds support in both houses of Congress (a dubious assumption after 1935),[94] he could not count on approval by the legislatures of the requisite thirty-six states. The child labor amendment, after all, had been sent to the states in 1924 for the express purpose of overturning two Supreme Court decisions, yet by 1937 it was still a dozen states short.[95] Moreover, even if eventually approved by the states, a proposed amendment might not be ratified soon enough to be of help to a president already in his second term.

The fourth option focused on the root cause of FDR's troubles: the justices themselves. Could not something be done to assure a Court majority more agreeable to the president's programs? Unlike options that hinged on one or more constitutional amendments, this one could be achieved by statute because the number of justices was fixed by Congress, not the Constitution. Mentioned by Roosevelt as early as January 1935 in the context of the Gold Clause Cases,[96] enlargement of the bench had become his preferred solution by January 1937.[97]

Thus, on February 5, just three days after the president had entertained the justices at dinner in the East Room,[98] FDR made his move by unveiling the Judicial Reorganization Act. Justifying his plan on the basis of judicial efficiency—the decrepit bench being unable to keep abreast of its work—Roosevelt proposed to appoint one justice for each current justice over the age of seventy who did not retire, up to a maximum bench size of fifteen. Because there were six justices in this category, FDR would have been able to make six appointments at once. Amazingly, the president gave no hint of wishing to stem the tide of anti-New Deal decisions. He tendered the hemlock cup to the elderly jurists on the elevated ground that they slowed the dispatch of judicial business. To obfuscate the Court-packing motive even further, the plan called for additional lower court judges (also based on the age of sitting jurists), temporary reassignment of lower court judges to overworked courts, and appointment of someone to oversee the flow of federal litigation.[99]

Opposition developed immediately, both across the nation and in Congress.[100] Tellingly, some Democrats who had themselves been critics of the Court came out against the plan. Republican senators and representatives could keep quiet and enjoy the ruckus, thus denying FDR the chance to blame them for his troubles. Closing ranks with bar associations, newspapers lined up almost solidly against the plan. The idea implicit in the bill, that the Court should change constitutional doctrine to meet national needs, was called as "false in theory, as it would be ruinous in practice." "The President wants to control the Supreme Court"[101] was the theme hammered incessantly. "[N]o one can conclude other than that the President seeks not to secure a Supreme Court that will find in accordance with the Constitution as it now stands," emphasized former President Herbert Hoover. "He wants one that will revise the Constitution so it will mean what he wishes it to mean."[102] Were the plan to be adopted, averred the anti-New Deal press, "not a thing would stand between the ambitions of an unscrupulous man . . . in becoming absolute dictator of this country."[103] The press and the bar hit a responsive chord. "No issue so great or so deep," wrote Walter Lippmann, "has been raised in America since secession."[104] FDR's disingenuousness lent credence to the opposition. "Because he is adroit and not forthright," William Allen White reflected, "he arouses irritating suspicions, probably needlessly, about his ultimate intentions as the leader of his party and the head of the Government." "Too clever, too damned clever," commented one pro-administration newspaper.[105]

Sensing that his initial approach had been a blunder, Roosevelt confronted the real issue on March 4 when he addressed a Democratic dinner. Likening the judiciary to an unruly horse on the government gang plow, unwilling to pull with its executive and legislative cohorts, he declared that the crucial question was not whether the Court had kept up with its calendar but whether it had kept up with the country. A "Fireside Chat" on March 9 put all sophistry aside: "The Court has been acting not as a judicial body, but as a policymaking body."[106]

Repackaging, however, further blurred the issue and never succeeded in getting the president off the defensive. Deception had generated too much ill will. This was made all the more apparent by the generally favorable reaction that greeted the chief justice's offensive. On March 22, in response to an invitation from Senator Burton Wheeler, Hughes sent a letter to the Senate that thoroughly refuted FDR's claim that the "old men" were not abreast of their docket. Moreover, he suggested that an enlarged bench would be less efficient and that a bench that heard cases in panels might run counter to the Constitution's stipulation of "one Supreme Court."

Hughes's letter put one more crimp in the president's project. Nothing FDR could do rallied public opinion to his side. The Gallup Poll reported 48–41 percent against the plan on March 1, 45–41 percent in favor on March 29, followed by a slide to 44–31 and 50–35 against on May 17 and June 7, respectively.[107] On June 14, the Senate Judiciary Committee voted 10–8 against the bill, and in a move that was almost anticlimactic, the full Senate voted 70–20 on July 22 to recommit a watered-down version[108] of the bill to committee, thus sealing the plan's fate.[109]

The president had miscalculated badly in several ways. Besides being duplicitous, he had excluded important constituencies, most especially Congress and the public. He had deliberately not made the Court an issue in the campaign, but then construed his overwhelming victory as a mandate to tame the Court.[110] "We gave warning last November that we had only just begun to fight," he declared defensively on March 4. "Did some people really believe we did not mean it? Well—I meant it, and you meant it."[111] "If these [New Deal] reforms were endorsed by the sovereign people as absolutely necessary for the general welfare . . . ," thundered Jim Farley, "then we expect the mandate . . . to be carried out."

> Eleven million majority of the American people expect it. Forty-six of the 48 sovereign States demand it. And if reforms in the judiciary are required to make all branches of the Government reasonably responsive to the will of the sovereign people, American democracy will demand that they be made.[112]

Moreover, apparently to preserve the element of surprise, FDR left his legislative allies and close advisers as much in the dark as the electorate. No one in Congress was consulted in advance. Perhaps only Attorney General Cummings was fully apprised of the president's intentions. Solicitor General (and future justice) Stanley Reed was surprised,[113] as was FDR's confidant Felix Frankfurter.[114] In short, there was no vetting of the plan's merits and demerits and no groundwork in place.[115] With key legislators locked out, no one on Capitol Hill had a personal stake in the plan. Many allies gave it lukewarm support at best.

Finally, the plan was more than a speedy means to a desired end. It represented a fundamental change in the political system, creating a way, Benjamin Cohen wrote to Justice Brandeis on July 30, "to resolve conflicts which recurrently arise between the Court and Congress during periods of social and economic change."[116] Except for those who remained thoroughly wedded to the Jacksonian and Progressive ideals of popular sovereignty, the plan struck even Roosevelt's sincerest admirers as inherently dangerous for personal freedom.

The Switch in Time

As much as any factor, the Supreme Court's own decisions assured the plan's demise. On March 29 in *West Coast Hotel Co.* v. *Parrish*,[117] five justices voted to uphold a minimum wage law from Washington State that was constitutionally indistinguishable from the New York statute invalidated ten months earlier in *Tipaldo*. Only Justice Roberts switched sides. Because the case had been argued in mid-December and because Roberts had let Hughes know promptly how he would vote, the Court-packing plan was not a factor, but the November election most probably was.[118] Clearer indication that FDR's assault was having some effect came on April 12 in *National Labor Relations Board* v. *Jones & Laughlin Steel Corp.*,[119] which had been argued on February 10–11, less than a week after the president had unveiled his plan. Now, Roberts and Hughes were part of the five-justice majority that upheld the Wagner Labor Act against objections that, among other things, Congress had exceeded its authority under the commerce clause. Despite striking similarities to the objections that had prevailed in *Schechter* and *Carter Coal*, the chief justice declared that those cases "are not controlling here."[120] But for the dissenters they most certainly were controlling. "Every consideration brought forward to uphold the Act before us was applicable to support the Acts held unconstitutional in cases decided within two years," McReynolds correctly admonished.[121] Then on May 24, the Court by votes of 5–4 and 7–2 upheld the unemployment compensation and old age benefits provisions, respectively, of the Social Security Act of 1935, effectively rejecting the reasoning in *Butler* that had entombed the AAA.[122] The New Deal was prevailing in Court at last.

"Constitutional Revolution Ltd."[123]

"In politics the black-robed reactionary Justices had won over the master liberal politician of [their] day," opined Attorney General Robert H. Jackson shortly before FDR named him to the Supreme Court. "In law the President defeated the recalcitrant Justices in their own Court."[124]

Yet Jackson may have been only about two-thirds right. True, the Court-packing plan never became law. Equally true, the Court rendered the decisions FDR wanted. Still, the president's plan cost him dearly because it was one of the factors energizing an emerging conservative coalition in Congress.[125] "At a moment when critics of the administration felt timid and insecure, Roosevelt had given them the confidence to strike at him." Death of the Court bill in July dealt the New Deal "a humiliating defeat from which it never fully recovered" by shattering FDR's image of invulnerability that had been one of his major assets.[126] Roosevelt would remain in office until his death in April 1945, but progress of the New Deal, as measured by passage of reform bills, had ground to a halt well before the nation went to war in December 1941.

Ironically, without the help of the Court-packing bill the president soon got his long-awaited chance to remake the Court. Justice Van Devanter announced his retirement on May 18, 1937, after Roosevelt had signed legislation on March 1 that sweetened retirement benefits by providing full salary to those who retired at age seventy. Before the election of 1940, Sutherland, Cardozo, Brandeis, and Butler were gone, too. In their seats were Hugo L. Black, Stanley F. Reed, Felix Frankfurter, William O. Douglas, and Frank Murphy, respectively. When FDR took the oath of office for an unprecedented third term in January 1941, only McReynolds, Stone, Hughes, and Roberts remained from the "old Court" of 1936–1937, and by late spring McReynolds and Hughes had retired. The president now had "his" Court.

Effects of FDR's assault on the Court went far beyond a string of pro-New Deal rulings. Had there been nothing more than this, the confrontation between FDR and the Court in 1937 would be important but hardly epochal. The event marked a constitutional divide in two principal respects.

First, a majority of the justices soon revealed that they had abandoned a half-century or more of jurisprudence that accorded property rights and, to a lesser extent, state prerogatives a preferred place in the hierarchy of constitutional values. *United States* v. *Carolene Products Co.*[127] illustrated the judicial metamorphosis that was under way. At issue was the constitutionality under the Fifth Amendment's due process clause of a congressional enactment banning the interstate shipment of "filled milk" (which had vegetable fat such as palm oil substituted for the butterfat). "Regulatory legislation affecting ordinary commercial transactions is not to be pronounced unconstitutional," explained Justice Stone, "unless in the light of the facts made known or generally assumed it is of such a character *as to preclude the assumption* that it rests upon some rational basis within the knowledge and experience of the legislators."[128] In other words, the government would no longer have to justify a regulation by convincing the justices of the need for its enactment. Reasonableness would be assumed from the fact that a legislature had acted. Thus, an approach to constitutional interpretation going back as far as 1890—the show-us-why-this-infringement-on-economic-liberty-is-necessary way of thinking—was discarded.[129]

With determination of reasonableness left to legislatures, what was the future of the commerce clause and the Tenth Amendment as limits to national power? The extent of this first phase of the constitutional revolution became fully apparent within four years. *United States* v. *Darby*[130] in

1941 not only upheld the Fair Labor Standards Act of 1938, which fixed minimum wages and maximum hours and banned child labor, and overruled *Hammer* v. *Dagenhart*,[131] but also relegated the Tenth Amendment to nothing more than a "truism that all is retained which has not been surrendered."[132] Thus, once Congress exercised one of its powers, the Tenth Amendment furnished no independent limitation even if the national statute interfered with matters historically within the purview of the states.

The significance of *Darby* became apparent one year later in *Wickard* v. *Filburn*[133] which sustained application of crop restrictions in the Agricultural Adjustment Act of 1938 to a farmer who had grown excess wheat for consumption only on his own farm. Even though the wheat never left his premises—even though it never "moved" in interstate commerce—the home-grown and home-consumed wheat nonetheless took the place of wheat the farmer would have purchased. The farmer's wheat "affected" interstate commerce and fell under congressional control. By such generous construction, it was hard to imagine any local activity that did not affect interstate commerce in some way. *Filburn* was light-years removed from *Carter Coal*.

The impact of decisions such as *Carolene Products*, *Darby*, and *Filburn* has been lasting. They show that the Court, not just the parties, had been swept up in realignment. Since 1937, the number of commercial regulations that the Supreme Court has struck down on grounds of Fifth or Fourteenth Amendment unreasonableness has been exactly zero. It was not until 1976 that the Court invalidated another law on Tenth Amendment grounds,[134] and not until 1995 did as many as five justices conclude that Congress had exceeded its authority under the commerce clause.[135]

But the constitutional revolution has had a second dimension independent of the first: the Court unveiled a new set of constitutional values that would replace the old. An early clue was appended as a footnote to Stone's sentence on the new judicial understanding of constitutional reasonableness in *Carolene Products*. The footnote's three paragraphs floated three exceptions to the Court's newly professed tolerance for majority rule. The first was legislation that "appears on its face to be within a specific prohibition of the Constitution, such as those of the first ten amendments." The second was legislation "restricting those political processes which can ordinarily be expected to bring about repeal of undesirable legislation." The third was legislation "directed at particular religious . . . or national . . . or racial minorities." Such "prejudice against discrete and insular minorities may be a special condition which tends seriously to curtail the operation of those political processes ordinarily to be relied upon to protect minorities, and which may call for a correspondingly more searching judicial inquiry."[136]

The first point in Stone's footnote suggested that the Court was still prepared to check majority rule if legislatures contravened specific (i.e., text-based) prohibitions in the Constitution. The second assumed a special responsibility for the Court as defender of freedoms prerequisite to the democratic process, as guardian of the channels of political change. The third suggested an exception to the second: a close look at laws discriminating against historically repressed groups helpless to defend themselves in the rough-and-tumble of majoritarian politics.

Under the freshly acquired banner of self-restraint, property rights and states' rights would be left to the ballot box. Judicial activism old-style was dead; judicial activism new-style was just around the corner. Thanks in no small measure to FDR, the Court rewrote its job description. New concerns—nonproperty aspects of the Bill of Rights and the Fourteenth Amendment—would replace the old. Paradoxically, the Court's strategy for extracting itself from political controversy in the late 1930s would eventually reentangle the institution in partisan strife afresh, as the fifth party system drew to a close.

CHAPTER 7

The Election of 1968: Partisanship Destabilized

T
he Supreme Court was embroiled in the election of 1936 because
it thwarted change. In contrast, the Court was enveloped in the
election of 1968 because it fostered change. A new type of judicial
activism gained ascendancy during the 1950s and 1960s that embodied the
programmatic liberalism that was reshaping the Democratic party. In its
legislative form in the mid-1960s, called the "Great Society," the new liberalism declared war on racial discrimination, and broadened and strengthened in nearly revolutionary fashion economic and social programs inherited from the New Deal. In its judicial form the new liberalism went to previously unsurpassed heights in defense of constitutional rights. Liberal
policy objectives were now deemed not merely constitutionally permissible
but constitutionally required. Particularly in combination with its embrace
by the Supreme Court, this metamorphosis contributed to three profound
changes in the political system: the dethroning of the reigning Democratic coalition; the onset of an era of party dealignment; and a struggle for
control of the Supreme Court.

THE DECLINE OF THE FIFTH PARTY SYSTEM

The second, third, and fourth party systems ended abruptly. The fifth party
system—defined as the unprecedented thirty-six years of nearly unbroken
Democratic control of the national government following the election of
1932—had a different fate. First, Democrats in 1968 were not suddenly
turned out of office in droves, as Republicans had been in the 1930s, and
consigned to minority status for a generation. The years since 1968 have
been a Republican era only in a limited sense. More often than not, Republicans have won the White House, and Democrats have controlled Con-

gress. Second, the decline of the fifth party system was occasioned by no single catastrophe but was partly attributable to developments within the party system itself and the increased saliency of issues that cut across traditional party lines. Ironically, the persistence of the fifth party system for thirty-six years may have been due to the delayed effects of the realignment that brought it into being.

In Northern and Western states, party strength in presidential elections after 1936 largely reflected class and ideology as prosperity returned.[1] Moreover, in state and congressional races the new alignment filtered downward. Because Democrats had become the party of reform and economic liberalism, and the heirs of the Progressive tradition, former Republicans now voting Democratic in presidential races soon adjusted to the idea of voting Democratic in these local races, too.[2] Republicans thus not only remained the conservative party but also saw their own progressive wing diminish bit by bit. Accepting most of the New Deal by 1940, Republicans differed from Democrats on domestic policy chiefly in advocating less spending, modest agendas, and a slower pace.

They succeeded in capturing the White House only twice between 1932 and 1968. The popular vote tallies of war hero Dwight Eisenhower in 1952 and 1956 were of Rooseveltian proportions (55 and 57 percent, respectively), but Ike's coattails were short. His impressive numbers produced a Republican Congress just once (the 83d, 1953–1955). Except for eagerness to exploit Democratic blunders in foreign policy, particularly the threat of communism, as in 1952,[3] Republicans had difficulty differentiating themselves from the opposition without appearing once more as "[t]hose gluttons of privilege."[4] A passage from Nixon's acceptance speech at the 1960 Republican National Convention might just as appropriately have been uttered at any of the five previous national gatherings: "All Americans regardless of party want a better life for our people. What is the difference then? . . . The difference is in the way we propose to reach these goals."[5]

Republicans may have done no better nationally in challenging Democrats because the reordering of the electorate by class and ideology, accomplished relatively quickly in the North and West, moved slowly in the South. The result was less a two-party system and more a party/half-party system; Democrats entered any national race with a Dixie-based congressional or electoral college head start.[6]

The pace of change was slow for several reasons. For white Southerners at midcentury, the Republican name carried more opprobrium than had afflicted the Democratic name in Northern states in past decades. It was easier for a long-time Republican in the Northeast to vote Democratic than for a long-time Democrat in the South to vote Republican. Moreover, Southern states had much to lose by leaving the Democratic ranks. Their congressional delegations enjoyed disproportional influence due to the system of committee seniority. Even if conservative Southern Democrats were disenchanted with their party's direction on domestic policy after 1932, they might moderate its extremes. Consequently, Republican organization in most Southern locales was practically nonexistent, as most political races were decided in the Democratic primaries. Most Southern voters lived full lives without ever having seen or heard a Republican candidate for state or local office.

Nonetheless, the Southern Republican vote in presidential races gradually increased because of two not entirely unrelated forces at work. The first, particularly evident in urban areas, was the appearance of "metropolitan Republicans"[7]—white-collar newcomers from the North and Southern locals who found Democratic social programs unappealing.[8] For the latter group, ideology trumped tradition. The trend became unmistakable in 1952 when each of the eleven Southern states recorded a percentage gain for Eisenhower that surpassed the national Republican average gain of 10 percent.

The second force at work was race, or more specifically, what the Democratic party proposed to do about racial discrimination. Initially race did not drive Southern Democrats into Republican ranks so much as it loosened their historic attachment and eased the resistance to a later bolt.

Discrimination against African Americans in virtually all aspects of life in the 1940s and 1950s was hardly confined to the South. Yet it was in the South that discriminatory practices, especially segregated public services such as education and denial of access to the ballot box, were most deeply embedded in law and custom. Responding to Northern blacks (who could vote) and an impatient Democratic left, President Truman appointed a Commission on Civil Rights that in October 1947 called for radical change.[9]

Advisers counseled Truman that the "Negro voter has become a cynical, hard-boiled trader." With third-party challenger Henry Wallace as well as Republicans bidding for the Northern urban black vote,[10] they argued for an aggressive presidential initiative, noting that "as always, the South can be considered safely Democratic. And in formulating national policy, it can be safely ignored."[11] Accordingly, in his State of the Union address in January 1948, Truman announced the goal of "secur[ing] fully the essential

human rights of our citizens," and recommended legislation on employment, lynching, and voting rights.[12]

The message ruffled white Southern sensibilities. "The President must
cease attacks on white supremacy or face full-fledged revolt in the South,"[13]
the Southern Governors' Conference declared. The White House then
delayed introduction of the bills, and in its draft of the 1948 Democratic
platform merely drew from the relatively mild reference to civil rights in
the 1944 platform.[14] This hesitation caused Hubert Humphrey of Minnesota, one of the party's new programmatic liberals, to lead a fight at the
convention in Philadelphia in July that succeeded in inserting a more vigorous plank. Upon its adoption, the entire Mississippi delegation and half
the Alabama delegation walked out of the convention hall.[15] By the end of
the month Truman issued executive orders to end racial discrimination in
the armed forces and the federal civil service.

Insisting that they were still Democrats, disgruntled Southerners convened in Birmingham, Alabama, and nominated Governor Strom Thurmond of South Carolina for president and Governor Fielding Wright of
Mississippi for vice president. Their objective was not to launch a third
party but to have state parties place Thurmond and Wright onto ballots as
the true Democratic candidates, in place of Truman and Alben Barkley.
The stratagem worked only in Alabama, Louisiana, Mississippi, and South
Carolina—the four states that Thurmond carried in the November election.

As events unfolded, Dixiecrats[16] returned to the Democratic party
(Thurmond himself was a delegate to the 1952 national convention).
Where else would they go? The platforms of both major parties insisted on
federal action to protect civil rights, differing only on details.[17] Moreover,
Southern influence in Congress seemed sufficient to resist any civil rights
legislation of substance. Without some event of seismic proportions to
focus the national consciousness on racial discrimination, Southern
realignment might well have proceeded more slowly, driven by economic
and social welfare issues alone.

An upheaval originated in perhaps the least likely of places: the United
States Supreme Court. On May 17, 1954, in *Brown v. Board of Education*,[18]
a unanimous bench, through an opinion by Eisenhower appointee Chief
Justice Earl Warren, declared racially segregated public schools unconstitutional. Leaping far ahead of the official civil rights positions of Democrats and Republicans, the Court called for revolutionary change in the pattern of education for 8 million white and 2.5 million black public school

students, not only in the seventeen mainly Southern and border states (plus the District of Columbia) where laws required racial segregation but also in four other states where segregation was permitted by local option. More-over, if segregation in public schools was incompatible with the Constitu-tion, as the Court said it was, then any other form of race-based public pol-icy was by implication also intolerable. An entire social system and decades-old way of life were pronounced illegitimate. Never had the Court directly touched so many Americans in matters of child-rearing and asso-ciation. *Brown* endowed racial discrimination with unprecedented saliency in national politics and in no small measure energized the modern civil rights movement in all its dimensions, from continued legal attacks on racism to the direct action of marches, sit-ins, and other forms of mass demonstrations.

Yet at first, *Brown* sparked no stampede of Southern Democrats into the Republican party. First, while the Court was heavily Democratic, consist-ing mainly of Roosevelt and Truman appointees, it was a Republican chief justice who spoke for the Court in *Brown*, as George Wallace would remind voters fourteen years later in his bid for the presidency.[19] Second, the shock of the pronouncement was softened because the Court waited a full year before revealing what the states would be expected to do as a result of the May 17 decision. By directing the school districts to "admit to pub-lic schools on a racially nondiscriminatory basis with all deliberate speed the parties to these cases," the 1955 enforcement decree[20] not only embod-ied a gradualist approach but also created ample opportunities for delay. With few signs of speedy enforcement on the horizon, some white South-erners believed that the future was less bleak than they had first feared.

Third, there was little empathy elsewhere in the nation for the segrega-tionist cause. Unpopular as the decision was among white Southerners, public opinion elsewhere generally supported the Court. Even though nineteen senators and seventy-seven representatives in Congress from the Southern states signed a "Southern Manifesto" challenging the correctness of *Brown*,[21] few of their colleagues from either side of the aisle came to the white South's defense. In a speech some months before the 1956 election, Vice President Nixon went so far as to claim Republican party credit for *Brown*.[22] The Democratic platform of 1956 condemned "the use of force to interfere with the orderly determination of these matters by the courts," and the Republican platform "accept[ed] the decision of the U.S. Supreme Court that racial discrimination in publicly supported schools must be pro-gressively eliminated."[23] Finally, when Arkansas Governor Orval Faubus deployed his state's national guard to resist a federal court order to integrate Little Rock's Central High School, it was a Republican, President Eisenhower, who dispatched the 101st Airborne Division to the city to affirm the authority of the local federal court's decree. Ike's action was remarkable in two respects. It won him few friends among Southern whites, and it was one of the few affirmative measures taken by the national government between 1955 and 1960 to support the judiciary in defense of *Brown*.

If the two national parties had differed little during the 1950s in their posture toward Southern segregationists, a noticeable gap opened after Democrats regained control of the presidency in the election of 1960. First, through a series of "Great Society" measures in the mid-1960s, the Democratic party moved decidedly to the left, enacting social welfare programs rivaling FDR's in significance. In combination with other legislation, the comprehensive Civil Rights Act of 1964 not only banned most forms of racial discrimination but also contributed to the first serious implementation of *Brown* in the deep South.[24] Then the Voting Rights Act of 1965 resulted in a marked increase in voting by blacks, particularly in the Southern states.

Second, programmatic conservatives gained ascendancy in the Republican party, selecting Arizona Senator Barry Goldwater to head the ticket against Lyndon Johnson in the election of 1964. These counterparts to northern Democratic liberals were philosophically opposed to the New Deal and its extensions that the latter embraced. For the first time since 1936, the Republican party built a national campaign around states' rights and challenged the expanded role of the national government in the life of the nation. Furthermore, Goldwater was the first Republican nominee to concoct a victory plan based on carrying the South. His appeal to Southerners drew from both forces that had been at work: rebellion against economic liberalism and social welfare, and the Democratic party's commitment to civil rights.[25] Moreover, because of serious rioting, burning, and looting, mainly by blacks in Northern cities in the summers of 1963 and 1964, Republicans had "the social issue"[26] that they hoped would attract Democrats. The words "crime in the streets" and "law and order" entered the lexicon of American presidential politics, as Goldwater emphasized the national government's responsibility to combat the former and to promote the latter. For some people the words were code phrases for racism. Intellectually, public safety and racism were certainly separable, but many listeners may not have separated them.

Because of a poorly conceived campaign, his tendency to appear "trigger-happy" on military policy, and an opposition eager to exploit both, Goldwater failed badly, collecting not quite 39 percent of the popular vote and handing Johnson a landslide win. Goldwater "represented a minority faction of the minority party and conducted a campaign which specialized in raising settled questions of American policy in a manner so self-destructive as to seem almost deliberately perverse."[27] The Southern strategy worked too well. Except for his home state of Arizona, Goldwater carried only the five deep South states (most of which had gone for Kennedy in 1960), almost an exact inversion of the election of 1924. Yet an important transition had occurred: over the span of four presidential elections, every Southern state had voted Republican at least once.

The party that had seemed practically moribund on the morning of November 4, 1964, however, recovered remarkably by 1968. Republican fortunes waxed as Democratic ones waned. The majority party found itself in disarray occasioned by President Johnson's withdrawal from the race and by an ever louder chorus of antiwar Democrats. The social issue was again prominent, including mainly crime and violence but also pornography, drug use, and religious exercises in public schools.[28] The social issue intersected with the growing public apprehension over the war in Vietnam as opposition to America's role in the conflict erupted in unruly protests—some of the most violent literally outside the Democrats' 1968 convention hall in Chicago—all conveyed via television to the living rooms of nearly every household in the land. Because the Supreme Court had recently rendered decisions touching many of the public's anxieties, it was dragged into the mayhem. And the year was made all the more unforgettable with the assassinations of civil rights leader Martin Luther King in April and of probable Democratic presidential nominee Robert F. Kennedy in June.

Amid the tumult the Republican ticket of former Vice President Richard Nixon and Governor Spiro Agnew of Maryland eked out a narrow victory over Democratic presidential candidate Humphrey and running mate Senator Edmund Muskie of Maine. Five Southern states cast their electoral votes for third-party candidate former Governor George Wallace of Alabama. Democrats won but a single Southern state—Texas, by only 40,000 votes. In five of the other ten states of the South, the Humphrey/Muskie ticket finished third.

The familiar bases of the fifth party system seemed in a shambles, but 1968 provided few clues as to what might take its place. While the combined vote for Wallace and Nixon meant that 57 percent of the voters rejected the Democratic heir to the Johnson presidency, there had been no headlong rush to the Republicans.

THE STONE, VINSON, AND WARREN COURTS

The combined tenures of Chief Justices Harlan Stone (1941–1946), Fred Vinson (1946–1953), and Earl Warren (1953–1969) coincided almost exactly with the fifth party system. Moreover, the bench that found itself enveloped in the election of 1968 had been shaped by four of the system's five presidents. Tom Clark, the last of the four Truman designees, had retired in 1967; Hugo Black and William Douglas, the most senior, were the survivors of Roosevelt's nine appointees. Four of the five Eisenhower appointees remained: Warren, John Marshall Harlan, William Brennan, and Potter Stewart. The three most junior were Byron White, one of two named by Kennedy, plus Johnson appointees Abe Fortas and Thurgood Marshall. They reflected the outcome of the election of 1936 and the "constitutional revolution" of 1937: acceptance of government's authority at all levels to enact economic and social welfare legislation.[29]

Into this consensus, however, protruded two jurisprudential fault lines. By the 1960s, decisive shifts along each moved the Court further into programmatic liberalism and deeper into partisan controversy. One fault line roughly paralleled footnote 4 from the Carolene Products case, discussed in the previous chapter. If courts were supposed to allow legislators wide latitude on social and economic matters, did constitutional tolerance extend to laws that restricted liberty in other ways? During the fifth party system, justices offered competing answers to that question, as illustrated by the flag-salute controversy of the early 1940s.

When Jehovah's Witnesses objected on First Amendment religious grounds to a compulsory flag salute in the public schools, eight justices sided with the local school board in defense of the rule. "[T]he courtroom is not the arena for debating issues of educational policy," admonished Justice Felix Frankfurter's majority opinion in *Minersville School District* v. *Gobitis*. "It is not our province to choose among competing considerations in the subtle process of securing effective loyalty to the traditional ideals of democracy. . . . So to hold would in effect make us the school board for the country."[30] But for Justice Stone in dissent, the majority had "surrender[ed] . . . the constitutional protection of the liberty of small minorities to the popular will." Democracy, he maintained, meant more than process. "It is also . . . a command that freedom of mind and spirit must be preserved."[31] When the Court reconsidered the issue three years later in *West Virginia Board of Education* v. *Barnette*, Frankfurter was in the minority; Stone's position now commanded six votes. "If there is any fixed star in our constitutional constellation," Justice Robert Jackson proclaimed, "it is that no official, high or petty, can prescribe what shall be orthodox in politics, nationalism, religion, or other matters of opinion or force citizens to confess by word or act their faith therein. If there are any circumstances which permit an exception, they do not now occur to us."[32]

The turnabout in *Barnette* symbolized a new hierarchy of constitutional rights. The revolution of 1937 effectively wrote traditional property rights out of the Constitution. In their place the Court—tentatively in the 1940s and aggressively in the 1960s—exalted nonproperty rights derived from the Bill of Rights and the Fourteenth Amendment. The hierarchy meant that the government had not only to justify each restriction on a preferred liberty, but also ordinarily to do so to a greater degree than had been required for regulations on property before 1937.

The second fault line revealed differences over the meaning of the due process clause of the Fourteenth Amendment. Since 1791 the Fifth Amendment had barred the national government[33] from depriving "any person . . . of life, liberty, or property without due process of law." Since 1868 the Fourteenth Amendment had directed the same limitation against "any State." To what degree, if at all, did the Fourteenth Amendment make provisions of the Bill of Rights applicable to the states? The question was of profound importance. If the Bill of Rights applied only to the national government, citizens ordinarily would have no recourse under the federal Constitution against most alleged abuses of power by the states. (Then, as now, when governments act in this country, more often than not it is action by a state government or one of its municipal subdivisions.) If the Bill of Rights applied to the states, individuals would have recourse under the national Constitution, in addition to whatever protections their state constitution might provide. The rights or right in question would thus be "federalized" or "nationalized."

Not until 1897, however, did the Court acknowledge that the Fourteenth Amendment made any part of the Bill of Rights applicable to the states.[34] "Incorporation" of the First Amendment's speech, press, and assembly/petition clauses followed in 1925, 1931, and 1937, as did the free exercise and establishment clauses in 1940 and 1947, respectively.[35] Most of the provisions of the Bill of Rights, however, address criminal justice, and with three exceptions, none was made applicable to the states until the 1960s.[36]

Justices inclined along the first fault line toward a rigorous protection of individual liberties were usually also those who favored rapid Fourteenth Amendment incorporation. As these justices more and more frequently controlled the outcome of decisions during the Warren Court, the effect was twofold: a broadening of "the substantive content of the rights guaranteed, giving virtually all personal rights a wider meaning than they had theretofore had in American law,"[37] and their application to every state, county, city, and crossroads in the land. Critics and supporters alike of these new rights-centered public policies by necessity converged on the Supreme Court.

JUDICIAL ACTIONS

The Court-packing fight of 1937 followed two years of judicial decisions hostile to Roosevelt's New Deal. Each case involved the same issue: government regulation of the economy. In contrast, the whirlwind that encircled the Court in 1968 stemmed from a series of decisions arising from at least five issues spanning fourteen years.

The most stubborn of these involved race. Although *Brown* instantly acquired landmark status in 1954, it was far stronger on promise than on results. A decade later, through a combination of dilatory and sometimes defiant tactics by local officials,[38] outright intimidation of would-be plaintiffs, President Eisenhower's widely discerned belief that *Brown* was ill-advised,[39] and a mainly indifferent Congress, less than 1 percent of black children in the Southern states attended school with white children.[40] In many locales "all deliberate speed" proved to be a turtle's pace. Even after President Johnson signed the Civil Rights Act in 1964, it remained unclear exactly what compliance with *Brown* entailed. In 1966, only 12.5 percent of black students in the South were enrolled in integrated schools. By the start of 1968, a larger number attended all-black schools than in 1954,[41] and public schools in the region remained the most segregated in the nation.[42]

Local officials knew that extreme measures such as shutting down a public school system were unacceptable,[43] but for systems once segregated by law, was it constitutionally sufficient merely to remove color barriers and to allow students to attend schools of their choice or those nearest their homes? The Supreme Court's answer arrived in early spring of 1968 in *Green*

v. *School Board of New Kent County*.[44] This rural Virginia county was about evenly divided between blacks and whites, and living patterns reflected little residential segregation. Under a "freedom-of-choice" plan, the "white school" had become 85 percent white, and the "black school" remained 100 percent black. The Supreme Court ruled unanimously that results, not means, mattered. In a restatement of what *Brown* required, school districts had "the affirmative duty to take whatever steps might be necessary to convert to a unitary system in which racial discrimination would be eliminated root and branch. . . . The burden on a school board today is to come forward with a plan that promises realistically to work, and promises realistically to work *now*."[45] Mere desegregation was not enough; integration was the law of the land, at least in the South.[46] In most locales, compliance with *Green* meant assignment and transportation of pupils to achieve some degree of racial balance. "Busing" became synonymous with racial integration, and entered the lexicon of state and national politics.[47] As refashioned by *Green*, *Brown* quickly became a reality throughout the Southern states. By 1976 public schools in the South were the most integrated in the nation.[48]

Soon after *Brown*, the Court faced another constitutional quandary: conflict between security and freedom. Since the onset of the Cold War in 1946, the menace of international communism, combined with Soviet and Chinese aggression in eastern Europe, Korea, and elsewhere, had preoccupied the United States. Domestically this preoccupation manifested itself in fears of Communist subversives and their sympathizers who would undermine the republic and seize power. Both parties took strong stands against communism; indeed, the principal issue in the 1960 presidential campaign was the accusation by Democrats that the Eisenhower administration had allowed the Soviets to gain the upper hand in military might, particularly in offensive missiles.

By 1956, while the most severe forms of political witch-hunting (collectively called "McCarthyism")[49] had dissipated, fear of the "Red Menace" had not. Thus, when the Court rendered a series of decisions limiting the authority of both state and federal governments to investigate and to penalize suspected subversives,[50] critics accused Chief Justice Warren and the bench of following the "Communist line." "I'm not accusing . . . Warren of being a [Communist] Party member," declared Mississippi Senator James Eastland, "but he takes the same position they do when he says the Communist Party is just another political party."[51] Southerners, already perturbed over *Brown*, now acquired new allies in their campaign against the Supreme Court.

What followed was the first significant national debate on the Supreme Court since 1937, outside as well as inside Congress. Alongside protests such as the "Impeach Earl Warren—Save the Republic" billboards erected by the John Birch Society[52] were mainstream attacks on Warren and the Court, as happened at a London meeting of the American Bar Association in 1957, to which the chief justice had been invited. Warren was so embarrassed and offended that he resigned his long-standing membership in the ABA, the largest organization of lawyers in the nation.[53] Another unprecedented rebuke followed in 1958 when the Conference of State Chief Justices (an association of the presiding judges of the highest courts in each state) overwhelmingly adopted six resolutions that highlighted questionable decisions. "It has long been an American boast that we have a government of laws and not of men," read a report that the conference adopted. "We believe that any study of recent decisions of the Supreme Court will raise at least considerable doubt as to the validity of that boast."[54] Former Justice James Byrnes called for Court-curbing.[55]

On Capitol Hill, Senator William Jenner of Indiana introduced a measure that would have stripped the Court of its appellate jurisdiction in several classes of national security cases. Other senators and representatives tried to reverse particular decisions that they found objectionable. The Senate defeated the Jenner bill 49 to 41, and another anti-Court bill failed by the close vote of 41 to 40. By late summer of 1958 only one relatively mild reprimand had actually become law.[56] Nonetheless, the Court had been taken to the congressional woodshed.[57] Members of Congress had seriously "engaged in a determined effort . . . fundamentally to limit the Court's powers of judicial review."[58]

Congressional virulence waned only when the Court moderated its stance in late 1958 and 1959, avoiding further high-profile national security rulings that went against the government.[59] Had the pattern of 1956–1957 persisted, the Court might well have been an issue in the 1960 election. Instead, the campaign was virtually silent on the Court. Nonetheless, with results that had hitherto eluded *Brown*-distressed, Court-baiting Southerners, the episode tarnished the constitutional role of the judiciary. The tempest was prelude to other controversies soon to emerge. Two of these involved the First Amendment: religion and obscenity.

In 1962 *Engel* v. *Vitale*[60] invalidated the use in New York's public schools of a short prayer, approved by the Board of Regents, that was recited during daily opening exercises. A year later, *School District of Abington Township* v. *Schempp*[61] held that Bible reading and recitation of the Lord's Prayer

in public school classrooms violated the Constitution. It made no difference that the religious exercises were nondenominational. In the majority's
interpretation of the establishment clause, public support of religion in
general was just as heinous as support for one religious belief over another.
Both cases nationalized debates over the role and content of public education, and cast the Court as villain in many quarters.[62]

"I fear for the very survival of the spiritual and moral values which set
our and other nations so far apart from the sterile materialism of our Communist enemies," asserted Representative Edwin Dooley of New York.[63]
Many Southerners were as displeased with these manifestations of judicial
power as they had been with *Brown*. "They put the Negroes in the schools,"
declared Alabama Congressman George Andrews, "and now they're driving God out."[64] Between January 1963 and September 1964, members
introduced 151 measures in the House to reverse the religion decisions, and
167 signed a discharge petition to force a vote on a constitutional amendment allowing school prayer.[65] Had Representative Emanuel Celler, chair
of the House Judiciary Committee, not strenuously opposed these measures, they might well have passed. What did pass the House remains in
place for all to see: the words "In God We Trust" were placed above the
speaker's chair in the House chamber. The drive to correct *Engel* and
Schempp waned as the 1964 election approached and the brawl over reapportionment[66] intensified, but school prayer would periodically reemerge
as an issue in national politics during the next thirty years.

The Supreme Court first seriously examined obscenity laws in 1957,
making clear what had long been assumed: the speech protected by the
First Amendment did not encompass obscenity. But the Court also
attempted for the first time to define obscenity, as a way of delineating sexually explicit material that could be suppressed from that which could not,
and soon found itself at odds with public opinion.[67] By 1966, the Court's
rulings in more than fifty obscenity cases pointed to three conclusions.
First, states and municipalities could no longer operate censorship boards
that previewed and licensed films before they could be shown.[68] Second, in
sharp contrast to the scope of the laws of most states in 1960, obscenity was
confined to "hard-core pornography," although the Court had difficulty
specifying exactly what the term encompassed.[69] Third, the Court became
an exceedingly tolerant board of censors for the nation. Staff obligingly set
up a viewing room in the basement of the Supreme Court building, but in
almost all instances, at least five justices rejected the rulings of courts below
and deemed the salacious material not obscene.[70]

The Court's decisions animated the national debate over obscenity. For 58 percent of the public, obscenity laws were "not strict enough," reported the Gallup Poll in 1965.[71] In 1967 Congress created an eighteen-member, presidentially appointed Commission on Obscenity and Pornography to make recommendations on policy, even though the Court had left open few constitutionally acceptable options.[72] For those concerned about public decency, the Court had become part of the problem, not the solution. "[M]anners and morals seemed unbound by the sweeping permissiveness of a Supreme Court which, apparently, found Bible-reading in schools illegal, but pornography permissible in or out of class."[73]

While these controversies were churning, the Supreme Court was in the midst of the "due process revolution"—a restructuring of the American system of criminal justice that made the Court for the first time the constitutional supervisor of almost every aspect of local law enforcement in each of the fifty states. A look at the Court's docket as late as the 1940s and mid-1950s revealed only a scattering of criminal cases from state courts. Unless local police or courts engaged in especially egregious conduct, states enjoyed wide discretion in the Court's eye in their choice of law enforcement practices. The Warren Court abandoned this tradition.

In *Mapp* v. *Ohio*,[74] for example, six justices placed significant restrictions on searches and arrests by applying the Fourth Amendment's exclusionary rule to the states by way of the Fourteenth Amendment.[75] The majority reasoned that unless illegally seized evidence was barred from trial, the Fourth Amendment right to be free from "unreasonable searches and seizures" would mean little. The exclusionary rule had been a fixture in federal courtrooms since 1914,[76] but in 1961 nearly half the states still allowed the introduction of illegally acquired evidence. *Mapp* was the linchpin for much of the due process revolution, both because the encounters that most people have with law enforcement authorities are with state or local police and because the Court was now obliged to lay down even more rules defining correct police procedure. As much as any other single decision, *Mapp* put the Supreme Court in charge of day-to-day police work. While *Mapp* might deter police misconduct, critics charged that its social costs were too high: an individual would not benefit directly from its operation *unless* incriminating evidence was found.

Cases in 1964 and 1966 dealt with testimonial evidence gleaned from interrogations. Since 1936 the Supreme Court had overturned state convictions that were based on "coerced confessions." By the 1960s some justices wondered whether interrogations, even those not involving "third-degree" tactics, were unavoidably coercive if an accused person was shut up in a room with only police present. Because the Constitution required that counsel be present at trial,[77] perhaps counsel should also be present for an interrogation. What a suspect might say to police in the station house might well have a determining effect later on what happened in the courthouse. This at least seemed to be the premise of *Escobedo* v. *Illinois*,[78] where a bare majority of five suppressed a confession after police denied the suspect's request to have his lawyer (who was waiting outside the interrogation room) present for the questioning. The decision, however, left police unclear as to their precise constitutional obligations.

On June 13, 1966, the Court, again by a 5–4 vote, clarified its intentions. While *Mapp* had rewritten the rules of criminal procedure in about half the states, *Miranda* v. *Arizona*[79] called for changes in police practices in all of them. It remains the most significant criminal procedure decision ever rendered by the Supreme Court in terms of its impact on the political system.

Because interrogations without the presence of counsel were inherently coercive, reasoned Chief Justice Warren, confessions elicited under such conditions amounted to compelled self-incrimination in violation of the Fifth Amendment. This was true even if, as in Miranda's own interrogation, the confession seemed entirely voluntary. Henceforth confessions would be admissible only if police had fully advised the suspect, prior to any questioning, of certain particulars: (1) the right not to answer any questions, (2) the warning that anything the suspect said might be used against him as evidence, (3) notification of one's right to have an attorney present if she chose to answer questions, and (4) the offer of a court-appointed attorney if the suspect was unable to retain one.

Dissents by Justices Harlan and White anticipated the tongue-lashing the Court received. "[T]he Court has not [made] and cannot make the powerful showing that its new rules are plainly desirable in the context of our society, something which is surely demanded before those rules are engrafted onto the Constitution and imposed on every State and county in the land . . . ,"[80] declared Harlan. For White the decision would have ruinous consequences. "[I]n some unknown number of cases" it would "return a killer, a rapist or other criminal to the streets and to the environment which produced him, to repeat his crime whenever it pleases him," and so would have a "corrosive effect on the criminal law as an effective device to prevent crime."[81]

While some press commentary on the ruling was favorable, much was incendiary. The Court was "an ally of the criminal element in America," claimed the *Richmond Times-Dispatch*. While deploring beatings, bullying, and badgering by police, the *Chicago Daily News* thought that the Court had gone too far. "[A]n era of drastically rising crime has also proved to be an era in which the Supreme Court has piled decision on decision to make convicting and punishing the guilty more difficult and less certain."[82]

As policy *Miranda* was surely debatable. More "i's" for police to dot might mean more dismissed prosecutions, and experts might disagree over the degree to which *Miranda* actually advanced personal freedom. Yet with nothing more, *Miranda* might not have become a constitutional pariah. Instead, *Miranda* shortly became for the Supreme Court a "self-inflicted wound."[83]

A week later the Court announced *Johnson* v. *New Jersey*,[84] which decreed that *Miranda* would apply to new *trials* beginning after June 13, rather than to *interrogations* occurring after that date. Thus confessions already in hand for trials about to begin were inadmissible, and for prosecutions in which a confession was absolutely essential, calamitous. The effect was unsettling. Across the nation self-confessed criminals walked out of jail in numbers large enough to generate eye-catching headlines: "Bronx Man Who Admitted Rape Set Free Under Miranda Ruling"; "Miranda Rule Voided 72 Maryland Confessions"; "Confessed Slayer of Wife and 5 Children Freed."[85] People wondered whether "[n]ice people have some rights, too."[86] (The Court apparently learned a lesson from its retroactivity blunder. When *United States* v. *Wade*[87] on June 12, 1967, required, 5 to 4, the presence of counsel at identification police lineups, the Court made clear that the ruling would apply only to identifications made after that date.)

Anti-*Miranda* sentiment welled up in Congress, too, as members lost little time in peppering the Court. When the president introduced his Omnibus Crime Control and Safe Streets Act[88] in early 1968, senators added provisions to overrule or modify three of the Court's most controversial decisions as they might apply in federal criminal prosecutions. Regarding *Miranda*, confessions would ordinarily be admissible if deemed "voluntary" by the trial judge according to the circumstances of the interrogation. Regarding *Mallory* v. *United States*[89] (discussed below), a confession made by a person while in police custody was not to be inadmissible solely because of a delay in arraignment. Regarding *Wade*, the testimony of an eyewitness identifying the accused was to be admissible as evidence at trial. The House scheduled a vote for June 6, 1968, to decide whether to accept the Senate version or to commit the bill to conference, where liberal Democrats might have removed the anti-Court sections. But twelve hours before the vote, Senator Robert Kennedy was murdered in California. The House then accepted the Senate bill as it stood, 368 to 17.[90] Despite the inclusion of these provisions that Johnson opposed, the bill became law. In form at least, Congress had corrected the Court.[91]

THE CAMPAIGN OF 1968

The election year was noteworthy in several respects. Debates over economic policy that routinely shape national campaigns were present but in the backseat.[92] After Democratic Senator Eugene McCarthy made a respectable showing in the New Hampshire primary, incumbent Lyndon Johnson, the probable Democratic nominee, announced on March 31, 1968, that he would not seek reelection. Having brought down the president, however, McCarthy did not get the nomination, which went to Vice President Humphrey in a convention marred by violence. Humphrey became the last nominee of either major political party not to have entered a single presidential primary. For the last time two liberals—George Romney and Nelson Rockefeller—seriously sought the nomination of the Republican party, which went instead to Richard Nixon, whose only challenge on the right came from California Governor Ronald Reagan. Not since Democrats nominated Bryan in 1908 had a major party turned to a defeated former candidate for president after an interval of more than four years. For the first time since 1948 a third-party candidate (George Wallace) was positioned to affect the outcome by winning electoral votes. And for the first time since 1936, the Court was part of the campaign.

Second only to the Vietnam war, crime, race, and societal disintegration dominated the presidential campaign of 1968. Sometimes the issues blended into one, as happened when protests over the war became heated with advocacy and acts of civil disobedience and violence. The Court seemed connected to the cultural chaos because its decisions had nationalized some of the issues that now beset the nation. Moreover, by giving constitutional answers to social questions that were dividing the nation, the Court frustrated the political process by taking certain options off the table. Never before had the Court been in so much "trouble for insisting that the *substance* of democracy must be fulfilled as well as the form."[93]

Then, as now, the Supreme Court is ill-equipped to defend itself in the court of public opinion. Traditionally, justices speak through their published opinions, and are reticent to comment publicly on their reasoning or its implications. The Court's public information office may be the only one in Washington that does no more than its name implies: it adds no "spin" nor explanation to the announcements and documents it releases. Instead, the Court has long depended on allies in the political, academic, and legal communities to explain or to defend, as the need arises. By 1968, the Court seemed short of allies, at least outspoken ones, as the public's perception of the justices turned sour. In 1967, 45 percent of people rated the Supreme Court as "excellent" or "good," a figure that declined to 36 percent in 1968.[94]

On school integration, Nixon explained in August that he was opposed to busing to achieve racial balance in schools, and would appoint as judges those "who attempted to interpret, not make law" and who did not think it proper to act as local school boards.[95] In an interview for telecast in the Carolinas on September 12, he announced that he opposed withholding federal funds from school districts that had not desegregated. "I believe that [Brown] was a correct decision, but on the other hand, while that decision . . . said that we should not have segregation, when you go beyond that and say that it is the responsibility of the federal government and the federal courts to, in effect, act as local school districts . . . then I think we are going too far." His syntax may have been weak, but his message was clear. "Our schools are for education, not integration," he told reporters two days later.[96] Emphasis on local control of schools fit well with the focus of his campaign: an appeal to the middle class, "the forgotten Americans, the non-shouters, the non-demonstrators" who were perplexed by the strife and confusion across the country. These were the "good people," the "decent people," who "work and . . . save . . . and pay their taxes . . . and care."[97]

On race Wallace and his American Independent party platform dropped any pretense of subtlety. Federal "operation and control of the public school systems of the several states" amounted to a "derogation and flagrant violation" of the Tenth Amendment of the Constitution. The Civil Rights Act of 1964 "set race against race and class against class, all of which we condemn."[98] Supreme Court justices "have endangered the lives of our children" at school, Wallace asserted.[99] "You can't read a simple Bible verse in school—but you can send obscene literature through the mails."[100]

But it was on crime that criticism of the Court was most strident.[101] The AIP platform decried "a beguiled judiciary" that displayed "solicitude for the criminal and lawless element of our society" by "shackl[ing] the police and other law enforcement agencies" with "arbitrary and unreasonable restrictions."[102] The mugger "is out of jail before the victim is out of the hospital," Wallace often said in his stump speeches.[103]

Court decisions "have inhibited law-enforcement officials and encouraged criminals," Nixon claimed in March as he advocated passage of the 1968 crime bill with its anti-Court measures. Then, in words that he would repeat many times during the next eight months, he added, "Some of our courts have gone too far in weakening the peace forces as against the criminal forces."[104] In May, Nixon accused the Supreme Court of giving the "green light" to "the criminal element" in the nation. Mentioning *Miranda* specifically, he claimed that some decisions accounted in part for "the 88 percent increase" in crime in the Kennedy and Johnson administrations.[105] "The right to be free from domestic violence has become the forgotten civil right," he announced later.[106]

The correlation between the Court and crime was telling. Supreme Court decisions significantly expanding the rights of persons accused of crimes had come just prior to or during a time of increased and highly visible street crime and unprecedented urban ghetto riots.[107] In 1968 "crime and lawlessness" was cited most frequently as the "most important problem," second only to the Vietnam war. In the same year 63 percent of the public believed that courts dealt with criminals "not harshly enough."[108] Here, as with lesser issues like school prayer and obscenity, Nixon and others could plausibly argue that the Supreme Court had contributed to moral breakdown and social dissolution.

Just days before the election, Nixon talked at length about his criteria for judicial appointments. Among the "qualifications I would consider would be experience or great knowledge in the field of criminal justice. . . . [T]he abused in our society deserve as much protection as the accused [and] any justice I would name would carry to the bench a deep and abiding concern for these forgotten rights." A Nixon Court would abandon the judicial activism that been the vehicle for programmatic liberalism. "[N]ominees to the high court . . . would be strict constructionists who saw their duty as interpreting law and not making law. They would see themselves as caretakers of the Constitution and servants of the people, not super-legislators with a free hand to impose their social forces and political viewpoints on the American people."[109]

Promises "to end the war in Vietnam" formed perhaps the only common ground among the three candidates (although, even here, they advocated different means). Democrats resisted Republican and AIP emphasis on escalating crime and an unchecked judiciary by stressing the reality of prosperity, pledging to protect the "great gains" in civil rights, opposing "lawlessness in all its forms," and vowing an "attack on the root causes of crime and disorder" that was joined with a reminder that "[l]awlessness cannot be ended by curtailing the hard-won liberties of all Americans."[110] On the stump Humphrey condemned Wallace for a "calculated campaign to deliberately inflame the fears, frustrations, and prejudices of our people." Nixon's "attacks on our courts" seemed certain, Humphrey continued, to "set group against group and race against race. . . . Those attacks have stockpiled the ingredients for civil explosion."[111]

Humphrey trailed Nixon badly during most of the campaign. In mid-September, the Gallup Poll gave the latter a commanding twelve-point lead, with Wallace at 19 percent and undecided voters at 7 percent.[112] Republicans talked of a Nixon landslide. From then until Election Day, Nixon's share held constant. Humphrey drew gradually from the Wallace and undecided groups, especially after organized labor worked hard to reverse the rank-and-file defections to Wallace.

The outcome on November 5 was among the closest of the century, with Nixon's popular vote total a bare half-million above Humphrey's. Wallace's 13.5 percent ranked just below La Follette's third-party share in 1924 and well below Theodore Roosevelt's 27.4 percent in 1912. Unlike La Follette, Wallace garnered electoral votes by carrying five states. Had Wallace not been in the race, one pair of analysts calculated that the Nixon-Humphrey split would have been 53 to 47 percent,[113] noticeably larger than the razor-thin edge Kennedy had over Nixon in 1960. The full meaning of the tally was less clear, however: Democrats suffered only slight or modest reductions in their majorities in the House and the Senate, making Nixon the first new president since 1848 to confront an entire Congress in the hands of the other party.

EFFECTS

The results of the campaign of 1968 marked the end of the party system in place since 1932, yet presaged no major realignment of the parties in the traditional sense. The campaign was significant, instead, in that it was the first time since 1912 that social issues had a measurable effect nationally on the outcome of the race. Moreover, the Supreme Court contributed mightily to the saliency of those issues. Second, the unprecedented turbulence of the campaign year, as well as Humphrey's nomination that had been opposed by the peace Democrats, led to a reformation of that party's nomination procedures by 1972 that conveyed power to those most skilled in the "retail politics" of primaries and caucuses. Republicans modified their procedures somewhat later, more slowly, and to a lesser extent. Third, the century-old allegiance of the Southern states to the Democratic party was shattered. The election accelerated the transformation of the South into a region that leaned Republican, first in presidential races and later in other contests.[114]

Fourth, the campaign of 1968 firmly established Republicans as the more socially conservative of the two major parties, just as they had been the more economically conservative party since 1932. Fifth, while social issues did not transform large numbers of Democrats outside the South permanently into Republicans, those concerns weakened the attachment of many Democrats and a much smaller number of Republicans to their parties. Called "dealignment," this phenomenon was so pronounced that by 1972 "independent voters," on whom neither party could confidently count for support, accounted for more than a third of the electorate, up from 23 percent in 1964.[115] Split-ticket voting became habitual, resulting in a form of political schizophrenia known as divided government. Voters were reluctant to give either party the lasting control of the reins of power that had distinguished previous party systems.

The campaign was also a watershed event for the Supreme Court both institutionally and jurisprudentially. It inaugurated an era of conspicuous politicization of the judiciary that was in part the consequence of dealignment: Republicans did not fully acquire the dominance in national affairs that Democrats lost. The result was a bench that did not discard, but sometimes moderated and sometimes extended, the programmatic liberalism that it inherited.

The Supreme Court of course has been politically important since the 1790s. Previous chapters have shown how particular decisions have affected the political process and how contending partisan forces have deemed control of the Court essential to their success. But these episodes were ordinarily short-lived. Ordinarily the Court succeeded in keeping its policy-making role in the background and its traditional dispute-resolution or "courtly" role in the foreground.[116] For several reasons the post-1968 period proved different.

First, for at least fourteen years the Supreme Court had set policy on a range of questions that were now salient issues in American national politics. Just as it had in 1936, the Court's ideology plainly mattered. Second, appointments might well determine whether Warren Court policy persisted or faltered, especially because some of the Warren Court's most controversial rulings were decided by margins of 5 to 4 or 6 to 3. With Democrats now identified with programmatic liberalism and Republicans with programmatic conservatism, the occupant of the White House and the future of the Court were linked each time a vacancy opened on the bench.

Second, presidential candidates made that link obvious by making discussion of judicial appointments a routine part of their campaigns. Rhetoric that had once been exceptional became common.[117] Accordingly, the ideological stakes in each presidential election and judicial vacancy were manifest. Third, discussion of the ideological impact of a nominee could hardly be avoided because eight of the eleven appointments made by Republican presidents after 1968 required the approval of a Senate in Democratic hands. The overtly politicized Court of 1968 and beyond contributed to a renewed interest in the Senate's "advice and consent," as both a departing and an arriving president soon discovered.

On June 26, 1968, President Johnson announced Chief Justice Warren's intention to retire upon Senate confirmation of a successor. With Democrats in disarray and with the probability of a Republican victory in November, the timing of Warren's departure was calculated.[118] As Warren expected, Johnson promptly picked Justice Abe Fortas, the president's close friend, for the center seat. The news was the opening offensive in a persistent struggle for the Supreme Court, eased only by an occasional truce. The first of the Court wars kept the judiciary in political combat for more than two years.

First-term Republican Senator Robert Griffin of Michigan mobilized opposition to the Fortas nomination immediately, hoping to save the vacancy for Nixon.[119] In hearings before the Senate Judiciary Committee and in floor remarks between July and September, Republicans and Southern Democrats took both Fortas and the Warren Court to task. They charged the former with various improprieties, including participation in White House strategy sessions on the Vietnam war, drafting of legislation, and acceptance of high lecture fees raised by wealthy business executives who happened to be clients of Fortas's former law partner, Paul Porter.[120]

Reflecting the presidential campaign then under way, Fortas's opponents took aim at the Court for its decisions on obscenity and criminal justice. Senator Thurmond arranged for members to see sexually explicit films and magazines that the Court had allowed to remain in circulation.[121] Testimony of one witness that was left unrefuted claimed that Fortas had cast the deciding vote in fifty-two cases in which the Court had overturned censorship verdicts.[122] Obscenity destroyed community morals, claimed

Iowa's Senator Jack Miller, and "Fortas stood for obscenity."[123] Thurmond went so far as to pillory Fortas for a decision handed down eight years before he went on the Court. Referring to *Mallory* v. *United States*, in which the Court had freed a confessed rapist because police held him too long before arraignment, the South Carolinian asked, "Do you believe in that kind of justice? . . . Does not that decision, *Mallory*—I want that word to ring in your ears . . . shackle law enforcement?" he bellowed. "Mallory, a man who raped a woman, admitted his guilt, and the Supreme Court turned him loose on a technicality?" Was not that decision "calculated to encourage more people to commit rapes and serious crimes?"[124]

When debate on the motion of Majority Leader Mike Mansfield to take up the nomination began on September 25, opposition senators launched a four-day filibuster. A cloture motion on October 1 fell fourteen votes short of the two-thirds needed to end debate. Two days later, at Fortas's request, Johnson withdrew the ill-fated justice's name. For the first time, a filibuster blocked a Supreme Court appointment, and for only the second time in the twentieth century the Senate failed to approve a president's choice for the Court. For unknown reasons,[125] Johnson declined to submit another name, leaving the choice of Warren's successor to Nixon.

Just five months after Nixon became president, the judicial fat was again in the political fire. Under pressure from colleagues, members of Congress, and the Justice Department, Fortas resigned on May 16, 1969—the only justice to leave the Court under fire—after *Life* magazine revealed that he had received (although several months later returned) the first of what was to be an annual $20,000 stipend from the Family Foundation of Louis Wolfson, who was then serving a prison term for selling unregistered stock.[126] Nixon now had two vacancies to fill simultaneously. In place of Warren, who left the Court on June 23, Nixon picked Warren Earl Burger, chief judge of the Court of Appeals for the District of Columbia Circuit and a vocal critic of the Warren Court's rulings on criminal justice.[127] Senate confirmation of Burger by a 74–3 vote followed the nomination by just eighteen days! It appeared that the new president would have little difficulty building his Court.

For the Fortas seat, Nixon selected Clement Haynsworth, a federal appeals judge from South Carolina. "With this one," Nixon is reported to have said, "we'd stick it to the liberal Ivy League clique who thought the Court was their own private playground."[128] The nomination, critics charged, was confirmation of the Republican party's "Southern strategy." Civil rights organizations claimed that Haynsworth was racially biased and

pointed to cases in which he had taken a restrictive view of school desegregation. Organized labor argued that Haynsworth was unfit because of
antiunion rulings. Yet ideological objections alone or even combined with
hard feelings among liberal Democrats stemming from the Fortas resignation would probably have been insufficient to defeat Haynsworth. Looking
for another way to scuttle the nomination, Birch Bayh of Indiana, leader of
the anti-Haynsworth senators, seized upon his insensitivity to judicial proprieties—specifically two cases in which Haynsworth arguably should have
disqualified himself. Because ethics had been central to calls for Fortas's
resignation, Bayh's strategy of combining ethics and ideology worked:
fifty-five senators, including some Northern Republicans but no Southern
Democrats, voted against confirmation.[129]

Nixon countered with the nomination of Judge G. Harrold Carswell of
the Fifth Circuit Court of Appeals, a Floridian with a tough law-and-order
record. Described by Attorney General John Mitchell as "too good to be
true,"[130] the nominee combined avowed racism (which he now disavowed)
with minimal professional qualifications. Verifying the latter criticism,
Senator Roman Hruska of Nebraska gallantly attempted to convert the liability into an asset. "Even if he is mediocre, there are a lot of mediocre
judges and people and lawyers. They're entitled to a little representation
aren't they, and a little chance? We can't have all Brandeises and Frank-
furters and Cardozos and stuff like that there."[131] The 51–45 vote against
Carswell marked the first time since the second Cleveland presidency in
1893 and 1894 that the Senate refused to accept two nominees for the same
Supreme Court vacancy.

In a televised address on April 9, 1970, Nixon accused the Senate of
regional discrimination, concluding, "with the Senate as presently constituted—I cannot successfully nominate to the Supreme Court any federal
appellate judge from the South who believes as I do in the strict construction of the Constitution."[132] The administration's failures may well have
reinforced the Republican strategy of gaining support in the South. Nixon
could blame the defeats on an ensconced liberal elite determined to maintain the Court as its own reserve.[133]

The president then turned to Chief Justice Burger's longtime Minnesota friend, Harry Blackmun of the Eighth Circuit Court of Appeals, a
jurist of moderately conservative views with solid professional credentials.
Arousing little concern, "old number three" (as Blackmun later called himself) passed the Senate 94–0. When he joined the Court on June 9, nearly
thirteen months had elapsed since Fortas's departure.

Piqued by the Haynsworth/Carswell debacle, congressional defenders led by Representative Gerald Ford of Michigan launched a drive for the impeachment of Justice William O. Douglas, the first serious effort to remove a member of the Supreme Court since 1804. An unfailing and outspoken liberal, and a man of unconventional habits with a proclivity for younger wives, Douglas seemed an inviting target. Ford detailed various improprieties, including conflict-of-interest activities, being a "well-paid moonlighter," work for the "leftish" Center for the Study of Democratic Institutions, and authorship of an "inflammatory volume" entitled *Points of Rebellion*,[134] which was linked in spirit to "the militant hippie-yippie movement."[135] Aside from boosting sales of the book by a factor of ten,[136] the call for an investigation of the justice accomplished little. Fortunately for Douglas, the impeachment resolution went to the House Judiciary Committee (still chaired by Democrat Celler) rather than to a select committee that might have been hostile. A five-person subcommittee issued a 924-page, largely exculpatory report on Douglas in September,[137] with the three Democratic members concluding in December (after the midterm election) that no grounds for impeachment existed.[138]

Jurisprudentially the campaign of 1968 and its aftermath had mixed results for the seventeen years of the Burger Court, despite additional changes in the Court's personnel[139] that left only three members of the Warren Court—Brennan, White, and Marshall—still sitting when Burger retired in 1986. The Burger Court did far less damage to the Warren Court's record than the latter's supporters had feared and its critics had hoped. Indeed, most of the Warren legacy survived intact.

On equality issues the Burger Court—to the surprise of the White House[140]—almost immediately reaffirmed the far-reaching directive from *Green*, forbade further delays in integration,[141] and moved beyond the Warren Court in a series of cases, most of which were decided by a unanimous or nearly unanimous bench. In 1971 it extended *Green* to sprawling Southern urban school districts,[142] and in 1973 applied *Green* to public schools outside the South in situations where attendance zones, not laws, had produced segregated student bodies.[143] On employment discrimination in the private sector, the Court gave a generous reading to Title VII of the Civil Rights Act of 1964. Banned were not only "overt discrimination but also practices that are fair in form, but discriminatory in operation."[144] Two additional decisions gave at least qualified approval to racially based affirmative action plans in medical school admissions and private employment.[145] In the first "benign" race-conscious districting case to reach the

High Court, the Court held that such efforts to increase minority representation were not only appropriate under the Voting Rights Act but also permitted by the Constitution.[146] Moreover, for the first time the Court held a statute invalid because of gender discrimination.[147] In two decisions that might well have been decided differently by the Warren Court, five justices (including the four Nixon appointees) refused to invalidate local property tax funding of public education where that resulted in inequalities between school districts,[148] and overturned an integration decree requiring busing among fifty-four urban and suburban school districts in Michigan.[149]

On First Amendment issues, the Court divided 5–4 to provide less constitutional protection in obscenity cases,[150] but generally was inclined to provide as much protection for free speech and press as had the Warren Court. In one high-profile case in 1971, for example, the Nixon administration suffered a stunning defeat when six justices, with Burger, Blackmun, and Harlan in dissent, refused to enjoin the *New York Times* and the *Washington Post* from publishing a purloined classified study of decision-making in the Vietnam war.[151] When the Court revisited school prayer a year before Burger's retirement, six justices opposed an officially sanctioned moment of silence for prayer and meditation; Burger, Rehnquist, and White would have allowed the practice.[152] Moreover, it was the Burger Court that was the first to invalidate state funding for sectarian schools, as a violation of the establishment clause.[153]

On criminal justice, however, there were substantial changes. While the Burger Court overturned no major Warren Court precedent outright, criminal defendants fared less well.[154] After declaring in 1972 that capital punishment as then administered in the United States was unconstitutional (with all four Nixon justices in dissent), seven justices approved it in principle four years later after states made changes in sentencing procedures.[155] *Miranda* survived, but the Court was more inclined to admit confessions in situations where, arguably, a violation of *Miranda* had occurred.[156] The exclusionary rule from *Mapp* continued, but in 1984 six justices for the first time approved a "good faith exception" in situations where police conducted a search with a warrant that later proved defective.[157] The Court rejected opportunities to expand the scope of warrantless searches where automobiles were involved,[158] but stretched a Warren Court decision that had narrowed the scope of a warrantless search incident to an otherwise lawful arrest.[159] On assistance of counsel, the Burger Court was as rigorous as the Warren Court,[160] even broadening the right to encompass misdemeanors where punishment included a jail sentence.[161] In litigation arising from the 1968 crime act, the Nixon administration suffered a setback when all eight participating justices refused to approve warrantless electronic surveillance in domestic national security cases.[162]

The Burger Court did not reverse the course of the Warren Court's judicial activism.[163] The balance of the decisions suggested the Burger Court's willingness—like its predecessor—to use judicial power in pursuit of particular social objectives, whether in curtailing or extending precedent or in venturing out onto new fields.[164] And more often than not, programmatic liberalism prevailed in the Court. Perhaps dealignment gave the Court new latitude. That part of the "constitutional revolution" of 1937 that preached a modest or retiring role for the Court in the political process, thus leaving policy-making to legislators, seemed to have vanished. Going beyond merely keeping open the channels of political change, or setting only very broad limits on legislative choices, the other part of the revolution of 1937 seemed firmly entrenched: for nonproprietarian issues affecting individual rights, the Court would dictate constitutionally acceptable policy.

In the Watergate tapes case[165] that ended his political career by a vote of 8–0, President Nixon learned the hard way that "his" Court might be no more deferential to elected officials than the Warren Court. Perhaps Nixon had warning of what awaited him. In 1973 three of his appointees had joined the majority in going where no Court had gone before, in striking down virtually every abortion law in the United States.[166] In so doing, as the next chapter will show, the Court refocused the electoral system on itself.

CHAPTER 8

The Elections of 1980 and 1984: Whose Constitution?

D uring the 1970s the Burger Court not only refrained from discarding, but also enthusiastically embraced, much of its predecessor's accomplishments. Would the Court again find itself snarled in partisan controversy? When the justices joined the abortion debate, the answer to that question became clear. Arguably, no single judicial decision since *Dred Scott*[1] in 1857 electrified the political system to a greater extent than *Roe* v. *Wade*.[2] Acting precisely as the two major parties were undergoing profound changes, the Court ignited the most extensive debate since the 1930s on the judiciary's role in democratic government.

A DIFFERENT PARTY SYSTEM

If widespread agreement prevails on the demarcations and nomenclature of previous party systems, the years since 1968 elude similar consensus. The reason is plain: no realignment in the traditional sense has occurred. Republicans have not sent Democrats into hiding; Democrats have not regained their dominance.

Transformation of the Southern states into a two-party region leaning Republican is noteworthy, of course, as have been the five Republican victories in presidential elections from 1968 through 1996. Nonetheless, Democrats won the White House with Southern governors at the top of the ticket: Jimmy Carter of Georgia in 1976 and Bill Clinton of Arkansas in 1992 and 1996. Carter carried all states of the old Confederacy, save Virginia, in a close race with President Gerald Ford. In more convincing electoral vote[3] triumphs, Clinton claimed four Southern states in 1992 and 1996.[4]

Moreover, and pivotal for the Supreme Court, during the thirty years from 1969 through 1998 Democrats dominated the U.S. House of Representatives for all but four years and the Senate for all but ten. A pattern of divided rule confronted each Republican president (Richard Nixon in 1968 and 1972, Ronald Reagan in 1980 and 1984, and George Bush in 1988) with a Democratic Congress, except for Reagan's good fortune in having a Republican Senate for six years. The same fate awaited Democrat Bill Clinton after his party stumbled badly in the 1994 midterm elections. When Republicans maintained control of Congress in 1996, Clinton became the first Democrat to be reelected president without a Democratic Congress. Not since 1928 and 1930 had voters chosen a Republican House of Representatives in consecutive elections. (And despite a narrow win in 1930, Republicans promptly lost control of the House because of post-election deaths.)

The pattern of post-1968 politics suggests that something important has occurred.[5] One may view the period as a sixth party system that reflects a new "stability";[6] voters, large numbers of whom are detached from either party, are only sometimes willing to entrust the national government to a single party; they seem slightly more likely to prefer a Republican to a Democratic president; yet they appear more likely to prefer Democratic to Republican Congresses. Described in this way, the sixth party system might easily persist for another decade or more. Alternatively, one may view the prolonged turbulence and indecisiveness since 1968 as an interlude to a Republican ascendancy or a Democratic revival.[7] In the nature of realignments, however, one must await the outcomes of the next two or three presidential elections. In either event, the era will be remembered as one in which both parties were transformed.

The changes within the parties are perhaps best understood by examining the several sectors or components of a political party: the party-in-the-electorate, the formal party organization, and the party-in-the-government.[8] The word "dealignment" captures much of the change in the first. Through the early 1960s more than 75 percent of the electorate identified strongly or weakly with one of the two major parties. By the late 1970s only about 60 percent did so, and more than a third said they were independents. Moreover, voters were less likely to see parties in favorable terms and to vote according to party identification. Such numbers made it easier for independent or third-party presidential candidates John Anderson (1980) and Ross Perot (1992 and 1996) to achieve vote shares of 7, 19, and 8 percent, respectively. Only during the nation-rending controversy over slavery was there another sixteen-year period in which as many third-party candidates received at least 7 percent of the popular vote. Ironically, as voters became estranged from the two parties in general, they became more "politically motivated by issues and ideology to a greater extent than they had been in the 1950s."[9] Increasingly voters became aligned with myriad single-issue interest groups on the right and left that sought to mobilize adherents through direct mail and other devices to influence elections and the lawmaking process.

Composition of the Democratic and Republican parties underwent changes as well. Ideologically, the parties moved apart: fewer liberal voters called themselves Republicans, just as fewer conservatives called themselves Democrats.[10] As the electorate shifted rightward on fiscal and some social matters, economic issues (such as taxes, deficits, and trade) remained important, to be sure, as did foreign policy, until the 1990s. But a variety of social issues—most of them newcomers to the national political agenda— were also salient: feminism, the environment, drug use, abortion, welfare, affirmative action, homosexuality, religion in public schools, flag protection, and immigration, as well as crime. Many of these became lumped into what would be called the "family values" agenda.

Demographically, Ronald Reagan's victorious presidential campaigns in 1980 and 1984 not only rested on strong support from white Southerners but elsewhere attracted working-class people, Catholics, and some Jews from the old Democratic coalition. Christian fundamentalists and evangelicals from the West and Midwest as well as the South backed Reagan in large numbers, many having been drawn into politics for the first time by Carter's candidacy in 1976.[11] By 1989, the Republican party remained fiscally conservative but was less "Eastern" and more "Sun Belt," less upperclass and "big business" and more middle- and working-class and entrepreneurial. For the first time since 1932, almost as many voters considered themselves Republican as Democratic, with voters twenty-eight and under favoring the Republicans 52 to 38 percent.[12] As of 1994, individuals and groups collectively labeled the "Christian Right," who were largely motivated by the family values agenda, had gained "substantial" or "dominant" influence in thirty-one of the fifty state Republican party organizations.[13] This was not the Republican party of Eisenhower's day, or even of Nixon's.

As manifested in the government and in organization, the national parties underwent functional and procedural changes as well. First, Democrats and Republicans in Congress became more ideologically distinct. The conservative bloc of Democrats diminished, as did the number of liberal Republicans, particularly in the House.[14] Second, within the electoral arena broadly defined, the parties found some of their traditional activities, such as mobilizing voters and bankrolling candidates, taken over by single-issue interest groups and political action committees (PACs—the political funding arms of interest groups, labor unions, and corporations). In 1985 the Supreme Court allowed PACs to assume an even larger role. If PACs spent money "independently" of a candidate's campaign, the usual federal limitations on campaign contributions did not apply.[15]

Third, national parties acquired new influence at the expense of state party organizations in at least two ways. More so than Republicans, Democrats after 1968 centralized and standardized preconvention procedures for nominating presidential candidates. New rules for the composition of the quadrennial summer conventions transferred control over the choice of a nominee from state party delegations selected under state party rules to voters in presidential primaries and caucuses who selected convention delegates under national rules and guidelines.[16]

However, greater national direction ironically resulted in a diminished role for party organization at all levels. Due partly to advances in technology, parties no longer held an "effective monopoly on the resources—the capital, the labor, and the flow of information—that were necessary to run an effective campaign."[17] "Plebiscitary appeals in terms of single issues, personality, or ideology"[18] replaced the traditional role of party leaders in the choice of a party's presidential candidate. The convention became less a decision-making body and more an assembly to ratify the results of five months of primaries and caucuses. A party-based nomination system shifted to media-oriented and candidate-centered politics. A would-be nominee could succeed independently of state party organizations by building a candidate-focused organization and hiring political consulting firms. Indeed, among Democrats, party leaders and elected officials are now assured of some voice at the national nominating convention *only* because of the creation in the 1980s of a class of "superdelegates" who, in 1996, amounted to 18 percent of voting delegates.[19]

Nonetheless, national party organizations eventually assumed an important place for themselves in the postconvention phase of the presidential election cycle. True, the introduction of public financing of presidential campaigns (with the corresponding prohibition on spending of other funds by a nominee's campaign) following Republican excesses in 1972 at first seemed to reinforce the relatively minor role that national party organizations had come to play in presidential politics.[20] Then a 1979 law allowed state parties to spend unlimited sums of money (much of which was provided by the national parties) for voter registration and get-out-the-vote drives.[21] Federal law also allowed the national parties to deploy such "soft money" for advertisements supporting or opposing candidates' stands or issues, a practice upheld by the Supreme Court, so long as the commercial did not expressly urge a vote for or against a particular candidate.[22] In 1996 even that limitation may have vanished when the Court applied its 1985 decision on PACs to the parties themselves: the latter could spend unlimited funds in support of a candidate, provided the media blitz remained "independent" of the nominee's own campaign organization.[23] Party hierarchy may no longer determine the presidential ticket, but it excels at generating cash for candidates who flourish in the new politics. Candidates are no longer in service to their parties; rather, parties are in service to their candidates.[24]

THE BURGER AND REHNQUIST COURTS

The Supreme Court that figured prominently in the elections of 1980 and 1984, like the Court of 1968, was a product of no single party or administration. The bench in 1980 reflected the handiwork of five presidents, and in 1984, of six. Justices William Brennan and Potter Stewart were the most senior in 1980, dating from the Eisenhower years. Justices Byron White and Thurgood Marshall, appointed by Kennedy and Johnson, respectively, also were holdovers from the Warren era. Next in rank were the four Nixon appointees: Chief Justice Warren Burger and Justices Harry Blackmun, Lewis Powell, and William Rehnquist. Justice John Stevens was President Ford's lone addition, in place of William O. Douglas. With one exception this same cast remained in place until the summer of 1986: Justice Stewart retired in mid-1981, opening the way for President Reagan's nomination of Sandra Day O'Connor.

The stability of this roster was remarkable. Between the swearings-in of Powell and Rehnquist in January 1972 and the retirement of Burger in the summer of 1986—fourteen and a half years—only two new faces appeared on the bench. One must go back to the Marshall Court in the early 1800s for anything comparable.[25] Given that Supreme Court vacancies occur, on average, about once every two years, it did not require the skills of an actuary to conclude that presidents elected in the 1980s might well be able to remake the Court.

Events proved the statisticians correct. To replace Burger, Reagan

turned to Rehnquist, making the fourteen-year veteran only the third sitting justice in Supreme Court history to become chief justice of the United
States.[26] Appeals Court Judge Antonin Scalia was the president's choice
for Rehnquist's seat. Reagan was thus not only the first president to name
a woman to the Supreme Court but also the first to select an Italian American. Anthony Kennedy was the third Reagan justice (as well as third
choice), after a protracted battle over Powell's successor in 1987. President
Bush's selections of Court of Appeals judges David Souter in 1990 and
Clarence Thomas in 1991, in place of Brennan and Marshall, respectively,
brought the total to five.

Beyond the new faces, the Burger/Rehnquist Court of the 1980s was
different in at least one major respect from the Warren Court. A new constitutional fault line opened, dividing the Court and constitutional scholars over the correct approach to constitutional interpretation, particularly
regarding the source of rights deemed worthy of special judicial guardianship. Expressed differently, this dispute derived from different answers
given to a deceptively simple question: What is "the Constitution" that is
interpreted? On one side of the divide is an approach called "interpretivism" that discerns the meaning of the Constitution from its words (the
text) and their historical context, including the intent of those who wrote
the Constitution and its amendments, and perhaps those who ratified
them. On the other side is "noninterpretivism." Its advocates do not deny
the usefulness of text and context, but rely as well on such things as principles derived from both, historical practice, natural law, and moral philosophy.[27] Neither approach necessarily produces a politically liberal or conservative result, although noninterpretivists have usually been associated
with the former and interpretivists with the latter.[28]

Evidence of this breach preceded the Burger/Rehnquist years, of
course.[29] But it was in the 1970s and 1980s that the debate acquired promi-
nence, defining constitutional discourse, dominating debates over Supreme
Court nominees, and filtering into presidential campaigns.

JUDICIAL ACTIONS

Had the Supreme Court continued merely to consolidate, modify, and
refine landmark rulings of the Warren Court, even the continuing debate
over some of them might have been insufficient to make the Court, once
again, a campaign whipping boy. Yet the Court fell into the briers of pres-

idential politics in 1980 and 1984 after a pronouncement on a single subject: abortion. The aftershocks of that case still roil the political system.

The Supreme Court is rarely precipitate. If decisions sometimes seem to be a surprise, they almost always rest to some degree on precedent. The past provides doctrinal steps that, even though they do not lead inexorably to a single destination, logically connect the outcome in one case with what has gone before. So it was with *Roe* v. *Wade* in 1973. Privacy had been a peripheral concern in several decisions,[30] but it was not until *Griswold* v. *Connecticut*[31] in 1965 that the Court first formally recognized privacy as a constitutional right. Held invalid in this landmark case was a state law that criminalized the use of "any drug, medicinal article or instrument for the purpose of preventing conception."

Abortion laws also affected the decision to bear a child. If a state could not proscribe birth control devices, could it nonetheless ban abortions? Most state governments believed that they could. Indeed, by 1972 only four states had repealed criminal penalties for most abortions.[32] Debated for decades, abortion remained an issue that sharply divided the American people, and an issue on which some held intense views. Depending on how one phrased the question, no more than 50 percent of the population was prepared to leave the abortion decision entirely to the woman and her doctor, and then only in the first three months of pregnancy.[33]

In the spring of 1972, challenges to abortion laws from Texas and Georgia were pending at the Supreme Court. Dating from the nineteenth century and similar to laws in twenty other states, the Texas statute was the more restrictive. All abortions were criminal except those necessary to preserve the life of the pregnant woman. Similar to those in about two dozen states, the Georgia statute embodied many of the recommendations of the American Law Institute's Model Penal Code of 1962 and allowed therapeutic, but not elective, abortions.

Because oral arguments in these cases had occurred in late 1971, the Court ordinarily would have decided them prior to its June adjournment. But this was no ordinary term. The departures of Hugo Black and John Harlan in September had left the bench two justices short, and replacements Powell and Rehnquist did not take their seats until January. Although five of the remaining seven justices seemed prepared to affirm the lower court rulings that had invalidated both the Texas and the Georgia laws, Chief Justice Burger, who was the most tenuous member of the pro-abortion bloc, persuaded the Court in the spring to set the cases for reargument before a full bench in the following term. But for Burger's tenacity, the Court would have announced *Roe* v. *Wade* and its Georgia companion, *Doe* v. *Bolton*[34] a few weeks before the Democratic and Republican national conventions. Had the Court not hesitated, future presidential campaigns might have unfolded differently.

As it was, abortion remained largely in the background as an election issue in 1972. Neither party platform mentioned it, although Democrats considered and voted down a pro-abortion minority plank, 1,570 to 1,103. Nixon was already on record as opposing "abortion on demand" but advocated no action by the federal government. In separate statements during the winter and spring of 1972, McGovern spoke of abortion as "a private matter which should be decided by a pregnant woman and her own doctor." Nonetheless, abortion was "a matter to be left to the state governments," which had "sole jurisdiction."[35] Seemingly, abortion was a subject too contentious for presidential politics.

What the national political process shunned, the Supreme Court embraced. Ten weeks after McGovern lost to Nixon in a landslide, seven justices announced that both the Texas and the Georgia abortion statutes were at odds with the Constitution. "[W]hether it be founded in the Fourteenth Amendment's concept of personal liberty . . . , as we feel it is, or . . . in the Ninth Amendment's reservations of rights to the people, [the right of privacy] is broad enough to encompass a woman's decision whether or not to terminate her pregnancy," wrote Justice Blackmun for the majority.[36] Being a fundamental right, privacy could be restricted only for "compelling" reasons, and in the context of abortion the state's interest in protecting "potential life" became compelling only in the third trimester of pregnancy. While a state's interest in guarding the health of the pregnant woman was sufficient to sustain certain medical regulations during the second trimester, at no point before the twenty-fifth week could a state ban abortion.

The Supreme Court in *Roe* occupied a position at odds with both parties, their 1972 presidential candidates, public opinion, and, the laws of forty-six states. Moreover, by lodging a protection for abortion in the Constitution, the Court dramatically expanded the abortion war. Activists on both sides had been accustomed to skirmishes on a state-by-state basis. As of 1973, opponents of abortion liberalization faced the stark reality that they had lost on a grand scale; they now had to think nationally as well as locally. Pro-abortion forces had captured the strategic high ground of constitutional law. No longer would a state's abortion laws be the product of clashing interests within its own legislature or judicial system. The battle between those who believed *Roe* was right and those who believed it was wrong soon would be joined in the federal courts, Congress, and presidential campaigns.[37]

Several years passed before the Supreme Court spoke again on the practical meaning of the newly declared abortion right. Cases arose because those who wanted to curtail abortions succeeded in enacting measures in many states to limit the availability of abortions and generally to discourage their use. Thus, in the only major abortion decisions between 1973 and the 1976 presidential election, *Planned Parenthood of Central Missouri* v. *Danforth*[38] and *Bellotti* v. *Baird (I)*[39] effectively nullified parental consent requirements for minors by prescribing a "judicial bypass" in circumstances where parents withheld consent or where the minor chose not to consult her parents. The former also invalidated a more comprehensive series of regulations.[40] Handed down on July 1, 1976, the pair signaled that the Court would subject abortion regulations to careful scrutiny but came too late to play a large role in that year's presidential campaign.

The rulings were among the first of a series of decisions through the summer of 1986 that declared, usually by votes of 6 to 3 or 5 to 4, most regulatory schemes constitutionally flawed. For example, because high expenses discourage abortions, locales could require abortions to be performed in hospitals after the first trimester only if "hospitals" were defined to include abortion clinics and outpatient surgical centers.[41] Also deemed unacceptably burdensome, usually on economic or psychological grounds or because of vagueness, were several varieties of "informed consent" rules,[42] parental notification rules[43] (but for minors in certain circumstances, states could mandate parental notification, "if possible," by the performing physician[44]), a twenty-four-hour waiting period between the signing of the consent form and the abortion,[45] a stipulation for disposal of fetal remains in a "humane and sanitary manner,"[46] reporting of all abortions to the state[47] (*pathological* reports for each abortion were deemed acceptable),[48] and fetal protection requirements[49] (but a second doctor could be mandated for postviability abortions.)[50]

Constitutionally, cost mattered less when public funds were at issue. In 1977 six justices upheld Connecticut's policy that denied Medicaid reimbursement for elective abortions while reimbursing expenses for childbirth, even though opponents of the measure argued that the policy forced poor women to carry an unwanted pregnancy to full term.[51] Three years later five justices extended that ruling to Congress. The recently enacted Hyde Amendment (so named for its sponsor, Republican Representative Henry

Hyde of Illinois) went a step beyond Connecticut's restriction and barred the spending of federal Medicaid funds even for most medically necessary abortions.[52] The majority reasoned that the ban placed no obstacle in the way of an abortion. A poor woman was no worse off than had no Medicaid funds been made available for any medical procedures.

These concessions to legislative majorities aside, it was evident by 1980 and unmistakable by 1984 that the Court envisaged no retreat on *Roe* v. *Wade*. Those who longed for *Roe*'s demise realized that significant state legislative barriers to abortion were doomed. If the existing Court would not change its mind, they would have to change the Constitution, or the Court.

THE CAMPAIGNS OF 1980 AND 1984

Pro-choice groups such as the National Abortion Rights Action League, the Planned Parenthood Federation, the National Organization for Women, and the American Civil Liberties Union were probably less well organized politically at the grass roots in the mid-1970s than were antiabortionists, but for the former it mattered less. Their influence had always stemmed from their legal staffs and their central offices,[53] and they now had the Constitution on their side. Defense requires less exertion than offense.

Abortion foes such as the U.S. Catholic Conference, the National Committee for a Human Life Amendment that it created, the National Council of Catholic Bishops, the Right to Life party and the Moral Majority (both organized in 1978), and the Pro-Life Action League realized the necessity of a crusade on a national scale. They needed candidates for the presidency and other offices who were fully committed to the antiabortion stance.[54] And they needed time.

The post-Watergate midterm elections of 1974 had already witnessed the defeat or retirement of some leading antiabortion champions. The Senate in 1975 tabled a proposal that would have ended federal Medicaid funding for abortions and voted down several constitutional amendments, pending for two years, that would have overturned *Roe*.[55] Another anti-*Roe* amendment, pushed strongly in the Senate by North Carolina Republican Jesse Helms, failed in March 1976.[56] Moreover, abortion as an issue was virtually absent from Senate hearings in December 1975 on Ford's nomination of John Stevens as associate justice.[57]

In 1976 Democratic presidential contender Jimmy Carter personally disapproved of abortion but opposed a constitutional amendment to end the practice, as did Republican incumbent Ford. Instead, Ford favored the status quo ante—an amendment that would return abortion policy to the states. Of major contenders for the Democratic and Republican nominations, only Ronald Reagan was uncompromising in his criticism both of abortion and of policies that countenanced the practice.[58] Indeed, with Ford claiming a lead of barely sixty delegates in the days before the Republican convention, Reagan tried to woo uncommitted delegates by claiming, among other things, that Ford was duplicitous on the issue.[59]

With Ford and Carter heading their respective tickets, neither pro- nor antiabortion rights activists could point to an outspoken champion in the fall campaign. Both men avoided polarizing extremes and played down the issue in their campaigns. However, the middle ground that both tried to occupy was reflected more in the Democratic than in the Republican platform. The latter bore the mark of Reagan's unsuccessful candidacy. Acknowledging "the question of abortion" to be "one of the most difficult and controversial of our time," Republicans protested "the Supreme Court's intrusion into the family structure through its denial of the parents' obligation and right to guide their minor children" (an oblique reference to *Bellotti* and *Central Missouri*), and supported "the efforts of those who seek enactment of a constitutional amendment to restore protection of the right to life for unborn children." Yet they took note of those who "assumed a stance somewhere in between polar positions," and called for "a continuance of the public dialogue on abortion."[60] Considerably more briefly, Democrats "fully recognize[d] the religious and ethical nature of the concerns which many Americans have on the subject of abortion. We feel, however, that it is undesirable to attempt to amend the U.S. Constitution to overturn the Supreme Court decision in this area."[61]

Democratic Catholics opposed to abortion thus had only a mild incentive to vote for Ford. Indeed, Carter's share of the Catholic and labor vote was more than enough to move states such as New York and Pennsylvania into the Democratic column, without which Ford would have won.[62] Apolitical or Democratic-leaning Protestant evangelicals had little reason not to vote for Carter. A self-proclaimed "born-again" Southern Baptist who taught a Sunday school class, Carter "mobilized the evangelicals as no candidate had done before."[63]

An intelligent man to whom voters consistently gave high marks for honesty and integrity, Carter came to the White House with broader experience than many of his predecessors. By mid-1979, however, his presidency had fallen upon hard times. The economy was in severe recession, and there were long lines at gasoline stations. The administration seemed inept. In the summer and fall Carter's approval rating in the polls hovered at 30–32 percent.[64]

A sign of Carter's shaky standing within his own party was Senator Edward Kennedy's announcement on November 7 that he would challenge Carter for the 1980 Democratic presidential nomination.[65] The declaration came only three days after Iranians overran the U.S. embassy in Tehran, taking American personnel hostage, and seven weeks before the Soviet Union invaded Afghanistan on December 27. Because the American people typically rally around the president in the early stages of an international crisis, the Tehran event alone doubled Carter's approval rating. This, along with the usual advantages of incumbency, gave Carter a boost that lasted long enough for him to finish first in fourteen of the nineteen presidential primaries from February through May. After the U.S. military mission to rescue the hostages failed on April 24, with eight Marines dying in the Iranian desert, Carter's standing sagged again, allowing Kennedy to win five of the remaining seven contests.[66] By this time, however, it was too late to derail the president's renomination even though his approval rating was again 30 percent.[67] Carter had amassed enough delegates, and fought back an attempt by Kennedy to force an "open convention"—to repeal the party rule that bound delegates to support their candidates.[68]

Carter hoped that columnist James Reston had been right. If Republicans nominated Ronald Reagan, Reston wrote in March, they would be choosing "Carter's favorite opponent. . . . Seldom in the history of American politics has a party out of power shown so much generosity to a President in such deep difficulty."[69] Republicans appeared to accommodate Democrats by nominating Reagan in July, an outcome that had seemed near-certain after Reagan outpaced moderate contenders George Bush (whom Reagan would choose as his running mate) and John Anderson (who launched an independent campaign for the presidency on April 24) in the midspring primaries. The man who had placed Barry Goldwater's name in nomination at the 1964 Republican convention, Reagan was the favorite of his party's right, dominant now as it had not been since that debacle. New delegate selection rules worked to Reagan's advantage in 1980, just as they had almost brought about an upset of Ford in 1976.

The New Right, as it was called, had two principal contingents: social and cultural conservatives and entrepreneurial conservatives. The former owed much of their political influence to Reverend Jerry Falwell and his

Moral Majority. They were animated by a family values agenda that abhorred the Supreme Court's decisions on abortion and school busing, and its steadfast adherence to Warren Court rulings on matters such as school prayer. They were convinced that, morally, the country was headed in the wrong direction and that the government had to do something about it. Reagan's mantra captured their concerns: "family, work, neighborhood, peace and freedom."[70] The entrepreneurial faction was driven by the prospects of renewed economic prosperity based on less regulation and lower taxes. Both were joined by traditional Republican believers in fiscal conservatism and a strong defense. "Reaganism," James Q. Wilson wrote a month before the election, "stands in opposition to those who believe in the unrestrained right of personal self-expression and the need for government to rationalize all other aspects of human affairs by rule and procedure."[71]

In their platform Republicans promised to reverse "America's international humiliation and decline," claimed "economic growth and full employment without inflation" as the party's "foremost goal," and sought "a rebirth of liberty and resurgence of private initiatives." For the first time Republicans failed to endorse ratification of the Equal Rights Amendment. Moreover, they not only reiterated the 1976 document's support "of a constitutional amendment to restore protection of the right to life for unborn children," but also called on "Congress to restore the right of individuals to participate in voluntary, non-denominational prayer in schools and other public facilities." The party "condemn[ed] the forced busing of school children to achieve arbitrary racial quotas . . . [that] has been a prescription for disaster," and demanded "the appointment of judges at all levels of the judiciary who respect traditional family values and the sanctity of innocent human life."[72] The meaning of that final pledge was unmistakable: one's stand on *Roe* v. *Wade* was to be a litmus test for appointments to the federal courts.[73]

The contrast with the Democratic platform was stark: "The Democratic Party supports the 1973 Supreme Court decision on abortion rights as the law of the land and opposes any constitutional amendment to restrict or overturn that decision."[74] Moreover, against Carter's wishes and the Hyde Amendment, the convention endorsed the federal Medicaid funding for abortions that the Supreme Court had declined to decree in June.[75]

Reagan's success at the July convention was now his problem and Carter's hope. Would 1980 repeat the results of 1964? He secured the nomination by amassing delegates, and to win delegates he had to appeal to the few—to the comparatively small number of conservative voters in Republican primaries and caucuses. But winning the election would require an appeal to the many—to independents and Democrats, all the while retaining his Republican base. Reagan sought to accomplish this objective through a five-point strategy. The campaign downplayed the agenda of the social conservatives,[76] instead depicting Republicans as the "party of jobs" and Democrats as the "party of recession."[77] The nation needed to restore competence in the Oval Office and American prestige abroad, yet the campaign tried to allay doubts that Reagan was a trigger-happy cold warrior, all the while reassuring skeptics that he had no intention of tampering with New Deal legacies such as Social Security.[78]

Democrats countered by portraying Reagan as a danger to the country and a tool of the right who stood well outside the mainstream. In remarks to the annual NAACP convention in July, Carter reminded members of what was at stake. "[C]onsider very carefully and very seriously how this nation's future will be affected by the . . . United States Supreme Court." The Court had been "a final bulwark of freedom" for blacks, but Republicans had "made a profound impact" on the Court in recent years. "You just think what will happen with another three or four appointments."[79]

The Republican "litmus test" handed Democrats a court-packing issue. Reagan's election would endanger the Court as the "center of gravity of fairness, equality, and humaneness," charged Jack Greenberg, head of the NAACP Legal Defense Fund, raising the "prospect of a wide swing in judicial orientation toward right-wing ideology." In contrast to President Carter's appointments to the federal bench that "deserve[d] high marks," Reagan would attempt to "ensure ideological purity. . . . Those who object to one or another of the Carter policies . . . must ask whether four or five Reaganites on the Court will transform it into the kind of Court that will help create the kind of America they want to live in, and have their children live in, for the next generation—not merely the next four years."[80]

The organized bar joined the chorus. Leonard Janofsky, former president of the American Bar Association, labeled the Republican position "improper . . . very dangerous and out of order." "I can't conceive of anyone in his right mind—lawyer or nonlawyer—conceiving of such an insidious, such an insidious thing," added Albert Jenner, former chair of the ABA's judicial selection committee.[81] The ABA's House of Delegates voted overwhelmingly to oppose the selection of judges on the basis of ideological criteria.[82] With Harvard Law School's Laurence Tribe and former Kennedy administration assistant Harris Wofford among the signatories, a group called Americans Concerned for the Judiciary sponsored an advertisement in the *New York Times* that was reminiscent of the campaign of 1896: depicted was "The Class of '81"—nine Ronald Reagan look-alike justices wielding a "right wing 'philosophic' test."[83] Justice Blackmun confided to Justices Brennan and Marshall that "the forces of emotion and professed morality are winning some battles.... I earnestly hope that the 'war' ... will not be lost."[84]

The alarm drove Republicans to countermeasures. Despite Reagan's observation that *Roe* v. *Wade* was "an abuse of power worse than Watergate,"[85] his campaign denied the use of any litmus test and insisted that, without regard for "race, creed, or color," he would seek judges with "integrity" who believed in "judicial restraint."[86] To divert the Democratic attack, Reagan moved forthrightly on October 14: "I am announcing today that one of the first Supreme Court vacancies in my administration will be filled by the most qualified woman I can find. ... "[87] Prominent conservatives in the bar such as Robert H. Bork and Antonin Scalia sponsored an advertisement in the *New York Times* promising that Reagan would "take partisan politics out of judicial selection." Claiming that Carter's appointees to the federal bench agreed with him on a wide range of policy questions,[88] conservatives contrasted Reagan, who sought merely a "broad compatibility" with his judicial philosophy of self-restraint to allow the people, not judges, to govern.[89]

Carter's defeat on November 4 was not a total surprise. The economic outlook remained gloomy, and Americans remained hostage in Iran a year after their capture. However, the margin of Reagan's victory was unexpected. With 51 percent of the popular vote, his sweep was nationwide, leaving Carter with only six states plus the District of Columbia. Without Anderson's fiscally conservative but socially liberal independent candidacy that amassed 7 percent of the vote, Carter perhaps would have carried several Northeastern states but the results of the race would have been unchanged. Reagan ran only eight points behind Carter among labor union households; 65 percent of the voters comprising the Christian Right supported Reagan, compared with 55 percent of white voters as a whole. Among Catholics, Reagan ran five points ahead of Ford's 1976 share.[90]

Republicans ran well in Congress, too. The party's net gain of thirty-three seats in the House of Representatives left it still in a minority but was the largest increase for Republicans since 1966. Results in Senate races were even more impressive: with fifty-three members, Republicans would be in the majority for the first time since 1953–1955.

The enlarged Republican presence on Capitol Hill and a sympathetic president begot the most Court-curbing bills in over a decade: twenty-three in the House and four in the Senate, all by late spring of 1981. Dealing variously with abortion, school prayer, and school busing, these bills and others that followed fell into three categories. The first group called for overturning objectionable decisions by constitutional amendment.[91] Because of the supermajorities stipulated by the Constitution for ratification, this tactic was the least likely to succeed, although it was probably the most dispositive if it did.

Pointing to Congress's power to define the appellate jurisdiction of the Supreme Court, others would withdraw the Court's authority—and/or the authority of lower federal courts, too—to hear certain types of cases. State supreme courts would thus possess the final authority on the meaning of particular parts of the Constitution in their respective states, but this tactic would not affect what the state court rulings would be. Assuming that Congress had the authority to take such drastic steps—itself a point of contention—even some of the Court's critics were troubled by the precedent that would be set, perhaps jeopardizing the Court's role in the constitutional system.[92]

In the third category was the Human Life Bill that arose from Blackmun's confession in *Roe* v. *Wade* of judicial inability to decide when life begins. Resting on Congress's authority, under section 5 of the Fourteenth Amendment, to enforce the rights granted therein (one of them being the right to "life"), this measure declared plainly that life began at conception and directed states to regulate abortions as they chose. Moreover, the lower federal courts would be denied jurisdiction over cases challenging the constitutionality of state abortion laws, although appeals in abortion cases could still be taken from a state supreme court to the U.S. Supreme Court. Although it avoided the practical difficulties of a constitutional amendment, the Human Life Bill held out a potentially empty promise. Nothing would prevent a determined Supreme Court from finding it, or any state law pursuant to it, unconstitutional.[93]

Focusing on its economic agenda during most of 1981, the Reagan administration at first delayed serious support for some Court-curbing legislation. Accordingly, the nomination of Sandra Day O'Connor to replace retiring Justice Stewart on the Supreme Court in the summer of 1981 encountered no difficulty in the Senate, where she was confirmed 99–0 on September 21. The only opposition came from the right: Reverend Jerry Falwell's Moral Majority and antiabortion groups claimed that she was "unsound" on abortion.

Two months later, Attorney General William French Smith signaled growing administration interest in reining in the judiciary. Addressing the Federal Legal Council, Smith noted "three areas of judicial policy-making" that had "led to some constitutionally dubious and unwise intrusions upon the legislative domain" and were of "particular concern": "the erosion of restraint," "analysis of so-called 'fundamental rights,'" and "the extravagant use of mandatory injunctions and remedial decrees. . . . No one should doubt," he concluded, "that this Administration's adherence to the constitutional principle of separation of powers will exact from us the same degree of obedience and moderation that we will urge upon the courts."[94]

Smith's remarks highlighted another way in which the administration hoped to move its social agenda: legal advocacy. Solicitor General Rex Lee and his successor, Charles Fried, advanced the administration's views in cases before the Supreme Court. Even when the United States was not party to a case, the "SG" could file a brief as amicus curiae, or friend of the court. At the start of the Supreme Court's 1983 term, for example, the Justice Department had expressed its views to the justices on more than half the 113 cases already set for argument.[95]

While the administration achieved some of its objectives in court (as discussed in the next section), none of the Court-curbing proposals passed Congress.[96] Indeed, while the party division in the Senate remained largely unchanged in 1983 and 1984, the Republican position was weaker in the House because Democrats gained twenty-six seats in the 1982 midterm elections. Barring a dramatic increase in their strength in both houses in the 1984 contests, Republicans realized that any significant corrective steps would probably have to come from the Court itself. Thus, for Democrats and Republicans alike the forthcoming presidential election would be a struggle for the Supreme Court.

The reasons for this were plain. The Reagan administration had demonstrated its intent to advance its social agenda judicially. Moreover, the collective age of the Supreme Court was the second oldest in history, just behind the "Nine Old Men" who had plagued Franklin Roosevelt during his first term. By Inauguration Day 1985, five of the nine justices would be seventy-six or older, and these five comprised all but one of the remaining votes on the bench in defense of *Roe* v. *Wade*. Those who in 1980 had stressed Reagan's probable impact on the Supreme Court knew that his first term was marked by a single judicial vacancy. Democratic campaign oratory that seemed urgent then was apocalyptic now. Constitutionally, the election seemed the most compelling since 1936.

"We must win to save the Supreme Court of the United States," cried future Democratic nominee Walter Mondale in December 1983. "If that Court is replaced by Mr. Reagan, it could well be that our great cause of justice will be doomed for the lifetime of everyone in this room."[97] Campaigning in the New Hampshire primary, Democratic Senator John Glenn of Ohio warned that Reagan would reshape the Court in his "far-right political ideology." The age of the Court "is one of the great issues in this Presidential campaign."[98] Staff at the *New York Times* inquired of each justice as to the state of his or her health.[99] "It takes a bit longer for a President to turn the tide of constitutional interpretation than to reduce taxes and social programs," observed Stuart Taylor. "But Ronald Reagan is working on it."[100] Justice Rehnquist, the most reliably conservative of Nixon's quartet of appointments, entered the fray, minimizing the impact of any president on the Court. "Presidents who wish to pack the Supreme Court, like murder suspects in a detective novel, must have both motive and opportunity," he asserted at the University of Minnesota. Even with both, "a number of factors militate against a president having anything more than partial success."[101]

Appointments of conservative jurists such as Robert Bork, Antonin Scalia, and Kenneth Starr to the lower federal courts were important, too.[102] The White House's Committee on Judicial Selection, advised judicial scholar Sheldon Goldman, provided "the most consistent ideological or policy-orientation screening of judicial candidates since the first term of Franklin Roosevelt."[103]

Democratic trepidations and Republican aspirations reflected the dilemma of the conservative judges sought by the Reagan administration. Judicial restraint—the new order of the day—would not necessarily serve conservative values. "Fundamental structural principles of constitutional law would almost certainly be re-examined and perhaps replaced," cautioned Professor Tribe.[104] On abortion and school prayer, for example, deference to the past would only preserve the status quo Reaganites disdained. To be effective, the new breed of judge would have to be activist, even "radical," toppling pillars of "long-settled constitutional law," wrote Floyd Abrams in a newspaper duel with Attorney General Smith.[105] "[T]he President has taken issue with the Bill of Rights itself,"[106] Abrams claimed. "The personal policy preferences of the individuals in the black robes have nothing to do with the meaning of the Constitution and have no place in judicial decisions," replied Smith. Moreover, "the fact that a constitutional doctrine is long settled does not make it correct or unalterable." Besides, "decisions on abortion and school prayer, as well as the Warren Court's holdings in the criminal law area, are all less than 25 years old—not long at all in constitutional or historical terms. . . . [T]hey have always been, and remain, controversial."[107] Others spoke with less circumspection. "One person, one vote," *Roe* v. *Wade*, and *Miranda*, "all that's going to go out the window," exclaimed former Justice Department official Bruce Fein, who gleefully predicted the "greatest change in direction since 1937."[108]

The candidates' positions and the platforms of their respective parties reflected the polarity. "God never should have been expelled from America's classrooms," Reagan proclaimed in his 1983 State of the Union address.[109] By denying "the value of certain human lives," *Roe* v. *Wade* was as wrong as the decision in *Dred Scott*, he maintained.[110] "[A] fetus is already protected by the Constitution," he said in his first televised debate with Mondale. In contrast, Mondale endorsed the 1973 abortion decision and landmarks on school prayer.[111]

"The hard truth," warned the Democratic platform, "is that if Mr. Reagan is reelected our most vigorous defender of the rule of law—the United States Supreme Court—could be lost to the cause of equal justice for another generation." Reaffirming support for affirmative action and for "the 1973 Supreme Court decision on abortion rights as the law of the land," and pledging resistance to "all efforts to weaken decisions" on church and state, Democrats saw "little doubt that a Supreme Court chosen by Ronald Reagan would radically restrict constitutional rights and drastically reinterpret existing laws. . . . No one knows the full extent of the damage Reagan could wreak on this country in another term. But we do know one thing: we cannot afford to find out."[112]

Republicans "commend[ed] the President for appointing federal judges committed to the rights of law-abiding citizens and traditional family values. . . . In his second term, President Reagan will continue to appoint Supreme Court and other federal judges who share our commitment to judicial restraint." Including identical language on abortion from the 1980 platform, they added that "[t]he unborn child has a fundamental individual right to life which cannot be infringed." Calling for economic opportunity, they opposed "efforts to replace equal rights with discriminatory quota systems and preferential treatment." "Mindful of our religious diversity," they reaffirmed commitment "to the freedoms of religion and speech" and supported "the rights of students to openly practice [*sic*] the same, including the right to engage in voluntary prayer in schools."[113]

The constitutional stakes in the election were considerably greater than suspense about its outcome.[114] With 59 percent of the vote and the electoral votes of every state save Mondale's Minnesota (and the District of Columbia), Reagan's personal triumph was of historic proportions. The Court issue probably helped Democrats to energize party regulars but cost Reagan few votes. Mondale's promise to reverse swelling budget deficits with a tax increase stood little chance against Reagan's promise not to raise taxes. Mondale's effort to paint Republicans as the party of the rich ran into Republican charges that he was the tool of "the special interests." Even Geraldine Ferraro's vice presidential candidacy—marking the first time that a major party had placed a woman on the national ticket—was offset by questions about her finances and her husband's real estate business. Reagan received 80 percent of the born-again Christian vote, 61 percent of the Catholic vote, and a slim majority of the votes from union households.[115]

The landslide, however, all but missed Congress. Democrats achieved a net gain of two seats in the Senate, but remained in the minority. Republicans gained only fourteen seats in the House, fewer than they lost in 1982. The new rules of electoral combat that had transformed presidential nomination politics allowed constituent groups to maintain issues salient to them in the forefront of a campaign. And by dividing control of the government between the parties, dealignment had struck again.

EFFECTS

In contrast to the election of 1968, the Supreme Court and social issues, as conspicuous in the campaign as they were, did not measurably affect the outcome of the election of 1984. Reagan's popularity was sufficiently great to have defeated Mondale had social issues such as abortion not energized some of Reagan's ardent supporters. Many voters picked Reagan in spite of, not because of, his stand on abortion. The role of social issues in the election of 1980 is more problematic. The Supreme Court's decision in Roe v. Wade single-handedly nationalized abortion, in much the same way that the justices already had nationalized crime, school prayer, and other concerns. Indeed, it is difficult to visualize how presidential politics would have unfolded after 1976 had Roe v. Wade never happened. The saliency of abortion surely contributed to Reagan's near success in 1976 and to his nomination in 1980. Without Reagan's emphasis on social issues through the spring of 1980, Anderson's independent candidacy might never have materialized. Reagan might have beaten Carter, but without the social issues he might not have had the chance. Someone else at the head of the Republican ticket might not have run as well against Carter.

More evident are the effects on the parties. In 1973 *Roe* v. *Wade* was neither "Democratic" or "Republican" because the Court aligned itself with the position of neither party, and presidents of both parties had appointed the justices in the *Roe* majority. Instead, abortion was a crosscutting issue that encouraged some voter realignment while it motivated some people to become politically active for the first time. By rallying behind *Roe* v. *Wade*, Democrats became not only the pro-choice party but also the party of choice for those for whom the issue of reproductive freedom was highly salient. Combined with the advent of candidate-centered presidential nomination politics, the decision transformed the GOP. It is not merely that the party has appealed to common folk who in an earlier decade would have voted Democratic, or not voted at all. Rather, the party's antiabortion plank that followed *Roe* has cemented social conservatives into the Republican electoral base. The phenomenon that seemed aberrant in 1964 and possibly ad hoc in 1968 (because it was temporarily useful to Nixon) is now both a fixture and a defining force. Without *Roe* v. *Wade*, coming as it did five years after the convulsive campaign of 1968, social conservatives might not have taken up residence mainly in the GOP, thus hastening the decline of "me-too Republicanism."

The Court's entanglement in partisan controversy after 1973 also ignited a debate that moved beyond case-specific critiques of its work. "We are dealing with a question of power: Who is to govern in our democracy, who is to make policy decisions for the nation—a group of unelected and virtually unaccountable Justices or the elected representatives of the people, indeed, the people themselves?"[116] Along with assertions that cases reached the wrong results were fundamental objections to the role the Supreme Court assumed after 1937 as the architect, guardian, and arbiter of individual liberty. The conflict has been as much a matter of who decides as it has been of what is to be decided. Statistics offer a hint of the magnitude of the debate. Between September 1970 and August 1973, English-language legal periodicals (consisting almost entirely of law reviews published by U.S. law schools) printed only five articles dealing generally with theories of American constitutional interpretation. Between September 1985 and August 1988, the number swelled to seventy-seven.[117]

This juristic combat has most often erupted along the fault line of interpretivism versus noninterpretivism (sometimes also called textualism versus nontextualism). Advocates of the former are frequently among the

Court's harshest critics, and advocates of the latter are among its most ardent defenders. The controversy centers on the response one makes to "silences" in the Constitution. For interpretivists, unless constitutional text or history speaks clearly, judges are obliged to defer to the will of the majority as expressed in state and national laws. "The original Constitution was devoted primarily to the mechanisms of democratic choice," counseled Judge Robert Bork. "Constitutional scholarship today is dominated by the creation of arguments that will encourage judges to thwart democratic choice." Accordingly, "the framers' intentions with respect to freedoms are the sole legitimate premise from which constitutional analysis may proceed."[118] A decision like *Roe* v. *Wade* was "the assumption of illegitimate judicial power and a usurpation of the democratic authority of the American people."[119]

In 1985 Edwin Meese, Smith's successor as attorney general in the Reagan administration, revealed the momentous implications of this approach when he called for a "jurisprudence of original intention" to replace the "jurisprudence of idiosyncrasy" that had licensed judges to decide cases on what they believe "constitutes sound public policy." Placed in doubt were not only the abortion and church–state rulings but also the long line of decisions, stretching back over a half-century, applying the Bill of Rights to the states. "A Constitution . . . viewed as only what the judges say it is, is no longer a constitution in the true sense."[120] Echoing laments of Presidents Jackson and Lincoln, he denied that Supreme Court decisions are "binding on all persons and parts of the government, henceforth and forever more." The Court's decisions are not, like the Constitution itself, the "law of the land."[121]

Brennan was one of the first to respond to Meese,[122] in a defense of the Court's role by a sitting justice that was the most striking since Chief Justice John Marshall's day. Meese's "view emphasizes not the transcendent historical authority of the framers but the predominant contemporary authority of the elected branches of government," argued Brennan. Interpretivists were guilty of "facile historicism" and established

> a presumption of resolving textual ambiguities against the claim of constitutional right. . . . This is a choice no less political than any other; it expresses antipathy to claims of the minority to rights against the majority. Those who would restrict claims of right to the values of 1789 . . . turn a blind eye to social progress and eschew adaptation of overarching principles to changes of social circumstance.[123]

For Brennan the Constitution's open-ended phrases were a mandate for judges to infer rights from general principles implied by the Constitution.

Echoes of the Meese–Brennan debate continue,[124] and may well influence the next generation of legal scholars and judges. What is certain is that this constitutional maelstrom profoundly affected the politics of nomination and confirmation to the Supreme Court for the next six years. The vortex may also have affected the pace of appointments, giving Court liberals all the more reason to "hang on" as long as physically and mentally possible.[125]

When Chief Justice Burger announced his retirement in June 1986, Reagan promptly nominated Justice Rehnquist for the center seat and federal appeals judge (and former law professor) Antonin Scalia as associate justice.[126] Although Republicans still held a small majority in the Senate as a result of the 1984 elections, liberal Democrats tried to derail both nominations by opposing Rehnquist. Republicans replied that Rehnquist's views on the Constitution, revealed in nearly fifteen years of judicial opinions, were irrelevant. Preferring to forget their party's opposition to Abe Fortas in 1965 and 1968, they wanted to confine the debate to character and merit. Democrats disagreed. If the president took a nominee's views into account, should not the Senate do the same? Other opponents directed questions to surrogate issues,[127] some of which had been vetted in his 1971 hearings, that cast doubt on his fitness to serve. Hearings on Rehnquist consumed four days, and Senate floor debate, five. Confirmation, 65–33, in September was the first since Taney's in 1836 whereby a nominee for chief justice was approved by a ratio of less than 2:1.

With Democratic energy exhausted on Rehnquist, Scalia's nomination generated only mild turbulence: two days of hearings and floor debate of only five minutes preceded a confirmation vote of 98–0. Although Reagan got his way, liberals knew that even with the addition of Scalia, the Court's alignment on the all-consuming abortion question remained unchanged. The original 7–2 split in *Roe* v. *Wade* had shifted to 6–3 with O'Connor's arrival in 1981 and then to 5–4 after Burger switched sides in 1983.

Justice Powell's retirement in 1987, however, was different. *Roe*'s future seemed to rest on the vote of his successor. With an opportunity to advance his social agenda judicially, Reagan turned to federal appeals judge Robert Bork. With Bork known as the nation's most prolific critic of the constitutional underpinnings of *Roe*, the nomination was guaranteed to be rancorous. The elections of 1986 had shifted control of the Senate to the

Democrats for the first time in six years. Joseph Biden, not Strom Thurmond, chaired the Judiciary Committee. Two of the Democrats on that committee (Biden and Paul Simon) were running for president. Moreover, Reagan himself was politically weaker in mid-1987 than in mid-1986. Intervening was the Iran–contra affair,[128] which had distracted, and shaken public confidence in, the administration.

Before the Judiciary Committee began its record-setting twelve days of hearings (Bork would testify and be questioned on five of them), battle lines had already been drawn. Hesitation expressed in 1986 over close scrutiny of a nominee's judicial philosophy all but vanished. Biden and other Democrats announced well before the hearings began that they would vote against Bork.

Cooperating with Democrats was the Leadership Conference on Civil Rights, an umbrella organization of nearly 200 groups. It coordinated a massive public relations drive to galvanize public opposition. Nearly 2,000 law school professors signed a petition urging rejection (only 300 had publicly opposed Carswell in 1970). Direct mail, television and newspaper advertisements, and other techniques of modern interest-group politics for the first time were aimed squarely against a Supreme Court nominee. Not since President Woodrow Wilson nominated Louis Brandeis in 1916 had confirmation politics been so vitriolic. On October 23, Bork's opponents prevailed, 58–42, a larger negative vote than either Haynsworth or Carswell had endured.

On October 29, Reagan next turned to Judge Douglas Ginsburg, one of Bork's colleagues on the District of Columbia Circuit, but conflict-of-interest questions about Ginsburg surfaced immediately. When Ginsburg acknowledged using marijuana while a member of the Harvard Law faculty in the 1970s, his nomination went up in a puff of smoke. On November 7 he withdrew his name from consideration.

Time was critical. Reagan was about to start his last year in office. "Lame duck" talk abounded. Like Johnson with Fortas in 1968, the vacancy might carry over to his successor in 1989. On November 10, Reagan made his third move, picking long-time acquaintance Judge Anthony Kennedy of the Ninth Circuit Court of Appeals, in whom a fatigued Senate could find little fault. An hour's floor debate on February 3, 1988, preceded the vote to confirm, 97–0.

Bork's defeat dictated strategy for President George Bush in 1990 when Justice Brennan retired. With a Senate still in Democratic hands, Bush was in no position to advance a contentious nominee. Instead, he picked recently confirmed First Circuit Appeals Judge David Souter, whom Chief of Staff Sununu, as New Hampshire's governor, had once named to that state's supreme court. With no paper trail of articles and speeches and with only brief service on the federal bench, Souter—a political protege and close friend of New Hampshire's U.S. Senator Warren Rudman—was an unknown, "the stealth candidate," said Alabama's Senator Howell Heflin. Bush denied asking Souter his views on abortion or anything else, but Democrats on the Judiciary Committee unabashedly asked the questions Bush presumably had not, leaving no doubt that abortion was the ever-present issue at the hearings. While Souter answered some questions on constitutional interpretation, he remained silent on the abortion right. Having denied opponents a chance to mobilize the kind of opposition that had worked against the effusive Bork, he was confirmed 90–9 on October 2.

Thurgood Marshall, the Court's first black justice and the surviving member of the Warren Court's liberal majority, retired in 1991. More than any other living American, he was as much a symbol of, as he had been an initiator of, the civil rights revolution. The irony created by Marshall's departure escaped few. As an outspoken opponent of racial quotas, would Bush name a black person in Marshall's place? The suspense was short-lived, as Bush announced the nomination of Clarence Thomas, a prominent African-American Republican, whom Bush had placed on the Court of Appeals for the D.C. Circuit only one year before. The nominee was on record as rejecting much of what Marshall had strived for: busing to achieve racial integration and race-based preferences, among other things. During five days of hearings in the Senate, however, Democrats were no more successful with Thomas than with Souter in drawing out his view on the right to abortion.

Objection to what Democrats suspected Thomas's constitutional values to be, combined with concern over his qualifications, led the Judiciary Committee to split 7–7. The nomination thus went to the floor without a recommendation, but supporters expected confirmation because Southern Democrats who had opposed Bork now felt pressure from some black constituents to support Thomas. Then events took an unexpected turn. A "leak" revealed that Professor Anita Hill of the University of Oklahoma School of Law, who had worked for Thomas at the Department of Education and the Equal Employment Opportunity Commission, had lodged charges of sexual harassment with the Judiciary Committee.

Back went the nomination to the Judiciary Committee. What followed was a television spectacle: twenty-eight hours of additional hearings marked by lurid details, bitter charges and countercharges, and equally bitter denials and counterdenials. The charges were potentially fatal for the nomination. Thomas, after all, had headed the agency responsible for enforcing the law against sexual harassment. The charges undercut his principal asset. Without a record of legal scholarship or lengthy judicial service, the nomination had rested all along on character—precisely what Hill called into question. On October 15, such doubts helped to make the Senate's vote to confirm, 52–48, one of the closest for a successful Supreme Court nominee. Only the approval of Stanley Matthews, 24–23, in 1881, generated a higher percentage of negative votes.

President Bush never anticipated the catalytic effects of the Thomas nomination. The hearings gave high visibility to sexual harassment in the workplace,[129] cast Republicans in the role of those who did not appear to take the matter seriously, and in the 1992 election constituted one of several factors leading to increased participation by women candidates, contributors, and voters, mostly on the Democratic side.[130]

The twelve Reagan-Bush years allowed Republicans to place five new justices on the Supreme Court in addition to Rehnquist, exactly what Democrats had feared in 1980 and 1984. Yet the impact of those twelve years on constitutional law is decidedly mixed. Social conservatives who came to power with Reagan in 1981 wanted no less than a judicial revolution, comparable with the events of 1937–1943. They wanted fundamentally to alter the Court's position in American government. They failed. At most they achieved a Court that moderated its decisions, but abandoned neither its direction nor its role.[131] Had the novel terrain of the post-1968 party system made the Supreme Court largely impervious to the vicissitudes of campaigns and elections?

As Democrats regained the presidency in 1993, there were at most only four usually consistent votes for the conservative position: from Rehnquist, Scalia, Thomas, and White. For them to prevail, they had to attract at least one (or two, after White's 1993 retirement) from the Court's center: O'Connor, Kennedy, and Souter. Cases involving three issues—religious exercises in public schools, affirmative action, and abortion—illustrate this process at work. With the first, they fell short. Justices O'Connor, Souter, and Kennedy joined Stevens and Blackmun in barring a rabbi's invocation at a middle school commencement.[132] On the second, they succeeded. Rejecting arguments advanced by the Clinton administration, Justices

O'Connor and Kennedy joined Rehnquist, Scalia, and Thomas in recasting the law. All racial classifications imposed by the federal as well as state governments would now be subject to "strict scrutiny" (the most exacting standard), and thus constitutionally acceptable only if narrowly tailored to further a compelling governmental interest.[133]

On the third, they succeeded only incrementally. The first clue that appointments alone did not a revolution make came in 1989 in *Webster* v. *Reproductive Health Services*. True, a majority of five (Rehnquist, White, O'Connor, Scalia, and Kennedy) sustained regulations that, between 1973 and 1986, would have been invalidated. Moreover, five votes no longer seemed present for the position that abortion laws implicated a "fundamental" constitutional right. However, O'Connor refused to join her four colleagues in overturning *Roe* v. *Wade* outright, as the attorney general's special representative (and former solicitor general) Fried had asked. For her, regulations were permissible unless they imposed an "undue burden" on a woman's access to abortion.

The arrivals of Souter and Thomas in place of *Roe* stalwarts Brennan and Marshall in 1990 and 1991 appeared to make O'Connor's views irrelevant. Indeed, it was Souter's vote in place of Brennan's that accounted for the outcome in *Rust* v. *Sullivan*,[134] which upheld regulations banning abortion counseling by family planning clinics receiving federal funds. Thus both the pro- and antiabortion rights camps awaited the outcome of *Planned Parenthood of Southeastern Pennsylvania* v. *Casey* in the midst of the 1992 presidential campaign.

As expected, the Court upheld most of the statute: provisions on informed consent, a twenty-four-hour waiting period, parental (but not spousal) consent, and record-keeping. Moreover, Justices Souter, Kennedy, and O'Connor confessed "reservations" about the correctness of *Roe* in 1973. Nonetheless, the trio unexpectedly "reaffirmed" what they termed "the central holding" of *Roe:* that abortion entailed a constitutionally protected liberty that states were forbidden to burden unduly.[135] Thus any ban on abortions before the twenty-fifth week would remain unconstitutional. The fifth vote to overturn *Roe* did not come forth. With *Roe* defenders Blackmun and Stevens, who found virtually the entire statute defective, the awkward alignment left *Roe's* avowed opponents (Rehnquist, White, Scalia, and Thomas) in the minority. Once again the judicial fat was in the political fire. "The constitutional right to choose is hanging by a thread," warned Bill Clinton in the campaign. "We are only one justice away from an outright reversal of *Roe*."[136]

Having altered the presidential campaign landscape in *Roe*, the Court may have done it again in *Casey*. Clinton's appointments of Justices Ginsburg and Breyer (each pro-choice) in 1993 and 1994, replacing abortion antagonists White and Blackmun, respectively, shored up the tenuous "truce" of 1992. Future campaigns would reveal whether the Court had reduced the saliency of abortion as a driving and transforming issue in American politics.

CHAPTER 9

Presidential Campaigns and the Supreme Court

hapter 1 gave fair warning: the Constitution provides means to ensure "independence" in the federal judiciary, as Alexander Hamilton acknowledged,[1] but the Supreme Court has nonetheless been susceptible to electoral entanglement. Such occasions include or are adjacent to every election that students of politics commonly designate as realigning events. These are the contests that stand out as landmarks in the history of American political parties: 1800, 1828, 1860, 1896, 1936, and, to an extent, 1968. Realigning elections give life to new party systems, signaling not only a widespread and long-lived shift of power from one party to the other but also sometimes the birth and demise of parties. The perception of national elections as a series of contests mainly between Republicans and Democrats obscures the role of Federalists, National Republicans, and Whigs whom events displaced, as well as the sometimes pivotal, if usually brief, place of the Free Soilers, Populists, Progressives, Socialists, and followers of George Wallace and Ross Perot. And most political parties successful enough for opponents to notice at the polls, it seems, have had something to say about the Supreme Court. That fact is equally apparent in those other Court-conscious campaigns—of 1912, 1924, 1980, and 1984—that did not mark a realignment.

CONFIGURATIONS

There should be little surprise that Court-focused campaigns occur at or adjacent to these realigning events. Deciding constitutional cases entails taking sides on vexing issues of the day, and issue-driven shifts within the electorate are the raw material of realignment. Taking sides in turn may lead to at least four political configurations. In each, the Court influences the issue agenda from which voters make their choice.

If the forces that precipitate a realignment involve long-running issues, the judiciary through its decisions may already have become identified with one side or another. This may mean that the Court is perceived as being part of the dominant coalition or party in power, as happened in the late 1850s when, in declaring the organizing principle of the Republican party illegitimate, the 7–2 margin in *Scott* v. *Sandford*[2] reinforced an image of the Court as an agent of pro-slavery forces in particular and the Democratic party in general.

The Court's position on a salient question, or its constitutional orientation generally, may also place it at odds either with the views of a recently ensconced ruling group or with a persistent and articulate minority that fails to achieve majority status. The first occurred when the Marshall Court's decisions in the Bank Cases[3] and its doctrine of national supremacy stood in contrast to Andrew Jackson and his Democratic party's states' rights orientation. Recall that constitutional issues drove the 1832 campaign, in contrast to the personality-heavy campaign that secured the White House for Jackson in 1828. The second describes the standoff between the Court and its critics in 1896 and well into the fourth party system. Both episodes suggest, too, that major expansions of judicial power are likely to be accompanied by outbursts of opposition to it. By the 1820s, for example, the Court's identification as a revisionist force against state court rulings hostile to national power had become clear. Similarly, the prolonged agitation among Progressives against judicial power followed the Court's conversion of the Fourteenth Amendment into a weapon against various social reforms.

A third configuration arises when, after a period in which the Court's reading of the Constitution has proven unexceptionable to dominant groups within both major parties, events transform one party, differentiate it in a new way from the other party, and set it against the Court. This was the state of affairs in 1935 and 1936 when the Court waged legal war against the Roosevelt administration and the Democratic party. The transforming event had been the Great Depression. The party that Roosevelt headed and the electoral coalition that he forged were vastly different from the Democratic party that had nominated John W. Davis in 1924. And while both parties had progressive elements that had long been critical of the Court, the Court enjoyed ample support in the ranks of each party. Between 1900 and 1932, neither party tried to dislodge the justices from the constitutional perch that they had occupied since 1890.

The fourth configuration unfolds when the Court creates a political issue or nationalizes an existing one. Widespread disapproval among some voters and approbation among others may lead candidates and parties to take positions not only on the issue but also on the correctness of the Court's decision. Those in favor praise the Court for defending the Constitution; those in opposition call for remedies. Thus the unprecedented appearance of social issues in the 1964 and 1968 campaigns resulted partly from decisions by the Supreme Court on criminal justice and racial equality. *Roe* v. *Wade*[4] in 1973 in turn allowed the cores of the Democratic and Republican parties to develop polar positions within a few years on a question that both parties had officially avoided at the national level as late as 1972. Control of the Supreme Court became central to each. Positions taken by candidates on questions from crime prevention to abortion led straight to the Marble Palace[5] and helped to define the major parties for a generation.

These four configurations aside, no eternal verity of political science dictates that the Court must be electorally ensnared during every realigning period. Indeed, it is entirely possible that a realigning event could transpire from which the Court is completely removed. Just as realignment may take place without entangling the Court, so judicial entanglement may be wholly divorced from realignment. As preceding chapters have shown, however, this happens only infrequently. By definition, periods of realignment present opportunities for candidates to lead voters to a new party identity. Judicial decisions thus may provide or contribute to the wedge issues that make that shift possible. In contrast, in election campaigns within a party system—that is, between alignments—candidates draw from their party's core support in the electorate while making an appeal to "independent" voters as well. There is the absence of the wedge issue to which judicial decisions historically have been connected.

THE COURT AS TARGET

Plainly, the Court has long been an appealing target for vote-hungry politicians. This is so not merely because a Supreme Court decision will occasionally touch a public nerve, allowing a candidate or officeholder to fuse the Court with an unpopular ruling. The Court's susceptibility to entanglement has *necessarily* been a characteristic of American politics because of the constitutional role that the justices have assumed for themselves. Indeed, this may have been John Marshall's most important contribution as chief justice. Perhaps more than anyone, he "legalized" the Constitution,[6] treating the fundamental law as *law*: a text amenable to exegesis in order to discover its meaning. Meaning in turn would resolve disputes over allocations of power. This transformation did not take place overnight. Marshall's assertion and defense of judicial review in *Marbury* v. *Madison*[7] as a solemn duty of the Court stated more possibility than reality. Nonetheless, once the view of the Constitution as a juridical document took root, the Court relinquished whatever immunity it might otherwise have enjoyed from political controversy.

Operationally, when the Court strikes down a statute, the justices place a particular public policy out of the reach of ordinary majoritarian politics. That policy is no longer "in play," no longer an option among the range of things that government or the voters may do through a vote of 51 percent in the legislature or in a referendum. To overcome the Court's decision, opponents must move to a higher plane of political activity by attempting one or more extraordinary measures: (1) amending the Constitution to allow that which has been judicially disallowed; (2) expediting a judicial change of mind, perhaps through the appointment of "right-thinking" justices; and (3) institutionally or jurisdictionally crippling the judiciary's capacity to do further harm.

The Court also becomes a target because, alongside almost all other institutions of government, it is *different*. Those constitutional fire walls that bar a diminution in salary and make removal of justices and other federal judges exceedingly difficult, combined with the Court-proclaimed authority to set aside decisions made by popularly elected representatives, contribute to the Court's "otherness." They also mark an institution that sometimes appears, or that can be made to appear, at odds with a political system founded on "the consent of the governed."[8] Whether it is a Progressive movement intent on social reform or a New Deal redefining the scope of government, the Court may foster doubts about its own legitimacy when it stands in the way of the popular will. Americans disagree over programs that Congress and the presidency should undertake, to be sure, but rarely have those debates reflected the fundamental misgivings that have dogged the Court across much of its history.

Additionally, practically every stage of the decision-making process and every step in the way the Court conducts its business set the judicial function apart from the legislative and executive functions. The justices seem not just different but aloof, even mysterious. One journalist has called the Court "at once one of the most open and one of the least accessible of the major institutions of government."[9] It is open because the public has access to nearly all legal documents that are filed and to the oral argument of cases. Yet the decisions themselves emerge from a deliberative process cloaked in secrecy. Leaks prior to official announcements of decisions are so rare that they make headlines when they occur. "The very idea of cooking up opinions in conclave, begets suspicions that something passes which fears the public ear," Thomas Jefferson protested to Justice William Johnson.[10] The Court's penchant for secrecy may even occasionally fuel the "paranoid style in American politics," which "evokes the qualities of heated exaggeration, suspiciousness, and conspiratorial fantasy."[11] And the Supreme Court's aversion to televised or broadcasted proceedings and to still photography in the courtroom makes even its most public activity seem set apart. "The only groups who don't appear on television," observes journalist Fred Graham, "are the Supreme Court and the Mafia."[12]

Once decisions "come down," the Court speaks almost exclusively through its opinions. Justices infrequently give interviews and never hold press conferences to answer questions about their decisions. Instances in which individual justices have personally defended their handiwork in public are rare. Even when they do so, they are likely to do so in very general terms. Recall from chapter 3 that Marshall's newspaper defense of *McCulloch* v. *Maryland* was carried on under a pseudonym. In contrast to other offices and agencies in Washington, from the White House to Congress and into the bureaucracy, the public relations bureau at the Supreme Court (accurately named the Public Information Office) is rudimentary and little more than a conduit for distribution of decisions, opinions (as they are announced in the courtroom upstairs), and other raw information. It offers no interpretation of decisions, only rarely arranges photo opportunities, attempts no "spin" on events, corrects no "misstatements" a justice may have made, engages in no defense of the institution or what it does, and points out no errors or distortions in comments politicians and journalists make about the Court. Today, as in Marshall's time, the Court relies on the intelligence and good faith of others in conveying its decisions to the people.

Not only does it offer no public defenses of its actions once a decision has precipitated an attack, but it does not "fight back" as do other officials and agencies that have been scorned or scourged. The Court lacks nearly all routine tools of political sparring: appropriations, ostentatiousness, jobs, contracts, and investigation. Indeed, any such forays by the Court into "politics as usual" would damage its legitimacy by calling into question its independence and impartiality. Instead, the Court is left with little more than occasional speech-making by the justices, combined with defenses— spontaneous or arranged[13]—that might be mounted by their champions outside the Marble Palace.

Vulnerability is unavoidable in another sense as well. In constitutional litigation the Court applies principle to facts. While the principle in question (free speech, for instance) may enjoy wide appeal, the beneficiary of a particular ruling is often no hero. Decisions may align the Court in the public's mind with unpopular or even unsavory individuals and groups. Justice Felix Frankfurter once said that "the safeguards of liberty have frequently been forged in controversies involving not very nice people."[14] He had criminal defendants in mind, but litigants who have sought the Court's approval, assistance, and protection at various points in American history and who have also been held in low esteem by some substantial number of people extend well beyond the universally disparaged confessed rapist or murderer: slaveholders,[15] strikebreakers,[16] the rich,[17] child-labor profiteers,[18] big business,[19] abortionists,[20] opponents of school prayer,[21] suspected Communists,[22] flag burners,[23] purveyors of sexually explicit materials,[24] and defenders of racial quotas.[25]

IN RETROSPECT

Previous chapters reveal the degree to which the record of Court-centered presidential campaigns has confirmed the expectations or propositions laid out at the beginning of this book. The Court's entanglement in the electoral process has assumed so many shapes under such widely varying circumstances that one should not be surprised to discover that some propositions have been substantiated across time to a greater extent than others.

Proposition # 1: Negation and Validation

The Court is more likely to become ensnared in partisan combat when it has negated, rather than upheld, a policy choice made by a state government or another branch of the national government.

Pivotal words in the first proposition include "more likely." Episodes of electoral entanglement occurring after the justices have struck down laws should outnumber those that have been sparked after the justices have upheld them.

As the first chapter suggested, this phenomenon is to be expected for at least three reasons. The public's awareness of Supreme Court decisions seems to be higher when the justices strike down a policy.[26] Greater awareness in turn means that any politician hoping to capitalize on disenchantment has less work to do at the outset. The rudiments of a groundswell of protest may already be in place. Second, when the Court affirms a policy made by a legislature, the political playing field remains the same. Opponents are worse off only in that the Court has resolved constitutional doubt in the statute's favor. From the perspective of the disgruntled, the Court may be party to the legislature's misdeeds, but remedies are close at hand: the ballot box and more persuasive lobbying of lawmakers. Third, invalidation of a law is, in principle at least, negation of the people's will. Constitutionalism trumps popular sovereignty, allowing the antimajoritarian Court to become an electoral scapegoat. Campaigns and elections, after all, are quintessentially appeals to the majority.

The record supports the first proposition. With four exceptions, negations of legislation precipitated the occasions when the judiciary was the target of electoral fire: (1) support of the Sedition Act between 1798 and 1800 by Supreme Court justices sitting as circuit judges; (2) the enthusiastic defense in *McCulloch* v. *Maryland* of the implied powers of Congress; (3) Supreme Court review of state court decisions in *Cohens* v. *Virginia*;[27] and (4) the extraordinary effort in 1895 to sustain the federal contempt conviction of Eugene Debs in the aftermath of the Pullman strike. Of the four, *McCulloch* and *Cohens* are admittedly mixed decisions. While the Court sustained the congressional statute in the former, it struck down Maryland's destructive tax on the bank. In *Cohens*, the Court was pilloried even though it upheld the Virginia law at issue and the convictions under it. *Cohens* was irritating to Virginia because of the authority the justices acknowledged for themselves in relation to state courts under Section 25 of the 1789 Judiciary Act.[28]

Ironically, of the instances in which validation led the Court into controversy, all but In re *Debs* occurred before judicial review in its modern form had taken shape. As late as 1832, the Court's place in the political system as constitutional arbiter was still as much promise as fact. Yet critics assailed the Court in those early imbroglios for *not* using its power to resist the elected agents of the people.

Proposition # 2: Conflict and Reaction

When the Court is on the "losing side" in an election in which it has been an issue, ensuing Court decisions in the short term will generate conflict between the Court and the new governing majority, resulting in presidential and/or congressional efforts to curb or otherwise to change the Court.

The second proposition assumes two conditions. The first of these is that the Court is widely, if figuratively, perceived to have "won" or "lost" an election when the presidential candidate and/or party that assails the Court is defeated or emerges victorious. If one or more decisions prior to the election were sufficiently at odds with the views of the party that emerges victorious to have played a role in the presidential campaign, the postcampaign Court represents both symbolically and substantively the policies and party that voters have rejected. Among the campaigns explored in previous chapters, the Court by this measure lost the elections of 1800, 1832, 1860, 1936, 1968, 1980, and 1984, and won in 1896, 1912, and 1924.

Second, short of a wholesale turnover in personnel, the Court stays its preelection course at least in the short term, creating a "lag" period in which the Court is at odds with the new majoritarian forces.[29] Accordingly, the new administration will presumably be no happier after the election than before with the direction of the Court's decisions, and will be compelled to take steps to secure more favorable judicial pronouncements.

Proposition 2 matches the record only in part. As for continuation of "old regime" policies by the Court for several years after a "new regime" has assumed control of the elected branches, events after 1800, 1832, 1860, and 1936 argue otherwise. The overt Federalist partisanship so visible before the election of 1800 prudently moderated after Jefferson assumed the presidency, as the Court redefined its "independence" to include partisan detachment as well as the constitutionally conferred institutional defenses from congressional and executive onslaughts. Enthusiastic application of the Sedition Act, so prevalent before the election of 1800, ceased to be an option for anyone once the statute expired in March 1801. And however else they might be read, the early Marshall Court's decisions in *Marbury* v.

Madison and *Stuart* v. *Laird*[30] went out of their way to avoid confrontations with Jefferson and the Republican Congress.

Once Jackson secured reelection in 1832, no further decisions by the late Marshall Court antagonized the president and his followers to the degree that *McCulloch* and other intrusions into state affairs, such as the more recent Cherokee Indian Cases,[31] had done. The potentially troublesome Charles River Bridge Case,[32] in which "new money" prevailed over "old money" in the guise of a contract clause dispute, was not decided until 1837 even though it had first been argued in 1831. The delay allowed Marshall's successor, Jackson appointee Roger Brooke Taney, to write the opinion for a 4 to 3 majority against the vested interests at stake.

Similar patterns followed the elections of 1860 and 1936. Whatever the Taney Court *might* have done to needle the new Republican administration, had the unpleasantness at Fort Sumter not occurred, was overwhelmed by the pressures of civil war. The full Court took constitutional issue with no wartime measure until after hostilities ceased, and the few Reconstruction policies, like the test oaths, that encountered a hostile bench were either relatively minor or, like legal tender, quickly reinstated. In contrast to Lincoln, President Franklin Roosevelt and his New Deal encountered stiff and unprecedented resistance at the Court, but all of the administration's defeats occurred *prior to*, not after, the election of 1936.

Only with the elections of 1968, 1980, and 1984 does conflict prevail between the Court's jurisprudence and the executive. With the exception of some holdings on criminal justice that it modified but did not overrule, the Burger Court continued, and even built upon, the Warren Court landmarks that had made the Court a lightning rod in the 1968 campaign. And with the arrival of Ronald Reagan in 1981, the Court hardly flinched on the newest of the social issues to inflame presidential campaigns, the constitutional protection afforded abortion as symbolized by *Roe* v. *Wade*. In fact, the Court delivered one of its most enthusiastic reaffirmations of *Roe* halfway through Reagan's second term.[33] Yet one distinctive feature of all three of these elections, in contrast to the contests of 1800, 1832, and 1860, was their indeterminateness: no complete transfer of power from one party to another.[34] Democrats held Congress throughout the 1970s and 1980s, except for the Senate during six of Reagan's years.

The second proposition, however, correctly conforms to the behavior of the elected branches. But this is a reaction based less on what the Court actually does after the election and more on what the elected branches anticipate the Court will do. Jefferson expected a hostile judiciary after

1801, and Congress acted accordingly in passing the Repeal Act and the Judiciary Act of 1802. Even the attempted removal of Justice Samuel Chase can be seen nearly as much as a warning shot as payback for Chase's unflagging efforts to skewer Republicans before 1801. While efforts in Congress to repeal Section 25 waned after 1832, Jackson's relationship with the Court prior to that year's election crystallized his thinking about the judiciary's place in the constitutional system. His four second-term appointments allowed Old Hickory to shape the Court for a generation.

Judicial discretion after the election of 1860, coupled with an abundance of vacancies in quick succession, avoided Court-curbing measures that Congress might otherwise have enacted. Nonetheless, Congress effectively reversed *Dred Scott* by statute in 1862, and the series of postwar constitutional amendments and civil rights acts expanded national power at the expense of state prerogatives that underlay much of the Taney Court's jurisprudence. Moreover, Congress's creation of a tenth seat on the Court must be regarded, at least partly, as a means to ensure an obliging bench.

What the Court avoided by way of institutional threat after 1860, however, it squarely faced after 1936. His patience exhausted, Roosevelt made the boldest and most overt move by any president to alter the Court. Remove this benchmark, and Republican labors in 1968–1971 to change constitutional law by transforming the Court would loom even larger than they do. This tumult had barely subsided when Congress gave serious attention to a rash of Court-curbing bills between 1980 and 1984, while Reagan administration officials pressed for the most sweeping refashioning of constitutional law since 1937.[35]

Proposition # 3: Policy Change

When the Court has been on the "losing side" in, or adjacent to, a realigning election, the Court will make significant policy changes within a decade that bring it into accord with the "winning side."

Like the previous proposition, the third proposition rests on several assumptions. First, going into an election in which the party out of power has attacked the bench, the disputed decisions reflect the values of the party in power. Second, an election that finds the Court on the losing side results in a clear shift of control to the new majority party in the elected branches of the federal government. The third proposition also assumes that the president of the party that comes to power in a realigning election will take advantage of vacancies on the Court to appoint justices who reflect the views of the new ruling coalition. Because retirements and deaths have occurred on average about once every two years since President Washington filled the first six seats,[36] a decade will probably yield about five occasions (enough for a majority) for a president and one or more successors to make High Court appointments. Even were the number only three or four, a president might still be able to build a favorable majority if the Court's membership already included one or two "friendly" justices.

On initial consideration, the proposition seems accurate, if judged solely against the raw total of congressional statutes struck down by the Supreme Court—about 140. The Marshall and Taney courts combined invalidated only two (although the decision in each instance was epochal). Of the remaining 138, about 10 percent fell between 1934 and 1936. With the latter group excluded, the pace of invalidation amounts to about one statute per year since 1864, suggesting that the Court is almost always a team player.

These numbers, however, mask what the Supreme Court has done with state legislation. For most of the Court's history, challenges to state laws (including local ordinances) have far outnumbered challenges to acts of Congress, just as the volume of annual state legislation far exceeds the number of bills that Congress passes each session. Moreover, since the Court negated its first state law on constitutional grounds in 1810,[37] the justices have rarely extended to states the degree of deference ordinarily shown to Congress. The number of state laws struck down exceeds invalidated national laws by about a factor of ten. As with invalidations of congressional acts, most have occurred well within party systems, not just at their junctures. Thus, while the Court upholds most challenged legislation, it has also invalidated some legislation in almost every decade.[38]

While the proposition corresponds to events following the election of 1936, it does not accurately depict jurisprudential affairs after the election of 1800 and does so only partly for 1832 and 1860. Moreover, the fit with 1968, 1980, and 1984 is awkward at best. Indeed, these recent Court-centered campaigns cast doubt on the conclusion of a study completed shortly past the midpoint of the fifth party system: "policy views dominant on the Court are never for long out of line with the policy views dominant among the law making majorities of the U.S."[39]

Several factors kept the Court and the "law making majorities" apart on issues that were central to the campaigns of 1968, 1980, and 1984. First, dealignment has divided the elected branches between the parties in most years since 1968. Indeed, the indeterminateness of the elections of 1968, 1980, and 1984 and the persistence of dealignment cast doubt on the applicability of the third proposition for the foreseeable future. If that proposition does not always account for events in eras of alignment, it is even less apt to do so in an era of dealignment. Of course dealignment will not defuse the explosiveness of some issues that confront the Court or shield the bench from campaign involvement, but it adds to the Court's imperviousness to the consequences of elections.

Second, the reluctance even by some new justices to depart from the Court's own precedents (the force of stare decisis, "the everyday work rule of our law"[40]) has argued more for modification of past decisions instead of outright rejection. Unpredictability is a third factor. For example, Nixon's four appointees between 1969 and 1971 made the Court less disposed toward criminal defendants, but had Chief Justice Burger and Justices Blackmun and Powell voted otherwise in *Roe* v. *Wade*, Texas's Civil War-era abortion law might still be in force. A fourth factor that is always at work is the irregularity of Supreme Court vacancies. Recall that from the winter of 1971–1972 until the summer of 1986, while a debate raged on the Court's role in the political system, there were but two justices (Stevens and O'Connor) named to the bench. Moreover, three members of the *Warren* Court (Brennan, White, and Marshall) were still sitting when Ronald Reagan left the White House in January 1989, twenty years after both Warren's retirement and the death of the president who named him chief justice.

As for 1800, 1832, and 1860, proposition 3 masks important jurisprudential developments. Consider its inappositeness to the Marshall Court. Together, Democratic–Republican Presidents Jefferson, Madison, and Monroe made six appointments to a bench that after 1807 had seven justices, and that after 1811 contained a majority of Democratic–Republican members. Yet with few exceptions most of the legendary decisions that exasperated Jefferson's party—rulings on federal judicial power, the implied powers of Congress, the commerce clause, and limitations on the states—were decided after 1815. If Jefferson and his two successors wanted a bench opposed to Federalist–Hamiltonian ideas, they were singularly unsuccessful. Significant shifts in doctrine had to await the arrival of Jackson's six appointees, a number only one less than the total number of justices named by his four White House predecessors.

The Jackson legacy, moreover, shows the ambiguity that can lurk even within periods when the Court appears to adhere to the party line. True, upon leaving office in 1837, Jackson bequeathed a Supreme Court more to his liking than the one he inherited in 1829. Constitutional jurisprudence under Taney became more solicitous of state prerogatives. But in important respects it departed from Jacksonian notions of popular sovereignty. As Taney's dual federalism displaced Marshall's national supremacy in governing relationships between state and national governments, judicial power and the role of the Supreme Court were enhanced, not diminished. That was surely an unintended consequence of Jacksonian democracy. Moreover, the pace of invalidation of state legislation quickened under Taney, as additional commerce and contract clause cases, some of which were related to the oncoming sectional crisis, reached the Court.[41]

The five Lincoln appointees (a number equal to those of his five predecessors combined) reacted differently to the new constitutional questions that the Court encountered in the third party system. While the bench did little to obstruct either the war or the major elements of Reconstruction during the 1860s, the Court that emerged under Lincoln and Grant was not always friendly to national power. Barely thirteen years after the election of 1860, the Chase Court denied that the Fourteenth Amendment applied to state infringement of most essential civil liberties.[42] In 1876 a unanimous bench narrowly construed federal authority under the Enforcement Act of 1870, making it difficult to secure voting rights of the newly freed slaves in the states of old Confederacy.[43] Seven years later, the Court, with only one dissent, altogether denied Congress authority under the Civil Rights Act of 1875 to ban racial discrimination in businesses such as hotels and theaters that were open to the public.[44] Arguably such decisions merely reflected a new mood in the nation that states should have wide latitude in dealing with black citizens, but the explanation is probably more complicated: Congress passed the public accommodations statute only a year before the Court nearly emasculated the Enforcement Act. As far as national power was concerned, the justices may have been more willing to accept the political adjustments wrought by war than the fundamental changes embodied in constitutional amendments.

Moreover, the issues of national power that related to Reconstruction promptly gave way to another constitutional question that consumed the Court for half a century: the degree to which the Fourteenth Amendment (ratified three years after Lincoln's death) limited the authority of states to enact health, safety, social, and economic regulations. As Chief Justice William Rehnquist observed a century later:

> Neither the President nor his appointees can foresee what issues will come before the Court . . . , and it may be that none had thought very much about these issues. Even though they agree as to the proper resolution of current issues, they may well disagree as to future cases involving other questions.[45]

The same variable—a changing agenda—produced still a different phenomenon on the heels of Roosevelt's triumph over the Supreme Court in 1936–1937. The "old Court's" 180-degree turn in 1937 was made secure after FDR made five appointments within three years. The president got the Court he wanted: with one accord the Roosevelt Court not only placed the constitutional seal of approval on the New Deal but also withdrew almost completely from appraising the reasonableness of economic and social regulation. But unanimity disappeared as the second component of the "constitutional revolution" emerged. The Court split in its reaction to violations of nonproprietarian civil liberties and civil rights. The Court's docket today and the divisions among the justices continue to reflect both seismic shifts from the late New Deal era.

Proposition # 4: Campaign Impact

The Court may facilitate the definition and clarification of candidates' and parties' positions on critical issues in a campaign.

This proposition is plausible because of the two avenues along which the Supreme Court ordinarily enters or is pulled into campaign warfare. First, the Court generates an issue on which candidates and parties then take different positions. This does not mean that the Court literally invents a dispute by causing division on a subject where none previously existed. Rather, the Court thrusts an existing subject about which people hold conflicting views into national politics by proclaiming one side or another as constitutionally correct. When this occurs, the Court is said to have "nationalized" an issue. The second path unfolds when the Court takes sides on a question that has previously divided the parties at the national level. In this instance, the Court stokes the controversy, but the issue exists independent of the Court. In both, the Court's actions allow one party to wrap itself in the Constitution while the other party goes on the attack against the judiciary. In both, the Court may thereby contribute to party realignment on the occasions when that occurs.[46]

More often through the second rather than the first avenue, the fourth proposition fairly fits all Court-entangled campaigns. Consider the contest of 1800, in which statements and actions by Supreme Court justices allowed Jeffersonian Republicans to distinguish themselves more clearly from Federalists. The Sedition Act would surely have been an issue had Federalist judges not appeared so partisan in its administration, but their partisanship made it easier for Republicans to depict Federalists as a threat to individual liberty. By 1832, controversy over the Bank of the United States, in its first or second incarnation, had been a staple of political debate since President Washington's first term. Yet the Supreme Court's pro-Bank decisions helped to crystallize thinking within the second party system that was emerging not only about the Bank itself but also about the place of the states in the federal system. Indeed, Marshall became the foil to Jacksonian Democrats in their opposition to the Bank and to Jackson himself in rejecting the Court as the final authority on the meaning of the Constitution.

In contrast, both variations of entanglement were in play in the events prior to the campaign of 1860. The Supreme Court hardly invented the national controversy over slavery. Congress, after all, had been grappling intermittently with the future of slavery in the territories for about a decade prior to *Dred Scott*, and neither Democrats nor Whigs were entirely of one mind as to what should or could be done. Moreover, there were the antecedent Northwest Ordinance of 1787 and Missouri Compromise of 1820. Not until 1856 did the two major parties take diametrically opposite positions on slavery. Yet *Dred Scott* in March 1857 not only assured that slavery was henceforth a subject that no major party could ignore, but also made congressional authority over slavery in territories—and by implication in the states—entirely a matter of constitutional law. By declaring the primary Republican objective invalid, the Court served the new party well not only by becoming a symbol of the adversary but also by dividing the Democrats, opening the door to Lincoln's victory.

More like the situation in 1832, issues of the 1896 campaign were not judicially spawned, but the Sugar Trust, income tax, and *Debs* decisions[47] enabled Democrats and Populists to transform the Court into a symbol of evil forces that gripped the land. The tactic handed Republicans a scare issue. They turned Democratic attacks to their advantage by portraying the Court as the barrier between upright Americans and radicals. Although Republicans were the decided beneficiaries of this election for more than a generation, alliance with or against the Court allowed each party to present clearer and more contrasting images of itself to the electorate.

The proposition applies even to 1912 and 1924, though the Court was not truly an issue between the major parties. Nonetheless, judicial decisions surely helped TR's and La Follette's Progressive candidacies to define and clarify positions regarding remedial measures to safeguard social reform legislation. Not only had the Court struck down desirable programs, but the threat of the judicial veto could be blamed for the political system's failure to do more to alleviate social ills.

FDR's campaign for reelection in 1936 would have been a referendum on the New Deal with or without the Supreme Court's intransigence. Yet judicial resistance to the New Deal fused the Court even more tightly with the Republican party. The Court was a symbolic standard-bearer for the party and defined the party's center. Where else would Republicans find legitimacy for their position? Persistent judicial declarations of the unconstitutionality of the New Deal and the destruction of American federalism became rallying points for Landon's crusade. To be sure, the realignment that 1936 confirmed would have taken place even had the justices consistently sustained the president's programs. Yet to the degree that the Court made the Republican position seem ever more unbending, the Court may actually have added to voter defections into Democratic ranks.

In contrast to 1936, it is difficult to comprehend the shape of the campaigns or even the candidates of 1968, 1980, and 1984 without the Supreme Court. Along with national security and economic concerns in each race, social and cultural issues achieved salience. They were salient not because voters had only recently developed opinions on race discrimination, criminal justice, school prayer, and abortion, but because the Court had thrust these and other matters into the cauldron of national politics by draping each in constitutional garb. The Court became a target of opportunity for Republicans, who identified Democrats with liberal rulings of the Warren and Burger Courts. Simultaneously, Republicans became decidedly the party of social conservatives, with a noticeable Southern tint. It seemed light-years since 1964, when a Democratic Congress was able to pass the Civil Rights Act only with significant Republican support.[48]

Proposition # 5: Court, Nation, and Judicial Review

Instances when the Court becomes an issue in a presidential campaign tend to coincide with widespread debate over the legitimacy of judicial review and the Court's role in political system.

The proposition does not suggest that entanglement in a presidential campaign causes the debate. Rather, criticism of the Court that is sufficiently broad and intense to become the stuff of a presidential campaign may draw from, as well as fuel, doubts about the legitimacy of what the Court has done. This situation arises from the Court's triple debility: (1) ambivalent authority (Did the framers really intend the Court to have a major hand in policy-making?); (2) antidemocratic function (The unelected branch negates an action of the elected branches); and (3) aloofness (The Court's constitutional decisions can be corrected only through extraordinary political measures).

In different ways and to varying degrees, the campaigns examined in the previous chapters support the fifth proposition. Indeed, every serious debate over judicial review in this country has occurred during a time that encompasses one of these campaigns. The controversy provoked by the Sedition Act, its enforcement, and the election of 1800 continued into Jefferson's first term as opinion varied on who or what should determine the meaning of the Constitution. When the judiciary next moved to the center of conflict in the 1820s and early 1830s, the Court's critics advanced apparently contradictory positions on judicial power. On the one hand, the Court was insufficiently energetic in wielding judicial review against acts of Congress (as in the Bank Cases); on the other hand, judicial review stood contrary to the principle of popular sovereignty. Furthermore, a vocal school of thought rejected the Court's supervisory role under Section 25 as final arbiter of the meaning of the Constitution.

Republican critics of the Court after 1857 did not share the general Jacksonian aversion to judicial power. Their complaints were case-specific: the nation could not tolerate pro-slavery decisions such as *Dred Scott* and *Ableman* v. *Booth*.[49] Although they possessed no principled objections to judicial review itself, their outlook might have changed had the Civil War not settled the status of slavery (and with it, the subordinate status of the states) so abruptly. Still, there was a flurry of anti-Court proposals in Congress, and circumstances compelled Lincoln in his first inaugural address to embrace the Taney-inspired Jacksonian (and un-Whiglike) position to deny the Court's exclusive authority to "say what the law is."[50]

The Court's assumption of an expanded role in overseeing public policy after 1890 led to a more prolonged reconsideration of judicial power, the most thorough dissection since Marshall's day. Some contenders in the debate probed the legitimacy of judicial review itself: whether the framers intended the Court to exercise the power. Others accepted judicial review in principle but divided over its scope: the circumstances in which it should be used. Still others pondered various institutional devices to discourage its use or to correct judges when people believed them to have erred. These were the ideas that Roosevelt and La Follette repackaged and rearticulated during their respective Progressive candidacies of 1912 and 1924, and that stimulated new jurisprudential movements such as legal realism.[51]

The confrontation between the Supreme Court and the New Deal in the 1930s reopened the controversy but yielded few ideas that had not been upturned in the post-1890 exhumation. Yet the results were astounding. The bulk of the many anti-Court measures introduced in Congress, including FDR's own pièce de résistance, reflected consensus. Blame for the confrontation in 1935–1936 derived not from a horse-and-buggy Constitution but from justices who gave it a horse-and-buggy interpretation. The significance of the "switch in time" on the part of Chief Justice Hughes and Justice Roberts in 1937 that catapulted the Court forward into a new era was matched only by the promise of footnote 4 in *United States v. Carolene Products Co.*,[52] a year later, which outlined an altogether new judicial duty. Such ground-shaking change, only partly hastened by the appointment of new justices, remains unprecedented in the annals of the federal judiciary and no doubt reflects the intellectual ferment of the day, inside and outside the Court.

The course of constitutional interpretation presaged by footnote 4 led to the politically unsettling decisions of the Warren Court in the 1950s and 1960s. A revived debate did not center merely on the merits of policies that the justices rejected or mandated. (The latter, after all, was the jurisprudential novelty of the Warren era. Some decisions called for more than the cessation of unconstitutional actions; compliance dictated affirmative steps that frequently amounted to entirely new policies and ways of conducting the public's business.) Both preceding and accompanying the tumultuous campaign of 1968 was a serious exchange inspired by members of the Court itself: judicial activism versus judicial restraint.[53]

Even if the policies dictated by the Warren Court were desirable in and of themselves, should they derive from unelected judges or from popularly elected legislators? If a law represented the will of the majority, one side reasoned, then a judicial order invalidating that law must represent the will of a minority. According to this view that was closely linked to Justices Frankfurter and John Marshall Harlan, democratic government and a respect for federalism argued that judges should refrain from imposing their values upon elected representatives except in the clearest and most egregious cases. With those exceptions, judges ordinarily should defer to the elected branches because balancing of political interests was primarily a legislative, not a judicial, task. Or as Justice Harlan admonished, "The Constitution is not a panacea for every blot upon the public welfare, nor should this Court, ordained as a judicial body, be thought of as a general haven for reform movements."[54]

The competing view, closely identified with Chief Justice Warren and Justices Black, Brennan, and Douglas, understood democracy as much in terms of a healthy respect for minority rights as for majority rule. They accepted the additional responsibilities suggested by footnote 4: protecting fundamental values, keeping open the channels of political change, and watching over minorities powerless to protect themselves in the rough-and-tumble of majoritarian politics. Besides, as some political scientists pointed out, majorities were less a monolith and more a shifting coalition of minorities.[55] Studies of the legislative process also revealed that laws often embodied less the expression of the majority's will and more the preference of politically well-connected minorities.[56] Some minorities would therefore find themselves more effectual in the statehouse and others more so in the courthouse. The argument was less about what government should do and more about what part of government should do it.[57]

The activism-restraint dispute was prelude to the searching and long-running inquiry into constitutional interpretation and the role of the Court that began less than a decade later in the wake of *Roe* v. *Wade*. Matching if not exceeding in scope and intensity previous intellectual storms over the judiciary, the debate has had at least two dimensions. Both bodies of opinion begin with an assumption about the legitimacy of judicial review: in striking down a statute, judges act on the authority of the supreme will of the people as embodied in the Constitution. They part company in deciding how one discerns that supreme will, particularly in the Constitution's open-ended provisions and in what the Constitution does not say.

One side limits the search to the Constitution's text and the intent of those who drafted (and perhaps ratified) the document, along with what one can fairly imply from both. Going beyond these limits allows judges to disguise their own values (or the values from another extraconstitutional source) as the people's supreme will. If text, history, and implication do not yield a meaning, the appropriate judicial response is to defer to the elected branches.

The other side recognizes the importance of text and history, but is skeptical that those sources speak with a clear enough voice truthfully to eliminate judicial discretion.[58] Moreover, questions arise today that were not anticipated one or two centuries ago or that were not assessed in constitutional terms. Open-ended phrases in particular presumably did not enter the Constitution with their meaning set in stone; otherwise, the framers would have substituted specificity. Later generations are entitled to infuse the words with new meaning as a sign of "contemporary ratification" of the Constitution. Moreover, the absence of a knowable intent empowers, not disempowers, the judiciary to supply meaning from broad principles that emanate from, or are consistent with the purposes of, the document.

The less obvious and talked-about dimension of this Court-inspired debate is that the judicially approved or mandated policies that one approach yields may be very different from the policies yielded by the other. Because the former approach, more often than not, results in more deference to the elected branches, individuals and groups desiring policies (such as stringent protection for abortion rights and lifestyle choices) not likely to be adopted by a legislature would rationally pursue them in court, and so would prefer the latter approach to constitutional interpretation. In this, as in every preceding Court-centered debate from 1798 onward, constitutional interpretation and public policy are inextricably linked. Policy may dictate the preferred interpretive method as much as the chosen method may yield the preferred policy.

PROSPECTS

Though both infrequent and sporadic since 1800, attacks on the Court in the context of presidential elections will remain part of American political life. The prediction seems safe. Little has occurred in recent years to thicken the Court's insulation from campaign politics on a permanent scale. Moreover, the opportunities for judicial entanglement have expanded. The range of potentially contentious matters that routinely occupy the Court's time is considerably broader than that found during the nineteenth and early twentieth centuries. Campaigns and television news dominated by "sound bites" and a public averse to thorough coverage of most issues[59] make the Court perhaps even more vulnerable to those who would turn the institution to partisan advantage.

Only two plausible developments hold out the promise of a different political future with respect to presidential campaigns and the Supreme Court. The first seems more probable than the second.

Using the congressionally authorized certiorari process that allows the Court to decide which cases it will decide, the justices might act positively to distance themselves from potential campaign entanglement by accepting fewer politically disputatious cases. While every case that the Court decides is of immense importance to the litigants, most cases do not contain the fuel of campaign oratory. Many of the approximately 100 decisions each term with published opinions seem specialized. They concern a particular profession, the rulemaking authority of an administrative agency, a segment of the business community, or a paragraph in the Internal Revenue Code. While the general public might well be affected in some way by these decisions, the effects are usually indirect and often too complex to employ in a campaign. Were the Court to accept more such cases, and therefore fewer cases stuffed with salient controversy, prospects for electoral entanglement would recede. Alexander Hamilton's "least dangerous" branch would be the "least noticed" one. Yet routinely forswearing the conflict-heavy would mean that the Court had decided to leave final resolution of those issues to other courts and agencies. And Congress could respond to such uncharacteristic meekness by mandating High Court review of certain issues, thus tossing the justices back into the political briar patch.

Alternatively, the Court might forthrightly attempt to denationalize the most quarrelsome issues. Just as the justices "nationalized" liberty of contract a century ago and abortion in 1973, so future justices could declare (as the Court did with the former after 1937) that regulation of those spheres of activity no longer implicated the United States Constitution to any important degree. However, unless the Court were following a colossal transformation in public opinion, the probability of conflict around the judiciary might not diminish. Denationalization or its prospect could also electrify the electoral process, because it would remove not only the Supreme Court but also other federal courts as decision makers and assign the "last word" to other institutions, such as state governments. Interests that would be helped or hurt would hardly be indifferent to the change.

Finally, recall the four configurations that, outlined at the beginning of this chapter, can arise when the Court is perceived as having taken sides on one or more "hot button" issues. One should ponder the effects of the varieties of electoral entanglement depicted in preceding chapters on the functioning of the American political system. Are such episodes (1) cause for alarm (and therefore to be avoided); (2) another manifestation of politics as usual (and therefore to be regarded with indifference); or (3) evidence of a healthy, robust politics (and therefore to be welcomed)? Clearly, the answer to the question must begin with recognition of the values that underlie one's conception of a "healthy" political system. Two values or principles that surely underlie what many people believe to be the "essence" of American democratic government are the rule of law ("a government of laws and not of men"[60]) and popular sovereignty ("government by the people"[61]).

The first emphasizes the importance of separating rulers from rules— that the latter have an existence and meaning apart from those who interpret and apply them. Although Americans seem savvy enough to recognize that judges cannot fully distance themselves from the law, they are nonetheless expected to try. Indeed, justices of the United States Supreme Court succeed as credible constitutional authorities to the degree that they are persuasive that it is the Constitution, not their individual preferences, that speaks.[62] If the people continue to see their political destiny unfolding within the Constitution, one may easily be disturbed when the very institution that has evolved as the guardian of the Constitution is embroiled in campaign controversy. The sight may be even more troubling when one recalls that combat over the Court in the context of a campaign occurs for the express purpose of assuring voters that the winning side will (or will not) take steps to change the Court. The risk is that winners and losers alike will see a game that has been rigged. "[B]y making [the Court] a topic of party and electioneering discussion and representing it to the people . . . as a despotic department of the Government," advised Senator David Barton in 1830, "it loses its great utility in quieting instead of inflaming the public mind."[63]

The other essential principle declares that ultimately "the people" are properly in control of their national destiny. The Constitution may embody the supreme will of the people, but the Constitution is not synonymous with the Court; "however the Court may interpret the provisions of the Constitution, it is still the Constitution which is law and not decisions of the Court."[64] Moreover, if infallibility is not an attribute of elected officials, there is no evidence that it adheres any more tightly to appointed ones. Thus popular sovereignty demands that voters be able to attempt, however indirectly and imprecisely, to "correct" a Court that, as past chapters demonstrate, is realistically unresponsive to all but a handful of political checks.[65]

So far, then, as one considers the effects of judicial entanglement in campaigns on the "health" of the political system, the key to maximizing both principles may lie in moderation. A High Court of the sort that has developed in the United States, were it to be thoroughly and consistently insulated from partisan attack, would endanger popular sovereignty. A High Court that was routinely the target of partisan attack and the focus of presidential campaigns might well diminish the strength of limited government that Chief Justice Marshall "deemed the greatest improvement on political institutions."[66] So the prospect of electoral entanglement must remain, but one hopes that it materializes infrequently. More than once a generation may well prove unhealthful.

APPENDIX I

The Presidency and Congress, 1789–1999

YEAR	CANDIDATES[a]	PARTY[b]	ELECTORAL VOTE	POPULAR VOTE[c]	ELECTED VICE PRESIDENT[d]	CONGRESSES[e]
1789	**George Washington**	Federalist	69[d]		John Adams	1st H: Ad-38, OP-26 S: Ad-17, OP-9	2nd F-37, DR-33 F-16, DR-13
	John Adams		34			
	John Jay		9			
	Others		26			
1792	**George Washington**	Federalist	132		John Adams	3rd H: DR-57, F-48 S: F-17, DR-13	4th F-54, DR-52 F-19, DR-13
	John Adams	Federalist	77			
	George Clinton	Democratic-Republican	50			
	Thomas Jefferson		4			
	Aaron Burr		1			
1796	**John Adams**	Federalist	71		Thomas Jefferson	5th H: F-58, DR-48 S: F-20, DR-12	6th F-64, DR-42 F-19, DR-13
	Thomas Jefferson	Democratic-Republican	68			
	Thomas Pinckney	Federalist	59			
	Aaron Burr	Democratic-Republican	30			
	Others		48			

Sources: Adapted from D. Grier Stephenson, Jr., Robert J. Bresler, Robert J. Frederich, and Joseph J. Karlesky, *American Government*, 2nd ed. (New York: HarperCollins, 1992), pp. A27–A31; Office of the clerk of the U.S. House of Representatives.

[a] The name of the winning candidate is printed in boldface type.

[b] Party labels in presidential elections did not become sufficiently distinct until the election of 1796.

[c] Popular election of presidential electors was not the usual practice until the election of 1824. Percentages may not total 100% in an election because of rounding and the presence of other candidates who received popular votes.

[d] Until ratification of the Twelfth Amendment in 1804, each presidential elector had two votes and cast them for different persons. The person receiving the most votes from a majority of electors was elected president; the person with second largest number was vice president. Washington's 69 electoral votes in 1789 thus represented a unanimous choice of the 69 electors. Beginning with the election of 1804, electors voted separately for president and vice president.

[e] Data are provided for the majority and the principal minority party in the House of Representatives (H) and the Senate (S). Key to abbreviations of parties; Ad, Administration; AM, Anti-Masonic; C, Coalition; D, Democratic; DR, Democratic-Republican; F, Federalist; J, Jacksonian; NR, National Republican; Op, Opposition; R, Republican; W, Whig. Party data are for the beginning of the first session of each Congress.

YEAR	CANDIDATES[a]	PARTY[b]	ELECTORAL VOTE	POPULAR VOTE[c]	ELECTED VICE PRESIDENT[d]	CONGRESSES[e]
1800	**Thomas Jefferson**	Democratic-Republican	73[f]		Aaron Burr	7th H: DR-69, F-36 S: DR-18, F-13 8th DR-102, F-39 DR-25, F-9
	Aaron Burr	Democratic-Republican	73			
	John Adams	Federalist	65			
	Thomas Pinckney	Federalist	64			
	John Jay	Federalist	1			
1804	**Thomas Jefferson**	Democratic- Republican	162		George Clinton	9th H: DR-116, F-25 S: DR-27, F-7 10th DR-118, F-24 DR-28, F-6
	Charles C. Pinckney	Federalsit	14			
1808	**James Madison**	Democratic-Republican	122		George Clinton	11th H: DR-94, F-48 S: DR-28, F-6 12th DR-108, F-36 DR-30, F-6
	Charles C. Pinckney	Federalist	47			
	George Clinton	Independent Democratic-Republican	6			
1812	**James Madison**	Democratic-Republican	128		Elbridge Gerry	13th H: DR-112, F-68 S: DR-27, F-9 14th DR-117, F-65 DR-25, F-11
	DeWitt Clinton	Federalist	89			
1816	**James Monroe**	Democratic-Republican	183		Daniel D. Tompkins	15th H: DR-141, F-42 S: DR-34, F-10 16th DR-156, F-27 DR-35, F-7
	Rufus King	Federalist	34			
1820	**James Monroe**	Democratic-Republican	231		Daniel D. Tompkins	17th H: DR-158, F-25 S: DR-44, F-4 18th DR-187, F-26 DR-44, F-4
	John Q. Adams	Independent Democratic-Republican	1			

[f] Election of president decided by the House of Representatives.

YEAR	CANDIDATES[a]	PARTY[b]	ELECTORAL VOTE	POPULAR VOTE[c]	ELECTED VICE PRESIDENT[d]	CONGRESSES[e]
1824	**John Q. Adams**	Coalition	84[f]	113,122 (30.9%)	John C. Calhoun	19th H: Ad-105, J-97 S:Ad-26, J-20	20th J-119, Ad-94 J-28, Ad-20
	Andrew Jackson	Democratic-Republican	99	115,271 (41.3%)		
	William H. Crawford	Democratic-Republican	41	40,856 (11.2%)		
	Henry Clay	Democratic-Republican	37	47,531 (13.0%)		
1828	**Andrew Jackson**	Democratic-Republican	178	642,553 (56.0%)	John C. Calhoun	21st H: D-139, NR-74 S: D-26, NR-22	22nd D-141, NR-58 D-25, NR-21
	John Q. Adams	National Republican	83	500,897 (43.6%)		
1832	**Andrew Jackson**	Democratic	219	701,780 (54.5%)	Martin Van Buren	23rd H: D-147, AM-53 S: D-20, NR-20	24th D-145, W-98 D-27, W-25
	Henry Clay	National Republican	49	484,205 (37.6%)		
	John Floyd	S.C. Governor	11			
	William Wirt	Anti-Masonic	7	100,715 (7.8%)		
1836	**Martin Van Buren**	Democratic	170	764,176 (50.8%)	Richard M. Johnson[g]	25th H: D-108, W-107 S: D-30, W-18	26th D-124, W-118 D-28, W-22
	William Henry Harrison	Whig	73	550,816 (36.7%)		
	Hugh L. White	Whig	23	146,107 (9.7%)		
	Daniel Webster	Whig	14	41,201 (2.7%)		
1840	**William Henry Harrison**	Whig	234	1,275,390 (52.9%)	John Tyler[b]	27th H: W-133, D-102 S: W-28, D-22	28th D-142, W-79 W-28, D-25
	Martin Van Buren	Democratic	60	1,128,854 (46.8%)		
1844	**James K. Polk**	Democratic	170	1,339,494 (49.5%)	George M. Dallas	29th H: D-143, W-77 S: D-31, W-25	30th W-115, D-108 D-36, W-21
	Henry Clay	Whig	105	1,300,004 (48.1%)		

[f] Election of president decided by the House of Representatives.
[g] For the first (and thus far the only) time, the Senate selected the vice president, voting 33-16 for Richard M. Johnson, who fell one vote short of election by the electoral college.
[b] Became president upon the death of the president.

YEAR	CANDIDATES[a]	PARTY[b]	ELECTORAL VOTE	POPULAR VOTE[c]	ELECTED VICE PRESIDENT[d]	CONGRESSES[e]
1848	Zachary Taylor	Whig	163	1,361,393 (47.3%)	Millard Fillmore[b]	31st H: D-112, W-109 S: D-35, W-25	32nd D-140, W-88 D-35, W-24
	Lewis Cass	Democratic	127	1,223,460 (42.5%)		
	Martin Van Buren	Free Soil	0	291,501 (10.1%)		
1852	Franklin Pierce	Democratic	254	1,607,510 (50.8%)	William R. King	33rd H: D-159, W-71 S: D-38, W-22	34th R-108, D-83 D-42, R-15
	Winfield Scott	Whig	42	1,386,942 (43.9%)		
	John P. Hale	Free Soil	0	155,210 (4.9%)		
1856	James Buchanan	Democratic	174	1,836,072 (45.3%)	John C. Breckinridge	35th H: D-131, R-92 S: D-36, R-20	36th R-114, D-101 D-38, R-26
	John C. Fremont	Republican	114	1,342,345 (33.1%)		
	Millard Fillmore	Whig–American	8	873,053 (21.5%)		
1860	Abraham Lincoln	Republican	180	1,865,908 (39.8%)	Hannibal Hamlin	37th H: R-105, D-43 S: R-31, D-8	38th R-102, D-75 R-36, D-9
	John C. Breckinridge	Southern Democratic	72	848,019 (18.1%)		
	John Bell	Constitutional Union	39	590,901 (12.6%)		
	Stephen A. Douglas	Democratic	12	1,380,202 (29.5%)		
1864	Abraham Lincoln	Republican	212[i]	2,218,388 (55.0%)	Andrew Johnson[b]	39th H: R-149, D-42 S: R-42, D-10	40th R-143, D-49 R-42, D-11
	George B. McClellan	Democratic	21	1,812,807 (45.0%)		
1868	Ulysses S. Grant	Republican	214[j]	3,013,650 (52.7%)	Schuyler Colfax	41st H: R-149, D-63 S: R-56, D-11	42nd R-134, D-104 R-52, D-17
	Horatio Seymour	Democratic	80	2,708,744 (47.3%)		
1872	Ulysses S. Grant	Republican	286[k]	3,598,235 (55.6%)	Henry Wilson	43rd H: R-194, D-92 S: R-49, D-19	44th D-169, R-109 R-45, D-29
	Horace Greeley	Democratic, Liberal Republican	66[l]	2,834,761 (43.9%)		

[i] Eleven Southern states had seceded from the Union and did not vote.

[j] Three Southern states had not been readmitted to the Union.

[k] Congress refused to accept the electoral votes of the two states because of reconstruction turmoil.

[l] Greely died after the election but before the casting of electoral votes. Democratic electors thus divided their 66 votes among other candidates.

YEAR	CANDIDATES[a]	PARTY[b]	ELECTORAL VOTE	POPULAR VOTE[c]	ELECTED VICE PRESIDENT[d]	CONGRESSES[e]
1876	**Rutherford B. Hayes**	Republican	185[m]	4,034,311 (47.9%)	William A. Wheeler	45th H: D-153, R-140 S: R-39, D-36 — 46th D-149, R-130 D-42, R-33
	Samuel J. Tilden	Democratic	184	4,288,546 (51.0%)		
1880	**James A. Garfield**	Republican	214	4,446,158 (48.3%)	Chester A. Arthur[b]	47th H: R-147, D-135 S: R-37, D-37 — 48th D-197, R-118 R-38, D-36
	Winfield S. Hancock	Democratic	155	4,444,260 (48.2%)		
	James B. Weaver	Greenback	0	305,997 (3.3%)		
1884	**Grover Cleveland**	Democratic	219	4,874,621 (48.5%)	Thomas A. Hendricks	49th H: D-183, R-140 S: R-43, D-34 — 50th D-169, R-152 R-39, D-37
	James G. Blaine	Republican	182	4,848,936 (48.2%)		
	Benjamin F. Butler	Greenback	0	175,096 (1.7%)		
	John P. St. John	Prohibition	0	147,482 (1.5%)		
1888	**Benjamin Harrison**	Republican	233	5,543,892 (47.8%)	Levy P. Morton	51st H: R-166, D-159 S: R-39, D-37 — 52nd D-235, R-88 R-47, D-39
	Grover Cleveland	Democratic	168	5,534,488 (48.6%)		
	Clinton B. Fisk	Prohibition	0	249,813 (2.2%)		
	Alson J. Streeter	Union Labor	0	146,602 (1.3%)		
1892	**Grover Cleveland**	Democratic	277	5,551,883 (46.1%)	Adlai Stevenson	53rd H: D-218, R-127 S: D-44, R-38 — 54th R-244, D-105 R-43, D-39
	Benjamin Harrison	Republican	145	5,179,244 (43.0%)		
	James B. Weaver	Populist	22	1,024,280 (8.5%)		
	John Bidwell	Prohibition	0	270,770 (2.2%)		
1896	**William McKinley**	Republican	271	7,108,480 (51.0%)	Garret A. Hobart	55th H: R-204, D-113 S: R-47, D-34 — 56th R-185, D-163 R-53, D-26
	William J. Bryan	Democratic, Populist	176	6,511,495 (46.7%)		
	John M. Palmer	National Democratic	0	133,435 (1.0%)		
	Joshua Levering	Prohibition	0	127,072 (.9%)		

[m] The electoral votes of three states were disputed. A special Republican-controlled commission awarded them to Hayes.

YEAR	CANDIDATES[a]	PARTY[b]	ELECTORAL VOTE	POPULAR VOTE[c]	ELECTED VICE PRESIDENT[d]	CONGRESSES[e]	
1900	William McKinley	Republican	292	7,218,039 (51.7%)	Theodore Roosevelt[b]	57th	58th
	William J. Bryan	Democratic	155	6,358,345 (45.5%)		H: R-197, D-151	H: R-208, D-178
	John C. Woolley	Prohibition	0	209,004 (1.5%)		S: R-55, D-31	S: R-57, D-33
	Eugene V. Debs	Socialist	0	86,935 (.6%)			
1904	Theodore Roosevelt	Republican	336	7,626,593 (56.4%)	Charles W. Fairbanks	59th	60th
	Alton B. Parker	Democratic	140	5,082,898 (37.6%)		H: R-250, D-136	H: R-222, D-164
	Eugene V. Debs	Socialist	0	402,489 (3.0%)		S: R-57, D-33	S: R-61, D-31
	Silas C. Swallow	Prohibition	0	258,596 (1.9%)			
1908	William Howard Taft	Republican	321	7,676,258 (51.6%)	James S. Sherman	61st	62nd
	William J. Bryan	Democratic	162	6,406,801 (43.1%)		H: R-219, D-172	D-228, R-161
	Eugene V. Debs	Socialist	0	420,380 (2.8%)		S: R-59, D-32	R-49, D-42
	Eugene W. Chafin	Prohibition	0	252,821 (1.7%)			
1912	Woodrow Wilson	Democratic	435	6,293,152 (41.9%)	Thomas R. Marshall	63rd	64th
	Theodore Roosevelt	Progressive	88	4,119,207 (27.4%)		H: D-291, R-127	D-230, R-196
	William Howard Taft	Republican	8	3,486,333 (23.2%)		S: D-51, R-44	D-56, R-40
	Eugene V. Debs	Socialist	0	900,369 (6.0%)			
1916	Woodrow Wilson	Democratic	277	9,126,300 (49.2%)	Thomas R. Marshall	65th	66th
	Charles E. Hughes	Republican	254	8,546,789 (46.1%)		H: D-210, R-216[r]	R-240, D-190
	Allan L. Benson	Socialist	0	589,924 (3.2%)		S: D-53, R-42	R-49, D-47
	J. Frank Hanly	Prohibition	0	221,030 (1.2%)			
1920	Warren G. Harding	Republican	404	16,133,314 (60.3%)	Calvin Coolidge[b]	67th	68th
	James M. Cox	Democratic	127	9,140,884 (34.2%)		H: R-301, D-131	R-225, D-205
	Eugene V. Debs	Socialist	0	913,664 (3.4%)		S: R-59, D-37	R-51, D-43
	Parley P. Christensen	Farmer–Labor	0	264,540 (1.0%)			

YEAR	CANDIDATES[a]	PARTY[b]	ELECTORAL VOTE	POPULAR VOTE[c]	ELECTED VICE PRESIDENT[d]	CONGRESSES[e]
1924	**Calvin Coolidge**	Republican	382	15,717,553 (54.1%)	Charles G. Dawes	69th H: R-247, D-183 S: R-54, D-40 · 70th R-237, D-195 R-49, D-46
	John W. Davis	Democratic	136	8,386,169 (28.8%)		
	Robert M. La Follette	Progressive	13	4,814,050 (16.6%)		
	Herman P. Faris	Prohibition	0	54,833 (.2%)		
1928	**Herbert Hoover**	Republican	444	21,411,991 (58.2%)	Charles Curtis	71st H: R-267, D-167 S: R-56, D-39 · 72nd D-220, R-214[f] R-48, D-47
	Alfred E. Smith	Democratic	87	15,000,185 (40.8%)		
	Norman Thomas	Socialist	0	266,453 (.7%)		
	William Z. Foster	Communist	0	48,170 (.1%)		
1932	**Franklin D. Roosevelt**	Democratic	472	22,825,016 (57.4%)	John N. Garner	73rd H: D-310, R-117 S: D-60, R-35 · 74th D-319, R-103 D-69, R-25
	Herbert Hoover	Republican	59	15,758,397 (39.6%)		
	Norman Thomas	Socialist	0	883,990 (2.2%)		
	William Z. Foster	Communist	0	102,221 (.3%)		
1936	**Franklin D. Roosevelt**	Democratic	523	27,747,636 (60.8%)	John N. Garner	75th H: D-331, R-89 S: D-76, R-16 · 76th D-261, R-164 D-69, R-23
	Alfred M. Landon	Republican	8	16,679,543 (36.5%)		
	William Lemke	Union	0	892,492 (2%)		
	Norman Thomas	Socialist	0	187,758 (.4%)		
1940	**Franklin D. Roosevelt**	Democratic	449	27,263,448 (54.7%)	Henry A. Wallace	77th H: D-268, R-162 S: D-66, R-28 · 78th D-218, R-208 D-58, R-37
	Wendell Willkie	Republican	82	22,336,260 (44.8%)		
	Norman Thomas	Socialist	0	116,827 (.2%)		
	Roger W. Babson	Prohibition	0	58,658 (.1%)		
1944	**Franklin D. Roosevelt**	Democratic	432	25,611,936 (53.4%)	Harry S Truman[b]	79th H: D-242, R-190 S: D-56, R-38 · 80th R-245, D-188 R-51, D-45
	Thomas E. Dewey	Republican	99	22,013,372 (45.9%)		
	Norman Thomas	Socialist	0	79,000 (.2%)		
	Claude A. Watson	Prohibition	0	74,733 (.2%)		

YEAR	CANDIDATES[a]	PARTY[b]	ELECTORAL VOTE	POPULAR VOTE[c]	ELECTED VICE PRESIDENT[d]	CONGRESSES[e]
1948	**Harry S Truman**	Democratic	303	24,105,587 (49.5%)	Alben W. Barkley	81st H: D-263, R-171 S: D-54, R-42	82nd D-234, R-199 D-49, R-47
	Thomas E. Dewey	Republican	189	21,970,017 (45.1%)		
	J. Strom Thurmond	State's Rights Democratic	39	1,169,134 (2.4%)		
	Henry A. Wallace	Progressive	0	1,157,057 (2.4%)		
1952	**Dwight D. Eisenhower**	Republican	442	33,936,137 (55.1%)	Richard M. Nixon	83rd H: R-221, D-211 S: R-48, D-47	84th D-232, R-203 D-48, R-47
	Adlai E. Stevenson	Democratic	89	27,314,649 (44.4%)		
	Vincent Hallinan	Progressive	0	140,416 (.2%)		
	Stuart Hamblen	Prohibition	0	73,413 (.1%)		
1956	**Dwight D. Eisenhower**	Republican	457	35,585,245 (57.4%)	Richard M. Nixon	85th H: D-233, R-200 S: D-49, R-47	86th D-283, R-153 D-64, R-34
	Adlai E. Stevenson	Democratic	73	26,030,172 (42.0%)		
	Eric Hass	Socialist Labor	0	44,300 (.1%)		
1960	**John F. Kennedy**	Democratic	303	34,221,344 (49.7%)	Lyndon B. Johnson[b]	87th H: D-263, R-174 S: D-65, R-35	88th D-258, R-177 D-67, R-33
	Richard M. Nixon	Republican	219	34,106,671 (49.6%)		
	Eric Hass	Socialist Labor	0	47,552 (.1%)		
	Harry F. Byrd		15[n]	0		
1964	**Lyndon B. Johnson**	Democratic	486	43,126,584 (61.1%)	Hubert H. Humprey	89th H: D-295, R-140 S: D-68, R-32	90th D-247, R-187 D-64, R-36
	Barry M. Goldwater	Republican	52	27,177,838 (38.5%)		
1968	**Richard M. Nixon**	Republican	301	31,785,148 (43.4%)	Spiro T. Agnew	91st H: D-243, R-192 S: D-57, R-43	92nd D-254, R-180 D-54, R-44
	Hubert H. Humprey	Democratic	191	31,274,503 (42.7%)		
	George C. Wallace	American Independent	46	9,901,151 (13.5%)		

[n] "Unpledged" Democratic electors cast votes for Senator Harry F. Byrd of Virginia.

YEAR	CANDIDATES[a]	PARTY[b]	ELECTORAL VOTE	POPULAR VOTE[c]	ELECTED VICE PRESIDENT[d]	CONGRESSES[e]	
1972	**Richard M. Nixon**[c]	Republican	520	47,170,179 (60.7%)	Spiro T. Agnew[p]	93rd H: D-239, R-192 S: D-56, R-42	94th D-291, R-144 D-60, R-37
	George McGovern	Democratic	17	29,171,791 (37.5%)			
	John G. Schmitz	American	0	1,090,673 (1.4%)			
	Benjamin Spock	People's	0	78,751 (.1%)			
1976	**Jimmy Carter**	Democratic	297	40,831,000 (50.1%)	Walter F. Mondale	95th H: D-292, R-143 S: D-61, R-38	96th D-276, R-158 D-58, R-41
	Gerald R. Ford	Republican	240	37,148,000 (48.0%)			
	Eugene McCarthy	Independent	0	756,691 (1.0%)			
1980	**Ronald Reagan**	Republican	489	43,904,0000 (50.7%)	George Bush	97th H: D-243, R-192 S: R-53, D-46	98th D-269, R-166 R-54, D-46
	Jimmy Carter	Democratic	49	35,484,000 (41.0%)			
	John Anderson	Independent	0	5,720,060 (7.1%)			
	Ed Clark	Libertarian	0	921,299 (1.1%)			
1984	**Ronald Reagan**	Republican	525	52,609,797 (59.0%)	George Bush	99th H: D-253, R-182 S: R-53, D-47	100th D-258, R-177 D-55, R-45
	Walter F. Mondale	Democratic	13	36,450,613 (41.0%)			
	David Bergland	Libertarian	0	235,619 (.3%)			
1988	**George Bush**	Republican	426	48,886,097 (53.4%)	J. Danforth Quayle	101st H: D-260, R-175 S: D-55, R-45	102nd D-267, R-167 D-56, R-44
	Michael S. Dukakis	Democratic	111[q]	41,809,083 (45.6%)			
	Ron Paul	Libertarian	0	431,616 (.5%)			
1992	**Bill Clinton**	Democratic	370	43,718,275 (43%)	Al Gore	103rd H: D-258, R-176 S: D-57, R-43	104th R-236, D-197, I-1 R-53, D-47
	George Bush	Republican	168	36,167,416 (38%)			
	Ross Perot	Independent	0	19,237,247 (19%)			
	André Marrou	Libertarian	0	291,627 (.3%)			

o Resigned in 1974; succeeded by Vice President Gerald R. Ford (see note p).

p Resigned in 1973; replaced under the Twenty-fifth Amendment by Gerald R. Ford. When Ford became president upon Nixon's resignation in 1974, Nelson Rockefeller was selected as vice president, according to the Twenty-fifth Amendment.

q Lloyd Bentsen, the Democratic candidate for vice president, polled one electoral vote for president, cast by an elector from West Virginia.

YEAR	CANDIDATES[a]	PARTY[b]	ELECTORAL VOTE	POPULAR VOTE[c]	ELECTED VICE PRESIDENT[d]	CONGRESSES[e]
1996	**Bill Clinton**	Democratic	379	45,628,667 (49%)	Al Gore	105th 106th[f]
	Bob Dole	Republican	159	37,869,453 (41%)		H: R-227, D-207, I-1 R-223, D-211, I-1
	Ross Perot	Patriot	0	7,874,283 (8%)		S: R-55, D-45 R-55, D-45
	Harry Browne	Libertarian	0	485,120 (.5%)		

[a] Democrats controlled the House with the help of other parties.

[b] The 1930 elections gave Republicans a two-seat majority in the House. Subsequent departures, however, handed control of the House to Democrats, with John Nance Garner as speaker.

[f] Unofficial results, as of November 12, 1998.

APPENDIX 2

Presidents and Justices, 1789–1999

PRESIDENT	JUSTICE APPOINTED	YEARS OF SERVICE	AGE AT START OF TERM
Washington (F)*		1789–1797	57
	Jay (F)**	1789–1795	43
	J. Rutledge (F)@	1789–1791	50
	Cushing (F)	1789–1810	57
	Wilson (F)	1789–1798	47
	Blair (F)	1789–1796	57
	Iredell (F)	1790–1799	38
	T. Johnson (F)	1791–1793	58
	Paterson (F)	1793–1806	47
	J. Rutledge (F)**$	1795	55
	S. Chase (F)	1796–1811	54
	Ellsworth (F)**	1796–1800	50
Adams, J. (F)		1797–1801	61
	Washington (F)	1798–1829	36
	Moore (F)	1799–1804	44
	J. Marshall (F)**	1801–1835	45
Jefferson (DR)		1801–1809	57
	W. Johnson (DR)	1804–1834	32
	Livingston (DR)	1806–1823	49
	Todd (DR)	1807–1826	42
Madison (DR)		1809–1817	57
	Duval (DR)	1811–1835	58
	Story (DR)	1812–1845	32

Source: Adapted from Alpheus Thomas Mason and Donald Grier Stephenson, Jr., American Constitutional Law: Introductory Essays and Selected Cases, 11th ed. (Upper Saddle River, N.J.: Prentice-Hall, 1996), pp. 693–697

PRESIDENT	JUSTICE APPOINTED	YEARS OF SERVICE	AGE AT START OF TERM
Monroe (DR)		1817–1825	58
	Thompson (DR)	1823–1843	55
Adams, J.Q. (DR)		1825–1829	57
	Trimble (DR)	1826–1828	49
Jackson (D)		1829–1837	61
	McLean (D)	1829–1861	43
	Baldwin (D)	1830–1844	49
	Wayne (D)	1835–1867	45
	Taney (D)**	1836–1864	58
	Barbour (D)	1836–1841	52
	Catron (D)	1837–1865	51
Van Buren (D)		1837–1841	54
	McKinley (D)	1837–1852	57
	Daniel (D)	1841–1860	56
Harrison, W. (W)#		1841	68
Tyler (W)		1841–1845	50
	Nelson (W)	1845–1872	52
Polk (D)		1845–1849	49
	Woodbury (D)	1845–1851	56
	Grier (D)	1846–1870	52
Taylor (W)#		1849–1850	65
Fillmore (W)		1850–1853	50
	Curtis	1851–1857	42

PRESIDENT	JUSTICE APPOINTED	YEARS OF SERVICE	AGE AT START OF TERM
Pierce (D)		1853–1857	48
	Campbel (D)	1853–1861	41
Buchanan (D)		1857–1861	65
	Clifford (D)	1858–1881	54
Lincoln (R)		1861–1865	52
	Swayne (R)	1862–1881	57
	Miller (R)	1862–1890	46
	Davis (R)	1862–1877	47
	Field (D)	1863–1897	46
	S. P. Chase (R)**	1864–1873	56
Johnson, A. (D)#		1865–1869	56
Grant (R)		1869–1877	46
	Strong (R)	1870–1880	61
	Bradley (R)	1870–1892	56
	Hunt (R)	1872–1882	62
	Waite (R)**	1874–1888	57
Hayes (R)		1877–1881	54
	Harlan, I (R)&	1877–1911	44
	Woods (R)	1880–1887	56
Garfield (R)		1881	49
	Mathews (R)	1881–1889	56
Arthur(R)		1881–1885	50
	Gray (R)	1881–1902	53
	Blatchford (R)	1882–1893	62

PRESIDENT	JUSTICE APPOINTED	YEARS OF SERVICE	AGE AT START OF TERM
Cleveland (D)		1885–1889	47
	L. Lamar (D)	1888–1893	62
	Fuller (D)**	1888–1910	55
Harrison, B. (R)		1889–1893	55
	Brewer (R)	1889–1910	52
	Brown (R)	1891–1906	54
	Shiras (R)	1892–1903	60
	H. Jackson (D)	1893–1895	60
Cleveland (D)		1893–1897	55
	E. White (D)@	1894–1910	48
	Peckham (D)	1896–1909	57
McKinley (R)		1897–1901	54
	McKenna (R)	1898–1925	54
Roosevelt, T. (R)		1901–1909	42
	Holmes (R)	1902–1932	61
	Day (R)	1903–1922	53
	Moody (R)	1906–1910	52
Taft (R)		1909–1913	51
	Lurton (D)	1909–1914	65
	Hughes (R)@	1910–1916	48
	E. White+ (D)**	1910–1921	65
	Van Devanter (R)	1910–1937	51
	J. Lamar (D)	1910–1916	53
	Pitney (R)	1912–1922	54

PRESIDENT	JUSTICE APPOINTED	YEARS OF SERVICE	AGE AT START OF TERM
Wilson (D)		1913–1921	56
	McReynolds (D)	1914–1941	52
	Brandeis (R)	1916–1939	59
	Clarke (D)	1916–1922	59
Harding		1921–1923	55
	Taft (R)**	1921–1930	63
	Sutherland (R)	1922–1938	60
	Butler (D)	1922–1939	56
	Sanford (R)	1923–1930	57
Coolidge (R)		1923–1929	50
	Stone (R)@	1925–1941	52
Hoover (R)		1929–1933	54
	Hughes (R)**	1930–1941	68
	Roberts (R)	1930–1945	55
	Cardozo (D)	1932–1938	61
Roosevelt, F. (D)		1933–1945	51
	Black (D)	1937–1971	51
	Reed (D)	1938–1957	53
	Frankfurter (Ind)	1939–1962	56
	Douglas (D)	1939–1975	40
	Murphy (D)	1940–1949	49
	Byrnes (D)	1941–1942	62
	Stone* (R)**	1941–1946	68
	R. Jackson (D)	1941–1954	49
	W. Rutledge (D)	1943–1949	48

PRESIDENT	JUSTICE APPOINTED	YEARS OF SERVICE	AGE AT START OF TERM
Truman (D)		1945–1953	60
	Burton (R)	1945–1958	57
	Vinson (D)**	1946–1953	56
	Clark (D)	1949–1967	49
	Minton (D)	1949–1956	58
Eisenhower (R)		1953–1961	62
	Warren (R)**	1953–1969	62
	Harlan, II (R)&	1955–1971	55
	Brennan (D)	1956–1990	50
	Whittaker (R)	1957–1962	56
	Stewart (R)	1958–1981	43
Kennedy (D)		1961–1963	43
	B. White (D)	1962–1993	44
	Goldberg (D)	1962–1965	54
Johnson, L. (D)		1963–1969	55
	Fortas (D)	1965–1969	55
	T. Marshall (D)	1967–1991	58
Nixon (R)		1969–1974	56
	Burger (R)**	1969–1986	61
	Blackmun (R)	1970–1994	61
	Powell (D)	1971–1987	64
	Rehnquist (R)@	1971–1986	47
Ford (R)		1974–1977	61
	Stevens (R)	1975–	55
Carter (D)#		1977–1981	52

PRESIDENT	JUSTICE APPOINTED	YEARS OF SERVICE	AGE AT START OF TERM
Reagan (R)		1981–1989	70
	O'Connor (R)	1981–	51
	Rehnquist+ (R)**	1986–	61
	Scalia (R)	1986–	50
	Kennedy (R)	1988–	51
Bush (R)		1989–1993	64
	Souter (R)	1990–	51
	Thomas (R)	1991–	43
Clinton (D)		1993–	46
	Ginsberg (D)	1993–	60
	Breyer (D)	1994–	55

* Letter following name indicates political party affiliation.

(F)—Federalist

(DR)—Democrat-Republican

(D)—Democratic

(W)—Whig

(R)—Republican

(Ind)—Independent

** Denotes appointmnet as chief justice.

@ Later appointed chief justice.

+ Indicates appoinment from associate to chief justice.

# Indicates no appointments to Supreme Court.

Holding a recess appointment, John Rutledge presided over the Supreme Court at the August term, 1795, but was denied confirmation by the Senate in December 1795.

& John Marshall Harlan (I) was a grandfather of John Marshall Harlan (II) and is thus far the only justice to have had a lineal descendant who also became a justice.

NOTES

I. THE CONSTITUTION, POLITICS, AND THE SUPREME COURT

1. Joan Bethke Elshtain, "Issues and Themes: Spiral of Delegitimation or New Social Covenant?" in Michael Nelson, ed., *The Elections of 1992* (Washington, DC: Congressional Quarterly Press, 1993), p. 123, n. 8.

2. *Congressional Quarterly Weekly Report*, August 22, 1992, p. 2567.

3. 410 U.S. 113 (1973).

4. The Supreme Court first clearly acknowledged a constitutional right of privacy in striking down a statute in *Griswold* v. *Connecticut*, 381 U.S. 479 (1965). However, a right of privacy (defined as a right of personal autonomy or personhood) was at least a peripheral concern in several decisions before *Griswold*. See William M. Beaney, "The Constitutional Right to Privacy in the Supreme Court," 1962 *Supreme Court Review* 212.

5. *Webster* v. *Reproductive Health Services*, 492 U.S. 490 (1989). The last unequivocal victory in the Supreme Court for proponents of abortion rights was *Thornburgh* v. *American College of Obstetricians and Gynecologists*, 474 U.S. 809 (1986), in which the Court, by a vote of 5 to 4, invalidated a comprehensive Pennsylvania regulatory scheme regarding consent, information, record-keeping, determination of viability, care of the fetus, and the presence of a second physician in postviability abortions.

6. *Planned Parenthood of Southeastern Pennsylvania* v. *Casey*, 505 U.S. 833 (1992).

7. In the Supreme Court's hierarchy of values, it makes a difference when a right is denominated as "fundamental." Government may restrict fundamental rights only when the regulation in question is "necessary" to achieve a "compelling" interest. Restrictions on liberties that are less than fundamental require correspondingly less justification.

8. 505 U.S. at 966.

9. Ibid., 943. Justice Blackmun retired from the Supreme Court in the summer of 1994.

10. Ibid., 1000–1001.

11. Barbara Hinkson Craig and David M. O'Brien, *Abortion and American Politics* (Chatham, NJ: Chatham House, 1993), p. 169. Reagan denied use of a strict litmus test, but it strains credulity to believe that his administration would have proposed someone for the Supreme Court who was openly supportive of *Roe*. After Clinton won the 1992 election but before he took office, none other than Justice Blackmun, the author of the Court's opinion in *Roe*, counseled the president-elect, during a lengthy conversation at a retreat in South Carolina, not to apply a litmus test on abortion in filling judicial vacancies. Statement by Lyle Denniston of the *Baltimore Sun* to the author, September 10, 1993.

12. To be sure, the Court figured more prominently in some elections than in others. As chapter 5 will show, Progressive criticism of judicial power in 1912 was aimed more at state courts and the lower federal courts than at the Supreme Court itself. The Court was certainly an issue in the 1992 election, but as chapter 8 explains, it was less involved than in 1980 and 1984.

13. As James Madison explained in *Federalist*, No. 10, "The friend of popular governments never finds himself so much alarmed for their character and fate as when he contemplates their propensity to [faction]. . . . Among the numerous advantages promised by a well-constructed Union none deserves to be more accurately developed than its tendency to break and control the violence of faction."

14. John H. Aldrich, *Why Parties?* (Chicago: University of Chicago Press, 1995), pp. 28–29.

15. Walter Dean Burnham, "Party Systems and the Political Process," in William Nisbet Chambers and Walter Dean Burnham, eds., *The American Party Systems* (New York: Oxford University Press, 1967), p. 289.

16. Walter Dean Burnham, *Critical Elections and the Mainsprings of American Politics* (New York: W. W. Norton, 1970), p. 10.

17. Between 1933 and 1999, Republicans were a majority in the House of Representatives only in 1947–1949, 1953–1955, and after January 1995; in the same period Republicans controlled the Senate only in 1947–1949, 1953–1955, 1981–1987, and after January 1995.

18. As commonly used in American political thought, "the people" refers to the political community—those persons who possess (or who should possess) the right to vote at a given time. In 1787 that community included, at most, white adult males; today the political community includes almost all persons above the age of seventeen.

19. Adams popularized the phrase shortly before the Revolutionary War. It was later incorporated into the Massachusetts Constitution, the oldest of the American state constitutions still in force.

20. *Van Horne's Lessee* v. *Dorrance*, 2 U.S. (2 Dallas) 304, 308 (C.C. Pa. 1795).

21. 5 U.S. (1 Cranch) 137 (1803).

22. Ibid., 178.

23. *Osborn* v. *Bank of the United States*, 22 U.S. (9 Wheaton) 738, 866 (1824).

24. Speech at Elmira, New York, May 3, 1907, in Charles Evans Hughes, *Addresses of Charles Evans Hughes*, 2d ed. (New York: G. P. Putnam's Sons, 1916), p. 185.

25. Donald E. Stokes and John J. DiIulio, Jr., "The Setting: Valance Politics in Modern Elections," in Michael Nelson, ed., *The Elections of 1992* (Washington, DC: Congressional Quarterly Press, 1993), pp. 1–20.

26. Alexis de Tocqueville, *Democracy in America*, vol. 1, Henry Reeve, trans. (New York: Colonial Press, 1899), p. 284.

27. Congress established the Court's first discretionary or "certiorari" jurisdiction in 1891, as part of a major judicial reorganization that created the United States Courts of Appeals. Congress greatly expanded certiorari jurisdiction in 1925; in 1988, Congress all but eliminated the remaining categories of cases the Court was required by law to decide.

28. 60 U.S. (19 Howard) 393 (1857).

29. U.S. Constitution, Article II, Section 1.

30. *Ashwander* v. *T.V.A.*, 297 U.S. 288 (1936).

31. For example, see *Carter* v. *Carter Coal Co.*, 298 U.S. 238 (1936).

32. Robert H. Jackson, *The Struggle for Judicial Supremacy* (New York: Vintage Books, 1941), p. 315.

33. See, for example, Richard Funston, "The Supreme Court and Critical Elections," 69 *American Political Science Review* 795 (1975); David Adamany, "The Supreme Court's Role in Critical Elections," in B. Campbell and R. Trilling, eds., *Realignment in American Politics* (Austin: University of Texas Press, 1980), pp. 246–247; and John R. Schmidhauser, *Constitutional Law in American Politics* (Monterey, CA: Brooks/Cole, 1984), p. 614.

34. Craig and O'Brien, *Abortion and American Politics*, ch. 2.

35. 2 U.S. (2 Dallas) 419 (1793).

36. 158 U.S. 601 (1895).

37. 400 U.S. 112 (1970).

38. *Texas* v. *Johnson*, 491 U.S. 397 (1989); *United States* v. *Eichman*, 496 U.S. 310 (1990).

39. Arguably, the Court has been reversed six times by constitutional amendment. In addition to the Eleventh, Fourteenth, Sixteenth, and Twenty-sixth amendments, the Nineteenth Amendment of 1920 reduced to nothing the Court's holding forty-six years before that the Fourteenth Amendment was no bar to state laws that excluded women from the franchise. *Minor* v. *Happersett*, 88 U.S. (21 Wallace) 162 (1874). The Twenty-fourth Amendment of 1964 partly displaced the Court's rejection twenty-seven years earlier of a Fourteenth Amendment challenge to poll taxes: *Breedlove* v. *Suttles*, 302 U.S. 277 (1937). The Twenty-fourth Amendment, however, applies only to elections for national office. In *Harper* v. *Virginia Board of Elections*, 383 U.S. 663 (1966), the Court used the Fourteenth Amendment to invalidate poll taxes that were a prerequisite to voting in state elections.

40. *Zurcher* v. *The Stanford Daily*, 436 U.S. 547 (1978).

41. *Employment Division* v. *Smith*, 494 U.S. 872 (1990). See "Religion Bill," *National Law Journal*, November 15, 1993, p. 12.

42. *Sherbert* v. *Verner*, 374 U.S. 398 (1963).

43. 138 L.Ed. 2d 624 (1997).

44. B. Henschen, "Statutory Interpretations of the Supreme Court: Congressional Response," 11 *American Politics Quarterly* 441 (1983).

45. William N. Eskridge, Jr., "Overriding Supreme Court Statutory Interpretation Decisions," 101 *Yale Law Journal* 331 (1991).

46. Note, "Congressional Reversals of Supreme Court Decisions," 71 *Harvard Law Review* 1324 (1958).

47. 490 U.S. 642 (1989).

48. *Griggs* v. *Duke Power Co.*, 401 U.S. 424, 432 (1971).

49. Henry J. Abraham, *Justices and Presidents*, 3d ed. (New York: Oxford University Press, 1992).

50. William H. Rehnquist, *Grand Inquests: The Historic Impeachments of Justice Samuel Chase and President Andrew Johnson* (New York: William Morrow, 1992).

51. Bruce Allen Murphy, *Fortas: The Rise and Ruin of a Supreme Court Justice* (New York: William Morrow, 1988).

52. Letter to Thomas Ritchie, 1820, in Paul Leicester Ford, ed., *The Writings of Thomas Jefferson*, vol. 10 (New York: G. P. Putnam's Sons, 1892–1899), p. 170.

53. Ex parte *McCardle*, 74 U.S. (7 Wallace) 506 (1869).

54. *United States* v. *Klein*, 80 U.S. (13 Wallace) 128 (1872).

55. Robert J. Steamer, *The Supreme Court in Crisis* (Amherst: University of Massachusetts Press, 1971), p. 255.

56. 125 *Congressional Record* S4128 (April 5, 1979); 125 *Congressional Record* S4138 (April 9, 1979).

57. Felix Frankfurter and James M. Landis, *The Business of the Supreme Court* (New York: Macmillan, 1928); Peter G. Fish, *The Politics of Federal Judicial Administration* (Princeton: Princeton University Press, 1973).

58. Finley Peter Dunne, *Mr. Dooley's Opinions* (New York: Harper & Brothers, 1906), p. 26.

59. Robert A. Dahl, "Decision-Making in a Democracy: The Role of the Supreme Court as a National Policy-Maker," 6 *Journal of Public Law* 279, 285 (1957).

60. John B. Taylor, "The Supreme Court and Political Eras: A Perspective on Judicial Power in a Democratic Polity," 54 *Review of Politics* 345, 362 (1992).

61. John B. Gates, *The Supreme Court and Partisan Realignment: A Macro- and Microlevel Perspective* (Boulder, CO: Westview Press, 1992), p. 170.

62. For example, see *Hylton* v. *United States*, 3 U.S. (3 Dallas) 171 (1796).

63. Emphasis added.

2. THE ELECTION OF 1800: PARTISAN BEGINNINGS

1. Kenneth C. Martis, *The Historical Atlas of the Political Parties in the United States Congress: 1789–1989* (New York: Macmillan, 1989).

2. John F. Hoadley, *Origins of American Political Parties, 1789–1803* (Lexington: University Press of Kentucky, 1986).

3. Noble E. Cunningham, Jr., "The Jeffersonian Republican Party," in Arthur M. Schlesinger, Jr., *History of U.S. Political Parties*, vol. 1 (New York: Chelsea House, 1973), p. 244.

4. John H. Aldrich, *Why Parties?* (Chicago: University of Chicago Press, 1995), pp. 94–95. The nomenclature derives from V. O. Key, Jr., *Politics, Parties, and Pressure Groups*, 5th ed. (New York: Crowell, 1964), pp. 313, 455, 657.

5. This number includes John Rutledge, whom Washington picked in July 1795 to succeed John Jay as chief justice. The Senate rejected Rutledge's nomination in December because of his opposition to the Jay Treaty, but he is usually counted among the chief justices because, holding a recess appointment, he presided over the Court during the August 1795 term.

6. Several of the Court's decisions in its first decade anticipated later developments. *Hayburn's Case*, 2 U.S. (2 Dallas) 409 (1792), laid the foundation for the practice that the Court renders decisions only in actual "cases" and "controversies." *Chisholm* v. *Georgia*, 2 U.S. (2 Dallas) 419 (1793), declared that states could be defendants in a suit brought in federal court by a citizen of another state. While the holding was quickly overturned by the Eleventh Amendment, the Court had acted as if it could proclaim the authoritative construction of the Constitution. Similarly, *Hylton* v. *United States*, 3 U.S. (3 Dallas) 171 (1796), upheld the validity of a tax on carriages against the claim that Congress had exceeded its power to tax. The unarticulated assumption of course was that the Court possessed the power of judicial review. At least two decisions injected a new dimension into the Court's work: review of the validity of state laws. The day before *Hylton* was announced, *Ware* v. *Hylton*, 3 U.S. (3 Dallas) 199 (1796), struck down a confiscatory Virginia statute that ran counter to the Treaty of Paris. Arguing against the binding force of the treaty over state law was attorney John Marshall, who referred to "those who wish to impair the sovereignty of Virginia," words his opponents would hurl against him years later as chief justice. Two years later *Calder* v. *Bull*, 3 U.S. (3 Dallas) 386 (1798), upheld a Connecticut law that had set aside the decree of a probate court and called for a new hearing. Although the ruling was favorable to the state, it was significant because the Court sat in judgment on a decision of the Connecticut Supreme Court. In a provision with far-reaching implications for the Court and the union, Section 25 of the Judiciary Act of 1789 allowed Supreme Court review of decisions of state courts when the latter had rejected a claim under federal law.

7. Quoted in Charles Warren, *The Supreme Court in United States History*, rev. ed., vol. 1 (Boston: Little, Brown, 1926), p. 173. One study of the pre-Marshall era

that assigns more significance to the work of the Court than most accounts, notes that over half of the Supreme Court's decisions involved national security and foreign affairs, broadly defined. "The preponderance of such business was not happenstance but by the intent of the framers who envisioned the federal courts as national security courts." William R. Castro, *The Supreme Court in the Early Republic: The Chief Justiceships of John Jay and Oliver Ellsworth* (Columbia: University of South Carolina Press, 1995), p. 71.

8. Because the election brought Federalist dominance to an end, John Adams referred to it as the "revolution of 1801." Charles Francis Adams, ed., *The Works of John Adams*, vol. 10 (Boston: Little, Brown, 1850–1856), p. 162. For Jefferson, the "revolution of 1800" was "as real a revolution in the principles of our government as that of 1776 was in form; not effected indeed by the sword, as that, but by the rational and peaceable instrument of reform, the suffrage of the people." To Spencer Roane, September 6, 1819, in Paul Leicester Ford, ed., *The Writings of Thomas Jefferson*, vol. 10 (New York: G. P. Putnam's Sons, 1892–1899), p. 140.

9. Richard Hofstadter, *The Idea of a Party System* (Berkeley: University of California Press, 1969), p. 128.

10. Not until after ratification of the Twentieth Amendment in 1933 did congressional (and presidential) terms begin in January, following the fall elections.

11. Dumas Malone, *Jefferson and the Ordeal of Liberty* (Boston: Little, Brown, 1962), pp. 484–506.

12. Talleyrand, the French foreign minister, refused to receive the commissioners officially but communicated surreptitiously with them, even demanding payment of $250,000 in order for negotiations to begin. The name XYZ originated from the designations X, Y, and Z that the commissioners used to identify themselves in dispatches to the United States.

13. At that time there was no single day prescribed for congressional elections. There was instead a series of contests in one state after another, spread over several months. A uniform Federal election day was not set until 1845.

14. Act of June 25, 1798. 1 Statutes at Large 570. Section 6 of the statute specified that it would be in force for a term of two years from the date of its enactment. Thus, it expired before the end of Adams's term.

15. Woodrow Wilson, *History of the American People*, vol. 3 (New York: Harper & Brothers, 1903), p. 153.

16. Quoted in James Morton Smith, *Freedom's Fetters* (Ithaca, NY: Cornell University Press, 1956), pp. 124–125.

17. Among justices of the Supreme Court, Chief Justice Jay was on record in the affirmative, and Justice Chase was opposed. Francis Wharton, *State Trials of the United States* (New York: Burt Franklin, 1970; reprint of 1849 edition), pp. 92, 197. The question was significant because seditious libel had long been a crime at English common law, and judges defined the common law. Thus, a criminal dimension to common law would allow federal judges, not state legislators or

members of Congress, to determine those acts, punishable in England, that were also punishable in the United States. The Supreme Court eventually declared that no federal criminal common law existed in *United States* v. *Hudson and Goodwin*, 11 U.S. (7 Cranch) 32 (1812). All criminal acts were instead to be defined by Congress through statutes. Ironically, this case arose after Republican partisans pressed a prosecution of Federalist editors for libeling President Thomas Jefferson, the Sedition Act having expired in 1801.

18. The most famous was probably the prosecution of John Peter Zenger, a printer in New York, in 1735. 17 *Howell's State Trials* 675 (1735). Zenger's acquittal did not bring an end to prosecutions for seditious libel, but it surely heightened discussion of the subject.

19. Zechariah Chafee, Jr., *Free Speech in the United States* (Cambridge, MA: Harvard University Press, 1942), p. 22. Once the Sedition Act expired in 1801, Congress did not enact another until 1918, during World War I.

20. In practice, "truth as a defense" was of scant help to a defendant. Judges interpreted the provision to mean that defendants had to prove the veracity of their statements, not that the government had to prove that the comments were false. In Justice Chase's words, "he must prove it to the marrow. If he asserts three things, and proves but one, he fails; if he proves but two, he fails in his defence, for he must prove the whole of his assertions to be true." Charge to the jury in Cooper's case, April 19, 1800. Wharton, *State Trials*, p. 676.

21. Campaigning in the fall of 1798 for a seat in the U.S. House of Representatives from Virginia (one of the states where the Sedition Act was especially unpopular), Marshall explained, "I am not an advocate for the alien and sedition bills; had I been in Congress when they passed, I should . . . certainly have opposed them. Yet, I do not think them fraught with all those mischiefs which many gentlemen ascribe to them. I should have opposed them because I think them useless; and because they are calculated to create unnecessary discontents and jealousies at a time when our very existence, as a nation, may depend on our union—." "Marshall's Answers to Freeholder's Questions," reprinted in Albert J. Beveridge, *The Life of John Marshall*, vol. 2 (Boston: Houghton Mifflin, 1916), p. 577. The "Answers," dated September 20, 1798, were published in a newspaper on October 11.

22. For Fisher Ames, "No correct man,—no incorrect man, even,—whose affections and feelings are wedded to the government, would give his name to the base opposers of the law. . . . This he has done. . . . The moderates [like Marshall] are the meanest of cowards, the falsest of hypocrites." In Theodore Sedgwick's words, Marshall's opposition had aided "french villainy," and he had "degraded himself by a mean & paltry electioneering trick." Quoted in Beveridge, *The Life of John Marshall*, vol. 2, pp. 390–391. George Cabot, however, suggested that allowance had to be made "for the influence of the atmosphere of Virginia which doubtless makes every one who breathes it visionary and, upon the subject of free government, incredibly credulous." Quoted in Malone, *Jefferson and the Ordeal of Liberty*, p. 390.

23. The occasion was Marshall's "Address of the Minority," December 1798, on passage of the Virginia Resolves by the state legislature in opposition to the Alien and Sedition Acts. Beveridge, *The Life of John Marshall*, vol. 2, p. 404. The Virginia Resolution, as well as its forerunner in Kentucky, will be discussed below. Marshall was elected to the House of Representatives in 1798 and served in the Sixth Congress. When Republicans mounted a drive in Congress in January 1800 to repeal the Sedition Act, Marshall was the only Federalist member of the House to vote for repeal. Ibid., p. 451.

24. Wharton, *State Trials*, p. 333. The first person convicted under the Sedition Act was Matthew Lyon, a Republican member of Congress from Vermont: his offense was an accusation that "the Executive" had "swallowed up" the "public welfare" in a "continual grasp for power, in an unbounded thirst for ridiculous pomp, foolish adulation and selfish avarice." Ibid.

25. Ibid., p. 23.

26. In many instances insights into Jefferson's thinking come from his letters. He communicated his opinions to his followers thorough correspondence and fully intended them to pass along those ideas to others.

27. Smith, *Freedom's Fetters*, p. 186. Most of the indictments were issued in 1798 and 1799, and most of the cases went to trial in the spring of 1800.

28. Ibid.

29. Ford, ed., *The Writings of Thomas Jefferson*, vol. 8, p. 205.

30. By then Chief Justice Oliver Ellsworth had undertaken a diplomatic mission abroad at the behest of President Adams, as Chief Justice Jay had done for President Washington.

31. A decision by the Supreme Court on the constitutionality of the statute would have been highly unlikely. Not until near the end of the nineteenth century did the Court acquire appellate jurisdiction in criminal cases from federal courts. In 1800, the question of the constitutionality of the Sedition Act probably could have reached the Court only on certification from a division in circuit court on the point of law in dispute, or perhaps through an action on habeas corpus. Until creation of a separate and permanent second judicial tier in the form of the Circuit Courts of Appeals in 1891, effectively this arrangement meant that ordinarily there was no right of appeal in most federal criminal cases.

32. Smith, *Freedom's Fetters*, p. 183.

33. Callender's trial is recorded in Wharton, *State Trials*, pp. 688–721.

34. Charge of May 24, 1800, quoted in Beveridge, *The Life of John Marshall*, vol. 3, p. 30, n. 1, quoting 2 *Green Bag* 264 (1890) (emphasis in the original).

35. Beveridge, *The Life of John Marshall*, vol. 3, p. 42.

36. Wharton, *State Trials*, p. 334.

37. *Hylton* v. *United States*, 3 U.S. (3 Dallas) 171 (1796). The only question argued before the Court in this case was the constitutionality of the statute.

38. Wharton, *State Trials*, pp. 709, 716. Chase's defense of judicial review in

Callender's trial anticipates several of the points Marshall would later make in his opinion in *Marbury* v. *Madison*, 5 U.S. (1 Cranch) 137 (1803).

39. Wharton, *State Trials*, pp. 670–671.

40. "To make a little saving for our friend Marshall's address" in case of repeal of the Sedition Act, Ellsworth wrote to Pickering, "the preamble . . . should read thus: 'Whereas the increasing danger and depravity of the present time require that the law against seditious practices *should be restored to its full rigor*, therefore,' etc." Quoted in Beveridge, *The Life of John Marshall*, vol. 2, pp. 451–452 (emphasis in the original).

41. Warren, *The Supreme Court in United States History*, vol. 1, p. 274.

42. Ibid., p. 156.

43. Ibid., p. 275.

44. Ibid., pp. 158–159. Warren refers to neutrality, federal common law jurisdiction, and expatriation, as well as the Alien and Sedition Acts.

45. Jefferson had an understandable desire for secrecy. Because he was vice president, the resolves might have been grounds for impeachment.

46. Letter to James Madison, March 15, 1789, in Ford, ed., *The Writings of Thomas Jefferson*, vol. 4, p. 477.

47. Letter to A. H. Rowan, in ibid., vol. 7, p. 281.

48. Edward S. Corwin, *The Doctrine of Judicial Review* (Gloucester, MA: Peter Smith, 1963; reprint of 1914 edition), p. 55.

49. The statement accorded both with the revolutionary theory found in the Declaration of Independence and with the Republican theory that the Constitution was a compact of states, not a constituent act of the people of the United States.

50. The full text of Jefferson's draft is reprinted in John P. Foley, ed., *The Jefferson Cyclopedia*, vol. 2 (New York: Russell & Russell, 1967; reissue of 1900 edition), pp. 977–979. See also Alfred H. Kelly, Winfred A. Harbison, and Herman Belz, *The American Constitution*, 7th ed., vol. 1 (New York: W. W. Norton, 1991), p. 135.

51. In the mildest interpretation, the resolves can be seen as petitions to Congress for a redress of grievances. This approach was procedurally similar to the second method the Constitution provides for its own amendment, although the resolves did not call for an alteration in the language of the Constitution, but rather adherence to the language it already contained.

52. Madison seemed shortly to abandon the argument he made in 1798. In his *Report* to the Virginia legislature in 1799, he appeared to concede the finality of the judiciary's construction of the U.S. Constitution for the other branches of the national government. Gaillard Hunt, ed., *The Writings of James Madison*, vol. 6 (New York: G. P. Putnam's Sons, 1906–1910), pp. 341–406.

53. House and Senate of Massachusetts, "Address," February 9, 1799, reprinted in Jonathan Elliot, ed., *The Debates in the Several State Conventions on the Adoption*

of the Constitution, vol. 4 (Philadelphia: J. P. Lippincott, 1836), p. 233. Inconsistent with its rejection of state negations of federal statutes, the Massachusetts legislature went on to declare the Sedition Act consistent with the First Amendment. The same legislators also defended the law because it provided the executive and legislative branches the same power of self-protection the judiciary already possessed through the inherent authority to punish contempts.

54. Page Smith, *John Adams*, vol. 2 (Garden City, NY: Doubleday, 1962), pp. 1057–1058.

55. Smith, *Freedom's Fetters*, p. 431.

56. Wharton, *State Trials*, p. 26.

57. Letter to Elbridge Gerry, January 1799; quoted in Cunningham, "The Jeffersonian Republican Party," p. 254. Cunningham's estimate is that Jefferson was far more active than Adams in these behind-the-scenes activities. Noble E. Cunningham, Jr., "The Election of 1800," in Arthur M. Schlesinger, Jr., and Fred L. Israel, eds., *History of American Presidential Elections 1789–1968* (New York: Chelsea House, 1971), vol. 1, p. 115. Open campaigning was deemed to be improper by both Adams and Jefferson.

58. Quoted in Cunningham, "The Election of 1800," p. 120.

59. Reprinted as an appendix in ibid., p. 139.

60. "To the People of New-Jersey," reprinted in the appendix in ibid., p. 136.

61. "An Address to the Voters for Electors of President and Vice-President of the United States in the State of Virginia," reprinted in the appendix in ibid., p. 149 (emphasis added).

62. "A Short Address to the Voters of Delaware," reprinted in the appendix in ibid., p. 152 (emphasis in the original).

63. Quoted in Cunningham, "The Election of 1800," p. 122.

64. "A Candid Address to the Freemen of the State of Rhode-Island," reprinted in the appendix in ibid., pp. 141–142.

65. Clare Cushman, ed., *The Supreme Court Justices* (Washington, DC: Congressional Quarterly, 1993), p. 50. Some accounts of the Supreme Court during this period omit the precise date of Ellsworth's notice to Adams. As the text explains, the timing is significant. See, for example, Henry J. Abraham, *Justices and Presidents*, 3d ed. (New York: Oxford University Press, 1992), p. 81, as well as the entry on Ellsworth in Kermit L. Hall, ed., *The Oxford Companion to the Supreme Court of the United States* (New York: Oxford University Press, 1992), p. 252; see also Michael Kraus, "Oliver Ellsworth," in Leon Friedman and Fred L. Israel, eds., *The Justices of the United States Supreme Court 1789–1969*, vol. 1 (New York: Chelsea House, 1969), p. 234.

66. Or at least this seems to be a fair interpretation of Jefferson's letter to Madison on December 19, 1800: "Ellsworth remains in France for the benefit of his health. He has resigned his office of C.J. Putting these two things together, we cannot misconstrue his views. He must have had confidence in Mr. A continuance,

to risk such a certainty as he held." Quoted in Warren, *The Supreme Court in United States History*, vol. 1, p. 174.

67. Pinckney would live to 1825, Jay to 1829. Paterson, however, would die in 1806; thus, had Adams named him chief justice, Jefferson would have selected the new chief. Not dying until 1835, Marshall survived them all.

68. This was not Marshall's first invitation to sit on the High Court. When Justice James Wilson died in 1798, Adams unsuccessfully urged Marshall to accept an appointment.

69. Quoted in Henry J. Abraham, *The Judicial Process*, 6th ed. (New York: Oxford University Press, 1993), pp. 305–306. Marshall first sat with the Court on February 4, 1801, the same day he wrote to Adams that he hoped "never to give you occasion to regret having made this appointment." Marshall was as good as his word, as far as Adams was concerned. Some twenty-five years later Adams told Marshall's son, "My gift of John Marshall to the people of the United States was the proudest act of my life." Quoted in Warren, *The Supreme Court in United States History*, vol. 1, p. 178. Marshall once referred to Jefferson as the "great Lama of the mountains." Herbert A. Johnson, *The Chief Justiceship of John Marshall, 1801–1835* (Columbia: University of South Carolina Press, 1997), p. 77. Jefferson was the great-grandson and Marshall the great-great-grandson of William Randolph and Mary Isham Randolph. Beveridge, *The Life of John Marshall*, vol. 1, p. 10.

70. Donald O. Dewey, *Marshall Versus Jefferson: The Political Background of Marbury v. Madison* (New York: Knopf, 1970), p. 55.

71. Quoted in Corwin, *The Doctrine of Judicial Review*, p. 57.

72. Letter to from Thomas Jefferson to John Dickinson, 1801, in H. A. Washington, ed., *The Writings of Thomas Jefferson*, vol. 4 (Washington, DC: Taylor & Maury, 1853), p. 424.

73. Quoted in Beveridge, *The Life of John Marshall*, vol. 3, p. 22.

74. Dumas Malone, *Jefferson the President: First Term, 1801–1805* (Boston: Little, Brown, 1970), p. 117.

75. Quoted in ibid., p. 116.

76. Ford, ed., *The Writings of Thomas Jefferson*, vol. 9, p. 247.

77. Ibid., vol. 8, p. 123.

78. Warren, *The Supreme Court in United States History*, vol. 1, p. 195. Some newspaper accounts of the day credited the offending letter to Jefferson's newly appointed United States attorney for the District of Columbia. Ibid., n. 1.

79. The order was the opening round in *Marbury v. Madison*, to be discussed below.

80. Warren, *The Supreme Court in United States History*, vol. 1, p. 204.

81. Letter of December 24, 1801, to James Monroe, quoted in ibid.

82. Quoted in ibid., vol. 1, p. 216. It seemed to bother him not at all that his position in 1801 was flatly the reverse of his argument as a Kentucky state legislator in defense of the Kentucky Resolves three years earlier.

83. If one includes William Wirt's argument advanced in defense of James Callender at the latter's sedition trial before Justice Chase, there was a fourth answer: the jury. Wharton, *State Trials*, p. 709.

84. Letter to Jefferson, February 15, 1804, quoted in Warren, *The Supreme Court in United States History*, vol. 1, p. 287.

85. Lawyers from Georgia were apparently not considered; as Gallatin also advised Jefferson, "I am told that the practice is as loose in Georgia as in New England and that a real lawyer could not easily be found there. But South Carolina stands high in that respect, at least in reputation." Ibid.

86. State Department Archives, reproduced in Gaillard Hunt, "Office-Seeking During Jefferson's Administration," 3 *American Historical Review* 282 (1898). In fact Johnson was thirty-two years of age; he and Joseph Story, a Madison appointee, are the youngest persons ever placed on the Supreme Court. The Senate promptly confirmed Johnson, and the nominee accepted when news of the president's offer reached him in April. He began his federal judicial service at the beginning of May 1804.

87. An important exception was Johnson's views on the power of Congress under the commerce clause, revealed in his concurring opinion in *Gibbons* v. *Ogden*, 22 U.S. (9 Wheaton) 1 (1824), where he took a more nationalist position than Marshall. *Gibbons* is discussed in note 66 to chapter 3.

88. *Gilchrist* v. *Collector*, 10 Fed. Cas. 355, 356, No. 5420 (C.C. Dist. of S.C., 1808).

89. U.S. Constitution, Article II, Section 4.

90. John Quincy Adams's diary entry of December 21, 1804, quoted in Warren, *The Supreme Court in United States History*, vol. 1, p. 294.

91. See the account of Chase's indictment and trial in William H. Rehnquist, *Grand Inquests: The Historic Impeachments of Justice Samuel Chase and President Andrew Johnson* (New York: William Morrow, 1992).

92. He criticized the repeal even though the Supreme Court, without a published dissent, had upheld certain provisions of the law only two months before in *Stuart* v. *Laird*, 5 U.S. (1 Cranch) 299 (1803).

93. Quoted in Warren, *The Supreme Court in United States History*, vol. 1, p. 276.

94. Rehnquist, *Grand Inquests*, p. 126.

95. Quoted in Beveridge, *The Life of John Marshall*, vol. 3, p. 167. Indeed, on the day of Chase's acquittal, Congressman John Randolph introduced in the House a resolution for a constitutional amendment that followed Jefferson's preference: "The Judges of the Supreme Court and all other Courts of the United States shall be removed from office by the President on joint address of both Houses of Congress requesting the same." Warren, *The Supreme Court in United States History*, vol. 1, p. 295.

96. Letter to Spencer Roane, September 6, 1819, in Ford, ed., *The Writings of Thomas Jefferson*, vol. 7, p. 134.

97. G. Edward White, *The American Judicial Tradition* (New York: Oxford University Press, 1976), p. 9. See also Richard E. Ellis, *The Jeffersonian Crisis: Courts and Politics in the Young Republic* (New York: Oxford University Press, 1971).

98. *Marbury* v. *Madison*, 5 U.S. (1 Cranch) 137, 165–166 (1803) (emphasis added).

99. Ibid., p. 167.

100. Corwin, *The Doctrine of Judicial Review*, p. 59.

101. Because the Court in *Marbury* denied itself power by refusing to issue the writ, the decision was compatible with Jefferson's theory of departmental review, whereby each branch of government would be the judge of the constitutionality of its own actions.

102. Twenty years later, Jefferson explained his resentment to Justice Johnson: "The court determined, at once, that, being an original process, they had no cognisance of it; and there the question before them was ended, but the Chief Justice went on to lay down what the law would be, had they jurisdiction of the case, to wit, that they should command the delivery. The object was clearly to instruct any other court having the jurisdiction, what they should do, if Marbury should apply to them. Besides the impropriety of this gratuitous interference, could anything exceed the perversion of law? . . . Yet this case of Marbury and Madison is continually cited by bench and bar as if it were settled law, without any animadversion on its being merely an obiter dissertation of the Chief Justice." Letter of June 21, 1823, quoted in Donald G. Morgan, *Justice William Johnson: The First Dissenter* (Columbia: University of South Carolina Press, 1954), p. 45.

103. 5 U.S. (1 Cranch) 299 (1803).

104. Walter F. Murphy, *Congress and the Court* (Chicago: University of Chicago Press, 1962), pp. 9–11.

105. Letter to Justice Paterson, May 3, 1802, quoted in Warren, *The Supreme Court in the United States History*, vol. 1, p. 270. Marshall polled the justices in April and May to solicit their views on whether they should abide by the Repeal Act and hold their circuit courts. (They would not come together because Congress had abolished the June 1802 term.) Justice Chase then wrote to Paterson that he viewed the Repeal Act as unconstitutional. However, there were no dissents to Paterson's opinion in *Stuart* when it came down in 1803. (Marshall did not take part because he had sat on the case in the circuit court.)

106. Some Federalists approached Marshall about running against James Madison in 1812. The chief justice did not reject the proposition out of hand, but both he and party leaders evidently concluded that he was of far more value on the Supreme Court, particularly since an election victory was unlikely. Had Marshall actively sought the presidency, the Court could have been sucked into partisan conflict again, particularly had Marshall remained on the bench during the campaign. Norman K. Risjord, "Election of 1812," in Schlesinger and Israel, eds., *History of American Presidential Elections 1789–1968*, vol. 1, pp. 253–254.

107. Ex parte *Bollman and Swartwout*, 8 U.S. (4 Cranch) 75 (1807).

108. Letter to James Bowdoin, Jr., April 2, 1807, quoted in Morgan, *Justice William Johnson*, p. 57.

109. Statement of March 4, 1807, quoted in Dumas Malone, *Jefferson the President: Second Term* (Boston: Little, Brown, 1974), p. 288.

110. James D. Richardson, ed., *Messages and Papers of the Presidents*, vol. 1 (Washington, DC: U.S. Government Printing Office, 1896–1899), p. 429.

111. Letter to Thomas Ritchie, December 25, 1820, in Andrew A. Lipscomb and Albert E. Bergh, eds., *Thomas Jefferson, Writings*, vol. 15 (Washington, DC: Thomas Jefferson Memorial Association, 1903), pp. 297–298.

3. THE ELECTION OF 1832: PARTISANSHIP REVIVED

1. Page Smith, *John Adams* (Garden City, NY: Doubleday, 1962), vol. 1, p. 1109.

2. It was Thomas Jefferson who had most vigorously opposed Treasury Secretary Alexander Hamilton's plan for the first Bank of the United States, which Congress created in 1791, during George Washington's first term as president.

3. Richard P. McCormick, *The Second American Party System: Party Formation in the Jacksonian Era* (Chapel Hill: University of North Carolina Press, 1966), p. 3.

4. Quoted in Lynn W. Turner, "Elections of 1816 and 1820," in Arthur M. Schlesinger, Jr., and Fred L. Israel, eds., *History of American Presidential Elections 1789–1968* (New York: Chelsea House, 1971), vol. 1, p. 315.

5. From Monticello, Jefferson was fully aware of the significance of the issue as doubtless were his contemporaries. "This momentous question, like a fire bell in the night, awakened and filled me with terror. I considered it at once as the knell of the Union." Letter of April 1820 to John Holmes, in H. A. Washington, ed., *The Writings of Thomas Jefferson* (New York: J. C. Riker, 1853–1855), vol. 7, p. 159.

6. Michael F. Holt, "The Democratic Party 1828–1860," in Arthur M. Schlesinger, Jr., ed., *History of U.S. Political Parties* (New York: Chelsea House, 1973), vol. 1, p. 502.

7. This cabinet post had come to be seen as a stepping-stone to the presidency.

8. McCormick, *The Second American Party System*, p. 329.

9. Ibid., p. 14.

10. "Address to the People of Maryland," November 6, 1828, in Schlesinger and Israel, eds., *History of American Presidential Elections*, vol. 1, p. 479.

11. Robert V. Remini, "Election of 1828," in ibid., pp. 426–427.

12. Of the remaining twenty-two, four allowed popular election by district. In the other eighteen, voters marked a general ticket that produced a "winner-take-all" effect, as is the practice in forty-eight states today. In the election of 1820, by contrast, legislatures still picked presidential electors in nine of the twenty-four states.

13. See Michael Nelson, ed., *Guide to the Presidency* (Washington, DC: Congressional Quarterly, 1989), pp. 71, 155.

14. Lee Benson, *The Concept of Jacksonian Democracy* (Princeton: Princeton University Press, 1961), p. 29.

15. Ibid., pp. 38–39; Richard P. McCormick, "Political Development and the Second Party System," in William Nisbet Chambers and Walter Dean Burnham, eds., *American Party Systems* (New York: Oxford University Press, 1967), p. 101.

16. Benson, *The Concept of Jacksonian Democracy*, p. 62.

17. Edward S. Corwin, *The President: Office and Powers*, 4th ed. (New York: New York University Press, 1957), p. 20.

18. Writing to Jefferson in 1822, Justice Johnson gave Marshall much of the credit for leadership of the Court. Yet Johnson's estimate of some of his colleagues may be too harsh. Speaking of the bench he found in the first decade of the century, Johnson explained: "While I was on our state-bench I was accustomed to delivering seriatim opinions in our appellate court, and was not a little surprised to find our Chief Justice in the Supreme Court delivering all the opinions in cases in which he sat, even in some instances when contrary to his own judgment and vote. But I remonstrated in vain; the answer was he is willing to take the trouble and it is a mark of respect to him. I soon however found out the real cause. Cushing was incompetent. Chase could not be got to think or write—Patterson [*sic*] was a slow man and willingly declined the trouble, and the other two judges you know are commonly estimated as one judge." Johnson to Jefferson, December 10, 1822, in Donald G. Morgan, *Justice William Johnson* (Columbia: University of South Carolina Press, 1954), pp. 181–182.

19. As one study maintains, "a monolithic view of the 'Marshall Court' ignores important variations in constitutional interpretation and in Court leadership." Robert G. Seddig, "John Marshall and the Origins of Supreme Court Leadership," *Journal of Supreme Court History* 63, 82 (1991). See also, Gerald Garvey, "The Constitutional Revolution of 1837 and the Myth of Marshall's Monolith," 18 *Western Political Quarterly* 27 (1965).

20. Justice Joseph Story accounted for 194 (18 percent) of the Court's opinions filed during the Marshall era; Justice William Johnson wrote 109 (10 percent). The remaining 23 percent of the opinions were authored by the eleven other justices whose years of service overlapped Marshall's in whole or in part. These data are the author's, based on the opinions of the court reported in Linda A. Blandford and Patricia Russell Evans, *Supreme Court of the United States 1789–1980: An Index to Opinions Arranged by Justice*, vol. 1 (Millwood, NJ: Kraus International Publications, 1983). Marshall's chief justiceship spanned the years covered by volumes 1–9 of the Cranch, volumes 1–12 of the Wheaton, and volumes 1–9 of the Peters *Reports*, or, as now numbered, volumes 5–34 in the *United States Reports*.

21. 5 U.S. (1 Cranch) 137 (1803).

22. "No State shall . . . pass any Law impairing the Obligation of Contracts." U.S. Constitution, Article I, Section 10.

23. 17 U.S. (4 Wheaton) 316 (1819).

24. A central bank, Hamilton argued, "is not a mere matter of private property, but a political machine of the greatest importance to the State." That is, a national bank would in effect become a keystone in an alliance between government and business enterprise. "Report on a National Bank," in Henry Cabot Lodge, ed., *The Works of Alexander Hamilton*, (New York: G. P. Putnam's Sons, 1904), vol. 3, p. 424. See also Jacob E. Cooke, ed., *The Reports of Alexander Hamilton* (New York: Harper & Row, 1964), pp. vii–xxiii.

25. Paul Leicester Ford, ed., *The Writings of Thomas Jefferson* (New York: G. P. Putnam's Sons, 1892–1899), vol. 5, pp. 284–289; Dumas Malone, *Jefferson and the Rights of Man* (Boston: Little, Brown, 1951), pp. 342–343.

26. Contrary to the impression generated by the name of the institution, the Bank of the United States was not an agency of the national government; the national government did not operate the bank. Rather, the bank existed as a national entity because it held a corporate charter granted by Congress, because the federal government owned one-fifth of the bank's shares, and because the president appointed one-fifth of the bank's directors, subject to confirmation by the Senate. The federal government was the bank's largest depositor.

27. Arthur M. Schlesinger, Jr., *The Age of Jackson* (London: Eyre & Spottiswoode, 1946), p. 76. In 1829, Jackson told Nicholas Biddle, president of the Bank of the United States, "I do not dislike your Bank any more than all banks." Quoted in J. S. Bassett, *Life of Andrew Jackson* (New York: Macmillan, 1928), p. 599. Charles Jared Ingersoll wrote to Biddle in early 1832 that "General Jackson's antipathy is not to the Bank of the United States in particular, but to all banks whatever. He considers all the State Banks unconstitutional and impolitic and thinks that there should be no Currency but coin." Quoted in R. C. H. Catterall, *Second Bank of the United States* (Chicago: University of Chicago Press, 1902), p. 185n.

28. Bray Hammond, "The Bank Cases," in John A. Garraty, ed., *Quarrels That Have Shaped the Constitution*, rev. ed. (New York: Harper & Row, 1987), p. 39.

29. Congress shall have authority to "make all Laws which shall be necessary and proper for carrying into Execution the [foregoing enumerated] Powers." U.S. Constitution, Article I, Section 8.

30. Hammond, "The Bank Cases," p. 39.

31. Ohio, Tennessee, Georgia, North Carolina, and Kentucky also adopted antibank measures. Illinois and Indiana, two states where the Bank operated no branches, banned the establishment of any. The bank's main office was in Philadelphia. Ibid., p. 38. See the reference to Ohio's conflict with the bank (and the federal courts) in note 36 below.

32. The statute was worded generally to include "all banks, or branches thereof, in the state of Maryland, not chartered by the legislature." 17 U.S. at 316.

33. The tax rate on most denominations of bank notes was thus 2 percent of face value. However, the tax stamp to be affixed to the $20 note was $.30, or 1.5 percent. Thus, one would pay $.40 tax on four $5 notes or just $.30 tax on one $20 note.

34. Not helping the bank's public image at this time was the fact that McCulloch (cashier of the Baltimore branch) and others were involved in a money-lending scheme that amounted to embezzlement. Their shenanigans cost the bank at least $1.4 million, a huge sum for that day. Sufficient doubt about practices at the Baltimore branch surfaced in 1818 so that Congress in October ordered that an investigation take place. A committee report in January 1819 recommended that the bank be retained but that its abuses in Baltimore and elsewhere be corrected. Three persons involved in the Baltimore branch scheme were brought to trial in Maryland state court in 1821, but the county court concluded that no statute made their conduct a punishable offense. Holding that the offense was one punishable at common law, the court of appeals returned the case to trial, but a jury found the "traversers," as they were termed under Maryland law, not guilty. Hammond, "The Bank Cases," pp. 43, 50–51.

35. Marshall had taken this position fifteen years earlier in *United States* v. *Fisher* when the Court upheld the Bankruptcy Act of 1800: To say that "no law was authorized which was not indispensably necessary . . . would produce endless difficulties. . . . Congress must possess the choice of means and must be empowered to use any means which are, in fact, conducive to the exercise of a power granted by the Constitution." 6 U.S. (2 Cranch) 358, 396 (1804).

36. *Osborn* v. *Bank*, 22 U.S. (9 Wheaton) 738, 871–872 (1824). *Osborn* involved yet another attack on the Bank of the United States. Despite *McCulloch*, Ohio pushed ahead with enforcement of an anti-bank statute of its own. The result was a spirited seizure of specie, notes, and securities from the Chillicothe branch, their delivery into the hands of the state treasurer, and, eventually, their forcible recovery by federal agents from the state vault in Columbus. Rejecting the state's argument that *McCulloch* had been wrongly decided, the Supreme Court sided with the bank on all issues in the case.

37. 19 U.S. (6 Wheaton) 264 (1821).

38. One of the Cohen lotteries raised most of the funds for the Washington Monument, located in the middle of Charles Street in Baltimore, next to what is now Peabody Conservatory. W. Ray Luce, *Cohens v. Virginia (1821): The Supreme Court and State Rights, a Reevaluation of Influences and Impacts* (New York: Garland, 1990), p. 9.

39. The antilottery act was an outright ban. Earlier laws had required payment of a license fee for those selling tickets from out of state. Ibid., pp. 22–23.

40. Ibid., p. 38.

41. See C. Peter Magrath, *Yazoo* (Providence, RI: Brown University Press, 1966), pp. 50–60; David P. Currie, *The Constitution in the Supreme Court: The First Hundred Years 1789–1888* (Chicago: University of Chicago Press, 1985), p. 98n.

42. Marshall to Story, July 13, 1821, quoted in Albert J. Beveridge, *The Life of John Marshall*, vol. 4 (Boston: Houghton Mifflin, 1916), p. 365.

43. Luce, *Cohens v. Virginia*, p. 80–81.

44. Use of Section 25 was hardly novel. The first case to reach the Court under Section 25 was *Olney* v. *Arnold*, 3 U.S. (3 Dallas) 308 (1797); the first case under Section 25 in which the Supreme Court invalidated a state law was *Clerke* v. *Harwood*, 3 U.S. (3 Dallas) 342 (1797), where the Court held that a Maryland law conflicted with a treaty. *Fletcher* v. *Peck*, 10 U.S. (6 Cranch) 87 (1810), was the first case in which the Supreme Court invalidated a state act on constitutional grounds, but the case originated in federal, not state, court.

45. *Martin* v. *Hunter's Lessee*, 14 U.S. (1 Wheaton) 304 (1816). As John C. Calhoun, who was soon to become the high priest of states' rights, later observed, "If the appellate power from the State courts to the U[nited] States court provided by the 25th sec[tio]n did not exist, the practical consequence would be, that each government would have a negative on the other and thus possess the most effectual remedy, that can be conceived against encroachment." Calhoun to Littleton Waller Tazewell, August 25, 1827, in Clyde N. Wilson and W. Edwin Hemphill, eds., *The Papers of John C. Calhoun*, vol. 10 (Columbia: University of South Carolina Press, 1977), p. 301. Tazewell was a U.S. senator from Virginia.

46. Chief counsel for the state was U.S. Senator James Barbour of Virginia, who served without fee in the case. Senator Barbour's younger brother Philip was placed on the Supreme Court in 1836 by Andrew Jackson.

47. One difference between *Martin* and *Cohens* was that the latter was a criminal case; the former, civil. Virginia attempted, unsuccessfully, to distinguish the new case from the old one on that ground.

48. Beveridge, *The Life of John Marshall*, vol. 4, p. 343.

49. Bernard Schwartz, *A History of the Supreme Court* (New York: Oxford University Press, 1993), p. 45.

50. Ordinance of Separation, 1789, quoted in Beveridge, *The Life of John Marshall*, vol. 4, p. 375.

51. Morgan, *Justice William Johnson*, p. 217.

52. *Green* v. *Biddle*, 21 U.S. (8 Wheaton) 1 (1823). Marshall's biographer credits the delay in the announcement of the decision following reargument to the controversy that erupted over the first pronouncement. Beveridge, *The Life of John Marshall*, vol. 4, p. 380.

53. Justice Johnson concurred on state law grounds. Although the three absent justices probably agreed with the decision, the perception that a minority of the bench (three of seven justices) had invalidated the state enactment added to the controversy that surrounded the decision. See Herbert A. Johnson, *The Chief Justiceship of John Marshall, 1801–1835* (Columbia: University of South Carolina Press, 1997), pp. 78–81; and Charles Warren, *The Supreme Court in United States History*, rev. ed., vol. 1 (Boston: Little, Brown, and Co., 1926), p. 640n.

54. Reflecting the controversy the case had already created and anticipating reaction to the Court's ruling, Washington confessed alarm: "We hold ourselves answerable to God, our consciences and our country, to decide this question

according to the dictates of our best judgment, be the consequences of the decision what they may." 21 U.S. at 93.

The case also sparked a debate over constitutional interpretation. Jefferson denounced a resort to merely a literal interpretation of the text and stressed the importance of examination of the intent of the framers: "On every question of construction, carry ourselves back to the time when the Constitution was adopted, recollect the spirit manifested in the debates, and instead of trying what meaning may be squeezed out of the text, or invented against it, conform to the probable one in which it was past [*sic*]." Thomas Jefferson to Justice Johnson, June 12, 1823, reprinted in 1 *South Carolina Historical and Genealogical Magazine* 3, 10 (1900).

55. Maryland's tax on the bank was a separate issue. Upholding the constitutionality of the bank did not require negation of the state tax. For this reason, anger over the Court's position on the tax is more akin to that engendered by the compact case than it is to Marshall's pronouncement about the bank itself.

56. This might account for the move by opponents of the bank prior to the decision to get the House of Representatives to pass legislation revoking its charter. The effort fizzled when Congress adjourned on March 3, 1819, only days before Marshall announced the Court's decision.

57. By 1818, however, Congress had doubts about the constitutionality of internal improvements, and Marshall's opinion might fairly be read as an answer to those doubts as well as to doubts about the bank. In a fascinating letter that amounted to an advisory opinion, Justice Johnson explained to President Monroe the sense of the Court on the far-reaching nature of the bank decision of 1819: "They are all of opinion that the decision on the bank question completely commits them on the subject of internal improvement. . . . On the other points, it is impossible to resist the lucid and conclusive reasoning contained in the argument. The principle assumed . . . is that the granting of the principal power carries with it the grant of all adequate and appropriate means of executing it. That the selection of those means must rest with the General Government, and as to that power and those means the Constitution makes the Government of the U.S. supreme." Quoted in Morgan, *Justice William Johnson*, p. 123; Johnson's letter bore no date.

58. The bank had not been the subject of hostile legislation in Virginia, and some of those who were most critical of Marshall's opinion had close ties to the bank's branch in Richmond.

59. Roane had written the opinion for the Virginia Court of Appeals, denying the constitutionality of Section 25 of the Judiciary Act of 1789, that the U.S. Supreme Court reversed in *Martin* v. *Hunter's Lessee*, mentioned above in connection with *Cohens* v. *Virginia*.

60. Donald O. Dewey, *Marshall Versus Jefferson: The Political Background of Marbury v. Madison* (New York: Alfred A. Knopf, 1970), p. 175.

61. The exchange is reprinted in Gerald Gunther, ed., *John Marshall's Defense of McCulloch v. Maryland* (Stanford: Stanford University Press, 1969), pp. 52–214.

62. Robert J. Steamer, *The Supreme Court in Crisis* (Amherst: University of Massachusetts Press, 1971), p. 42.

63. John Taylor, *Construction Construed and Constitution Vindicated* (Richmond, Va.: Shepherd & Pollard, 1820), p. i.

64. *Tyranny Unmasked*, quoted in Warren, *The Supreme Court in United States History*, vol. 1, p. 545.

65. John Taylor, *New Views of the Constitution of the United States* (New York: Da Capo Press, 1971), p. 142 (reprint of 1823 edition published by Way & Gideon in Washington, DC).

66. Although it was generally popular because it was antimonopolistic, the famous steamboat case [*Gibbons* v. *Ogden*, 22 U.S. (9 Wheaton) 1 (1824)] took on added meaning in light of the doctrine of national supremacy that accompanied Marshall's expansive reasoning in *McCulloch*. In allowing competitive steamboat traffic in New York harbor, *Gibbons* gave the Marshall Court its first opportunity to construe Congress's power "[t]o regulate commerce . . . among the several States," as Section 8 of Article I in the Constitution declared. Typically, the Court did so generously, thus making Congress's authority to regulate commerce "the most important substantive power vested in the Federal Government in time of peace. . . . " Schwartz, *A History of the Supreme Court*, p. 47.

67. See, generally, Steamer, *The Supreme Court in Crisis*, pp. 34–50, and Warren, *The Supreme Court in United States History*, vol. 1, pp. 651–663.

68. Distrust of judicial power also accounted for the failure of any bills on judicial reform to pass. With westward migration, both new and reorganized circuits were needed. New circuits would mean additional justices for the Court. Advocates of modernization, however, were stymied by the probable consequences of change. Opponents of federal judicial power feared an enlarged national judiciary: more judges, coupled with more efficient organization of the circuits, would allow the federal courts to do more. After Jackson won the presidency, some earlier advocates of reform balked because they were apprehensive over the judges the new president might appoint. Similarly, some previous opponents of reform found themselves on the other side precisely because they expected that the new appointees would harbor views at variance with Marshall's. A majority on reform could not be had in both houses until the very end of Jackson's second term on March 3, 1837, when Congress created two new circuits and authorized two additional justices for the Supreme Court. Felix Frankfurter and James M. Landis, *The Business of the Supreme Court* (New York: Macmillan, 1928), pp. 46–48; Steamer, *The Supreme Court in Crisis*, p. 47.

69. Alfred H. Kelly, Winfred A. Harbison, and Herman Belz, *The American Constitution*, 7th ed. (New York: Norton, 1991), vol. 1, pp. 217–218.

70. From a speech by Hayne in the Senate in January 1830, quoted in Warren, *The Supreme Court in United States History*, vol. 1, p. 723 (emphasis added).

71. *Niles' Weekly Register*, June 22, 1822, quoted in G. Edward White, *The*

Marshall Court and Cultural Change, 1815–1835 (New York: Macmillan, 1988), p. 947.

72. Turner, "Elections of 1816 and 1820," James F. Hopkins, "Election of 1824," and Robert V. Remini, "Election of 1828," in Schlesinger and Israel, eds., *History of American Presidential Elections*, vol. 1, pp. 299, 349, 413.

73. Warren, *The Supreme Court in United States History*, vol. 1, p. 724.

74. See the "Coffin Handbill" of 1828, which described the "bloody deeds of General Jackson": the execution of six members of the militia in 1818, for which Jackson was claimed to be responsible, "in violation of the laws of the country and the usages of civilized society." The handbill is reprinted in Schlesinger and Israel, eds., *History of American Presidential Elections*, vol. 1, pp. 485–491.

75. "Address to the People of Virginia," January 17, 1828, ibid., vol. 1, pp. 465, 473.

76. Beveridge, *The Life of John Marshall*, vol. 4, p. 462. A Democratic paper in Baltimore claimed in March 1828 that Marshall had said that he considered "it a solemn duty . . . to go to the polls and vote at the next presidential election — for should Jackson be elected, I shall look upon the government as virtually dissolved." Quoted in ibid., p. 463. Marshall acknowledged having said that he would vote in the presidential election but denied having made the statement about Jackson.

77. Ibid., p. 462.

78. Book Review, "A History of the Colonies," 26 *North American Review* 10 (1828).

79. Letter to Ezekiel Bacon, August 3, 1828, in William W. Story, *The Life and Letters of Joseph Story*, vol. 1 (Boston: C. C. Little and J. Brown, 1851), p. 538.

80. Charles Francis Adams, ed., *Memoirs of John Quincy Adams*, vol. 7 (Philadelphia: J. B. Lippincott, 1875), p. 404. Jackson carried New York by about 5,000 votes; however, Thompson's efforts were not entirely unproductive. Since electors were not chosen on a statewide basis, the state's thirty-six electoral votes were divided, with twenty for Jackson and sixteen for Adams.

81. Gerald T. Dunne, *Justice Joseph Story and the Rise of the Supreme Court* (New York: Simon & Schuster, 1970), p. 182.

82. Judges on many other courts felt similarly, since their attitudes may well have reflected those of 1832. "The jurists of many of the states were cast more or less crudely in Marshall's image. All agreed in repeating his prejudices, though rarely with his profundity, and all, operating as a kind of high priesthood of the law, agreed in detesting Jacksonian democracy." Schlesinger, *The Age of Jackson*, p. 322.

83. Carl Brent Swisher, *Roger B. Taney* (New York: Macmillan, 1935), p. 126.

84. For example, Jackson did not disclose "his strong prejudice against banks and paper money or his highly conservative views about credit and specie" during the campaign. Remini, "Election of 1828," p. 419. However, Jackson did promise to "purify the government." This meant that once elected, as Daniel Webster cynically observed, "a greater a horde of office seekers descended upon Washington

than could be fed without a miracle." Webster to Mrs. Ezekiel Webster, February 19, 1829, in *Writings and Speeches of Daniel Webster*, National Edition, vol. 17 (Boston: Little, Brown, 1903), p. 470.

85. White, *The Marshall Court and Cultural Change*, p. 928.

86. Ibid., p. 950.

87. Steamer, *The Supreme Court in Crisis*, p. 46.

88. Warren, *The Supreme Court in United States History*, vol. 1, p. 642.

89. An article in 1820 by commentator Warren Dutton, a Boston lawyer, indicated that the potential was surely present. He acknowledged a "truth of fearful import" about those appointed to the Court. "[A]s a party or faction is the offspring of our institutions, and always the heir apparent to the throne, men may be selected for this high office *because* they are known to be devoted to a great political party, and ready to become the willing instruments of its ambition or its vengeance; and that no species of oppression is so hopeless or so terrible, as that which may be practised [*sic*] under the forms of justice." "Constitutional Law," 10 *North American Review* 83, 107 (1820) (emphasis in the original).

90. Ongoing debate about the Court made it easy for President Monroe to select Navy Secretary Thompson to succeed Justice Livingston. At the very least, anti-Marshall sentiment may have doomed the chances of former New York Chancellor James Kent, who, along with other judicial officials, had been ejected from office as a result of his state's constitutional convention of 1822. Kent's appointment would have been meritorious but probably rancorous in the Senate because of views too akin to the Federalists.' Gerald T. Dunne, "Smith Thompson," in Leon Friedman and Fred L. Israel, eds., *The Justices of the United States Supreme Court* (New York: Chelsea House, 1969), vol. 1, p. 481. That Kent authored the opinion for the New York court that the U.S. Supreme Court reversed in *Gibbons* v. *Ogden* was hardly enough to assuage states' rights concerns and, in any event, would have been a liability because it upheld a state-granted monopoly.

President Adams's selection of Trimble of Kentucky in 1826 did not go unopposed. The nomination of Trimble, the first person to come to the Supreme Court bench with prior federal judicial experience, generated a month's acrimony in the Senate. Opposed by several senators, including Kentucky's John Rowan because he was too Marshallian, he was finally confirmed by a vote of 27 to 5. Trimble died two years later, near the end of Adams's term, but when the president picked former Kentucky senator John J. Crittenden in December 1828, after the election, pro-Jackson sentiment in the Senate yielded a 23 to 17 vote to "postpone" consideration, thus leaving the choice to Jackson and consigning Crittenden's judicial future to oblivion. Henry J. Abraham, *Justices and Presidents*, 3d ed. (New York: Oxford University Press, 1992), pp. 93–94.

91. Robert V. Remini, "Election of 1832," in Schlesinger and Israel, eds., *History of American Presidential Elections*, vol. 1, p. 498.

92. Benson, *The Concept of Jacksonian Democracy*, p. 52.

93. Warren, *The Supreme Court in United States History*, vol. 1, p. 719.

94. Quoted in ibid., vol. 1, p. 722.

95. 29 U.S. (4 Peters) 410 (1830). Justices Johnson, Thompson, and McLean dissented.

96. U.S. Constitution, Article I, Section 10. In effect, the state had guaranteed the worth of the certificates as a kind of currency.

97. Letter of October 15, 1830, quoted in Warren, *The Supreme Court in United States History*, vol. 1, p. 727. The Court's decision in *Craig* had come down on March 12. The House Judiciary Committee reported out a bill in January 1831 to repeal Section 25; it failed by a vote of 138 to 51, with all but six of the minority votes coming from the Southern and Western states. Steamer, *The Supreme Court in Crisis*, p. 49.

98. The Tariff Act of 1828 was a political scheme gone awry. The bill, containing the highest tariff rates in American history, was pushed by Jackson Democrats thinking that even protectionists in the North would find it unacceptable. Upon its defeat, their candidate would thus be appealing to the South as a free trader and to the Middle Atlantic region as a protectionist. With a few modifications, enough New Englanders found it acceptable and the bill became law. It was this "tariff of abomination" against which Calhoun aimed the "Exposition."

99. Letter to John McLean, October 4, 1828, in Wilson and Hemphill, eds., *The Papers of John C. Calhoun*, vol. 10, p. 428.

100. "South Carolina Exposition," in ibid., vol. 10, p. 501.

101. Richard P. Longaker, "Andrew Jackson and the Judiciary," 71 *Political Science Quarterly* 341, 344 (1956).

102. Quoted in Warren, *The Supreme Court in United States History*, vol. 1, p. 754.

103. *Worcester v. Georgia*, 31 U.S. (6 Peters) 515 (1832).

104. As a slight nod in favor of compromise, but only after the state had had its way, the Georgia governor pardoned Worcester and Butler in 1833. Beveridge, *Life of John Marshall*, vol. 4, p. 552n.

105. Longaker, "Andrew Jackson and the Judiciary," p. 346. Some scholars of the Court, such as Charles Warren, maintain that Jackson lacked authority to enforce the Court's decision because, technically, the Court never issued a proper mandate. See Warren, *The Supreme Court in United States History*, vol. 1, pp. 761–762. Regardless, Jackson was hardly inclined to come to the Court's assistance.

106. Quoted in Horace Greeley, *The American Conflict* (Hartford, CT: O. D. Case, 1864), vol. 1, p. 106 (emphasis in the original).

107. Longaker, "Andrew Jackson and the Judiciary," p. 349.

108. Swisher, *Roger B. Taney*, p. 172.

109. The election of 1832 was the first to use the convention as a method for nominating presidential candidates. It was also the first to witness a third-party

candidacy for the presidency. Meeting in the Athenaeum saloon at the southwest corner of St. Paul and Lexington streets in Baltimore in September 1831—a gathering that Chief Justice Marshall attended—the Anti-Masonic party nominated William Wirt for president after Justice John McLean declined. The National Republicans used the same saloon for their convention in December 1831, as did the Democrats in May 1832. The latter, however, found the saloon too small and had to adjourn to the Universalist Church on St. Paul Street. The Democratic convention never formally nominated Jackson, but merely concurred in the nominations that had been received from conventions in the states. Remini, "Election of 1832," pp. 501–509.

110. Swisher, *Roger B. Taney*, pp. 191–192.

111. The veto message is reprinted in full in James D. Richardson, *Messages and Papers of the Presidents* (Washington, DC: Government Printing Office, 1896), vol. 2, pp. 576–591; and in part in Nelson, ed., *Guide to the Presidency*, pp. 1368–1370.

112. "Bank Bill Veto," in Richardson, *Messages and Papers of the Presidents*, vol. 2, pp. 581–582.

113. Benson, *The Concept of Jacksonian Democracy*, p. 52.

114. Jackson to Col. Anthony Butler, March 6, 1832, in John Spencer Bassett, ed., *Correspondence of Andrew Jackson*, vol. 4 (Washington, DC: Carnegie Institution, 1931), p. 415 (emphasis in the original).

115. Editorial of July 27, 1832, quoted in Robert V. Remini, *Andrew Jackson and the Course of American Democracy*, 1833–1845 (New York: Harper & Row, 1984), p. 317.

116. Dunne, *Justice Joseph Story*, pp. 301–302; Swisher, *Roger B. Taney*, p. 202. For Story, war on the bank and the Court no doubt made all the more urgent publication of his work on the Constitution, written for lay and legal readers alike, with a nationalist perspective on the Constitution that was both anti-Jefferson and anti-Jackson. *Commentaries on the Constitution of the United States*, 3 vols. (Boston: Hilliard, Gray, 1833).

117. Quoted in Remini, "Election of 1832," p. 510 (emphasis in the original).

118. Ibid., p. 511.

119. "Address of the National Republican Convention," reprinted in ibid., pp. 563–564.

120. Benson, *The Concept of Jacksonian Democracy*, p. 58.

121. Speech in the Senate on February 9, 1830, quoted in Warren, *The Supreme Court in United States History*, vol. 1, p. 724.

122. "Proclamation to the People of South Carolina," in Richardson, *Messages and Papers of the Presidents*, vol. 2, p. 623. Only six days before, the *Globe* uncharacteristically defended the Judiciary Act of 1789 and the supremacy of the federal courts. Longaker, "Andrew Jackson and the Judiciary," p. 360.

123. Letter of January 27, 1833, in Story, *Life and Letters of Joseph Story*, vol. 2, p. 119. The proclamation was followed in March 1833 by passage of the Force Act.

This measure not only specifically authorized the use of force to obtain compliance with federal law but also enlarged federal judicial authority by providing for removal into federal court of any state judicial action brought against a federal official in the enforcement of the revenue laws.

124. After the federal charter expired, the bank continued to operate in Pennsylvania under a state charter.

125. Combined service of the six on the Supreme Court totaled 111 years.

126. President Taft made six appointments during his one term in office, but one of these was the elevation of Associate Justice Edward White to the chief justiceship.

127. Abraham, *Justices and Presidents*, p. 99.

128. This turn of events should not have been surprising. Although he was Adams's postmaster general, McLean was able to cultivate Jackson supporters without unduly antagonizing the Adams people. Jackson kept McLean in his old post, but soon found him out of step with the administration's new patronage policy. Not wanting to anger McLean's friends in his home state of Ohio, Jackson moved him to the Court, where, presumably, he could do no harm.

129. Baldwin authored a short commentary that placed his views in contrast to Story's: *A General View of the Origin and Nature of the Constitution and Government of the United States* (New York: Da Capo, 1970) (reprint of the 1837 edition).

130. Morgan, *Justice William Johnson*, pp. 275–276.

131. Remini, *Andrew Jackson and the Course of American Democracy*, p. 339. See Jackson's letter to A. J. Donelson, May 12, 1835, reprinted on p. 339, where Jackson attempts to spell out his views.

132. This was true particularly in some cases involving state power under the commerce clause, as in *Passenger Cases*, 48 U.S. (7 Howard) 283 (1849), and *Cooley v. Board of Wardens*, 53 U.S. (12 Howard) 299 (1852). The Jacksonian view would have allotted ample local regulatory authority in spite of the commerce clause.

133. Swisher, *Roger B. Taney*, p. 322. Not until the Senate confirmed Associate Justice William Rehnquist as chief justice in 1986 would a successful nominee for the center chair receive proportionally as many negative votes. The vote on Rehnquist was 65 to 33.

134. Frank Otto Gatell, "John Catron," in Friedman and Israel, eds., *The Justices of the United States Supreme Court*, vol. 1, pp. 741–744. Jackson actually nominated a seventh justice. William Smith's name went to the Senate with Catron's (both nominations were possible because of the enlargement of the bench from seven to nine justices). Although the Senate confirmed Smith, he refused to accept, and the vacancy fell to Van Buren to fill.

135. Quoted in Warren, *The Supreme Court in United States History*, vol. 2, p. 10n (emphasis in the original).

136. Seddig, "John Marshall and the Origins of Supreme Court Leadership," p. 80.

137. 29 U.S. (4 Peters) 514 (1830).

138. *Providence Bank* was unanimous, as was *Willson* v. *Black Bird Creek Marsh Co.*, 27 U.S. (2 Peters) 245 (1829). Marshall spoke for the Court in each. The latter expressed greater tolerance of state laws adversely affecting interstate commerce, as contrasted with the Court's earlier holding in *Gibbons* v. *Ogden*.

139. 36 U.S. (11 Peters) 420 (1837). The case had first been docketed in 1834. Marshall's views about the case may have been essentially the same ones Taney advanced in his opinion in 1837. Stanley I. Kutler, *Privilege and Creative Destruction: The Charles River Bridge Case* (Philadelphia: Lippincott, 1971), pp. 172–179.

140. 36 U.S. (11 Peters) 102 (1837); 36 U.S. (11 Peters) 257 (1837).

141. During the twenty-eight years of the Taney Court, the justices invalidated twenty-one state laws, compared to nineteen in the thirty-four years of the Marshall Court. David M. O'Brien, *Storm Center*, 3d ed. (New York: Norton, 1993), p. 63.

142. 41 U.S. (16 Peters) 1 (1842).

143. *Steamboat Thomas Jefferson*, 23 U.S. (10 Wheaton) 28 (1825).

144. 53 U.S. (12 Howard) 443 (1852).

145. Alexis de Tocqueville, *Democracy in America*, J. P. Mayer and Max Lerner, eds., George Lawrence, trans. (New York: Harper & Row, 1966), pp. 129, 137. Tocqueville's work was first published in Paris in two parts, the first in 1835 and the second in 1840.

4. THE ELECTION OF 1860: LIMITS OF PARTISANSHIP

1. Letter to John Holmes, April 1820, in Paul Leicester Ford, ed., *The Writings of Thomas Jefferson*, vol. 10 (New York: G. P. Putnam's Sons, 1892–1899), p. 157.

2. Robert V. Remini, *Martin Van Buren and the Making of the Democratic Party* (New York: Columbia University Press, 1959), pp. 131–132.

3. James L. Sundquist, *Dynamics of the Party System*, rev. ed. (Washington, DC: Brookings Institution, 1983), pp. 52–53.

4. William M. Wiecek, *The Sources of Antislavery Constitutionalism in America, 1760–1848* (Ithaca, NY: Cornell University Press, 1977), pp. 20–61; James H. Smylie, *Scotch-Irish Presence in Pennsylvania* (University Park: Pennsylvania Historical Association, 1990), p. 26.

5. Aileen S. Kraditor, "The Liberty and Free Soil Parties," in Arthur M. Schlesinger, ed., *History of U.S. Political Parties*, vol. 1 (New York: Chelsea House, 1973), p. 741. William Lloyd Garrison delivered his first antislavery address in 1829 at Boston's Park Street Church.

6. Lewis Perry, "Versions of Anarchism in the Antislavery Movement," 20 *American Quarterly* 768, 779 (1968).

7. Lee Benson, *The Concept of Jacksonian Democracy: New York as a Test Case* (Princeton: Princeton University Press, 1961), pp. 140–207; Ronald P. Formisano,

The Birth of Mass Political Parties: Michigan, 1827–1861 (Princeton: Princeton University Press, 1971), p. 120.

8. Sundquist, *Dynamics of the Party System*, pp. 53–55.

9. Michael F. Holt, "The Democratic Party, 1828–1860," in Schlesinger, ed., *History of U.S. Political Parties*, vol. 1, p. 519.

10. The labels came from factions within New York's Democratic party that had developed a few years earlier over issues unrelated to slavery. Hunkers represented the party organization and were so named because they wanted the whole "hunk" of patronage. Barnburners were the antiorganization reformers who, like someone who would burn down a barn to get rid of the rats, were prepared to bolt, and possibly to destroy, the party in order to purify it.

11. Platform of the Free Soil party, 1848, reprinted in Schlesinger, ed., *History of U.S. Political Parties*, vol. 1, p. 876.

12. Resolutions of the Ohio State Independent Free Territory Convention of 1848, ibid., vol. 1, p. 848.

13. Platform of the Free Soil party, 1848, ibid., vol. 1, p. 877. Like the Liberty party before it, the Free Soil party was very nearly a single-issue party. Of the sixteen resolves in the platform of 1848, only four failed to mention slavery or the "Slave Power."

14. Frederick Judd Blue, "A History of the Free Soil Party," Ph.D. dissertation, University of Wisconsin (Madison), 1966, ch. 4.

15. First Republican platform, July 6, 1854, in Schlesinger, ed., *History of U.S. Political Parties*, vol. 2, pp. 1185–1188.

16. Quoted in Roy F. Nichols and Philip S. Klein, "Election of 1856," in Arthur M. Schlesinger and Fred L. Israel, eds., *History of American Presidential Elections*, vol. 2 (New York: Chelsea House, 1971), p. 1031.

17. Formed in New York as a secret, oath-bound, anti-immigrant, anti-Catholic society in 1849, its name came from the response "I know nothing" that members gave when questioned by outsiders about the society. The society's formal name was the Order of the Star-Spangled Banner, but it became the American party in 1854. Having both Northern and Southern followers, the Americans tried as unsuccessfully as the Whigs to straddle the slavery question and disappeared in 1857 as an organized national political group. In presidential and congressional politics, the Americans in the North then generally aligned themselves with the Republicans. Michael F. Holt, "The Antimasonic and Know Nothing Parties," in Schlesinger, ed., *History of U.S. Political Parties*, vol. 1, pp. 575–620.

18. Republican platform of 1856, ibid., vol. 2, pp. 1203–1205.

19. Democratic Platform of 1856, in Schlesinger and Israel, eds., *History of American Presidential Elections*, vol. 2, pp. 1035–1039 (emphasis in the original).

20. Particularly when going to the more distant circuits, the justices might often spend more time traveling than judging. Justice Peter V. Daniel used river boats, horse-drawn carriages, and railroads to journey from Washington, D.C., to

Little Rock, Arkansas, in the 1850s. Under the best of circumstances, the trip routinely consumed twelve–fourteen days, one way. John P. Frank, *Justice Daniel Dissenting* (Cambridge, MA: Harvard University Press, 1964), pp. 277–281.

21. Charles Warren, *The Supreme Court in United States History*, rev. ed., vol. 2 (Boston: Little, Brown, and Co., 1926), p. 206.

22. Robert G. McCloskey, *The American Supreme Court* (Chicago: University of Chicago Press, 1960), p. 84.

23. For accounts with varying amounts of detail, see John B. Gates, *The Supreme Court and Partisan Realignment* (Boulder, CO: Westview Press, 1992), pp. 42–43; Carl B. Swisher, *Roger B. Taney* (Washington, DC: Brookings Institution, 1935), pp. 347–411; Wallace Mendelson, *Capitalism, Democracy and the Supreme Court* (New York: Appleton-Century-Crofts, 1960), pp. 30–44; and Bernard Schwartz, *A History of the Supreme Court* (New York: Oxford University Press, 1993), pp. 69–104.

24. Data are derived from Lee Epstein, et al., *The Supreme Court Compendium* (Washington, DC: Congressional Quarterly, 1994), Table 3–1, p. 147

25. *Charles River Bridge* v. *Warren Bridge*, 36 U.S. (11 Peters) 420 (1837).

26. *Planters' Bank of Mississippi* v. *Sharp*, 47 U.S. (6 Howard) 301 (1848).

27. *Passenger Cases*, 48 U.S. (7 Howard) 283 (1849).

28. For example, *Holmes* v. *Jennison*, 39 U.S (14 Peters) 540 (1840), upheld exclusive federal power over extradition; *Dobbins* v. *Erie County*, 41 U.S. (16 Peters) 435 (1842), invalidated a state effort to tax the pay of federal officials; and *Almy* v. *California*, 65 U.S. (24 Howard) 169 (1861), disallowed a state tax on goods being shipped to outside markets.

29. 62 U.S. (21 Howard) 506 (1859).

30. 60 U.S. (19 Howard) 393 (1857).

31. *Luther* v. *Borden*, 48 U.S. (7 Howard) 1 (1849).

32. *Louisville Railroad Co.* v. *Letson*, 43 U.S. (2 Howard) 497 (1844).

33. 41 U.S. (16 Peters) 1 (1842).

34. *Swift* was overturned almost a century later in *Erie Railroad Co.* v. *Tompkins*, 304 U.S. 64 (1938).

35. *The Genesee Chief* v. *Fitzhugh*, 53 U.S. (12 Howard) 443 (1852).

36. The judicial serenity that prevailed was certainly not hurt by the tendency of most justices scrupulously to steer clear of partisan activities. The exception was Justice John McLean, a Jackson appointee, who after Story's death in 1845 became the senior associate justice. More than anything else, apparently, McLean wanted to be president. Accordingly, within wide limits, he was prepared to appeal to whatever party might give him a chance. In a record unmatched by any predecessor or successor, beginning in the 1840s and concluding in 1856 he unsuccessfully offered himself as a moderate Democrat, an Anti-Masonic, a Free Soiler, a Whig, and finally a Republican. No one should have been surprised at McLean's antics; they were nearly a lifetime pattern. Appointed postmaster general in the Monroe administra-

tion, he survived in that post through the Adams administration even though he had backed John C. Calhoun instead of Adams to be Monroe's successor. When Adams opposed Jackson in 1828, there was no doubt that McLean courted the challenger. Jackson had barely moved into the White House in March 1829 when McLean was named to succeed Robert Trimble on the Supreme Court in the "Western seat." Burnett Anderson, "John McLean," in Clare Cushman, ed., *The Supreme Court Justices* (Washington, DC: Congressional Quarterly, 1993), p. 103.

37. Robert J. Steamer, *The Supreme Court in Crisis* (Amherst: University of Massachusetts Press, 1971), p. 68.

38. 41 U.S. (16 Peters) 539 (1842).

39. U.S. Constitution, Article IV, Section 2.

40. There was confusion between the majority opinion and concurring opinions on whether states were prevented only from enacting laws that added requirements to the 1793 act or whether states were prevented from legislating independently on the subject at all. David P. Currie, *The Constitution in the Supreme Court*, vol. 1 (Chicago: University of Chicago Press, 1988), pp. 243–245. A majority of the Court decided ten years later that state laws assisting recaption were constitutional. *Moore* v. *Illinois*, 55 U.S. (14 Howard) 13 (1852).

41. Swisher, *Roger B. Taney*, p. 424; William M. Wiecek, *Liberty Under Law: The Supreme Court in American Life* (Baltimore: Johns Hopkins University Press, 1988), p. 75.

42. The 1850 act authorized the federal circuit courts to appoint federal commissioners who, concurrently with federal district judges who had been empowered under the 1793 law, could issue removal permits to owners or their agents upon proof of ownership. The 1850 statute provided for no jury trial, did not permit slaves to testify, and held that the commissioner's permit would supersede a writ of habeas corpus issued by a state court.

43. *Jones* v. *Van Zandt*, 46 U.S. (5 Howard) 215 (1847). Among other reasons, Chase based his argument on the absence in the 1793 law of procedural safeguards when runaway slaves were reclaimed, in violation of various provisions of the Bill of Rights.

44. Ibid., at 231.

45. 51 U.S. (10 Howard) 82 (1851).

46. California was assigned its own circuit with a separate judge in 1855, given the difficulty of travel to the west coast prior to completion of the transcontinental railroad. See Felix Frankfurter and James M. Landis, *The Business of the Supreme Court* (New York: Macmillan, 1928), pp. 49, 54–55.

47. Letter of January 1, 1857, quoted in Richard M. Johnson and William H. Browne, *Life of Alexander H. Stephens*, rev. ed. (Philadelphia: J. B. Lippincott, 1883), p. 318.

48. Don E. Fehrenbacher, *The Dred Scott Case* (New York: Oxford University Press, 1978), p. 240.

49. *Scott* v. *Emerson*, 15 Mo. 576 (1852).

50. In the Supreme Court records of the case, Sanford's name is spelled "Sandford."

51. Benjamin R. Curtis, ed., *The Life and Writings of Benjamin Robbins Curtis, LL.D.*, vol. 1 (Boston: Little, Brown, 1879), p. 236.

52. Not all of the other six members of the majority agreed with Taney on all points of his opinion. Nelson's opinion basically adhered to the original plan by falling back on *Strader*.

53. "[A]n Act of Congress which deprives a citizen of the United States of his liberty or property, merely because he came himself or brought his property into a particular Territory of the United States . . . could hardly be dignified with the name of due process of law." 60 U.S. at 450.

54. In both houses combined, the vote by party in Congress on passage of the Kansas–Nebraska Act was fifty-eight Northern and seventy Southern Democrats for, and forty-six and three, respectively, opposed; no Northern and twenty-two Southern Whigs for, and fifty-two and eight, respectively, opposed; there were also five Free Soil votes against the bill. The legislation was therefore carried mainly by Democratic votes.

55. Emphasis added.

56. Remarks of 1851, quoted in Warren, *The Supreme Court in United States History*, vol. 2, p. 223.

57. That President-elect Buchanan was aware of what the Court would say about the Missouri Compromise has long been part of the lore of the Dred Scott case. Swisher, *Roger Brooke Taney*, pp. 495–502. There were at least two letters to Buchanan prior to his inauguration, one from Catron and one from Grier. Both wrote of the Missouri Compromise. What remains intriguing, however, is the pertinent paragraph from Buchanan's inaugural address on March 4, 1857. Noting that Congress had applied the principle of majority rule to the question of slavery in the territories, he added: "A difference of opinion has arisen in regard to the point of time when the people of a Territory shall decide this question for themselves. This is happily a matter of but little practical importance. Besides, it is a judicial question which legitimately belongs to the Supreme Court of the United States before whom it is now pending, and will, it is understood, be speedily and finally settled. To their decision, in common with all good citizens, I shall cheerfully submit." James D. Richardson, ed., *Messages and Papers of the Presidents* (Washington, DC: U.S. Government Printing Office, 1913), vol. 4, p. 2962. Buchanan's point was addressed in neither of the extant letters from Catron and Grier.

Several possibilities present themselves. Perhaps reference to congressional power in the territories included the local "timing" question as well, so that the signals from Catron and Grier to the president-elect conveyed more information than they might appear to do. Perhaps Buchanan was confused about the issue the Dred Scott case raised, but this seems highly unlikely, given the widespread discussion about the case during the several weeks prior to the decision. Perhaps Taney himself (or someone else) communicated the scope of his opinion to Buchanan. Although no manuscript proof of a contact has emerged, this seems the most plausible explanation of this part of the inaugural address.

58. John C. Calhoun had argued exactly this point in a Senate resolution he introduced in 1847: "the doctrine of the self-extension of slavery into all the Territories by the self-expansion of the Constitution over them." Quoted in Warren, *The Supreme Court in United States History*, vol. 2, p. 208.

59. Arthur Bestor, "State Sovereignty and Slavery: A Reinterpretation of Proslavery Constitutional Doctrine," 54 *Journal of the Illinois State Historical Society* 117, 162–166 (1961); Samuel Eliot Morison, *The Oxford History of the American People* (New York: Oxford University Press, 1965), p. 603.

60. Senator George P. Marsh of Vermont had asked at the time, "Is that Court a fit tribunal for the determination of a great political question like this? . . . Could a tribunal which relies for its support upon moral force and public opinion alone, awes not by lictor and fasces, enforces its decrees by no armed satellites, dispenses no patronage, and is sustained by no Executive power, long withstand the malignant influence which would thus be brought to bear?" Quoted in Warren, *The Supreme Court in United States History*, vol. 2, pp. 212–213.

61. "Interested parties exerted pressure to secure an opinion on the more important political question involved. . . . Public opinion appeared to demand that the judges pronounce on it. . . . If they had not spoken, they would have been attacked as delinquent. If there had been no decision, men would probably ask, in the years to come, why the last peaceful means of settling the issue that precipitated the Civil War had not been tried." Vincent C. Hopkins, *Dred Scott's Case* (New York: Atheneum, 1967), pp. v–vi. Indeed, when the case was set for reargument, thus meaning that the decision would not come down until after the presidential election of 1856, the abolitionist *New York Tribune* commented that "the black gowns have come to be artful dodgers." Quoted in Warren, *The Supreme Court in United States History*, vol. 2, p. 285.

62. Speech at Galena, Illinois, July 23, 1856, in Roy P. Basler, ed., *The Collected Works of Abraham Lincoln*, vol. 2 (New Brunswick, N.J.: Rutgers University Press, 1953), p. 355.

63. *United States* v. *Booth* was the companion case to *Ableman* v. *Booth* and was decided by the Supreme Court at the same time.

64. According to Charles Warren, between 1831 and the late 1850s, the only legislative attempts to restrict the power of the Supreme Court had involved term limits proposals in the 1840s. Warren, *The Supreme Court in United States History*, vol. 2, p. 333n.

65. 62 U.S. at 517, 521.

66. Warren, *The Supreme Court in United States History*, vol. 2, p. 338.

67. "This judicial power was justly regarded as indispensable, not merely to

maintain the supremacy of the laws of the United States, but also to guard the states from any encroachment upon their reserved rights by the general government." 62 U.S. at 520.

68. Harold Holzer, ed., *The Lincoln–Douglas Debates* (New York: Harper-Collins, 1993), p. 1. The quotation is from the editor's introductory essay.

69. Being the incumbent, and therefore the one who had something to lose, Douglas dictated the terms. He and Lincoln would appear once in each of the state's congressional districts. Since, however, Lincoln and Douglas had already given speeches in Chicago and Springfield, even though they were not on the same platform, the joint debates were therefore limited to one in a community in each of the remaining seven districts: Ottawa, Freeport, Jonesboro, Charleston, Galesburg, Quincy, and Alton.

70. "The Seventh Joint Debate at Alton," October 15, 1858, in Holzer, ed., *The Lincoln–Douglas Debates*, p. 367.

71. "The Fifth Joint Debate at Galesburg," October 7, 1858. Ibid., p. 258.

72. Speech at Springfield, Illinois, June 16, 1858, in Basler, ed., *Collected Works*, vol. 2, p. 461 (emphasis in the original).

73. Speech at Springfield, Illinois, June 26, 1857, ibid., vol. 2, p. 401.

74. Fehrenbacher shows that Douglas had first enunciated what would be called his Freeport doctrine more than a year earlier, when it aroused little controversy. It would be Douglas's Lecompton connection that subjected the Freeport statement to attack by the Buchanan administration and Southern Democrats. *The Dred Scott Case*, pp. 456–457.

75. "Mr. Douglas' Reply," in "The Second Joint Debate at Freeport," August 27, 1858, in Holzer, ed., *The Lincoln–Douglas Debates*, p. 106.

76. Speech at Cincinnati, Ohio, September 17, 1859, in Basler, ed., *Collected Works*, vol. 3, p. 450.

77. Speech at Springfield, Illinois, June 16, 1858, ibid., vol. 2, p. 464.

78. The constitution was so named because Lecompton was the territorial capital. The basis of Douglas's opposition was not that the constitution was pro-slavery, but that the voters had not been given a real choice—that the process had been flawed.

79. Fehrenbacher, *The Dred Scott Case*, p. 486. Greeley's opinion changed dramatically. By the fall of 1858 he was a cheerleader for Lincoln, noting that he had transformed the race into "a contest for the Kingdom of Heaven or the Kingdom of Satan—a contest for advance or retrograde in civilization." Quoted in Holzer, ed., *The Lincoln–Douglas Debates*, p. 43. For Lincoln's comments on the advice from "outsiders," see "Notes for Speeches in Cincinnati and Columbus, Ohio, September 16, 17, 1859," in Basler, ed., *Collected Works*, vol. 3, p. 434.

80. Speech at Springfield, Illinois, June 16, 1858, in Basler, ed., *Collected Works*, vol. 2, pp. 465–466 (emphasis in the original).

81. "The First Joint Debate at Ottawa," August 21, 1858. Holzer, ed., *The Lincoln–Douglas Debates*, p. 74.

82. Speech at Springfield, Illinois, June 16, 1858, in Basler, ed., *Collected Works*, vol. 2, p. 467 (emphasis in the original).

83. Letter to Salmon P. Chase, September 21, 1859; speech at Chicago, March 1, 1859. Ibid., vol. 3, pp. 471, 369.

84. Such legislation would have countered the practical deficiencies that Douglas's Freeport doctrine had revealed in the constitutional assurances offered by *Dred Scott*.

85. Nearly a century and a half later, it may be difficult to understand why so much would have been wagered by all sides over the right of slave owners to carry their slaves even into regions probably unsuited for the Southern plantation system. Those fearing and favoring slavery must have known that the prospects for substantial expansion were small. Yet the political implications of one or two additional slave states were large. Symbolism was also a factor. A ban on slavery was a moral statement, even if the ban applied to places where slavery was unlikely to develop without the ban. For Southerners, a ban placed on their shoulders the weight of moral reprehensibility, a burden they did not want to bear.

86. Warren, *The Supreme Court in United States History*, vol. 2, p. 357. Fehrenbacher essentially concurs; *The Dred Scott Case*, p. 485.

87. "Constitutional Union Platform," in Schlesinger and Israel, eds., *History of American Presidential Elections*, vol. 2, p. 1127.

88. The Republican congressional committee, for example, widely distributed copies of a speech made by Maine Representative Israel Washburn on May 19, 1860: "[I]f the Dred Scott decision is good law, . . . the question of freedom or slavery in this country is irrevocably settled; the Constitution which the builders constructed is already overthrown, and the Union for liberty and republicanism . . . exists no longer, and the foundations of a Union for a grinding servitude on the one side, and an arrogant oligarchy on the other, to be erected upon its ruins, have been commenced." His address is one of three items reprinted in *The Dred Scott Case* (Plainview, NY: Books for Libraries Press, 1973), pt. 3, p. 7.

89. Republican platform, in Schlesinger and Israel, eds., *History of American Presidential Elections*, vol. 2, pp. 1125–1126. In contrast to 1856, the Republican platform of 1860 did not call for repeal of the Fugitive Slave Law; Lincoln thought that a debate on repeal might badly divide the convention, and without reference to repeal the party could present a more moderate image to the public. See Lincoln's letter to Salmon P. Chase, June 9, 1859, in Basler, ed., *Collected Works*, vol. 2, p. 384.

90. Due to secession and war, there was, of course, no sequel to *Dred Scott*. But even without secession and war, a ruling as Lincoln envisioned it seems improbable. The Court, however, undoubtedly would have faced other sensitive slave-status questions. Surely there would have been litigation challenging a territorial legislature's ban on slavery (the point addressed by Taney in *Dred Scott* but not technically decided in that case). There would also have been review of cases such as *Lemmon* v. *The People*, 20 N.Y. 562 (1860), in which the New York Court of

Appeals ruled that all slaves except fugitives became free as soon as they entered the state, no matter how briefly they might be present in the state.

91. Speech at New Haven, Connecticut, March 6, 1860, in Basler, ed., *Collected Works*, vol. 4, p. 29.

92. An indicator of the Court's overall stature, at least the chief justice's, is the fact that there was a discussion between Lincoln and his cabinet in 1864 as to whether they should attend Chief Justice Taney's funeral. Swisher, *Roger Brooke Taney*, pp. 577–578.

93. Letter to D. M. Perine, August 6, 1863. Quoted in Samuel Tyler, *Memoir of Roger Brooke Taney* (Baltimore: John Murphy & Co., 1872), p. 454.

94. Stanley I. Kutler, who tends to the latter pole, has reviewed the varying assessments in his *Judicial Power and Reconstruction Politics* (Chicago: University of Chicago Press, 1968), pp. 1–6.

95. A prudent attitude of deference, however, did not preclude moves in the other direction by Taney. Sitting as circuit judge in Baltimore, the chief justice challenged Lincoln's unilateral suspension of the writ of habeas corpus by issuing a writ to Union officers holding a suspected Maryland secessionist. On the president's instructions, the officers ignored the judicial directive. Ex parte *Merryman*, 17 Federal Cases 144 (C.C.D.Md. 1861). Moreover, in a posture of anticipation, Taney drafted opinions that he might have to issue on certain constitutional questions, were they to come before the Supreme Court. Harold M. Hyman and William M. Wiecek, *Equal Justice Under the Law* (New York: Harper & Row, 1982), p. 250.

96. *Prize Cases*, 67 U.S. (2 Black) 635 (1863); Ex parte *Vallandigham*, 68 U.S. (1 Wallace) 243 (1864). See David M. Silver, *Lincoln's Supreme Court* (Urbana: University of Illinois Press, 1998), pp. 104–118, 147–155 (reissue of 1956 edition).

97. These data are compiled from Epstein, et al., *The Supreme Court Compendium*, Tables 2–12 and 2–13, pp. 96–97, 100–101.

98. Charles Evans Hughes, *The Supreme Court of the United States* (New York: Columbia University Press, 1928), p. 50.

99. Salmon P. Chase, Taney's successor as chief justice, wrote the opinion of the Court in *Hepburn* v. *Griswold*, 75 U.S. (8 Wallace) 603 (1870). The reversal came in *Knox* v. *Lee*, 79 U.S. (12 Wallace) 457 (1871). As Lincoln's secretary of the treasury, Chase had supported the paper money law as a wartime necessity.

100. *Mississippi* v. *Johnson*, 71 U.S. (4 Wallace) 475 (1867); *Georgia* v. *Stanton*, 73 U.S. (6 Wallace) 50 (1868). Both cases were outright challenges to Reconstruction acts. In the first, a unanimous bench held that the Court was without authority to enjoin the president from enforcing an allegedly unconstitutional law; in the second, the Court concluded that the case involved political questions over which it had no jurisdiction. However, in other litigation the Court struck down both state and federal laws requiring test oaths. *Cummings* v. *Missouri*, 71 U.S. (4 Wallace) 277 (1867); Ex parte *Garland*, 71 U.S. (4 Wallace) 333 (1867).

101. 71 U.S. (4 Wallace) 2 (1866).

102. Ex parte *McCardle*, 74 U.S. (7 Wallace) 506 (1869).

103. The lone Democrat was also a tenth justice, Stephen J. Field of California, from the new (and temporary) Tenth Circuit. Lincoln concluded that Field's "real politics" matched his own. Henry J. Abraham, *Justices and Presidents*, 3d ed. (New York: Oxford University Press, 1992), p. 121.

104. Charles Fairman, *History of the Supreme Court of the United States*; vol. 6; *Reconstruction and Reunion 1864–88* (New York: Macmillan, 1971), pp. 160–169, 559–560.

105. In 1866 Johnson nominated Attorney General Henry Stanbery, a Republican from Ohio, to succeed Justice Catron, but the nomination fell victim to Congress's decision to downsize the Court.

106. Kutler, *Judicial Power and Reconstruction Politics*, p. 63.

107. William Lasser, *The Limits of Judicial Power* (Chapel Hill: University of North Carolina Press, 1988), pp. 101–103.

108. Finley Peter Dunne, in *Mr. Dooley's Opinions: The Supreme Court's Decision* (New York: Harper & Brothers, 1906), p. 26.

109. *Texas* v. *White*, 74 U.S. (7 Wallace) 700, 725 (1869). See Harold M. Hyman, *The Reconstruction Justice of Salmon P. Chase* (Lawrence: University Press of Kansas, 1997), pp. 140–150.

110. Act of June 19, 1862; 12 *Statutes at Large* 432.

111. As a wartime measure, the proclamation sought to free slaves only in areas under Confederate control. It expressly excluded parts of seceded states then under Union control. Lincoln issued his preliminary declaration of emancipation on September 22, 1862, after the battle of Antietam had placed Confederate forces on the defensive. Lincoln specified that union, and not abolition, was the objective of the war, and that he favored compensated emancipation overall. The official proclamation was issued on January 1, 1863.

112. Section 4 of the Fourteenth Amendment categorically placed any compensation for slave property out of reach.

5. THE ELECTIONS OF 1896, 1912, AND 1924: PARTISANSHIP REDIRECTED

1. In 1868 three Southern states still remained, practically speaking, out of the Union.

2. Republican candidate Rutherford Hayes, not Democrat Samuel Tilden, won the White House in 1876, despite the latter's popular vote margin of 3.1 percent. A special electoral commission awarded disputed electoral votes from some Southern states to Hayes.

3. Quoted in Mark D. Hirsch, "Election of 1884," in Arthur M. Schlesinger, Jr., and Fred L. Israel, eds., *History of American Presidential Elections*, vol. 2 (New York:

Chelsea House, 1971), p. 1578. The slander was not original with Burchard, however, since James Garfield had used the same phrase in 1876.

4. Ibid., p. 1570.

5. For a discussion of the impact of congressional measures on currency supply, see Irwin Unger, *The Greenback Era: A Social and Political History of American Finance* (Princeton: Princeton University Press, 1964).

6. This chapter does not attempt to chronicle all third-party activity. The Prohibition party, for instance, was politically significant for several decades.

7. John D. Hicks, *The Populist Revolt: A History of the Farmers' Alliance and the People's Party* (Minneapolis: University of Minnesota Press, 1931), ch. 13.

8. L. L. Polk of North Carolina, quoted in C. Vann Woodward, *Origins of the New South, 1877–1913* (Baton Rouge: Louisiana State University Press, 1951), p. 242.

9. 30 *Congressional Record* 410–411 (August 16, 1893).

10. James L. Sundquist, *Dynamics of the Party System*, rev. ed. (Washington, DC: Brookings Institution, 1983), p. 154.

11. As used here, "Progressive" or "Progressives" is capitalized when referring to the movement, to the political party that ran its own candidates for the presidency and vice presidency in 1912 and 1924, or to persons acting in their capacity as participants in this movement or party. Thus uppercase Progressives would include many Democrats and Republicans, as well as people who were specifically active in the Progressive party.

12. Organized labor pursued its own agenda. Leaders like Samuel Gompers eschewed a separate labor party and worked for unions that would be a match in strength for strong corporations. Other labor leaders preferred a separate labor party or cooperated with the Socialists.

13. Arthur S. Link, "Wilson: Idealism and Realism," in Arthur S. Link, ed., *Woodrow Wilson* (New York: Hill and Wang, 1968), pp. 169–170. Wilson owed a debt to chance. But for a rule that required a two-thirds vote for nomination, Democrats would have selected House Speaker Champ Clark of Missouri, who was decidedly less reform-minded than Wilson. Richard C. Bain and Judith H. Parris, *Convention Decisions and Voting Records*, 2d ed. (Washington, DC: Brookings Institution, 1973), pp. 184–191.

14. This tally counts Edward Douglass White only once; appointed associate justice by Cleveland in 1894, White was named chief by Taft in 1910, thus becoming the first sitting justice to be so elevated. Except for Andrew Johnson, whose administration, as explained in the preceding chapter, was marked by a shrinking Court allotment, each president made at least one appointment. Even James Garfield, who was shot by an assassin only four months after taking office, was able to appoint Stanley Matthews, thanks to Senate inaction on Matthews's nomination when first submitted by President Hayes.

15. David M. O'Brien, *Storm Center: The Supreme Court in American Politics*, 3d ed. (New York: Norton, 1993), p. 191.

16. For most cases, the old circuit courts, dating from 1789, had not been appellate tribunals; a case began in either the district or the circuit court depending on the subject matter. The old circuit courts were soon merged into the existing district courts.

17. The Court's certiorari jurisdiction was substantially enlarged in the Judges' Bill of 1925. As a result of another enlargement in 1988, almost all the Court's business each term is now discretionary.

18. U.S. Constitution, Article I, Section 10.

19. *Calder* v. *Bull*, 3 U.S. (3 Dallas) 386 (1798).

20. *Dartmouth College* v. *Woodward*, 17 U.S. (4 Wheaton) 518 (1819).

21. *Charles River Bridge Co.* v. *Warren Bridge Co.*, 36 U.S. (11 Peters) 420 (1837).

22. *Cooley* v. *Board of Wardens*, 53 U.S. (12 Howard) 299 (1852).

23. Slaughterhouse Cases, 83 U.S. (16 Wallace) 36 (1873).

24. 94 U.S. 113 (1877).

25. Ibid., 126.

26. Ibid., 132.

27. Ibid., 134.

28. *Chicago, Milwaukee & St. Paul Railway Co.* v. *Minnesota*, 134 U.S. 418 (1890).

29. Ibid., 457. A full consolidation of the railroad victory in 1890 followed in *Smyth* v. *Ames*, 169 U.S. 466 (1898), when the Court not only reaffirmed its decision in the Minnesota Rate Case but also held that the question of the reasonableness of rates depended upon the "fair value of the property being used by [the railroad] for the convenience of the public," and that the company was entitled to "a fair return upon the value of that which it employs for the public convenience." Ibid., 546–547.

30. In two other respects as well, the Supreme Court won few friends among agrarians. In some 150 decisions between 1870 and 1896, the justices vigorously opposed repudiation of bonds issued by local governments to aid railway construction, even where no construction occurred. Farmers shouldered a large part of the tax burden to make good on the indebtedness; the beneficiaries were typically high-income investors. Charles Warren, *The Supreme Court in United States History*, rev. ed., vol. 2 (Boston: Little, Brown, 1926), p. 679. See also John F. Dillon, *Commentaries on the Law of Municipal Corporations*, 4th ed. (Boston: Little, Brown, 1890), p. 580. In another series of cases the Court rebuffed those who attempted to reclaim millions of acres of public land that had been offered to companies as inducement for various internal improvements such as railroad construction. *United States* v. *Calif. and Ore. Land Company*, 148 U.S. 31 (1892). As Populist leader James Weaver declared, "The blackest pages in the history of legislative, administrative, and judicial procedure in this country are undoubtedly connected with the railroad land grant system." James B. Weaver, *A Call to Action* (Des Moines: Iowa Printing Co., 1892), p. 151.

31. *Gibbons* v. *Ogden*, 22 U.S. (9 Wheaton) 1 (1824).

32. 158 U.S. 546 (1895).

33. 157 U.S. 429 (first hearing) (1895); 158 U.S. 601 (rehearing) (1895).

34. 156 U.S. 1 (1895).

35. Homer Cummings and Carl McFarland, *Federal Justice* (New York: Macmillan, 1937), pp. 321–323.

36. Arnold M. Paul, *Conservative Crisis and the Rule of Law: Attitudes of the Bar and Bench, 1887–1895* (Ithaca, NY: Cornell University Press, 1960), p. 179.

37. 156 U.S. at 12.

38. 156 U.S. at 16.

39. Neither Democrats nor Populists, however, were enthusiastic defenders of the Sherman Act. The 1892 Democratic platform "denounce[d]" it "as a cowardly makeshift, fraught with possibilities of danger in the future, which should make all of its supporters, as well as its author, anxious for its speedy repeal." See Bryan's reference to this part of the platform in his speech to the House on August 16, 1893. 30 *Congressional Record* 410 (August 16, 1893). See also Owen M. Fiss, *Troubled Beginnings of the Modern State, 1888–1910* (New York: Macmillan, 1993), p. 111. While Democrats and Populists were opposed to monopoly, they thought the act offered insufficient protection against industrial and railroad monopolies. Populists in particular feared its application to farming and their own alliance groups. The latter fear may have been well-founded in light of the government's action in the Debs case, to be discussed below. Lawrence Goodwyn, *Democratic Promise: The Populist Movement* (New York: Oxford University Press, 1976), pp. 25–50. For a contrary view, see Alan F. Westin, "The Supreme Court, the Populist Movement and the Campaign of 1896," 15 *Journal of Politics* 3, 24 (1953).

40. Note, 29 *American Law Review* 293, 306 (1895).

41. For example, see *Northern Securities Co.* v. *United States*, 193 U.S. 197 (1904).

42. Warren, *The Supreme Court in United States History*, vol. 2, p. 733.

43. William Howard Taft, *The Anti-Trust Law and the Supreme Court* (New York: Harper and Brothers, 1914), p. 60.

44. Robert Higgs, *Crisis and Leviathan: Critical Episodes in the Growth of American Government* (New York: Oxford University Press, 1987), pp. 84–5.

45. 158 U.S. at 597.

46. "Debs Wildly Talks Civil War," *New York Times*, July 5, 1894, p. 2.

47. Higgs, *Crisis and Leviathan*, p. 95.

48. Westin, "The Supreme Court . . . ," p. 27.

49. 158 U.S. at 597.

50. David J. Brewer, "The Nation's Safeguard," address of January 17, 1893, in *Proceedings of the New York State Bar Association* (New York: Stumpf & Steurer, 1893), pp. 40, 46. The address is also found at 16 *Report of the N.Y. State Bar Association* 37 (January, 1893).

51. Alfred H. Kelly, Winfred A. Harbison, and Herman Belz, *The American Constitution: Its Origins and Development*, 7th ed., vol. 2 (New York: W. W. Norton, 1991), p. 400. The Norris-La Guardia Act of 1932 denied federal courts the authority to issue injunctions in labor disputes and thus greatly constricted the holding in *Debs*. See Felix Frankfurter and Nathan Greene, *The Labor Injunction* (New York: Macmillan, 1930), for a defense of the policy adopted by the 1932 statute. Violence sparked by laborers' demands persisted. In September 1897, for example, a sheriff's posse in Luzerne County, Pennsylvania, killed nineteen anthracite miners and wounded thirty-nine others as they marched toward Lattimer in support of fellow miners protesting company policies. Michael Novak, *The Guns of Lattimer* (New York: Basic Books, 1978). See also Brent D. Glass, "Massacre at Lattimer, an American Rite of Passage: An Interview with Michael Novak," 23 *Pennsylvania Heritage* 4 (Fall 1997).

52. *Springer* v. *United States*, 102 U.S. 586 (1881).

53. Robert Stanley, *Dimensions of Law in the Service of Order: Origins of the Federal Income Tax, 1861–1913* (New York: Oxford University Press, 1993), p. 133.

54. 157 U.S. at 533.

55. 157 U.S. at 596, 607.

56. A century before, *Hylton* v. *United States*, 3 U.S. (3 Dallas) 171 (1796), upheld a federal tax on carriages against the objection that it was a direct tax and had to be apportioned. In this decision, the Court suggested (but did not decide) that the category of direct taxes was limited to capitation and land taxes. The *Pollock* Court distinguished *Hylton* by saying that the carriage tax was not a tax on capital but on income from "business, privileges or employments" (158 U.S. at 635), thus *suggesting* (but not deciding) the indirectness, and hence the constitutionality, of a tax applied solely to earned income.

57. Loren P. Beth, *John Marshall Harlan: The Last Whig Justice* (Lexington: University Press of Kentucky, 1992), p. 242.

58. As Harlan noted in dissent, "No such apportionment can possibly be made without doing gross injustice to the many for the benefit of the favored few in particular States." 157 U.S. at 671.

59. 158 U.S. at 637.

60. *Allgeyer* v. *Louisiana*, 165 U.S. 578 (1897); on the same day the Court held that the due process clause required states to pay "just compensation" when property was taken by the states for a public use. This was the first step in "incorporating" the provisions of the Bill of Rights, which apply only to the national government, into the Fourteenth Amendment, making them applicable to the states. *Chicago, B. & Q. R. Co.* v. *Chicago*, 166 U.S. 226 (1897). The genesis of this way of thinking about due process of law may have originated in the seminal decision by the New York Court of Appeals in *Wynehamer* v. *State*, 13 N.Y. 378 (1856). See Edward S. Corwin, "The Doctrine of Due Process of Law Before the Civil War," 24 *Harvard Law Review* 366 (1911).

61. Similarly, a minimum wage law interferes with liberty of contract by stipulating that the wage for which one agrees to work must be at or above a certain amount. The Court proved to be even less tolerant of wage laws because they supposedly went to "the heart of the contract." *Adkins* v. *Children's Hospital*, 261 U.S. 525, 554 (1923).

62. *Holden* v. *Hardy*, 169 U.S. 366 (1898).

63. *Lochner* v. *New York*, 198 U.S. 45 (1905).

64. 198 U.S. at 57.

65. Ibid., at 59.

66. Stephen B. Wood, *Constitutional Politics in the Progressive Era: Child Labor and the Law* (Chicago: University of Chicago Press, 1968), pp. 11–13. The earliest child labor laws dated from the 1840s in a handful of states.

67. Claude G. Bowers, *Beveridge and the Progressive Era* (Boston: Houghton Mifflin, 1932), pp. 250–252.

68. State courts routinely upheld the constitutionality of state child labor laws, and the U.S. Supreme Court affirmed the states' prerogative in this area in *Sturges Manufacturing Co.* v. *Beauchamp*, 231 U.S. 320 (1913).

69. Wood, *Constitutional Politics in the Progressive Era*, p. 14.

70. *Champion* v. *Ames*, 188 U.S. 321 (1903).

71. *Hipolite Egg Co.* v. *United States*, 220 U.S. 45 (1911).

72. *Hoke* v. *United States*, 227 U.S. 308 (1913).

73. 247 U.S. 251 (1918).

74. Ibid., at 270.

75. Ibid., at 276.

76. *Bailey* v. *Drexel Furniture Co.*, 259 U.S. 20 (1922). The government had relied on *McCray* v. *United States*, 195 U.S. 27 (1904), which had upheld, 6–3, a tax of \$.10 per pound on colored oleomargarine, even though uncolored oleo was taxed at only \$.0025 per pound.

77. Sylvester Pennoyer, "The Income Tax Decision and the Power of the Supreme Court to Nullify Acts of Congress," 29 *American Law Review* 550, 558 (1895).

78. Quoted in Harry Barnard, *Eagle Forgotten: The Life of John Peter Altgeld* (New York: Duell, Sloan, and Pearce, 1938), p. 336.

79. Quoted in Westin, "The Supreme Court . . . ," p. 28.

80. William Jennings Bryan, "The Cross of Gold" Speech, July 8, 1896, in Schlesinger and Israel, eds., *History of American Presidential Elections*, vol. 2, p. 1847.

81. *Official Proceedings of the Democratic National Convention, Chicago, 1896* (Logansport, IN: Wilson, Humphreys, 1896), pp. 116–117.

82. "Democratic Platform of 1896," in Schlesinger and Israel, eds., *History of American Presidential Elections*, vol. 2, p. 1829.

83. Ibid., p. 1830.

84. Letter from Joseph Culbertson Clayton, *New York Herald Tribune*, September 18, 1896, p. 14. See also the excerpts from *Bankers' Magazine*, reprinted in 13 *Literary Digest* 551 (August 29, 1896).

85. "Democratic Platform of 1896," in Schlesinger and Israel, eds., *History of American Presidential Elections*, vol. 2, p. 1827. Significantly, perhaps, the constitutional basis of silver coin was not mentioned in the People's platform of 1892.

86. Quoted in Waldo Browne, *Altgeld of Illinois* (New York: B. W. Heubsch, 1924), p. 289.

87. *Official Proceedings*, p. 210.

88. Quoted in Sundquist, *Dynamics of the Party System*, p. 152.

89. "National Democratic Platform," in Schlesinger and Israel, eds., *History of American Presidential Elections*, vol. 2, p. 1838. Some silver Republicans had bolted their convention as well, and unsuccessfully attempted to foist their leader, Senator Henry Teller of Colorado, on the Democrats.

90. Quoted in 21 *Public Opinion* 297–298 (September 3, 1896).

91. 13 *Literary Digest* 776–77 (October 17, 1896).

92. Barnard, *Eagle Forgotten*, p. 385.

93. Sundquist, *Dynamics of the Party System*, p. 164.

94. Ibid., p. 165.

95. An exception was Senator Marion Butler's 1897 proposal calling for popular election of the federal judiciary, including Supreme Court justices. 31 *Congressional Record* 430 (January 7, 1897).

96. Address in Chicago, August 6, 1912, in Schlesinger and Israel, eds., *History of American Presidential Elections*, vol. 3, p. 2223.

97. For example, see Louis Boudin, "Government by Judiciary," 26 *Political Science Quarterly* 238 (1911).

98. "Democratic Platform of 1912," in Schlesinger and Israel, eds., *History of American Presidential Elections*, vol. 3, p. 2168.

99. "Republican Platform of 1912," in ibid., vol. 3, pp. 2178–2179.

100. Taft—former U.S. solicitor general and federal circuit judge as well as future chief justice—was unequivocal in opposition to judicial recall. In a veto on the Arizona and New Mexico statehood resolutions in 1911, the president denounced the device as "pernicious in its effect, . . . destructive of the independence of the judiciary, . . . likely to subject the rights of the individual to the possible tyranny of a popular majority, . . . injurious to the cause of free government." 47 *Congressional Record* 3964 (August 15, 1911). He commented gleefully, "By George, I am ready for them. I rejoice in the chance to give this recall business a blow." Quoted in Archibald Butt, *Taft and Roosevelt*, vol. 2 (New York: Doubleday, Doran, 1930), p. 742.

101. Letter of January 11, 1908, in E. E. Morison and John M. Blum, eds., *Letters of Theodore Roosevelt*, vol. 6 (Cambridge, MA: Harvard University Press, 1951), p. 904.

102. "Socialist Platform of 1912," in Schlesinger and Israel, eds., *History of American Presidential Elections*, vol. 3, pp. 2202–2203.

103. "Progressive Party Platform," in ibid., p. 2188.

104. Howard Gillman, *The Constitution Besieged: The Rise and Demise of Lochner Era Police Powers Jurisprudence* (Durham, NC: Duke University Press, 1993), p. 237. For example, the New York Court of Appeals invalidated the nation's first worker's compensation law as "a deprivation of liberty and property under the Federal and State Constitutions." *Ives* v. *South Buffalo Railway Co.*, 201 N.Y. 271, 294 (1911). See also John B. Gates, *The Supreme Court and Partisan Realignment* (Boulder, CO: Westview Press, 1992), p. 79.

105. Felix Frankfurter and James M. Landis, *The Business of the Supreme Court* (New York: Macmillan, 1928), pp. 197–198. Heretofore, appeal lay to the Supreme Court from the highest court of a state where the latter had ruled against the federal constitutional claim.

106. Address, "Charter of Democracy," reprinted in 100 *Outlook* 390 (February 24, 1912). Roosevelt was a contributing editor of *Outlook*, and the periodical was a pulpit for his views.

107. Ibid., p. 398.

108. In the elections of 1916 and 1920, none of the third-party candidates polled even a million votes.

109. *Adkins* v. *Children's Hospital*, 261 U.S. 525 (1923).

110. *Muller* v. *Oregon*, 208 U.S. 412 (1908), argued by Brandeis, and *Bunting* v. *Oregon*, 243 U.S. 426 (1917), argued by Felix Frankfurter.

111. Quoted in Archibald MacLeish and E. F. Pritchard, Jr., eds., *Law and Politics: The Occasional Papers of Felix Frankfurter, 1913–1938* (New York: Harcourt, Brace, 1939), p. 15.

112. "Progressive Party Platform," in Schlesinger and Israel, eds., *History of American Presidential Elections*, vol. 3, p. 2518.

113. Speech at Wheeling, West Virginia, September 1, 1924, in ibid., vol. 3, p. 2539.

114. "Full Text of La Follette's Speech Attacking Supreme Court," *New York Times*, September 19, 1924, sec. A, p. 2. According to the *Times* reporter who was present, La Follette quoted at length from Supreme Court opinions but soon desisted when members of the audience began to leave the hall in droves.

115. No detached observer could fairly regard the Supreme Court as hostile to most legislation in the first quarter of the twentieth century any more than the same observer would have found a Court hostile to most legislation in the last decade of the nineteenth. In the large majority of constitutional cases that came before the Court during the fourth party system, the justices upheld the statute in question. See the lists, compiled partly in response to La Follette, in Charles Warren, *Congress, the Constitution, and the Supreme Court* (Boston: Little, Brown, 1925), pp. 233–245.

116. Wilfred E. Binkley, *American Political Parties: Their Natural History*, 4th ed. (New York: Alfred A. Knopf, 1962), p. 350.

117. Sundquist, *Dynamics of the Party System*, p. 186.

118. G. Edward White, *Justice Oliver Wendell Holmes: Law and the Inner Self* (New York: Oxford University Press, 1993), pp. 327–328.

119. Quoted in *Guide to the U.S. Supreme Court* (Washington, DC: Congressional Quarterly, 1979), p. 843.

120. The traditional account of the Court during the fourth party system depicts most of the justices as intent on writing laissez-faire economics and social Darwinism into the Constitution. According to one essay, Brewer, for instance, "held to a strictly conservative, sometimes reactionary, position on the Court, opposing firmly the expansion of government regulatory power, state or federal. . . . [O]utspoken and doctrinaire . . . [h]e was for the Court of that era the right-wing opposite of . . . Harlan on the left . . . , and a worthy follower of his more famous conservative uncle on the Court, . . . Field." Arnold M. Paul, "David J. Brewer," in Leon Friedman and Fred L. Israel, eds., *The Justices of the United States Supreme Court 1789–1969: Their Lives and Major Opinions*, vol. 3 (New York: Chelsea House, 1969), p. 1515. Another account credits Brewer with leadership "of the ultra-conservative economic laissez faire advocates on the Court." Henry J. Abraham, *Justices and Presidents*, 3d ed. (New York: Oxford University Press, 1992), p. 149. See also Kelly, Harbison, and Belz, *The American Constitution*, p. 442. In his dissent in *Lochner*, Justice Holmes was among the first to popularize this view: "This case is decided upon an economic theory which a large part of the country does not entertain." 198 U.S. at 75.

Some recent scholarship, however, takes issue with this view. While not ordinarily defending the results reached in cases such as *Lochner*, this revisionist literature finds other values at work in the minds of the justices. Thus, while the results reached in some cases may have been consistent with laissez-faire economics, values other than laissez-faire thinking drove the decisions. For example, see Michael Brodhead, *David J. Brewer: The Life of a Supreme Court Justice, 1837–1910* (Carbondale: Southern Illinois University Press, 1994); Fiss, *Troubled Beginnings of the Modern State*, pp. 155–165; Gillman, *The Constitution Besieged*; Paul Kens, *Justice Stephen Field: Shaping Liberty from the Gold Rush to the Gilded Age* (Lawrence: University Press of Kansas, 1997), pp. 266–275.

For the purposes of this chapter, however, it makes little difference whether the traditional or the revisionist school is closer to the truth of what the justices thought they were really doing. What is important are the perceptions of the Court and its decisions widespread among reformers in the 1890s and in the first quarter of the twentieth century. And those perceptions generally accord with the traditional view.

121. William G. Ross, *A Muted Fury: Populists, Progressives, and Labor Unions Confront the Courts, 1890–1937* (Princeton: Princeton University Press, 1994).

122. One of the first of these was James Bradley Thayer, "The Origin and Scope of the American Doctrine of Constitutional Law," 7 *Harvard Law Review* 129 (1893).

123. For example, see Roscoe Pound, "The Scope and Purpose of Sociological Jurisprudence," 24 *Harvard Law Review* 591 (1911); the article continues into volume 25 in two further installments, at pages 140 and 489 (1912). Also see Roscoe Pound, *The Spirit of the Common Law* (Boston: Marshall Jones, 1921), pp. 170–171, where, in a reference to continental Europe, mechanical jurisprudence was said to make a court into a "sort of judicial slot machine." The facts may not "always fit the machinery, and, hence we may have to thump and joggle the machinery a bit in order to get anything out. But even in extreme cases of this departure from the purely automatic, the decision is attributed, not at all to the thumping and joggling process, but solely to the machine."

124. Jerome Frank, *Law and the Modern Mind* (New York: Brentano's, 1930), and Karl N. Llewellyn, *The Bramble Bush* (New York: Oceana, 1951); see also Julius Stone, *The Province and Function of Law* (London: Stevens & Son, 1961), pp. 414–417. Both realists and sociological jurisprudes trace their origins to parts of the address "The Path of the Law" that Oliver Wendell Holmes, Jr., delivered in 1897, reprinted in Holmes's *Collected Legal Papers* (New York: Harcourt, Brace, and Howe, 1920), p. 167.

125. See the lists of cases in Lee Epstein et al., *The Supreme Court Compendium: Data, Decisions and Developments* (Washington, DC: Congressional Quarterly, 1994), pp. 103–109.

126. D. Grier Stephenson, Jr., "The Supreme Court and Constitutional Change: *Lochner* v. *New York* Revisited," 21 *Villanova Law Review* 217, 233–236 (1975–1976).

127. James Willard Hurst, *The Growth of American Law* (Boston: Little, Brown, 1950), p. 72.

128. John F. Dillon, "Address of the President," in *Report of the Fifteenth Annual Meeting of the American Bar Association* (Chicago: American Bar Association, 1892), p. 211.

6. THE ELECTION OF 1936: A CONSTITUTIONAL DIVIDE

1. James L. Sundquist, *Dynamics of the Party System* (Washington, DC: Brookings Institute, 1983), p. 198.

2. Quoted in Frank Freidel, "Election of 1932," in Arthur M. Schlesinger, Jr., and Fred L. Israel, eds., *History of American Presidential Elections* (New York: Chelsea House, 1971), vol. 3, p. 2708.

3. "Democratic Platform of 1932," ibid., p. 2741.

4. "A Party for the People," *The Nation*, January 28, 1931, p. 88.

5. William Starr Myers, ed., *The State Papers and Other Public Writings of Herbert Hoover*, vol. 1 (Garden City, NY: Doubleday, Doran, 1934), pp. 429–430.

6. "Republican Platform of 1932," in Schlesinger and Israel, eds., *History of American Presidential Elections*, vol. 3, p. 2744.

7. Walter Lippmann, *Interpretations 1931–1932*, Allan Nevins, ed. (New York: Macmillan, 1932), p. 259.

8. Quoted in Frank Freidel, *Franklin D. Roosevelt: A Rendezvous with Destiny* (Boston: Little, Brown, 1990), p. 61.

9. Nonetheless, Roosevelt's campaign drew a contrast against Republicans in an important respect: if the former won, voters could expect a more active government. "Take a method and try it," FDR declared in Georgia; "if it fails, admit it frankly, and try another. But above all, try something." *Literary Digest*, June 4, 1932, p. 3. As a sign of willingness to depart from past practice, FDR was the first presidential nominee to arrive in the convention city (Chicago) by airplane and the first to deliver an acceptance speech at the convention itself. This may explain why FDR's speech reads like a campaign document and Hoover's, delivered in the traditional way, more like a position paper.

10. Freidel, "Election of 1932," p. 2735.

11. Otis L. Graham, Jr., "The Democratic Party 1932–1945," in Arthur M. Schlesinger, Jr., *History of U.S. Political Parties*, vol. 3 (New York: Chelsea House, 1973), p. 1941.

12. FDR thus placed third on the all-time victory list to that point, behind Harding's 60 percent in 1920 and Hoover's 58 percent in 1928. However, Hoover's 1932 total surpassed Al Smith's 1928 count by 758,000.

13. On the eve of the election Hoover had presciently characterized the choice facing the voters as "a contest between two philosophies of government." "This election is not a mere shift from the ins to the outs. It means determining the course our nation will take over a century to come." Events proved him to be perspicacious. *New York Times*, November 1, 1932, p. 12.

The term "New Deal" derived from FDR's acceptance speech at the 1932 convention, when he "pledge[d] a new deal for the American people . . . a new order of competence and of courage." *The Public Papers and Addresses of Franklin D. Roosevelt*, Samuel J. Rosenman, ed., vol. 1 (New York: Random House, 1938), p. 647.

14. *Literary Digest*, October 28, 1934, p. 6.

15. *Public Papers and Addresses*, vol. 4, pp. 16–17.

16. Coming in 1938, the FLSA was the last of these to be enacted. By this time there was less support in Congress for additional measures, and national security concerns increasingly occupied the president's time.

17. The qualification is important. By the standards of many countries, this was no revolution. Despite the rhetoric of class, sparked by higher taxes on the wealthy and abrogation of the gold contracts, that permeated much of the decade, political enemies were neither shot nor incarcerated; land was not seized and given to the landless; corporations were not seized and handed over to the workers. Charles and Mary Beard may have been right on this point: the New Deal was less a revolution and more a culmination of agitation over perceived economic inequities. *America in Midpassage*, vol. 1 (New York: Macmillan, 1939), p. 248.

18. In early 1936, owing probably to primitive polling techniques, FDR's reelection chances appeared less than certain. A poll in January by the American Institute of Public Opinion predicted a Roosevelt victory, but only by a margin of twenty-five electoral votes. "Not since Hughes battled Wilson in 1916," declared the *Literary Digest* midyear, "have the lines been so sharply drawn, the outcome so in doubt." Quoted in William E. Leuchtenburg, "Election of 1936," in Schlesinger and Israel, eds., *History of American Presidential Elections*, vol. 3, p. 2809. Despite its generally good record of electoral predictions based on polling techniques considered crude by today's standards, the *Literary Digest* ceased publication in February 1938 because of financial difficulties brought on in part by its woefully inaccurate prediction in the fall of 1936, of a Republican landslide. *New York Times*, February 25, 1938, p. 13. See note 25 below.

19. Phrases from speeches delivered between November 1935 and June 1936, in Herbert Hoover, *Addresses upon the American Road, 1933–1938* (New York: Scribner's, 1938), pp. 76, 88, 101, 105, 132, 175–178.

20. Sundquist, *Dynamics of the Party System*, p. 213.

21. "Democratic Platform of 1936," in Schlesinger, *History of U.S. Political Parties*, vol. 3, p. 1990.

22. "Acceptance Speech," June 27, 1936, in ibid., vol. 3, p. 1999.

23. Arthur M. Schlesinger, Jr., *The Politics of Upheaval* (Boston: Houghton Mifflin, 1960), p. 638.

24. *Public Papers and Addresses*, vol. 5, pp. 568–569.

25. The strong appeal of class seems to have accounted for the *Literary Digest's* gravely erroneous prediction of 42 percent for Roosevelt. The technique used in 1936 had come close in 1932 to the actual share Roosevelt received. But the magazine's sampling technique (using telephone directories and automobile registrations) had a bias toward upper-income groups. If one assumes that the Democratic share of the popular vote in 1932 was relatively uniform across all income groups, then the erroneous share forecast in 1936 suggests that FDR drew disproportionately from lower income voters, when compared to 1932. Walter Dean Burnham, *Critical Elections and the Mainsprings of American Politics* (New York: Norton, 1970), p. 56.

26. "Constitutional party" would have been a likely name. Clyde P. Weed, *The Nemesis of Reform: The Republican Party During the New Deal* (New York: Columbia University Press, 1994), p. 191.

27. Sundquist, *Dynamics of the Party System*, p. 227.

28. President from 1817 until 1825, Monroe did not make his first Supreme Court appointment until his second term.

29. Prior to 1869, the statutory allotment had briefly been as low as five and as high as ten. For most of the time between 1789 and 1869, the actual bench size ranged from six to nine.

30. The text of this address by FDR in Indianapolis is reprinted in the *New*

York Times, October. 26, 1932, p. 10. The theme of this address was the "Four Horsemen" of the present Republican leadership: "Destruction, Delay, Deceit, Despair." The equestrian metaphor was ironic because the four justices on the Supreme Court who would most consistently oppose FDR's legislative agenda were dubbed by their critics the "Four Horsemen" [of the Apocalypse: pestilence, war, famine, and death], from Revelation 6:2–8.

31. *New York Times*, October 29, 1932, p. 10. Hoover soon repeated the theme in a speech at New York City's Madison Square Garden: "If that is his intention, he is proposing the most revolutionary new deal, the most stupendous breaking of precedent, the most destructive undermining of the very safeguard of our form of government yet proposed by any Presidential candidate." *New York Times*, November 1, 1932, p. 12.

32. That concern had been responsible for most of the uproar when Hoover had picked Hughes to succeed Taft. The Senate confirmed Hughes 52 to 26 (with eighteen not voting), making the nomination the most contentious since Wilson picked Brandeis in 1916. The problem for this former New York governor, Supreme Court justice, and Republican presidential nominee was not party-inspired opposition but a bipartisan bloc of Progressives. For them, Hughes was a symbol of what the Supreme Court should not be. "Perhaps it is not far amiss," explained Senator George Norris, "that no man in public life so exemplifies the influence of powerful combinations in the political and financial world as does Mr. Hughes. . . . [M]en should not be elevated [to the Court] . . . who have lived this one-sided life." 72 *Congressional Record*, p. 3373 (February 10, 1930).

Hughes had been a progressive two-term governor of New York (although Theodore Roosevelt disliked him) prior to service on the Court between 1910 and 1916 that reflected a blend of both liberal and conservative views. Senate opposition in 1930 stemmed largely from the nature of his law practice after 1916. Burnette Anderson, "Charles Evans Hughes," in Clare Cushman, ed., *The Supreme Court Justices* (Washington, DC: Congressional Quarterly, 1993), p. 308; Henry Abraham, *Justices and Presidents*, 3d ed. (New York: Oxford University Press, 1992), p. 169.

The serious opposition to Hughes partly explains the defeat, 39 to 41, of Hoover's second nominee, Judge John Parker, to fill the vacancy created by Justice Sanford's death in 1930. The first twentieth-century Supreme Court nominee to be turned down, Parker drew fire from labor and civil rights groups. However, persistent apprehension over Hughes's confirmation most probably cost Parker his seat. This rejection accounts for Hoover's nomination of Roberts, which in contrast to Hughes's and Parker's, was approved by acclamation one minute after it was reported unanimously from the Judiciary Committee. Despite his background as a to-the-manner-born Philadelphia Republican and his close association with the Pennsylvania Railroad, he appealed to the Hughes and Parker naysayers because of his service as special prosecutor in the Teapot Dome oil scandals and his record of humanitarian pursuits.

33. 72 *Congressional Record* 3642 (February 14, 1930)

34. The words were party chairman Henry Fletcher's. *New York Times*, July 8, 1934, p. 18.

35. Roberts, Hughes, Brandeis, Stone, and Cardozo.

36. *Nebbia* v. *New York*, 291 U.S. 502, 537 (1934).

37. U.S. Constitution, Article I, Section 10.

38. See *Charles River Bridge* v. *Warren Bridge*, 36 U.S. (11 Peters) 420 (1837), discussed in chapter 3.

39. *Home Building & Loan Association* v. *Blaisdell*, 290 U.S. 398, 442. (1934).

40. Quoted in Richard A. Maidment, *The Judicial Response to the New Deal* (Manchester: Manchester University Press, 1991), p. 51.

41. 293 U.S. 388 (1935).

42. *Perry* v. *United States*, 294 U.S. 330, 361 (1935) (McReynolds dissenting). Also see Max Freedman, ed., *Roosevelt and Frankfurter: Their Correspondence, 1928–45* (Boston: Little, Brown, 1967), p. 256. The oral version was more vehement than the published dissent; an incomplete account of the former was published in the *Wall Street Journal*, February 23, 1935. A copy of this account, on which McReynolds made pencil corrections, is in the McReynolds Papers at the University of Virginia.

43. Elliott Roosevelt, ed., *F.D.R.: His Personal Letters 1928–1945*, vol. 1 (New York: Duell, Sloan and Pearce, 1950), p. 455. The text of the undelivered speech is on pp. 456–460.

44. *New Republic*, March 6, 1935, p. 100.

45. *Railroad Retirement Board* v. *Alton R.R. Co.*, 295 U.S. 330 (1935).

46. 295 U.S. 495 (1935).

47. Ibid., 553–554.

48. The fact that justices such as Cardozo were sometimes arrayed against the administration casts some doubt on the complete accuracy of the conventional interpretation that has explained judicial opposition to reform measures almost entirely in terms of politics and personal predilection, rather than of principled Constitution-based objections. Maidment, *The Judicial Response to the New Deal*, p. 95. For an example of the conventional interpretation, see Fred Rodell, *Nine Men: A Political History of the Supreme Court of the United States from 1790 to 1955* (New York: Random House, 1955), pp. 217–225.

49. Some liberals in the Brandeis mold disliked the law because it fostered both big business and monopoly. Philippa Strum, *Louis D. Brandeis: Justice for the People* (Cambridge, MA: Harvard University Press, 1984), pp. 339–353.

50. Quoted in William Lasser, *The Limits of Judicial Power* (Chapel Hill: University of North Carolina Press, 1988), p. 134.

51. Frankfurter to FDR, May 29, 1935, in Freedman, ed., *Roosevelt and Frankfurter*, p. 272 (emphasis in the original).

52. "High Court Meets Amid New Splendor," *New York Times*, October 8,

1935, p. 2. For the previous seventy-five years the Court had occupied the Old Senate Chamber in the Capitol.

53. *United States* v. *Butler*, 297 U.S. 1 (1936).

54. The law may not have been popular with the general population, however, according to the results of a Gallup poll issued the day before *Butler* came down. William E. Leuchtenburg, *The Supreme Court Reborn* (New York: Oxford University Press, 1995), p. 98.

55. Maidment, *The Judicial Response to the New Deal*, p. 105.

56. A measure of Roosevelt's attachment to the AAA was his comment to Charles E. Wyzanski, Jr., of Solititor General Stanley Reed's staff: "If the Court does send the AAA flying like the NRA, there might even be a revolution." Quoted in Schlesinger, *The Politics of Upheaval*, p. 453.

57. Van L. Perkins, *Crisis in Agriculture: The Agricultural Adjustment Administration and the New Deal* (Berkeley: University of California Press, 1969), p. 48.

58. U.S. Constitution, Article I, Section 8.

59. *Ashwander* v. *Tennessee Valley Authority*, 297 U.S. 288 (1936). Even though the TVA was controversial, constitutionally as well as politically, the Court seemed to go out of its way to assure a ruling for the government in this case by confining itself to the specific program being challenged, the sale of power from the Muscle Shoals Dam.

60. 298 U.S. 238 (1936). The majority struck down the price-fixing provisions of the law as inseparable from the constitutionally defective labor regulations, despite Congress's express insistence in the statute that the two parts were separable. Chief Justice Hughes in a separate opinion was prepared to allow the price-fixing part to stand but agreed that the labor provisions went "beyond any proper measure of protection of interstate commerce" (ibid., p. 320). Thus, on the major constitutional question at issue, the split within the Court was 6–3, not 5–4, as is sometimes reported. Justice Cardozo's dissent, joined by Brandeis and Stone, drew a contrary lesson from past decisions. "What the cases really mean is that the causal relation in such circumstances is so close and intimate and obvious as to permit it to be called direct without subjecting the word to an unfair or excessive strain. There is a like immediacy here" (ibid., pp. 328–329).

61. *United States* v. *E. C. Knight Co.*, 156 U.S. 1 (1895). See the discussion of this case in chapter 5.

62. 298 U.S. at 266.

63. 298 U.S. 587 (1936).

64. *Adkins* v. *Children's Hospital*, 261 U.S. 525 (1923). This case is discussed in chapter 5. In a posthumously published memorandum Roberts explained that he voted as he did not because he thought *Adkins* was correct but because New York had not explicitly asked the Court to overrule it. See Felix Frankfurter, "Mr. Justice Roberts," 104 *University of Pennsylvania Law Review* 311 (1955). However, Justice Stone's dissent in *Tipaldo* quoted tellingly from the state's petition that " 'the

circumstances prevailing under which the New York law was enacted call for a reconsideration of the *Adkins* case in the light of the New York act.' " 298 U.S. at 636.

65. 261 U.S. at 558.

66. 298 U.S. at 610–14.

67. Quoted in Alpheus Thomas Mason, *Harlan Fiske Stone: Pillar of the Law* (New York: Viking, 1956), pp. 425–426.

68. "Washington News and Comment," *Literary Digest*, July 13, 1935, p. 16.

69. However, while awaiting the decision in the Gold Clause Cases, Roosevelt publicly disavowed reports that the administration "was considering enlargement of the membership of the Supreme Court," adding that he had "no intention" of tampering with the membership of the Court. *New York Times*, January 31, 1935, p. 2.

70. *Public Papers and Addresses*, vol. 4, pp. 205, 215, 220–221 (paragraph breaks omitted).

71. In the fall of 1935, FDR mentioned to newspaper publisher Paul Block that he would "pack the Supreme Court" if necessary. Block then recounted the remark to the Toledo Bar Association and received a rebuke from Press Secretary Steve Early for doing so. Freidel, *Franklin D. Roosevelt*, p. 194.

72. *Complete Presidential Press Conferences of Franklin D. Roosevelt*, vol. 7 (New York: DaCapo Press, 1972), p. 280.

73. *Literary Digest*, June 13, 1936, p. 6.

74. Henry A. Wallace, *Whose Constitution: An Inquiry into the General Welfare* (New York: Reynal & Hitchcock, 1936). See especially pp. 212–239, 295–327. The book's theme is that the Constitution belongs to the people, not the Supreme Court.

75. Michael Nelson, "The President and the Court: Reinterpreting the Court-packing Episode of 1937," 103 *Political Science Quarterly* 267, 273 (1988), drawing on data in Stuart S. Nagel, "Court-Curbing Periods in American History," 18 *Vanderbilt Law Review* 926 (1965).

Consider this sample of the barrage of criticism of the Court in Congress and in periodicals such as *The Nation* and the *New Republic*: Representative Dobbins introduced a bill after *Schechter* requiring a two-thirds vote of the justices before an act could be declared unconstitutional. *Literary Digest*, May 25, 1935, p. 43. Representative Joseph Monaghan of Montana promised in early 1936 that he would introduce legislation to oust the justices if they struck down the TVA. Senator Norris declared, "The people can change the Congress, but only God can change the Supreme Court," adding that Congress could take corrective action against the judiciary "if it has the courage to do it." *Literary Digest*, February 22, 1936, p. 5. In the fall of 1935, Howard Lee McBain called the dispute over congressional powers "the largest constitutional issue that the American people have faced since 1787." *Literary Digest*, November 9, 1935, p. 42. See also Morris R. Cohen, "What to Do with the Supreme Court?" *The Nation*, July 10, 1935, p. 39; Max Lerner, "The Fate of the Supreme Court," *The Nation*, March 25, 1936, p. 379; Samuel Lubell, "Agriculture and the Constitution," 241 *North American Review* 57 (1936); "Liberty to Starve," *New Republic*, June 10, 1936, p. 116; Charles A. Beard, "Little Alice Looks at the Constitution," *New Republic*, July 22, 1936, p. 315.

76. Column of April 10, 1936. Arthur Krock, *In the Nation* (New York: McGraw-Hill, 1966), p. 36.

77. *Public Papers and Addresses*, vol. 4, p. 274.

78. "Republican Platform of 1936," in Schlesinger and Israel, eds., *History of American Presidential Elections*, vol. 3, p. 2857.

79. "The Texts of Governor Landon's Addresses at Madison Square Garden," *New York Times*, October 30, 1936, p. 16 (paragraph breaks omitted).

80. *Literary Digest*, June 13, 1936, p. 6.

81. "Republican Platform of 1936," in Schlesinger and Israel, eds., *History of American Presidential Elections*, vol. 3, p. 2859 (emphasis added).

82. "Inaugural Address," March 4, 1933, in *Public Papers and Addresses*, vol. 2, pp. 14–15.

83. "Self-Government We Must and Shall Maintain," address at Little Rock, Arkansas, June 10, 1936, in *Public Papers and Addresses*, vol. 5, pp. 200–201.

84. "Democratic Platform of 1936," in Schlesinger and Israel, eds., *History of American Presidential Elections*, vol. 3, p. 1994 (emphasis added).

85. 80 *Congressional Record* 644 (January 18, 1936).

86. "Annual Message to the Congress," January 6, 1937, in *Public Papers and Addresses*, vol. 5, p. 639.

87. Quoted in Alpheus Thomas Mason and Donald Grier Stephenson, Jr., *American Constitutional Law: Introductory Essays and Selected Cases*, 11th ed. (Upper Saddle River, NJ: Prentice-Hall, 1996), p. 242.

88. Quoted in Leonard Baker, *Back to Back: The Duel Between FDR and the Supreme Court* (New York: Macmillan, 1967), p. 8.

89. Actuarial tables of the Metropolitan Life Insurance Company accorded even the oldest justice another five years. Schlesinger, *The Politics of Upheaval*, p. 493.

90. For a thorough analysis of the amendment possibility, see David F. Kyvig, "The Road Not Taken: FDR, the Supreme Court, and Constitutional Amendment," 104 *Political Science Quarterly* 463 (1989).

91. Walter Lippmann, quoted in "Topics of the Day," *Literary Digest*, July 27, 1935, p. 3.

92. By statute, Congress could also withdraw review of certain statutes from the Supreme Court's appellate jurisdiction. This alone, however, would not prevent federal district or appeals judges from invalidating legislation.

93. Entry of December 27, 1935, in *The Secret Diary of Harold L. Ickes*, vol. 1 (New York: Simon & Schuster, 1953), p. 495.

94. Freidel, *Franklin D. Roosevelt*, p. 222.

95. See FDR's letter of January 7, 1937, to the governors of those states that had not ratified the child labor amendment, in *Public Papers and Addresses*, vol. 5, p. 657. The amendment was never ratified, but soon became unnecessary because of enactment of the Fair Labor Standards Act of 1938 which included a ban on the interstate shipment of goods produced or manufactured with child labor. See the discussion of the Supreme Court's reaction to this legislation in the text containing the reference to note 130.

96. Entry of January 11, 1935, in *The Secret Diary of Harold L. Ickes*, vol. 1, p. 274.

97. For a detailed account of FDR's manuevers against the Court, see Joseph Alsop and Turner Catledge, *The 168 Days* (Garden City, NY: Doubleday, Doran, 1938); and, Leuchtenberg, *The Supreme Court Reborn*, chs. 4 and 5.

98. The occasion reminded Senator William Borah of "the Roman Emperor who looked around his dinner table and began to laugh when he thought how many of those heads would be rolling on the morrow." *Time*, March 1, 1937, p. 13.

99. Besides promising to be a corrective that was both speedy and sure, the prospect of altering the Court's membership must have been personally satisfying to FDR. He had hardly forgotten *Humphrey's Executor* v. *United States*, 295 U.S. 602, decided on the same day that the Court struck down NIRA. Although the former case did not involve New Deal legislation, it held that subordinates—in this instance, a now deceased Hoover appointee to the Federal Trade Commission—vested with tenure by Congress were not subject to removal at the president's pleasure. More than any other decision that went against his administration, FDR took this ruling as a personal affront. Advisers later traced the origins of the plan he devised to that vexatious decision. Rexford G. Tugwell, *The Democratic Roosevelt* (Garden City, NY: Doubleday, 1957), p. 392.

Roosevelt also liked the plan because of its savory irony. Attorney General Homer Cummings had recently rediscovered a proposal Attorney General (now Justice) McReynolds had made in 1913, advocating the addition of one new federal judge, below the level of the Supreme Court, for each judge who reached seventy without retiring. Leuchtenburg, *The Supreme Court Reborn*, p. 120; Homer Cummings and Carl McFarland, *Federal Justice* (New York: Macmillan, 1937), p. 531.

100. *Reorganization of the Federal Judiciary*, hearings by the Senate Judiciary Committee on S. 1392, March 10–April 23, 1937, 75th Congress, 1st session (Washington, DC: Government Printing Office, 1937).

101. Quoted in Mason and Stephenson, *American Constitutional Law*, p. 243.

102. Speech of February 20, 1937, quoted in *The Memoirs of Herbert Hoover*, vol. 3 (New York: Macmillan, 1952), p. 374.

103. "Arouse and Beware," *American Agriculturist*, February 27, 1937, p. 1.

104. Quoted in Mason and Stephenson, *American Constitutional Law*, p. 243.

105. Quoted in Mason, *Harlan Fiske Stone*, pp. 443–444.

106. Fireside Chat of March 9, 1937, "Defending the Plan to 'Pack' the Supreme Court," in Russell D. Buhite and David W. Levy, *FDR's Fireside Chats* (Norman: University of Oklahoma Press, 1992), p. 88.

107. Gregory A. Caldeira, "Public Opinion and the U.S. Supreme Court: FDR's Court-Packing Plan," 81 *American Political Science Review* 1139, 1147 (1987).

108. After the Judiciary Committee's action, Roosevelt revamped the legislation, asking to appoint an additional justice per calendar year (instead of acting all at once) for each member of the Court who remained on the bench after the age of seventy-five (instead of seventy). Had this version been adopted, FDR would have been able to name three new justices by January 1938, because on May 18 Justice Van Devanter had announced his intention to retire.

109. The bill's demise in the Senate of course obviated the need for any action by the House of Representatives.

110. Nelson, "The President and the Court," p. 288.

111. Quoted in James MacGregor Burns, *Roosevelt: The Lion and the Fox* (New York: Harcourt Brace Jovanovich, 1956), p. 299.

112. Speech by James A. Farley to the Boston University Law School Alumni Association, April 22, 1937. Reprinted in 81 *Congressional Record* appendix, p. 1041. Farley was postmaster general, twice FDR's campaign manager, and in charge of patronage.

113. John D. Fassett, *New Deal Justice: The Life of Stanley Reed of Kentucky* (New York: Vantage Press, 1994), p. 161.

114. FDR did not consult Frankfurter in advance probably because he suspected divided loyalties, given Frankfurter's close relationship with Justice Brandeis. Also, in 1934 Frankfurter had warned the Court's critics in print against enlarging the bench. Melvin I. Urofsky, *Felix Frankfurter: Judicial Restraint and Individual Liberties* (Boston: Twayne, 1991), p. 42.

115. FDR's craving for secrecy makes little sense because he had already revealed his intentions in late December in an interview with journalist George Creel. " 'Then,' said the President, his face like a fist, 'Congress can enlarge the Supreme Court, increasing the number of justices so as to permit the appointment of men in tune with the spirit of the age.' " George Creel, "Roosevelt's Plans and Purposes," *Collier's*, December 26, 1936, p. 7. See also George Creel, *Rebel at Large* (New York: G. P. Putnam's Sons, 1947), p. 294. Roosevelt's comment on the Court attracted little attention at the time.

116. Quoted in Alan Brinkley, *The End of Reform: New Deal Liberalism in Recession and War* (New York: Alfred A. Knopf, 1995), p. 282, n. 10.

117. 300 U.S. 379 (1937).

118. Mason, *Harlan Fiske Stone*, p. 454.

119. 301 U.S. 1 (1937).

120. Ibid., 41.

121. Ibid., 77.

122. *Steward Machine Co.* v. *Davis*, 301 U.S. 548 (1937); *Helvering* v. *Davis*, 301 U.S. 619 (1937). The former had been argued on April 8–9; the latter, on May 5.

123. The term was coined by Princeton's Edward Corwin. See his *Constitutional Revolution, Ltd.* (Claremont, CA: Claremont Colleges, 1941). Ironically, it was Corwin who, on December 16, passed the Court-packing scheme to Attorney General Cummings, having received the idea from Harvard's Arthur Holcombe in a letter dated December 7, 1936. Corwin's involvement may have added persuasiveness to the idea not only because of his reputation as the nation's leading academic constitutional scholar but also because it offered a cover of administrative reform. "Once Corwin had blazed the path this far, . . . it did not take Cummings long to trace out the rest of the way." Leuchtenberg, *The Supreme Court Reborn*, p. 119. Corwin later publicly supported Roosevelt's proposal.

124. Robert H. Jackson, *The Struggle for Judicial Supremacy* (New York: Random House, 1941), p. 196.

125. James T. Patterson, *Congressional Conservatives and the New Deal* (Lexington: University Press of Kentucky, 1967), pp. 165, 325–337.

126. Brinkley, *The End of Reform*, p. 20. For Roosevelt to be down did not mean that he was out, however. Compare his failure on executive reorganization with his success on "pump priming" in 1938. Weed, *The Nemesis of Reform*, pp. 179–185. See also Sidney M. Milkis, *The President and the Parties: The Transformation of the American Party System Since the New Deal* (New York: Oxford University Press, 1993), pp. 52–53, 80–83.

127. 304 U.S. 144 (1938).

128. Ibid., 152 (emphasis added).

129. *Chicago, Milwaukee & St. Paul R.R. Co.* v. *Minnesota*, 134 U.S. 418 (1890); *Lochner* v. *New York*, 198 U.S. 45 (1905). Both cases are discussed in chapter 5.

130. 312 U.S. 100 (1941).

131. 247 U.S. 251 (1918).

132. 312 U.S. at 124.

133. 317 U.S. 111 (1942).

134. *National League of Cities* v. *Usery*, 426 U.S. 833 (1976), reversed in *Garcia* v. *San Antonio Metropolitan Transit Authority*, 469 U.S. 528 (1985).

135. *United States* v. *Lopez*, 514 U.S. 549 (1995).

136. 304 U.S. at 152, n. 4.

7. THE ELECTION OF 1968: PARTISANSHIP DESTABILIZED

1. Alan Brinkley, *The End of Reform: New Deal Liberalism in Recession and War* (New York: Alfred A. Knopf, 1995), p. 140. Between 1933 and 1953, Republicans controlled only a single Congress: the 80th, after the midterm election of 1946.

2. James L. Sundquist, *Dynamics of the Party System*, rev. ed. (Washington, DC: Brookings Institution, 1983), p. 241.

3. "It all fits into a pattern," exclaimed Nevada Senator George Malone. "We deliberately lose Manchuria, China, Korea, and Berlin. We follow the pattern of sometimes apparently unrelated events—but it all adds up to losing strategic areas throughout the world." Quoted in Barton J. Bernstein, "Election of 1952," in Arthur M. Schlesinger, Jr., and Fred L. Israel, eds., *History of American Presidential Elections 1789–1968*, vol. 4 (New York: Chelsea House, 1971), p. 3217.

4. Speech by President Harry S Truman, September 18, 1948, in ibid., p. 3200.

5. "Acceptance Speech by Vice-President Richard M. Nixon," July 28, 1960, in ibid., p. 3552.

6. Of the 266 electoral votes needed to win the White House in the 1940s, the eleven states of the old Confederacy accounted for 127, and during the fifth party system none was cast in the Republican column until 1952 when Ike carried Florida, Tennessee, Texas, and Virginia. The same four, plus Louisiana, went Republican in 1956 as well. Among the Southern congressional delegations in modern times, only Tennessee (with two) claimed Republican representatives prior to 1952. Republican representatives first appeared in North Carolina and Virginia in 1952, in Texas in 1954, in Florida in 1956, in Alabama, Georgia, and Mississippi in 1964, and in Arkansas and South Carolina in 1966. Louisiana did not send a Republican member to Congress until the 1970s. John Tower of Texas was the first Republican elected to the U.S. Senate from the South in the fifth party system. He won a special election in 1961 to fill the seat vacated by Lyndon Johnson, who had been elected vice president. Strom Thurmond of South Carolina was the second Southern Senate Republican. Elected as a Democrat in 1954, he switched parties in September 1964 and was reelected as a Republican in 1966. *Congress and the Nation*, vol. 2 (Washington, DC: Congressional Quarterly Service, 1969), pp. 33, 35.

7. Sundquist, *Dynamics of the Party System*, p. 277.

8. Donald S. Strong, "Durable Republicanism in the South," in Allan P. Sindler, ed., *Change in the Contemporary South* (Durham, NC: Duke University Press, 1963), pp. 174–181.

9. President's Commission on Civil Rights, *To Secure These Rights* (Washington, DC: U.S. Government Printing Office, 1947).

10. Irwin Ross, *The Loneliest Campaign: The Truman Victory of 1948* (New York: New American Library, 1968), pp. 64–65. Former Vice President Wallace decided in 1947 to challenge Truman. He led a reborn Progressive ticket in the 1948 campaign that Truman supporters feared would attract voters who might otherwise vote Democratic. On the ballot in all but three states, he drew 1.16 million votes.

11. Memorandum by Clark M. Clifford and James H. Rowe to the president, November 10, 1947. Quoted in ibid., pp. 22–23.

12. These measures would not be fully enacted until the 1960s. *Public Papers of the Presidents: Harry S Truman, 1948* (Washington, DC: U.S. Government Printing Office, 1964), pp. 3, 121–126.

13. Quoted in John M. Redding, *Inside the Democratic Party* (Indianapolis, IN: Bobbs-Merrill, 1958), pp. 113–114.

14. "We believe that racial and religious minorities have the right to live, develop and vote equally with all citizens and share the rights that are guaranteed by our Constitution. Congress should exert its full constitutional powers to protect those rights." "Democratic Platform of 1944," in Schlesinger and Israel, eds., *History of American Presidential Elections*, vol. 4, p. 3041. Southern delegates had not objected strenuously to this paragraph because of the important qualifying language it contained.

15. "We highly commend President Harry S. [*sic*] Truman for his courageous stand on the issue of civil rights. We call upon the Congress to support our President in guaranteeing these basic and fundamental American Principles: (1) the right of full and equal political participation; (2) the right to equal opportunity of employment; (3) the right of security of person; (4) and the right of equal treatment in the service and defense of our nation." "Democratic Platform of 1948," in ibid., vol. 4, p. 3154.

16. The label "Dixiecrat" seems to have originated when a newspaper editor in Charlotte, North Carolina, could not squeeze "States Rights Democrat" into a headline. Leonard Dinnerstein, "The Progressive and States' Rights Parties of 1948," in Arthur M. Schlesinger, Jr., *History of U.S. Political Parties*, vol. 4 (New York: Chelsea House, 1973), p. 3328, n. 1.

17. In their 1952 platform, Democrats carried over most of the 1948 provisions on civil rights and commended the Justice Department for pursuing "the elimination of many illegal discriminations, including those involving rights . . . to enroll in publicly supported higher educational institutions." "Democratic Platform of 1952," in Schlesinger and Israel, eds., *History of American Presidential Elections*, vol. 4, p. 3280. Republicans were at once both more and less bold. Advocating federal antilynching laws, abolition of poll taxes, the end of segregation in the District of Columbia, and laws banning "discriminatory employment practices," the party also recognized "the primary responsibility of each State to order and control its own domestic institutions," as well as the duty of the national government to "take supplemental action within its constitutional jurisdiction to oppose discrimination against race, religion or national origin." "Republican Platform of 1952," in ibid., p. 3291.

18. 347 U.S. 483 (1954).

19. Speaking in Atlanta, Wallace charged a "Republican Chief Justice" with "the destruction of every local institution in Georgia." *New York Times*, November 5, 1968, p. 30.

20. *Brown* v. *Board of Education*, 349 U.S. 294 (1955) (sometimes called *Brown II*).

21. "Declaration of Constitutional Principles Issued by 19 Senators and 77 Representatives of the Congress," *New York Times*, March 12, 1956, p. 19.

22. "Speaking for a unanimous Supreme Court, a great Republican Chief Justice, Earl Warren, has ordered an end to racial segregation in the nation's schools." *New York Times*, February 14, 1956, p. 18.

23. "Democratic Platform of 1956," in Schlesinger and Israel, eds., *History of American Presidential Elections*, vol. 4., p. 3384; "Republican Platform of 1956," in ibid., p. 3400.

24. Ironically, it took votes of moderate Republicans to break a Southern-led filibuster that had blocked a vote on the Civil Rights Act in the Senate. Without Republican help, the measure probably would not have become law until perhaps 1965.

25. Senator Goldwater based his vote against the Civil Rights Act of 1964 on constitutional, not racial grounds. Barry Goldwater, *Goldwater* (New York: Doubleday, 1988), pp. 172–174.

26. Richard M. Scammon and Ben J. Wattenberg popularized the term. *The Real Majority* (New York: Coward-McCann, 1970), p. 12.

27. David S. Broder, "Election of 1968," in Schlesinger and Israel, eds., *History of American Presidential Elections*, vol. 4, p. 3707.

28. In 1965, for the first time, Americans had listed street crime as one of the major problems facing the nation, second only to the need for improved schools. George H. Gallup, *The Gallup Poll: Public Opinion 1935–1971*, vol. 3 (New York: Random House, 1972), pp. 1764, 1842, 1908, 1939.

29. That position was so settled that it hardly rated reconsideration. For example, see *Ferguson* v. *Skrupa*, 372 U.S. 726 (1963). The only significant exception was continued scrutiny under the commerce clause of state and local commercial regulations that were "protectionist" or otherwise unduly interfered with interstate commerce. For example, see *Southern Pacific* v. *Arizona*, 325 U.S. 761 (1945), where a divided bench struck down a state train limit law. But there was no dispute over *Congress's* authority to enact such a statute, if it chose to do so.

30. 310 U.S. 586, 598 (1940).

31. Ibid., 606.

32. 319 U.S. 624, 642 (1943).

33. In *Barron* v. *Baltimore*, 32 U.S. (7 Peters) 243 (1833), the Supreme Court held without dissent that the provisions of the first ten amendments (the Bill of Rights) were applicable only to the national government.

34. *Chicago, B. & Q. R. Co.* v. *Chicago*, 166 U.S. 226 (1897), made the "just compensation" clause of the Fifth Amendment applicable to the states by way of the Fourteenth Amendment.

35. *Gitlow* v. *New York*, 268 U.S. 652 (1925); *Near* v. *Minnesota*, 283 U.S. 697 (1931); *DeJonge* v. *Oregon*, 299 U.S. 353 (1937); *Cantwell* v. *Connecticut*, 310 U.S. 296 (1940); *Everson* v. *Board of Education*, 330 U.S. 1 (1947).

36. This did not mean that, without incorporation, the Fourteenth Amendment gave the states an entirely free hand in administering their criminal justice

systems. As early as *Moore* v. *Dempsey*, 261 U.S. 86 (1923), the Court insisted that state court convictions influenced by the pressure of lynch mobs violated due process; in *Rochin* v. *California*, 342 U.S. 165 (1952), the Court overturned a conviction based on local police procedure that "shocks the conscience."

37. Bernard Schwartz, *A History of the Supreme Court* (New York: Oxford University Press, 1993), pp. 282–283.

38. J. W. Peltason, *Fifty-eight Lonely Men: Southern Federal Judges and School Desegregation*, rev. ed. (Urbana: University of Illinois Press, 1971), pp. 93–134.

39. David M. O'Brien, *Storm Center: The Supreme Court in American Politics*, 3d ed. (New York: Norton, 1993), p. 404.

40. Alan Westin, ed., *Freedom Now!* (New York: Basic Books, 1964), p. 133. However, in six border states and the District of Columbia, the figure was much higher: 52 percent.

41. J. Harvie Wilkinson, *From Brown to Bakke* (New York: Oxford University Press, 1979), p. 108; *New York Times*, January 12, 1968, p. 49.

42. See D. Grier Stephenson, Jr., et al., *American Government*, 2d ed. (New York: HarperCollins, 1992), fig. 5.1, p. 143.

43. *Griffin* v. *School Board of Prince Edward County*, 377 U.S. 218 (1964).

44. 391 U.S. 430 (1968).

45. Ibid., pp. 437–439 (emphasis in the original).

46. Between 1954 and 1968, *all* school cases in the High Court involved Southern and border states (plus Kansas) where racial segregation had been either required by state law or under local option. Thus, through the election of 1968 the dispute over school integration was still perceived nationally as a "Southern problem."

47. Students had been riding school buses for years, of course, sometimes even to maintain racially segregated schools.

48. Stephenson et al., *American Government*, fig. 5.1, p. 143.

49. The term derives from Republican Senator Joseph McCarthy of Wisconsin, who in the early 1950s excelled in breeding popular suspicion of treason in the highest echelons of government. Excesses precipitated his censure by the Senate in 1954.

50. The most controversial of these included *Slochower* v. *Board of Education of New York City*, 350 U.S. 551 (1956), holding that a public university could not dismiss a professor merely because he invoked the Fifth Amendment during questioning by a congressional committee; *Communist Party of the U.S.* v. *Subversive Activities Control Board*, 351 U.S. 115 (1956), refusing to accept the SACB's findings that the American Communist party was a "Communist action organization" under the Internal Security Act of 1950; *Pennsylvania* v. *Nelson*, 350 U.S. 497 (1956), holding invalid state laws punishing sedition against the United States, on grounds of federal preemption; *Jencks* v. *United States*, 353 U.S 657 (1957), overturning the conviction of a union official who had falsely sworn that he was not a member of

the Communist party, after defense counsel had been denied access to FBI reports on the key witnesses; *Watkins* v. *United States*, 354 U.S. 178 (1957), overturning a conviction for contempt of Congress of one who, on First Amendment free speech grounds, had refused to answer questions about former Communists asked by the House Committee on Un-American Activities, and boldly casting doubt on the constitutionality of Congress's investigatory power when used to expose someone's political beliefs; and *Yates* v. *United States*, 354 U.S. 298 (1957), reversing convictions for subversive activity under the Smith Act by requiring a higher level of proof for the "advocacy" of overthrow that the statute prohibited.

51. *New York Times*, June 27, 1956, p. 18.

52. Earl Warren, *The Memoirs of Earl Warren* (Garden City, NY: Doubleday, 1977), pp. 303–304. The billboards remained in place until Warren's last year on the Court.

53. Ibid., p. 325.

54. The text of the report and the resolutions was reprinted in *U.S. News & World Report*, October 3, 1958, p. 45. See also Charles S. Hyneman, *The Supreme Court on Trial* (New York: Atherton Press, 1963), pp. 22–24.

55. James F. Byrnes, "The Supreme Court Must Be Curbed," *U.S. News & World Report*, May 18, 1956, p. 50.

56. This law altered the *Jencks* decision (see note 50 above) by allowing the trial judge, not defense attorneys, to decide what material was properly relevant for the defense. See Walter F. Murphy, *Congress and the Court* (Chicago: University of Chicago Press, 1962), pp. 127–153, for an analysis of the various versions of the Jencks Act.

57. By comparison, in the Court-packing fight of 1937, Senator Joseph Robinson, the president's floor leader in the Senate, was never certain of more than thirty affirmative votes, even with the prestige of FDR behind him. Ibid., p. 200.

58. C. Herman Pritchett, *Congress Versus the Supreme Court* (Minneapolis: University of Minnesota Press, 1961), pp. vii–viii.

59. William Lasser, *The Limits of Judicial Power* (Chapel Hill: University of North Carolina Press, 1988), pp. 174–175. For example, see *Barenblatt* v. *United States*, 360 U.S. 109 (1959), which upheld a conviction for contempt of Congress by "distinguishing" *Watkins*.

60. 370 U.S. 421 (1962).

61. 374 U.S. 203 (1963).

62. William M. Beaney and Edward N. Beiser, "Prayer and Politics: The Impact of *Engel* and *Schempp* on the Political Process," 13 *Journal of Public Law* 475 (1964).

63. 108 *Congressional Record* 15991 (August 8, 1962).

64. Quoted in *New Republic*, July 9, 1962, p. 2.

65. *Congressional Quarterly Almanac* (Washington, DC: Congressional Quarterly News Features, 1964), pp. 400–401.

66. *Wesberry* v. *Sanders*, 376 U.S. 1 (1964), and *Reynolds* v. *Sims*, 377 U.S. 533 (1964), were two leading reapportionment decisions that effectively remade the political map of the United States. For the U.S. House of Representatives, as well as for both houses of state legislatures, states were constitutionally required to redraw district lines on the principle of numerical equality ("one man, one vote"). Except for the U.S. Senate, the apportionment of which is stipulated by the Constitution, hardly any elected representative body in the nation remained unaffected by the rulings. While not strictly an issue in the 1968 presidential campaign, the reapportionment decisions led to strenuous efforts to overturn what the Court had done by constitutional amendment. In both 1965 and 1966 antireapportionment amendments in the Senate fell only seven votes short of the two-thirds required by the Constitution. Twenty-eight states of the constitutionally mandated thirty-four petitioned Congress to convene a constitutional convention to overturn what the Court had done. *Congress and the Nation*, vol. 2, pp. 432–435. The anti-Court drive withered after 1966 because of speedy implementation of *Sanders* and *Sims*. State legislators and members of Congress elected under the new apportionment schemes were as advantaged as their predecessors had been disadvantaged by the 1964 rulings. Royce Hanson, *The Political Thicket* (Englewood Cliffs, NJ: Prentice-Hall, 1966), p. 91. Nonetheless, the row yet again produced a torrent of anti-Court invective and charges, even from principled quarters, of an audacious and meddlesome Supreme Court that, contrary to the framers' plan, had become "a general haven for reform movements." "[W]hen in the name of constitutional interpretation," Justice Harlan admonished, "the Court *adds* something to the Constitution that was deliberately excluded from it, the Court in reality substitutes its view of what should be so for the amending process." 377 U.S. at 625 (dissenting opinion; emphasis in the original).

67. *Roth* v. *United States*, 354 U.S. 476 (1957).

68. *Kingsley International Pictures Corp.* v. *Regents*, 360 U.S. 684 (1959).

69. Justice Stewart was the most candid, confessing that he "could never succeed in intelligibly doing so," but adding, "I know it when I see it." *Jacobellis* v. *Ohio*, 378 U.S. 184, 197 (1964) (concurring opinion). This case involved a French film entitled *The Lovers*.

70. *Redrup* v. *New York*, 386 U.S. 767 (1967).

71. Only 15 percent replied that they were "about right." Gallup, vol. 3, p. 1966.

72. *Congress and the Nation*, vol. 3, p. 413. The commission issued a series of recommendations in 1970, urging that laws "prohibiting the sale, exhibition, or distribution of sexual materials to consenting adults should be repealed."

73. Theodore H. White, *The Making of the President 1968* (New York: Atheneum, 1969), p. 34.

74. 367 U.S. 643 (1961).

75. *Wolf* v. *Colorado*, 338 U.S. 25 (1949), incorporated the Fourth Amendment into the Fourteenth, but did so without including the judicially crafted exclusionary rule, and so was of little help to criminal defendants in state courts.

76. The exclusionary rule was first applied to certain federal criminal prosecutions in *Weeks* v. *United States*, 232 U.S. 383 (1914).

77. *Gideon* v. *Wainwright*, 372 U.S. 335 (1963), mandated court-appointed counsel for all indigents charged with serious offenses in state courts. This pro-defendant decision of the Warren Court was unusual in that it was unanimous and widely applauded, both probably because *Gideon* called for changes in only a handful of states. The Supreme Court had mandated counsel for indigents in federal trials since 1938, and by 1963 almost all of the states had already adopted on their own the rule that *Gideon* declared to be constitutionally required.

78. 378 U.S. 478 (1964).

79. 384 U.S. 436 (1966).

80. Ibid., 515.

81. Ibid., 542–543.

82. See *New York Times*, June 19, 1966, sec. 4, p. 13, for these and other press comments from different parts of the nation.

83. Charles Evans Hughes introduced this term shortly before becoming chief justice. See his *The Supreme Court of the United States* (New York: Columbia University Press, 1928), p. 50. A self-inflicted wound, as the term implies, occurs when the Court sustains grave injury through its own handiwork. Fred P. Graham borrowed it for the title of his book on the Warren Court's criminal justice decisions. *The Self-Inflicted Wound* (New York: Macmillan, 1970), esp. pp. 153–193.

84. 384 U.S. 719 (1966).

85. Graham, *The Self-Inflicted Wound*, p. 185. For background on one of the jail deliveries, see the *New York Times*, February 21, 1967, p. 41.

86. *Killough* v. *United States*, 315 F.2d 241, 265 (DC Cir., 1962) (Miller, J., dissenting).

87. 388 U.S. 218 (1967).

88. The legislation was first introduced in 1967. The 1968 version provided millions of dollars in grants to local law enforcement and regulated firearms. Against the administration's wishes, Congress inserted an elaborate codification of procedures for wiretapping and eavesdropping, thus legitimizing electronic surveillance for the first time. *Congress and the Nation*, vol. 2, p. 323.

89. 354 U.S. 449 (1957).

90. The vote not to send the bill to conference was 60–318. See the summary in *Congressional Quarterly Weekly Report*, June 7, 1968, pp. 1433–1439. The 1968 law emphasized law enforcement. Ironically, this was in sharp contrast to the findings in the same year of the Kerner Commission, which had been appointed by President Johnson. In trying to account for recent civil unrest, the commission stressed the need for reining in law enforcement. Its report blamed aggressive patrolling by police, police brutality, and unwarranted use of deadly force as the primary sources of minority group hostility. National Advisory Commission on Civil Disorders, *Report* (Washington, DC: U.S. Government Printing Office, 1968).

91. It was a hollow victory. The Justice Department has not insisted on the use of any of the three anti-Court measures in federal criminal cases, and none of them applied to prosecutions in state courts.

92. *Congress and the Nation*, vol. 2, pp. 15–21.

93. Robert J. Steamer, *The Supreme Court in Crisis* (Amherst: University of Massachusetts Press, 1971), p. 260.

94. Gallup, *The Gallup Poll*, vol. 3, pp. 2068, 2147.

95. "Nixon Said to Bar Southerners' Bid," *New York Times*, August 7, 1968, p. 30.

96. Quoted in Broder, "Election of 1968," pp. 3741–3742.

97. "Acceptance Speech by Former Vice-President Richard M. Nixon," August 8, 1968, in Schlesinger and Israel, eds., *History of American Presidential Elections*, vol. 4, p. 3833.

98. "American Independent Platform," ibid., vol 4, p. 3798.

99. Robert Semple, Jr., "3 Presidential Aspirants Back Strong Local Rule," *New York Times*, August 1, 1968, p. 18.

100. "Wallace Denies His Support Is Slipping," *New York Times*, November 3, 1968, p. 77.

101. The Harris poll issued a week before the November election said "LAW AND ORDER: Perhaps more than any other, this issue finds Humphrey on the defensive." As to the candidate who would handle that issue best, Nixon led with 35 percent, to 26 and 24 percent for Humphrey and Wallace, respectively. Scammon and Wattenberg, *The Real Majority*, p. 183n.

102. "American Independent Platform," in Schlesinger and Israel, eds., *History of American Presidential Elections*, vol. 4, pp. 3797, 3799.

103. In a second version of this line, Wallace warned, "And if you walk out of this building tonite [*sic*], and someone knocks you in the head, the person who knocked you in the head will be out of jail if you don't watch out." Quoted in Jody Carlson, *George C. Wallace and the Politics of Powerlessness* (New Brunswick, NJ: Transaction Books, 1981), p. 129.

104. Robert B. Semple, Jr., "Nixon Withholds His Peace Ideas," *New York Times*, March 11, 1968, pp. 1, 33. Nixon used nearly the same phrasing in his acceptance speech in Miami on August 8.

105. *New York Times*, May 31, 1968, p. 18.

106. John W. Finney, "Nixon and Reagan Ask for War on Crime," *New York Times*, August 1, 1968, p. 1.

107. George F. Cole, *The American System of Criminal Justice*, 4th ed. (Monterey,CA: Brooks/Cole, 1986), p. 15.

108. Gallup, *The Gallup Poll*, vol. 3, pp. 2107–2108.

109. E. E. Kenworthy, "Nixon Scores Indulgence," *New York Times*, November 3, 1968, pp. 1, 79.

110. "Democratic Platform," in Schlesinger and Israel, eds., *History of American Presidential Elections*, vol. 4, pp. 3753–3780.

111. Robert B. Semple, Jr., "Humphrey Links Wallace to Fear," *New York Times*, October 2, 1968, p. 1.

112. *Congress and the Nation*, vol. 2, p. 19.

113. Scammon and Wattenberg, *The Real Majority*, p. 183.

114. Still the South was not as fully Republican as it had been Democratic for so long, especially prior to 1948. Earl Black and Merle Black, *The Vital South: How Presidents Are Elected* (Cambridge, MA: Harvard University Press, 1992), p. 217.

115. Stephen J. Wayne, *The Road to the White House 1996* (New York: St. Martin's Press, 1996), table 3–3 and fig. 3–1, pp. 73–74.

116. Robert M. McCloskey, *The American Supreme Court* (Chicago: University of Chicago Press, 1960), p. 20.

117. The campaign of 1968 and several others to follow were a long distance in propriety from the 1956 race when Vice President Nixon sought political profit from Republican Warren's leadership in *Brown*. Democratic presidential nominee Adlai Stevenson directly reprimanded Nixon for the remark, and even President Eisenhower indirectly chided his running mate for the "blunder" of seeking partisan advantage at the Court's expense. *New York Times*, February 16, 1956, p. 28; February 18, 1956, p. 10; March 1, 1956, p. 1.

118. Mark Silverstein, *Judicious Choices* (New York: Norton, 1994), p. 18. See also G. Edward White, *Earl Warren: A Public Life* (New York: Oxford University Press, 1982), pp. 306–313.

119. Even before word of Warren's impending departure, Republicans and conservative Democrats in the Senate had indicated that they would attempt to block a Johnson designee. Marjorie Hunter, "Senate Coalition May Block Action on Warren's Post," *New York Times*, June 23, 1968, p. 1.

120. Two biographies of Fortas indicate that the extent of Justice Fortas's White House advisory role was probably more extensive than even his critics claimed in 1968. See Bruce A. Murphy, *Fortas* (New York: William Morrow, 1988), and Laura Kalman, *Abe Fortas* (New Haven: Yale University Press, 1990). Neither book includes the revelation in Joseph A. Califano, *The Triumph & Tragedy of Lyndon Johnson* (New York: Simon & Schuster, 1991). According to this former Johnson adviser, during the Pennsylvania Railroad–New York Central merger affair in November 1966, Fortas, at Johnson's request, gave the president instructions on what the Justice Department should put in its brief. Later Fortas not only participated when the Court decided in March 1967 to remand the case to the Interstate Commerce Commission, but his dissent repeated the same point that he had urged for the government's brief. When the Court finally approved the merger in January 1968, Fortas wrote the opinion of the Court. Ibid., pp. 159–164.

121. John Corry, "Strom's Dirty Movies," *Harper's*, December 1968, p. 30.

122. United States Senate, Committee on the Judiciary, *Hearings on the Nominations of Abe Fortas and Homer Thornberry* (Washington, DC: U.S. Government Printing Office, 1968), pp. 292–297, 300.

123. Kalman, *Abe Fortas*, p. 344.

124. U.S. Senate, *Hearings*, p. 191. For a description of the committee scene, see Robert F. Shogan, *A Question of Judgment* (Indianapolis, IN: Bobbs-Merrill, 1972), p. 170.

125. Neil D. McFeeley, *Appointment of Judges: The Johnson Presidency* (Austin: University of Texas Press, 1987), p. 128.

126. William Lambert, "Fortas of the Supreme Court," *Life*, May 9, 1969, p. 82.

127. During the Burger hearings, Democratic Senator Robert Byrd of West Virginia quoted approvingly from a 1967 speech by Burger in which he questioned the rationality of a system that emphasized protection of citizens from police rather than protection of citizens from criminals. See Leonard W. Levy, *Against the Law: The Nixon Court and Criminal Justice* (New York: Harper & Row, 1974), pp. 20–21.

128. Stephen E. Ambrose, *Nixon: The Triumph of a Politician* (New York: Simon & Schuster, 1989), p. 296.

129. John P. Frank, an expert on judicial ethics and a scholar not disposed to Haynsworth's jurisprudence, concludes that the ethical charges were vastly overblown and served only as a cover for senators not willing openly to oppose Haynsworth on ideological grounds. *Clement Haynsworth, the Senate, and the Supreme Court* (Charlottesville: University Press of Virginia, 1991).

130. Henry J. Abraham, *Justices and Presidents*, 3d ed. (New York: Oxford University Press, 1992), p. 15.

131. Quoted in Richard Harris, *Decision* (New York: Dutton, 1971), p. 110.

132. The text of the address appears in *New York Times*, April 10, 1970, p. 1. In the midterm election seven months later, Republican opponents defeated Democratic Senators Albert Gore of Tennessee and Joseph Tydings of Maryland; in an earlier Texas primary, liberal Democratic Senator Ralph Yarborough lost to a conservative challenger. Their votes against Carswell contributed to their defeats.

133. Silverstein, *Judicious Choices*, p. 109.

134. William O. Douglas, *Points of Rebellion* (New York: Random House, 1969). See D. Grier Stephenson, Jr., Book Review, 119 *University of Pennsylvania Law Review* 536 (1971).

135. James F. Simon, *Independent Journey: The Life of William O. Douglas* (New York: Harper & Row, 1980), pp. 404–405.

136. Ibid., p. 406.

137. Committee on the Judiciary, U.S. House of Representatives, *Final Report by the Special Subcommittee on H. Res. 920* (Washington, DC: U.S. Government Printing Office, 1970).

138. The two Republican members did not call for the justice's impeachment but believed that the three Democrats had given inadequate attention to the propriety of some of Douglas's conduct. See *New York Times*, December 16, 1970, p. 20, and December 17, 1970, p. 43.

139. In January 1972 Lewis F. Powell (an attorney from Richmond, Virginia)

and Arizonan William H. Rehnquist (assistant attorney general for the Office of Legal Counsel) replaced Justices Black and Harlan, respectively. Ironically, Gerald Ford was president when Justice Douglas retired. Ford's choice was Seventh Circuit Appeals Judge John Stevens. President Ronald Reagan named Sandra Day O'Connor in 1981 to fill the seat vacated by Justice Potter Stewart.

140. Leon E. Panetta and Peter Gall, *Bring Us Together: The Nixon Team and the Civil Rights Retreat* (Philadelphia: Lippincott, 1971), pp. 301–304; Rowland Evans and Robert Novak, *Nixon in the White House* (New York: Random House, 1971), pp. 171–173.

141. *Alexander* v. *Holmes County Board of Education*, 396 U.S. 19 (1969). The unanimous per curiam order announced that "all deliberate speed" was no longer applicable to school integration. See Charles S. Bullock III and Charles M. Lamb, *Implementation of Civil Rights Policy* (Monterey, CA: Brooks/Cole, 1984), pp. 11–12, 58.

142. *Swann* v. *Charlotte-Mecklenburg School District*, 402 U.S. 1 (1971).

143. *Keyes* v. *School District of Denver*, 413 U.S. 189 (1973).

144. *Griggs* v. *Duke Power Co.*, 401 U.S. 424 (1971).

145. *Regents* v. *Bakke*, 438 U.S. 265 (1978); *Steelworkers* v. *Weber*, 443 U.S. 193 (1979).

146. *United Jewish Organizations* v. *Carey*, 430 U.S. 144 (1977).

147. *Reed* v. *Reed*, 404 U.S. 71 (1971).

148. *San Antonio Independent School District* v. *Rodriguez*, 411 U.S. 1 (1973).

149. *Milliken* v. *Bradley*, 418 U.S. 717 (1974).

150. *Miller* v. *California*, 413 U.S. 5 (1973).

151. *New York Times Co.* v. *United States*, 403 U.S. 713 (1971).

152. *Wallace* v. *Jaffree*, 472 U.S. 38 (1985).

153. *Lemon* v. *Kurtzman*, 403 U.S. 602 (1971).

154. Yale Kamisar, "The Police Practice Phases of the Criminal Process and the Three Phases of the Burger Court," in Herman Schwartz, ed., *The Burger Years* (New York: Penguin, 1987), p. 143.

155. *Furman* v. *Georgia*, 408 U.S. 238 (1972); *Gregg* v. *Georgia*, 428 U.S. 153 (1976).

156. *Harris* v. *New York*, 401 U.S. 22 (1971); *Rhode Island* v. *Innis*, 446 U.S. 291 (1980); *Oregon* v. *Elstead*, 470 U.S. 298 (1985).

157. *United States* v. *Leon*, 468 U.S. 897 (1984).

158. *United States* v. *Chadwick*, 433 U.S. 1 (1977); *Arkansas* v. *Sanders*, 442 U.S. 753 (1979).

159. *United States* v. *Robinson*, 414 U.S. 218 (1973).

160. *Brewer* v. *Williams*, 430 U.S. 387 (1977), applying the Warren Court's *Massiah* v. *United States*, 337 U.S. 201 (1964), under emotionally laden circumstances.

161. *Argersinger* v. *Hamlin*, 407 U.S. 25 (1972).

162. *United States* v. *United States District Court*, 407 U.S. 297 (1972).

163. Vincent Blasi, ed., *The Burger Court: The Counter-Revolution That Wasn't* (New Haven: Yale University Press, 1983).

164. Mark Tushnet, "The Warren Court as History: An Interpretation," in Tushnet, ed., *The Warren Court in Historical and Political Perspective* (Charlottesville: University Press of Virginia, 1993), p. 34.

165. *United States* v. *Nixon*, 418 U.S. 683 (1974).

166. *Roe* v. *Wade*, 410 U.S. 113 (1973).

8. THE ELECTIONS OF 1980 AND 1984: WHOSE CONSTITUTION?

1. *Scott* v. *Sandford*, 60 U.S. (19 Howard) 393 (1857).

2. 410 U.S. 113 (1973).

3. Clinton failed on both occasions to receive a majority of the popular vote. His share was 43 percent in 1992 and 49 percent in 1996. Independent candidate Ross Perot drew 19 percent in 1992 (the largest for a third-party candidate since 1912) and 8.5 percent in 1996.

4. Clinton's trophies were Arkansas, Louisiana, and Tennessee in both 1992 and 1996, plus Georgia in 1992 and Florida in 1996. Unlike Carter in 1976, Clinton would have won with no Southern states.

5. David G. Lawrence, *The Collapse of the Democratic Presidential Majority: Realignment, Dealignment, and Electoral Change from Franklin Roosevelt to Bill Clinton* (Boulder, CO: Westview Press, 1996), pp. 169–181.

6. John H. Aldrich, *Why Parties? The Origin and Transformation of Political Parties in America* (Chicago: University of Chicago Press, 1995), p. 262.

7. For different perspectives on the future, see Theodore Lowi, "The Party Crasher," *New York Times Magazine*, August 23, 1992, p. 28; Michel Lind, *Up from Conservatism* (New York: Free Press, 1996); Geoffrey P. Faux, *The Party's Not Over: A New Vision for Democrats* (New York: Basic Books, 1996); Daniel J. Balz, *Storming the Gates: Protest Politics and the Republican Revival* (Boston: Little, Brown, 1996); Mario M. Cuomo, *Reason to Believe* (New York: Simon & Schuster, 1995).

8. This distinction, a legacy of V. O. Key, Jr., originated in his *Politics, Parties, and Pressure Groups*, 5th ed. (New York: Crowell, 1964). It has been widely adopted by students of American politics. See, for example, Frank J. Sorauf and Paul Allen Beck, *Party Politics in America*, 6th ed. (Glenview, IL: Scott, Foresman, 1988).

9. Nicol C. Rae, *The Decline and Fall of the Liberal Republicans from 1952 to the Present* (New York: Oxford University Press, 1989), p. 123. See Norman H. Nie, Sidney Verba, and John R. Petrocik, *The Changing American Voter*, enl. ed. (Cambridge, MA: Harvard University Press, 1979), pp. 96–173.

10. Rae, *The Decline and Fall of the Liberal Republicans*, p. 200. See also Ronald Radosh, *Divided They Fell: The Demise of the Democratic Party, 1964–1996* (New York: Free Press, 1996).

11. Clyde Wilcox, *God's Warriors: The Christian Right in Twentieth Century America* (Baltimore: Johns Hopkins University Press, 1992), p. 118. See also Duane Murray Oldfield, *The Right and the Righteous: The Christian Right Confronts the Republican Party* (Lanham, MD: Rowman & Littlefield, 1996).

12. *New York Times*/CBS News poll, 1989, reported in D. Grier Stephenson, Jr., Robert J. Bresler, Robert J. Friedrich, and Joseph J. Karlesky, *American Government*, 2d ed. (New York: HarperCollins, 1992), p. 317.

13. Mark J. Rozell and Clyde Wilcox, *Second Coming: The New Christian Right in Virginia Politics* (Baltimore, MD: Johns Hopkins University Press, 1996), fig. 1, p. 5.

14. William R. Shaffer, *Party and Ideology in the United States Congress* (Washington, DC: University Press of America, 1980); Barbara Sinclair, *Congressional Realignment 1925–1978* (Austin: University of Texas Press, 1982), p. 174; Rae, *The Decline and Fall of the Liberal Republicans*, pp. 193–195.

15. *Federal Election Commission* v. *National Conservative Political Action Committee*, 470 U.S. 480 (1985).

16. Nelson W. Polsby, *Consequences of Party Reform* (New York: Oxford University Press, 1983).

17. Aldrich, *Why Parties?*, p. 269.

18. Rae, *The Decline and Fall of the Liberal Republicans*, p. 127.

19. Stephen J. Wayne, *The Road to the White House 1996* (New York: St. Martin's Press, 1996), p. 107.

20. David Broder, *The Party's Over* (New York: Harper & Row, 1972); Cornelius P. Cotter and Bernard C. Hennessy, *Politics Without Power: The National Party Committees* (New York: Atherton, 1964).

21. "Presidential Race Resuscitates Campaign Finance Debate," *Congressional Quarterly Weekly Report*, November 9, 1996, p. 3196.

22. Michael Nelson, ed., *Guide to the Presidency* (Washington, DC: Congressional Quarterly, 1989), p. 193.

23. *Colorado Republican Federal Campaign Committee* v. *Federal Election Commission*, 518 U.S. 604 (1996).

24. Aldrich, *Why Parties?* p. 282.

25. Between Joseph Story's appointment in early 1812 and Justice McLean's in early 1829, the seven-justice bench remained unchanged except for the arrivals of Smith Thompson in 1823 and Robert Trimble in 1826.

26. Justice Edward Douglass White was the first, in 1910, under President Taft; Justice Harlan Fiske Stone was the second, in 1941, during FDR's third term.

27. John Hart Ely, *Democracy and Distrust: A Theory of Judicial Review* (Cambridge, MA: Harvard University Press, 1980), pp. 1–9.

28. David M. O'Brien, *Constitutional Law and Politics*, 2d ed., vol. 1 (New York: Norton, 1995), p. 77.

29. As previous chapters have demonstrated, there was little discussion in the nineteenth century of theories of constitutional interpretation. Most who accepted

judicial review at all also accepted the English declaratory theory of the law. It was the task of the judiciary to say what the law is, wrote Chief Justice Marshall in *Marbury* v. *Madison*, 5 U.S. (1 Cranch) 137 (1803). Or, as Justice Joseph Story explained, "[t]he first and fundamental rule in the interpretation of all instruments is, to construe them according to the sense of the terms and the intention of the parties." Story, *Commentaries on the Constitution of the United States* (Durham, NC: Carolina Academic Press, 1987), p. 135 (reprint of the 1833 edition). Debates turned instead on whether the judge erred in discerning the "sense" and the "intention." Early in the twentieth century, critics of the Court's decisions frequently accused the justices of substituting their own values for those of the Constitution. Legal realists in the 1920s and 1930s built on this critique by playing down the force of formal rules and playing up the role of discretion present in virtually all judicial decisions. After the constitutional revolution of 1937, when the politics inherent in constitutional interpretation became too plain to deny, it was only a matter of time before attention would focus on the sources on which judges could properly rely in divining the meaning of the Constitution. If the Supreme Court was no longer an instrument of "revealed truth" but of "power" instead, what determined the legitimacy of its decisions? Alpheus T. Mason, *The Supreme Court: Instrument of Power or of Revealed Truth, 1930–1937* (Boston: Boston University Press, 1953). One of the clearest precursors in a Supreme Court decision of the forthcoming debate appeared in *Home Building & Loan Association* v. *Blaisdell*, 290 U.S. 398 (1934), in which the Court construed the contract clause to uphold, 5 to 4, a Minnesota statute temporarily suspending payments of a mortgage principal in a time of economic calamity. Justice McReynolds's dissent articulates "original intent"; Chief Justice Hughes's majority opinion expresses an adaptive approach derived from a principle of social cohesion.

30. *Meyer* v. *Nebraska*, 262 U.S. 390 (1923), overturned a state statute that both prohibited the teaching of subjects in any language other than English and forbade the teaching of foreign languages to any pupil who had not passed the eighth grade. Two years later, *Pierce* v. *Society of Sisters*, 268 U.S. 510 (1925), invalidated an Oregon law forbidding parents from sending their children to private schools. In 1942, *Skinner* v. *Oklahoma*, 316 U.S. 535 (1942), struck down a compulsory sterilization scheme mandated by the state for most classes of habitual criminals. The application of a Fourth Amendment exclusionary rule to the states in *Mapp* v. *Ohio*, 367 U.S. 643 (1961), was also proclaimed in the context of protecting privacy.

31. 381 U.S. 479 (1965).

32. David J. Garrow, *Liberty and Sexuality: The Right to Privacy and the Making of Roe v. Wade* (New York: Macmillan, 1994), pp. 456–457.

33. *New York Times*, October 28, 1971, pp. 1, 22; Gerald Lipson and Dianne Wolman, "Polling Americans on Birth Control and Population," 4 *Family Planning Perspectives* 39 (1972). The 50 percent figure represented a noticeable change in a short time. As recently as 1966, while most respondents accepted therapeutic

abortions, fewer than 20 percent were prepared to accept elective, or nontherapeutic, abortions. Hazel G. Erskine, "The Polls: The Population Explosion, Birth Control, and Sex Education," 30 *Public Opinion Quarterly* 490, 499 (1966); *New York Herald Tribune*, March 7, 1966, pp. 17, 19; *New York Times*, April 24, 1966, p. 83.

34. 410 U.S. 179 (1973).

35. "Campaign Issues: Statements by Nixon and McGovern," *Congressional Quarterly Weekly Report*, September 2, 1972, p. 2222.

36. 410 U.S. at 153.

37. In the decade before *Roe*, members introduced ten abortion-related bills in Congress. In the decade after *Roe*, the number rose to more than 500. Neal Devins, *Shaping Constitutional Values: Elected Government, the Supreme Court, and the Abortion Debate* (Baltimore: Johns Hopkins University Press, 1996), p. 78.

38. 428 U.S. 52 (1976).

39. 428 U.S. 132 (1976). The Court avoided a ruling on the merits in this case by remanding it for a determination whether the Massachusetts statute actually permitted a parental veto, but the Court left no doubt as to the eventual outcome if it did.

40. The regulations included (1) requiring a married woman to obtain consent of her spouse in most instances before undergoing an abortion; (2) banning abortion by saline amniocentesis; and (3) criminalizing a physicians's failure to preserve the life and health of a fetus, whatever the stage of pregnancy.

41. *Akron* v. *Akron Center for Reproductive Health*, 462 U.S. 416 (1983); *Simopoulos* v. *Virginia*, 462 U.S. 506 (1983).

42. *Akron* v. *Akron Center*, *Thornburgh* v. *American College of Obstetricians & Gynecologists*, 476 U.S. 747 (1986).

43. *Akron* v. *Akron Center*.

44. *H.L.* v. *Matheson*, 450 U.S. 398 (1981).

45. *Akron* v. *Akron Center*.

46. Ibid.

47. *Thornburgh* v. *American College of Obstetricians*.

48. *Planned Parenthood Association of Kansas City* v. *Ashcroft*, 462 U.S. 476 (1983).

49. *Thornburgh* v. *American College of Obstetricians*.

50. *Planned Parenthood of Kansas City* v. *Ashcroft*.

51. *Maher* v. *Roe*, 432 U.S. 464 (1977).

52. *Harris* v. *McRae*, 448 U.S. 297 (1980).

53. Barbara Hinkson Craig and David M. O'Brien, *Abortion and American Politics* (Chatham, NJ: Chatham House, 1993), p. 59.

54. Ibid., p. 43. The Moral Majority disbanded in the mid-1980s and was replaced as a political force by the Christian Coalition, organized by Reverend Pat Robertson, himself a candidate in Republican primaries in 1988.

55. Garrow, *Liberty and Sexuality*, pp. 618–619.

56. "Move to Take Up Abortion Amendment Fails," *Congressional Quarterly Weekly Report*, March 27, 1976, p. 712; also May 1, 1976, p. 1432.

57. The only reference to abortion came in testimony by Margaret Drachsler of the National Organization for Women. The group thought Stevens was insensitive to women's issues and opposed his nomination. In retrospect her testimony was ironic, for Stevens quickly became one of the Supreme Court's leading defenders of *Roe* v. *Wade*. U.S. Senate, Committee on the Judiciary, *Hearings on the Nomination of John Paul Stevens to Be a Justice of the Supreme Court* (Washington, DC: U.S. Government Printing Office, 1975), p. 80.

58. "Reagan Affirms Anti-Abortion Stand," *New York Times*, February 8, 1976, p. 44. Reagan acknowledged his mistake when, as California governor, he signed a bill in 1967 allowing therapeutic abortions. *New York Times*, February 4, 1976, p. 8.

59. "Ford and Reagan: Psychological Warfare," *Congressional Quarterly Weekly Report*, July 24, 1976, p. 2021.

60. "Republican Platform," *Congressional Quarterly Weekly Report*, August 21, 1976, p. 2298.

61. "Democratic Platform," *Congressional Quarterly Weekly Report*, July 17, 1976, p. 1918.

62. "Key States '76," *New York Times*, November 3, 1976, p. 22.

63. Wilcox, *God's Warriors*, p. 11.

64. Austin Ranney, "The Carter Administration," in Austin Ranney, ed., *The American Elections of 1980* (Washington, DC: American Enterprise Institute, 1981), p. 16.

65. At a White House dinner for sixty members of Congress on June 12, Carter was heard to say, "If Kennedy runs, I'll whip his ass." Quoted in Jonathan Moore, *The Campaign for President: 1980 in Retrospect* (Cambridge, MA: Ballinger, 1981), p. 264.

66. The approval rating remained in the 50 percent range through March, and fluctuated between 38 and 43 percent through May. It sagged into the low thirties in June. David Broder, "Democrats," in Richard Harwood, ed., *The Pursuit of the Presidency 1980* (New York: Berkley Books, 1980), p. 188.

67. Adam Clymer, "Approval of Carter's Foreign Policy Drops in Poll," *New York Times*, June 25, 1980, p. A-20.

68. Martin Plissner, "The Open Convention: A Kennedy Scenario," *Atlantic*, August 1980, p. 4.

69. James Reston, "Carter's Secret Weapon," *New York Times*, March 21, 1980, p. A-27.

70. Ronald Reagan, "Acceptance Speech," July 17, 1980, reprinted in Harwood, ed., *The Pursuit of the Presidency 1980*, p. 415.

71. James Q. Wilson, "Reagan and the Republican Revival," *Commentary*, October, 1980, p. 26.

72. "1980 Republican Platform Text," *Congressional Quarterly Weekly Report*, July 19, 1980, pp. 2030, 2031, 2034, 2035, 2046.

73. Reagan's stand on abortion was not sufficient to win the endorsement of the tiny Right-to-Life party. They ran cofounder Ellen McCormack, who had entered twenty-two Democratic primaries in 1976. Frank Lynn, "Anti-Abortion Groups Split on Reagan's Candidacy," *New York Times*, June 22, 1980, p. 28.

74. "1980 Democratic Platform Text," *Congressional Quarterly Weekly Report*, August 16, 1980, p. 2396. The platform also endorsed ratification of the Equal Rights Amendment and "oppose[d] efforts to undermine the Supreme Court's historic mandate of school desegregation." Ibid., p. 2404.

75. See Bella S. Abzug's discussion of the adoption by the Democratic convention of this minority position. Letter to the Editor, *New York Times*, August 30, 1980, p. 20.

76. In June, 57 percent of Reagan supporters opposed his stand favoring a constitutional amendment to outlaw abortions. Adam Clymer, "Approval of Carter's Foreign Policy Drops in Poll," *New York Times*, June 25, 1980, p. A-20.

77. Hedrick Smith, "G.O.P. Planning Drive as 'Party of Jobs,' " *New York Times*, July 5, 1980, p. 7. The phrase came from party chairman Bill Brock.

78. Richard Harwood, "Labor Day 1980," in Harwood, ed., *The Pursuit of the Presidency 1980*, pp. 286–287; Moore, ed., *The Campaign for President*, p. 145.

79. Steven R. Weisman, " 'Fanatics' in Regime in Tehran Blamed by Carter for Crisis," *New York Times*, July 5, 1980, p. 1.

80. Jack Greenberg, "A Reagan Supreme Court," *New York Times*, September 15, 1980, p. 23. Greenberg was a veteran of numerous legal and political battles over civil rights. See his memoir-style account in *Crusaders in the Courts* (New York: Basic Books, 1994).

81. Quoted in Greenberg, "A Reagan Supreme Court."

82. *New York Times*, August 8, 1980, p. 20.

83. *New York Times*, November 2, 1980, sec. IV, p. 8.

84. From Justice Marshall's papers, November 12, 1980, quoted in Garrow, *Liberty and Sexuality*, p. 638. Blackmun's reference was probably to *Harris* v. *McRae*, where Blackmun believed the majority had failed to apply *Roe*'s protections to Medicaid funding.

85. Quoted in Editorial, *New York Times*, October 1, 1980, p. 26.

86. The words came from Loren Smith, a Reagan spokesperson. Stuart Taylor, "Bell Says All-White High Court Is 'Unthinkable,' " *New York Times*, October 10, 1980, p. 18.

87. "Transcript of Ronald Reagan's Remarks," *New York Times*, October 15, 1980, p. 24. See also Douglas E. Kneeland, "Reagan Pledges Woman on Court," *New York Times*, October 15, 1980, p. 1. Carter treated Reagan's pledge as a jest: "He's promised to appoint, I think, an Italian-American as judge and he's still got three weeks to go." The announcement was "less than responsible" and "another

example of [Republican] pandering to special interest groups," added White House Counsel Lloyd Cutler. Terrence Smith, "Carter Challenges Reagan's Proposals on Economy," *New York Times*, October 15, 1980, p. 22.

88. Carter's judicial appointments—he remains the only president to have served at least a full term with no occasion to name anyone to the Supreme Court—were confined almost entirely to "moderate to liberal Democrats." *New York Times*, March 16, 1980, p. 20. The data were complied by Professor Sheldon Goldman of the University of Massachusetts. Goldman noted that, to date, Carter had appointed 40 percent of the judges sitting on the U.S. district courts and the U.S. courts of appeals.

89. *New York Times*, October 28, 1980, p. A20. On October 1, Reagan had stated that he would look for nominees whose views were "broadly similar" to his own. *New York Times*, October 2, 1980, sec. II, p. 13.

90. *Congress and the Nation*, vol. 5 (Washington, DC: Congressional Quarterly, 1981), p. 25; Wilcox, *God's Warriors*, p. 220; Wayne, *The Road to the White House 1996*, table 3–4, p. 78. Comparative data on voting by religious perspective are tenuous because the questions have not been worded the same from election to election. For example, not all fundamentalist Protestants (Pentecostals, for instance) consider themselves "evangelical," just as not all evangelicals consider themselves fundamentalist. "Born-again" Christians may include both Catholics and Protestants, and among the latter the term can also include members of mainline denominations as well as evangelical denominational congregants. Not all fundamentalists and evangelicals see themselves as part of the Christian Right. Indeed, some evangelicals belong to People for the American Way, which was organized to combat the political influence of the Christian Right. Clyde Wilcox, *The Latest American Revolution* (New York: St. Martin's Press, 1995), p. 83.

91. U.S. Senate, Subcommittee on Separation of Powers, Committee on the Judiciary, *Hearings on Court-Ordered School Busing*, 97th Cong., 1st. sess. (Washington, DC: U.S. Government Printing Office, 1981); U.S. Senate, Subcommittee on the Constitution, Committee on the Judiciary, *Hearings on the Fourteenth Amendment and School Busing*, 97th Cong., 1st sess. (Washington, DC: U.S. Government Printing Office, 1981); U.S. Senate, Subcommittee on the Constitution, Committee on the Judiciary, *Hearings on Voluntary School Prayer Constitutional Amendment*, 98th Cong., 1st sess. (Washington, DC: U.S. Government Printing Office, 1983).

92. U.S. Senate, Subcommittee on the Constitution, Committee on the Judiciary, *Hearings on Constitutional Restraints upon the Judiciary*, 97th Cong., 1st sess. (Washington, DC: U.S. Government Printing Office, 1981); Gerald Gunther, "Congressional Power to Curtail Federal Court Jurisdiction: An Opinionated Guide to the Ongoing Debate," 36 *Stanford Law Review* 201 (1984); Max Barcus and Kenneth R. Kay, "The Court Stripping Bills," 27 *Villanova Law Review* 988 (1982); Paul M. Bator, "Congressional Power over the Jurisdiction of the Federal Courts," 27 *Villanova Law Review* 1030 (1982).

93. See U.S. Senate, Committee on the Judiciary, *The Human Life Bill: Hearings Before the Subcommittee on Separation of Powers*, 2 vols., 97th Cong., 1st sess. (Washington, DC: U.S. Government Printing Office, 1981). In *Katzenbach* v. *Morgan*, 384 U.S. 641 (1966), Justice Brennan articulated the so-called "ratchet theory" in his opinion for the Court, upholding expanded protection of voting rights by Congress beyond what the Court itself had deemed constitutionally required. "Congress's power under §5 is limited to adopting measures to enforce the guarantees of the Amendment; §5 grants Congress no power to restrict, abrogate, or dilute these guarantees." Ibid., 651. For further discussion, see Henry J. Hyde, "The Human Life Bill: Some Issues and Answers," 8 *Human Life Review* 9 (1982); William Cohen, "Congressional Power to Interpret Due Process and Equal Protection," 27 *Stanford Law Review* 603 (1975); and, Jesse H. Choper, "Congressional Power to Expand Judicial Definitions of the Substantive Terms of the Civil War Amendments," 67 *Minnesota Law Review* 299 (1982). For floor debate on the Human Life Bill, see the *Congressional Record* for June 27 and 28, 1983.

94. "Excerpts from Attorney General's Remarks on Plans of Justice Department," *New York Times*, October 30, 1981, p. A22.

95. Elder Witt, *A Different Justice: Reagan and the Supreme Court* (Washington, DC: Congressional Quarterly, 1986), p. 117.

96. *Congress and the Nation 1981–1984*, vol. 6 (Washington, DC: Congressional Quarterly, 1985), pp. 691–692.

97. Linda Greenhouse, "Taking the Supreme Court's Pulse," *New York Times*, January 28, 1984, p. A8.

98. David Shribman, "Glenn Says Reagan, If Re-elected, Will Reshape High Court," *New York Times*, January 17, 1984, p. B7.

99. Greenhouse, "Taking the Supreme Court's Pulse."

100. Stuart Taylor, Jr., "The Reaganization of the Federal Courts," *New York Times*, August 23, 1984, p. B8.

101. Quoted in Alpheus Thomas Mason and Donald Grier Stephenson, Jr., *American Constitutional Law*, 11th ed. (Upper Saddle River, NJ: Prentice-Hall, 1996), p. 10. "[E]ven after 13 years inside the Court, he remains highly sensitive to the political storms outside," wrote one editor. Editorial, "Justice Rehnquist's Assurances," *New York Times*, October 23, 1984, p. A32. Another writer regarded the chief justice's intrusion into one of the "most controversial issues in a hotly fought campaign" as "extraordinary" and "injudicious activism." Herman Schwartz, "Rehnquist's Partisan Intrusion," *New York Times*, October 26, 1984, p. A35.

102. Stuart Taylor, Jr., "The One-Pronged Test for Federal Judges," *New York Times*, April 22, 1984, sec. IV, p. 5. Bork, Scalia, and Starr were named to the U.S. Court of Appeals for the District of Columbia, arguably the second most consequential court in the nation.

103. Quoted in Alpheus Thomas Mason and Donald Grier Stephenson, Jr., *American Constitutional Law*, 9th ed. (Englewood Cliffs, NJ: Prentice-Hall, 1990),

p. 8. Dennis Mullins of the Justice Department explained that prospective nominees would not be asked their views on abortion but whether they thought Justice Blackmun's analysis in *Roe* v. *Wade* was "sound." If nominees gave an affirmative answer, "that would give us real concern about their judicial philosophy." Quoted in Taylor, "The One-Pronged Test for Federal Judges." For a systematic study of selection of federal judges below the Supreme Court, see Sheldon Goldman, *Picking Federal Judges: Lower Court Selection from Roosevelt Through Reagan* (New Haven: Yale University Press, 1997).

104. Stuart Taylor, Jr., "Whoever Is Elected, Potential Is Great for Change in High Court's Course," *New York Times*, October 21, 1984, p. 30.

105. Floyd Abrams, "Supreme Court Justices: An Issue," *New York Times*, February 23, 1984, p. A23.

106. Floyd Abrams, Letter to the Editor, *New York Times*, March 25, 1984, sec. IV, p. 20.

107. William French Smith, Letter to the Editor, *New York Times*, March 18, 1984, sec. IV, p. 20.

108. Quoted in Taylor, "Whoever Is Elected . . . ."

109. Mason and Stephenson, *American Constitutional Law*, 11th ed., p. 513.

110. Ronald Reagan, *Abortion and the Conscience of the Nation* (Nashville, TN: Nelson, 1984), p. 19.

111. Taylor, "Whoever Is Elected . . . ."

112. "Text of 1984 Democratic Party Platform," *Congressional Quarterly Weekly Report*, July 21, 1984, pp. 1764–1767.

113. "Text of 1984 Republican Party Platform," *Congressional Quarterly Weekly Report*, August 25, 1984, pp. 2105, 2108, 2110–2111.

114. On the 1984 campaign generally, see Elizabeth Drew, *Campaign Journal* (New York: Macmillan, 1985).

115. *Congress and the Nation*, vol. 6, pp. 20–22; Wayne, *The Road to the White House 1996*, p. 79.

116. Raoul Berger, "The Role of the Supreme Court," 3 *University of Arkansas at Little Rock Law Review* 3 (1980).

117. Data compiled by the author, based on articles cataloged in the *Index to Legal Periodicals* for the months indicated. The count excludes articles on particular constitutional issues (substantive and procedural) as well as critiques of individual cases, in which references to constitutional interpretation might well have appeared.

118. Robert H. Bork, "Tradition and Morality in Constitutional Law," in Mark W. Cannon and David M. O'Brien, eds., *Views from the Bench* (Chatham, NJ: Chatham House, 1985), pp. 170–171.

119. Robert H. Bork, *The Tempting of America* (New York: Free Press, 1990), p. 116.

120. Edwin Meese III, Address to the American Bar Association, July 9, 1985.

This address has been reprinted in various places. See *Major Policy Statements of the Attorney General: Edwin Meese III 1985–1988* (Washington, DC: U.S. Government Printing Office, 1989), pp. 1–8; "The Attorney-General's View of the Supreme Court: Toward a Jurisprudence of Original Intention," 45 *Public Administration Review* 701 (1985). Meese offered his views in the context of a critique of the Supreme Court's 1984 term.

121. Edwin Meese III, "The Law of the Constitution," speech at Tulane University, October 21, 1986, quoted in William Lasser, *The Limits of Judicial Power* (Chapel Hill: University of North Carolina Press, 1988), p. 230.

122. See also comments by Justice Marshall. *Washington Post*, May 7, 1987, pp. A1, A18.

123. William J. Brennan, Jr., "The Constitution of the United States: Contemporary Ratification," speech at Georgetown University, October 12, 1985, reprinted in Alpheus Thomas Mason and Donald Grier Stephenson, Jr., *American Constitutional Law*, 8th ed. (Englewood Cliffs, NJ: Prentice-Hall, 1987), p. 609. For a short analysis of the Meese and Brennan arguments, see Stuart Taylor, Jr., "Meese v. Brennan," *New Republic*, January 6–13, 1986, p. 17.

124. See, for example, Peter Irons, *Brennan vs. Rehnquist: The Battle for the Constitution* (New York: Knopf, 1994); Lee Epstein, *Conservatives in Court* (Knoxville: University of Tennessee Press, 1985); Eugene H. Hickok, *Justice vs. Law* (New York: Free Press, 1993); Gary L. McDowell, *Curbing the Courts: The Constitution and the Limits of Judicial Power* (Baton Rouge: Louisiana State University Press, 1988); Terry Eastland, *Ending Affirmative Action* (New York: Basic Books, 1996); Bernard Schwartz, *Packing the Courts: The Conservative Campaign to Re-write the Constitution* (New York: Scribner's, 1988); Earl M. Maltz, *Rethinking Constitutional Law* (Lawrence: University Press of Kansas, 1994); Antonin Scalia, *A Matter of Interpretation* (Princeton: Princeton University Press, 1997) (a lengthy essay by Justice Scalia, probably the present Court's most articulate textualist, is followed by comments of several critics, including Laurence Tribe and Ronald Dworkin); David A. Schultz and Christopher E. Smith, *The Jurisprudential Vision of Justice Antonin Scalia* (Lanham, MD: Rowman & Littlefield, 1996); Richard Brisbin, *Justice Scalia and the Conservative Revival* (Baltimore: Johns Hopkins University Press, 1997).

125. Henry J. Abraham, *Justices and Presidents*, 3d ed. (New York: Oxford University Press, 1992), pp. 342–343.

126. Upon confirmation, Rehnquist became only the third chief justice to have been selected from the Court itself.

127. For example, as a Republican activist in Phoenix, Arizona, in 1962 and 1964 Rehnquist was supposed to have intimidated minority voters. He denied the charges. In a deed for a house that Rehnquist had purchased in Vermont in 1974, a 1933 covenant (legally unenforceable after 1948) barred sale or lease to a person of "the Hebrew race." Rehnquist explained that he was unaware of the existence of

the restriction and promised to have the offensive language removed. A third and potentially more serious charge turned on the propriety of Rehnquist's participation in a free speech case in 1972 (*Laird* v. *Tatum*, 408 U.S. 1) that, by a vote of 5 to 4, dismissed a suit challenging surveillance by the Army of domestic political groups. In October 1972 Rehnquist issued a sixteen-page statement explaining that he had had nothing to do with the surveillance policy while serving in the Justice Department and that he knew little about the evidence in question (Memorandum on Motion to Recuse, 409 U.S. 824). In August 1986, opponents claimed that Rehnquist knew more than he admitted about the case in 1972. On August 12, Rehnquist responded to questions from Senator Charles Mathias of Maryland, asserting that he had no recollection of any participation in formulating the policy in question.

128. Sometimes called the Iranian arms affair or Iranscam, this scandal in the Reagan administration followed disclosure in 1986 of secret American arms sales to Iran to obtain release of hostages in Lebanon. Some of the proceeds were diverted to the contras fighting the Communist government of Nicaragua, even though Congress had expressly ended American financial support for the contra rebels. Both National Security Adviser Admiral John Poindexter and senior National Security Council staff member Lieutenant Colonel Oliver North were convicted of lying to Congress about the operation.

129. By mid-1992, the EEOC reported that sexual harassment complaints filed in the first half of the fiscal year had increased by more than 50 percent, compared with the same period in the previous year. Jane Gross, "Suffering in Silence No More: Fighting Sexual Harassment," *New York Times*, July 13, 1992, p. A1.

130. Christopher E. Smith, *Critical Judicial Nominations and Political Change: The Impact of Clarence Thomas* (Westport, CT: Praeger, 1993), pp. 13–14, 85–87, 154.

131. James F. Simon, *The Center Holds* (New York: Simon & Schuster, 1995), p. 11. "[N]either pressure from the right wing . . . nor any later appointments are likely to undercut the prevailing judicial ethos of moderation." Ibid., p. 303.

132. *Lee* v. *Weisman*, 505 U.S. 577 (1992).

133. *Adarand Constructors, Inc.* v. *Peña*, 515 U.S. 200 (1995).

134. *Webster*, 492 U.S. 490 (1989); *Rust*, 500 U.S. 173 (1991).

135. Their reaffirmation was in reality a significant modification. Few of the regulations that were acceptable to them would have survived a challenge between 1973 and 1986. During *Roe*'s heyday, the Court invalidated most regulations that appeared to be "burdens," whether due or "undue." 500 U.S. 833 (1992)

136. Mason and Stephenson, *American Constitutional Law*, 11th ed., p. 17.

9. PRESIDENTIAL CAMPAIGNS AND THE SUPREME COURT

1. *The Federalist*, No. 78.

2. 60 U.S. (19 Howard) 393 (1857).

3. *McCulloch* v. *Maryland*, 17 U.S. (4 Wheaton) 316 (1819), and *Osborn* v. *Bank of the United States*, 22 U.S. (9 Wheaton) 738 (1824).

4. 410 U.S. 113 (1973).

5. This nickname for the Supreme Court became the title of a book about the Court by John P. Frank (New York: Knopf, 1958).

6. Sylvia Snowiss, *Judicial Review and the Law of the Constitution* (New Haven: Yale University Press, 1990), pp. 1–12, 113–121; Charles F. Hobson, *The Great Chief Justice: John Marshall and the Rule of Law* (Lawrence: University Press of Kansas, 1996), pp. 181–214.

7. 5 U.S. (1 Cranch) 137 (1803).

8. Declaration of Independence (1776).

9. Linda Greenhouse, "Press Coverage," in Kermit L. Hall, ed., *The Oxford Companion to The Supreme Court of the United States* (New York: Oxford University Press, 1992), pp. 666–667.

10. Letter of 1823. In Paul Leicester Ford ed., *The Writings of Thomas Jefferson* (New York: G. P. Putnam's Sons, 1892–1899), vol. 10, p. 248. Jefferson may have been less concerned with the secrecy of deliberations than with Marshall's practice of expressing the collective views of the Court through a single opinion, "the opinion of the Court," in contrast to the older practice of seriatim, or individual, opinions.

11. Richard Hofstadter, *The Paranoid Style in American Politics and Other Essays*, Vintage ed. (New York: Random House, 1967), p. 3.

12. Quoted in Edward J. Cleary, *Beyond the Burning Cross: The First Amendment and the Landmark R.A.V. Case* (New York: Random House, 1994), p. xiv.

13. Walter F. Murphy, *Elements of Judicial Strategy* (Chicago: University of Chicago Press, 1964), p. 128. As Henry Adams recorded, "the Chief Justice [Chase] was very willing to win an ally in the press who would tell his story as he wished it to be read." *The Education of Henry Adams* (Boston: Houghton Mifflin, 1918), p. 250.

It was the tradition of reticence at the Supreme Court that made Justice Clarence Thomas's 1998 address to the National Bar Association so remarkable. Speaking to the nation's largest organization of black attorneys, he vigorously defended his jurisprudence against those who criticized his views because they did not conform to what was expected from an African-American. "I refuse to have my ideas assigned to me because I am black." Neil A. Lewis, "Justice Thomas Suggests Critics' Views Are Racist," *New York Times*, July 30, 1998, p. A1.

14. *United States* v. *Rabinowitz*, 339 U.S. 56, 69 (1950) (dissenting opinion).

15. *Scott* v. *Sandford*.

16. In re *Debs*, 158 U.S. 564 (1895).

17. *Pollock* v. *Farmers' Loan & Trust Co.*, 158 U.S. 601 (1895).

18. *Hammer* v. *Dagenhart*, 247 U.S. 251 (1918).

19. *Carter* v. *Carter Coal Co.*, 298 U.S. 238 (1936).

20. *Akron* v. *Akron Center for Reproductive Health*, 462 U.S. 416 (1983).

21. *Engel* v. *Vitale*, 370 U.S. 421 (1962).

22. *Watkins* v. *United States*, 354 U.S. 178 (1957).

23. *Texas* v. *Johnson*, 491 U.S. 397 (1989).

24. *Roth* v. *United States*, 354 U.S. 476 (1957).

25. *Regents* v. *Bakke*, 438 U.S. 265 (1978).

26. John B. Gates, *The Supreme Court and Partisan Realignment: A Macro- and Microlevel Perspective* (Boulder, CO: Westview Press, 1992), p. 14. See also Walter F. Murphy, Joseph Tanenhaus, and Daniel L. Kastner, *Public Evaluations of Constitutional Courts* (Beverly Hills, CA: Sage, 1973).

27. 19 U.S. (6 Wheaton) 264 (1821).

28. A twentieth-century addition to that short list remains hypothetical, if only by a vote of 5 to 4. *Planned Parenthood of Southeastern Pennsylvania* v. *Casey*, 505 U.S. 833 (1992), sustained most regulations of Pennsylvania's abortion control law only a few weeks prior to the 1992 national nominating conventions. Although no configuration of five justices could unite behind a single opinion, the Court nonetheless gave something to both sides in this incessant dispute. Women retained the constitutional right to abortion, recognized nineteen years before in *Roe* v. *Wade*, free of prohibition by the government through the second trimester of pregnancy. States were nonetheless free to impose regulations on abortions, including regulations intended to discourage abortions, so long as a regulation did not impose "an undue burden" on the woman's right to terminate the pregnancy. Suppose, however, that the Court had sustained the Pennsylvania law by overturning *Roe* outright. In this eventuality abortion laws would implicate the Constitution no more than an ordinance banning parking on the north side of the street on Mondays. Had the Court moved in this direction—and it stopped short of doing so by a single vote—the Court and abortion would surely have loomed far larger in that year's campaign, dwarfing even what was said and done in 1980 and 1984. Of course a decision to strike down the law in its entirety would also have made the Court a more prominent campaign issue. However, as the previous chapter explained, this was a highly unlikely prospect, given the changed membership on the bench.

29. David Adamany, "Legitimacy, Realigning Elections, and the Supreme Court," 1973 *Wisconsin Law Review* 790 (1973); Richard Funston, "The Supreme Court and Critical Elections," 83 *American Political Science Review* 795 (1975).

30. 5 U.S. (1 Cranch) 299 (1803).

31. 31 U.S. (6 Peters) 515 (1832).

32. 36 U.S. (11 Peters) 420 (1837).

33. *Thornburgh* v. *American College of Obstetricians & Gynecologists*, 474 U.S. 809 (1986).

34. For two years after 1832 Jackson faced a Senate divided evenly along party lines, but with the tie-breaking vote of Vice President Martin Van Buren Democrats had control in principle.

35. The facts that the Court appears to give some ground against concerted opposition (or at least to slow an advance) and that Court-curbing measures are only rarely enacted perhaps may also be explained because of the benefits to warring factions to be derived from compromise and cooperation. "The existence of independent and rival seats of power . . . makes Court-congressional and Court-presidential relations . . . more analogous to a mixed-motive than to a zero-sum game." Murphy, *Elements of Judicial Strategy*, p. 174. Moreover, no branch of government can consider itself immune from the potential dangers that lurk within some kind of political upheaval. A massive struggle might get out of control and lead to results that no party to the conflict desires.

36. Through Stephen Breyer, 108 individuals have served on the Supreme Court. Subtracting Washington's initial 6 leaves 102 persons sent to the Court since 1790. One then divides the intervening years by 102.

37. *Fletcher* v. *Peck*, 10 U.S. (6 Cranch) 87 (1810).

38. Lee Epstein et al., *The Supreme Court Compendium* (Washington, DC: Congressional Quarterly, 1994), pp. 96–128.

39. Robert Dahl, "Decision-making in a Democracy: The Supreme Court as a National Policymaker," 6 *Journal of Public Law* 279, 285 (1957).

40. Benjamin N. Cardozo, *The Nature of the Judicial Process* (New Haven: Yale University Press, 1921), p. 20.

41. John R. Schmidhauser, "Judicial Behavior and the Sectional Crisis of 1837–1860," 23 *Journal of Politics* 615 (1961).

42. Slaughterhouse Cases, 83 U.S. (16 Wallace) 36 (1873).

43. *Cruikshank* v. *United States*, 92 U.S. 542 (1876).

44. Civil Rights Cases, 109 U.S. 3 (1883).

45. Quoted in Stuart Taylor, "Re: Shaping the Court," *New York Times*, July 2, 1988, p. 9.

46. This is a conclusion of the important study by Gates, *The Supreme Court and Partisan Realignment*, p. 181.

47. *United States* v. *E. C. Knight Co.*, 156 U.S. 1 (1895); *Pollock* v. *Farmers' Loan & Trust Co.*; In re *Debs*.

48. There were 289 affirmative votes in the House of Representatives, of which 136 (47 percent) came from Republican members. There were 73 affirmative votes in the Senate, of which 27 (37 percent) came from Republicans, despite the fact that presidential nominee-apparent Senator Barry Goldwater opposed the bill. "Civil Rights Act of 1964 Is Signed into Law," *Congressional Quarterly Weekly Report*, July 3, 1964, p. 1331.

49. 62 U.S. (21 Howard) 506 (1859).

50. 5 U.S. at 177.

51. In contrast to earlier periods, post-1890 debates reached well beyond the usual media of legislative floor remarks, stump speeches, pamphlets, and newspaper commentary. Technological improvements in publishing after the Civil War

brought down the cost of printing books and periodicals. The effect was a flowering of learned journals and opinion magazines beyond anything previously seen. As more rapid transport and communication became available, people in different parts of the United States, in greater numbers and in a shorter period of time than ever before, could learn about and think about the same issues and problems.

52. 304 U.S. 144 (1938).

53. David F. Forte, ed., *The Supreme Court in American Politics: Judicial Activism vs. Judicial Restraint* (Lexington, MA: D. C. Heath, 1972); Stephen C. Halpern and Charles M. Lamb, eds., *Supreme Court Activism and Restraint* (Lexington, MA: Lexington Books, 1982). On the importance of judicial decisions in 1941–1953 as an enabling transition to the Warren Court, see Melvin I. Urofsky, *Division and Discord* (Columbia: University of South Carolina Press, 1997).

54. *Reynolds* v. *Sims*, 377 U.S. 533, 624–625 (1964) (dissenting opinion).

55. Alpheus Thomas Mason, *The Supreme Court: Palladium of Freedom* (Ann Arbor: University of Michigan Press, 1962), p. 177.

56. Martin Shapiro, *Freedom of Speech: The Supreme Court and Judicial Review* (Englewood Cliffs, NJ: Prentice-Hall, 1966).

57. Or so the argument was cast. It is also part of political reality that deciding who will act is part of deciding what will be done, because one level or institution of government may well be more receptive to certain interests than to others.

58. In Justice Robert H. Jackson's words in the context of a dispute over the executive power, "Just what our forefathers did envision, or would have envisioned had they foreseen modern conditions, must be divined from materials almost as enigmatic as the dreams Joseph was called upon to interpret for Pharaoh." *Youngstown Sheet & Tube Co.* v. *Sawyer*, 343 U.S. 575, 634 (1952) (concurring opinion).

59. The Age of Indifference (Washington, DC: Times-Mirror Center for the People & the Press, 1990). See also the analysis of the "news interest index" in News Release (Washington, DC: Pew Research Center for the People & the Press, August 15, 1997), pp. 8–9.

60. Massachusetts Bill of Rights, Article XXX (1780).

61. Abraham Lincoln, "Gettysburg Address," November 19, 1863.

62. Jeffrey D. Hockett, *New Deal Justice: The Constitutional Jurisprudence of Hugo L. Black, Felix Frankfurter, and Robert H. Jackson* (Lanham, MD: Rowman & Littlefield, 1996), p. 291.

63. Quoted in Charles Warren, *The Supreme Court in United States History*, rev. ed. (Boston: Little, Brown, 1926), vol. 1, p. 724.

64. Ibid., pp. 748–749.

65. One presumes that the framers might have imposed more institutional and political checks on the federal judiciary had most of them clearly foreseen the large policy-making role that the Court would eventually play.

66. 5 U.S. at 178.

INDEX